The Limits of Affluence:
Welfare in Ontario, 1920–1970

ES STRUTHERS

The Limits of Affluence:
Welfare in Ontario, 1920–1970

A publication of the
Ontario Historical Studies Series
for the Government of Ontario
Published by the University of Toronto Press
Toronto Buffalo London

Printed in Canada

ISBN 0-8020-0622-1 (cloth)
ISBN 0-8020-7582-7 (paper)

Printed on acid-free paper

Canadian Cataloguing in Publication Data

Struthers, James, 1950–
    The limits of affluence : welfare in Ontario, 1920–1970

    (Ontario historical studies series)
    Includes bibliographical references and index.
    ISBN 0-8020-0622-1 (bound) ISBN 0-8020-7582-7 (pbk.)

    1. Public welfare – Ontario – History.   I. Title.
    II. Series.

HV109.054S88 1994   361.6'09713   C94-931964-3

This book has been published with the assistance of funds provided by the Government of Ontario through the Ministry of Culture, Tourism and Recreation.

For Betsy and Ned

Contents

The Ontario Historical Studies Series

For many years the principal theme in English-Canadian historical writing has been the emergence and the consolidation of the Canadian nation. This theme has been developed in uneasy awareness of the persistence and importance of regional interests and identities, but because of the central role of Ontario in the growth of Canada, Ontario has not been seen as a region. Almost unconsciously, historians have equated the history of the province with that of the nation and have often depicted the interests of other regions as obstacles to the unity and welfare of Canada.

The creation of the province of Ontario in 1867 was the visible embodiment of a formidable reality, the existence at the core of the new nation of a powerful if disjointed society whose traditions and characteristics differed in many respects from those of the other British North American colonies. The intervening century has not witnessed the assimilation of Ontario to the other regions in Canada; on the contrary, it has become a more clearly articulated entity. Within the formal geographical and institutional framework defined so assiduously by Ontario's political leaders, an increasingly intricate web of economic and social interests has been woven and shaped by the dynamic interplay between Toronto and its hinterland. The character of this regional community has been formed in the tension between a rapid adaptation to the processes of modernization and industrialization in modern Western society and a reluctance to modify or discard traditional attitudes and values. Not surprisingly, the Ontario outlook has been, and in some measure still is, a compound of aggressiveness, conservatism, and the conviction that its values should be the model for the rest of Canada.

From the outset, the objective of the Series' Board of Trustees has been to describe and analyse the historical development of Ontario as a distinct region within Canada. The Series includes biographies of several premiers and thematic studies on the growth of the provincial economy, educational institutions, labour, welfare, the Franco-Ontarians, the native peoples, and the arts.

The Limits of Affluence is a history of the response to poverty in a provincial society characterized until recently by abundance and rapid economic growth. In Ontario, poverty has been relieved by means-based social assistance programs beginning with mothers' allowances and culminating in the so-called War on Poverty of the 1960s from which emerged the Canada Assistance Plan. By 1993, one of every eight Ontarians was dependent on needs-tested social assistance. The recipients and their advocates remain convinced that the level of such help is inadequate; governments and the fully employed consider welfare programs the most controversial form of social spending. This continuing debate reflects the fact that the welfare system has a history, but does not embody a known and accepted rationale.

James Struthers has written a scholarly, perceptive, and compassionate account of the development of social assistance in Ontario, one that is informed by a thorough grasp of the relevant international literature. This work will be indispensable for all those involved in the comprehensive social policy review now being undertaken by the federal and provincial governments.

The editors and the Board of Trustees are grateful to James Struthers for undertaking this task.

Acknowledgments

Writing this book would not have been possible without the aid and support of many people to whom I am deeply indebted. Allan Irving shared my fascination with Ontario's social welfare history and provided continual encouragement that this project was worth doing. He also introduced me to some of the key social work pioneers interviewed for this book. At the University of Western Ontario, Peter Neary gave me gracious hospitality and an annual forum for exploring many of the ideas and arguments contained in this study as well as providing a close reading of its chapters. He also pointed me towards the rich London Welfare Department Record Collection in the Weldon Library as well as towards the Bernice Vincent painting for the book jacket. Desmond Glynn was a critical help in the early stages of research for this book, particularly with the extensive deputy minister's correspondence of James Band, and has served as sounding board for ideas throughout the writing. James G. Snell and Margaret Hillyard Little, during the course of completing their own major studies on, respectively, the history of old age and mothers' allowances in Canada, gave me generous access to their writing and valuable comments on draft chapters of this book. Joan Sangster and Christopher Armstrong shared my ongoing frustrations with attempting to extract archival records out of Ontario's poorly conceived and badly implemented Freedom of Information and Protection of Privacy Act. They also provided important help in locating sources at various points in my research.

I also wish to thank a number of other people for their assistance along the way. Elizabeth Wilton did excellent work as a research assistant on this project. In the Ontario Archives Freedom of Information unit, Hazel Blythe struggled with the restrictiveness of the province's 1988 privacy legislation to get material cleared for my research. George Wharton, at the Metropolitan Toronto Records and Archives, and Karen

Teeple, in the City of Toronto Archives, gave generously of their time to facilitate my access to crucial municipal records on social welfare. Bessie Touzel, one of the giants in Canadian social work from the 1920s onwards, provided me with four remarkable hours of conversation about the events and implications of social advocacy for better welfare standards in the 1930s and 1940s. I am also grateful to Dorothea Crittenden, Albert Rose, and Richard Splane for sharing their memories of some of the policies and people portrayed in this book. Goldwin French, Jeanne Beck, and Peter Oliver of the Ontario Historical Studies Series were strong believers in the importance of this project and provided ongoing advice and encouragement at every step of the way. At the University of Toronto Press, Rosemary Shipton was once again an outstanding editor. My special thanks as well to Bernice Vincent and the Blackburn Group for allowing me to use her richly evocative painting *Picnic* on the jacket of this book. I also wish to thank both the OHSS and the Social Sciences and Humanities Research Council of Canada for the financial support that made my research possible.

My deepest debts are, as always, to Betsy Struthers, my partner in life and in writing, and to our son Ned. They endured my frequent absences on research, my episodic frustrations with wrestling this book to completion, and, above all, helped me to keep the whole project in perspective. It is to them this book is dedicated.

The Limits of Affluence:
Welfare in Ontario, 1920–1970

Introduction

The image of Ontario has been shaped by affluence, best captured, perhaps, in the titles of two economic histories of the province in this series, *Progress without Planning* and *The Prosperous Years*. Sharing 'all the booms and only some of the busts of Canada's roller-coaster economy,' Ontario has been 'relatively easy to govern,' Desmond Morton reminds us. Other analysts of the province's political culture have pointed to the linkage between its 'politics of affluence' and the 'unusual durability of its governments.' Variously described as 'big, rich, and successful,' or as the 'smug defender of its own dominance,' Ontario since Confederation has been viewed primarily through the lens of its power, wealth, and privilege relative to the rest of Canada, or indeed the rest of the world.[1]

These prevailing images of abundance mask a grimmer side to the province's past. Although Ontario has been the hub of Canada's most dramatic economic growth throughout the twentieth century, it has also been home to one-quarter of its poor. Even in the years of most rapid economic expansion after the Second World War, enduring poverty 'among the fully employed living in relatively "normal" circumstances' coexisted side by side with burgeoning material abundance. So too did the plight of mothers, children, people with disabilities, the elderly, and the unemployed, subsisting outside the labour force on a bewildering variety of welfare programs. As K.J. Rea comments in his history of *The Prosperous Years*, 'it [is] surprising how little the actual distribution of income ... ha[s] changed since the 1930s.'[2]

The Limits of Affluence is about this other history of Ontario, a history of the response to poverty and need within a province experiencing abundance and rapid economic growth. In taking Ontario as its focus, the book departs from the prevailing framework of writing on the welfare state which has concentrated on transnational comparisons and the evolution of national policies and programs. Universal income security and contributory social programs such as unemployment insurance, family allowances, old age pensions, and medicare account by far for the largest share of Canada's social spending; they have been crucial breakthroughs in the fight against poverty and insecurity, and have helped to create a sense of social rights linked to national citizenship.[3] It is hardly surprising they should attract our attention.

However, this focus on universal programs and contributory social insurance schemes at the national level has obscured the extent to which needs-based programs most directly targeted towards the poor have been developed and administered by provinces and local governments. Houses of Refuge, mothers' allowances, a means-tested old age pension scheme, welfare, and unemployment relief formed the basis of a provincial welfare state more intimately connected with the lives of the poor than national social security policies aimed at the general population. During the Great Depression and the 'War on Poverty' of the 1960s, Ontario's two great cycles of welfare reform, the province and its municipalities, not the federal government, played the primary role in delivering programs to those in need. Moreover, as recent feminist writing on social policy has pointed out, the welfare state itself is a gendered, two-tiered construct in which 'rights-based' social insurance programs, both in design and in administration, typically serve a male wage-labour force. In contrast, discretionary 'needs-based' social assistance, along with its more intrusive tradition of casework intervention, responds to the particular vulnerabilities and moral expectations surrounding women's dependence within the family.[4] Understanding the gendered response to poverty in our past, then, requires a redirection of our attention to policy developments at subnational levels of government where needs-based programs predominate.

Means-tested social assistance programs, developed within Ontario over the critical half century between 1920 and 1970, form the subject of this book: mothers' allowances, the first income security and gender-specific welfare program, launched in 1920; means-tested old age pensions, the first major policy response to aging; unemployment relief, available during the Depression in the 1930s; and the post–Second World War evolution of welfare, culminating in the short-lived 1960s War on Poverty. During these fifty years, Ontario put in place the framework of a response to poverty which, despite increasing strain, remains more or less intact today. Over this period annual provincial spending on social assistance soared from $800,000 to more than $231 million, and the numbers dependent on it jumped from 0.37 per cent to more than 5 per cent of the provincial population. In the post–Second

World War era of most rapid growth between 1945 and 1970, welfare spending as a proportion of the total provincial budget grew by three and a half times. By 1993, in the midst of the worst economic crisis since the Depression, one out of every eight Ontarians was dependent on needs-tested social assistance. What was once envisaged as an increasingly 'residual' domain within a mostly univeralistic and non-stigmatizing welfare state has now re-emerged as our fastest-growing and most controversial form of social spending, particularly during an era in which universality itself is increasingly under attack.[5]

The rapid growth and scope of the Keynesian welfare state in the postwar era, and more importantly its perceived contribution to the fiscal crisis of governments in late twentieth-century capitalism, have produced an explosion of critical writing on the welfare state during the past two decades.[6] Despite this interest, particularly by political scientists and sociologists, the historical analysis of welfare itself – defined as means-tested social assistance – has received far less attention.[7] As Clarke Chambers, one of the leading American scholars in the field, recently observed, welfare historians 'have striven to define a field of scholarship that carries the stigma of its subjects.' Within a North American society obsessed with progress, growth, and material success, 'it has been awkward for scholars to credit the objective reality of failure, dependency, and poverty'; consequently, most writing on the welfare state has focused on the creation of alternatives to stigmatized, means-tested social assistance rather than on the relief system itself.

Moreover, much of the writing that has appeared reflects the 'top-down' bias of records and sources 'generated by guardian classes' or the professional orientation of social work 'with its emphasis on technical expertise ... and its perception of clients as victims either of circumstance or of social injustice, not as actors in their own right.'[8] Despite these limitations, a rich theoretical literature now exists as a context for new analyses of the origins and evolution of welfare policies and programs.

Theoretical Perspectives on Social Welfare

Over the past three decades at least six distinct interpretations of the origins and development of welfare state policies have emerged within the historical and social science literature. One of the earliest and most influential approaches can be termed the logic of industrialism school, associated most closely with the seminal work of Harold Wilensky. Looking at the comparative development of welfare state programs across many nations over time, Wilensky and others writing from this functionalist perspective in the late 1950s viewed welfare programs as a logical and inevitable response to the forces of industrialization, urbanization, and the expansion of a wage-earning labour force. Interested in comparative statistical indicators of development such as the gross national product, the degree of urbanization, and the percentage of workers engaged in industry rather than agriculture, functionalist theorists argued that the path of welfare state development was a smooth trajectory on which all industrial nations eventually converged, albeit at different rates and with a somewhat different mix and blend of programs. The most important explanatory variable was industrialism itself, which severed workers and their families from earlier kin-based networks of mutual aid, created the economic vulnerabilities associated with wage dependency, and generated the societal surplus needed to finance welfare state programs of redistribution and social insurance as well as the bureaucratic structure necessary to administer them.[9]

Comparative and functional analyses such as Wilensky's were helpful in undercutting an earlier idealist and Whiggish tradition of writing on welfare that viewed most programs as the product of enlightened and altruistic reformers. His work drew attention to the critical correlations between economic and bureaucratic growth as the necessary preconditions for the financing and implementation of welfare policy; he also stressed the functional fit between the welfare state and capitalism, structures previously assumed to exist in tension, if not opposition to each other. As Wilensky and Lebeaux put it in their well-known formulation of the distinction between residual and institutional approaches to welfare, through modernization 'social welfare becomes accepted as a proper, legitimate function of modern industrial society in helping individuals achieve self-fulfillment. The complexity of modern life is recognized. The inability of the individual to provide fully for himself, or to meet all his needs in family and work settings, is considered a "normal" condition; and the helping agencies receive "regular" institutional status.'[10] During the highwater mark of the Keynesian welfare state between 1945 and 1970, Wilensky's linkage between economic expansion and widening social entitlement seemed particularly persuasive.

However, functionalist interpretations of the welfare state left much that was unexplained. Although helpful in isolating necessary preconditions for welfare, they could not answer why particular policies, such as family allowances or health insurance, emerged in some nations and not in others, or why within individual nations sickness insurance might precede unemployment compensation. Even after more rigorous comparative analysis they could not account for the timing of welfare state developments among nations. If the level of industrialization was the key causal variable for understanding the growth of welfare, why did nations such as New Zealand and Australia lead the way in social experimentation around old age pensions while more advanced and affluent industrial societies such as the United States remained notorious welfare laggards? Functionalist theories were also unhelpful in explaining which groups within nations pushed for particular policies, or why they might succeed or fail.[11]

At the same time, a rival group of political cultural theorists emerged who viewed differences in the scope, timing, and nature of social entitlements as reflections of fundamental differences in national values. Associated most clearly with the work of Seymour Martin Lipset, Louis Hartz, and Gaston Rimlinger, this second group of scholars were interested in accounting for the strength of residualist and individualistic approaches to welfare in the United States, particularly in comparison with most European industrial nations or even neighbouring North American nations such as Canada. In contrast to Wilensky's economic approach to welfare, these cultural theorists laid great stress on a societal consensus around certain values, ideas, and core beliefs such as the strength of voluntarism or the liberal tradition. They explained that a liberal society such as the United States, with no feudal heritage and a deep suspicion of state power, was resistant to collectivist solutions to the problems of dependency and need posed by industrial societies.[12] Canadian variations on this theme held that Tory and feudal fragments within British North America explained the rise of third parties rooted in collectivism as well as a broader public acceptance for more paternalist state leadership in the solution of social problems.[13] Recent interpretations of Ontario's political culture by John Wilson, S.F. Wise, H.V. Nelles, and S.J.R. Noel have stressed particular pre-Confederation traditions of elite leadership, ascription, hierarchy, and trust in the state; these conservative values explain the traditions of one-party dominance within the province as well as the willingness among its citizens to look to the state for leadership in promoting economic and social development.[14]

Interpretations of the welfare state which take political culture as their starting point provide some explanation, unlike functionalist theory, for why levels of economic development may not correspond directly with social policy expenditure. For this reason they have most frequently been applied to understanding America's exceptionalism to the European model of more comprehensive social provision. They also acknowledge directly, in a way functionalist approaches do not, that social policy is about values, beliefs, and normative judgments, particularly concerning issues of self-reliance versus social solidarity, or charity versus entitlement. However, as 'holistic' interpretations of national or regional political cultures, they are not helpful in making connections between widely shared values and specific policy responses to particular social problems. As Theda Skocpol points out, such an approach will not tell us why public education was early and widespread in North America, but not in Europe, or to use Ontario as an example, why mothers' allowances preceded old age pensions as our first state response to providing income security. Nor will such an approach shed much light on the reasons for change within either program over time. Finally, interpretive understandings of the welfare state which assign primacy of place to national or core values are silent on the question of how such values are represented or enforced, particularly given prevailing class, ethnic, and gender inequalities. Whose values are these and how widely are they shared? And what, precisely, are they about?[15] As Nancy Fraser reminds us, within the arena of social welfare 'the interpretation of people's needs is itself a political stake, indeed sometimes the political stake ... since at the heart of such politics lie questions about what various groups ... really need and whose interpretations ... should be authoritative.'[16]

The 'social democratic' model is a more recent and powerful variant of political approaches to understanding the emergence of the welfare state. Articulated most prominently by European and particularly Scandinavian social theorists such as Walter Korpi and Gosta Esping-Andersen, its essential premise is that the welfare state is 'the product of the strength of labor in civil society.'[17] Simply put, welfare policies and programs are the programmatic response of the labour movement and its political allies. The level of any nation's or region's social policy development reflects the extent to which the working class, through trade union organization and political mobilization, can move the state to meet its needs rather than those of capital. Although no one has yet attempted an extended application of this third approach to Canada, numerous writings that posit the centrality of the CCF-NDP and its predecessors to major social policy breakthroughs – such as the achievement of old age pensions in 1927, unemployment insurance in 1940, family allowances in 1944, or state health insurance initiatives in Saskatchewan in 1944–62 – view the welfare state as the creation of 'pressure from the left.'[18]

Unlike the first two models, the social democratic model can be applied precisely to explain the specific timing of particular welfare initiatives within nations. It is a contingent rather than an essentialist approach to analysing the welfare state and it incorporates ample scope for understanding achievements as well as policy reversals, the conflictual nature of struggles over welfare entitlement, and the importance of agency, ideology, and class mobilization in winning welfare reforms. Examining the extent of trade union organization and socialist party strength is also a more accurate predictor of cross-national variations in levels of welfare state development than reliance on purely economic indicators or generalizations about national values. From the perspective of this model, it is hardly surprising that Sweden should have the most developed and the United States the least developed level of social provision among advanced industrial nations, given the vast differences in the strength of organized labour and social democratic parties within the two societies.

Despite these virtues, interpretations of the welfare state which concentrate exclusively on the degree of labour's industrial and political mobilization present an overly simplified framework for understanding why and how social policy gets made. As Jill Quadagno points out, 'state power through social democracy is not the only route to welfare state growth.' Programs and benefits instead may emerge through 'any number of different political coalitions' in which businessmen, farmers, women, ethnic and racial minorities, and regions may play critical roles.[19] By assigning all its explanatory power to the strength of labour, the social democratic framework is not helpful, within a Canadian context, in understanding the creation of mothers' allowances, where unions or leftist third parties did not play a key role, or in the pioneering of health insurance within a rural province such as Saskatchewan. Developed principally within a European setting, where highly centralized national governments are the norm, the model is also less sensitive to the decentralized federal nature of North American societies, where state power is more diffuse and it remains more difficult for labour and leftist parties to exert influence at the centre.[20] Nor is the social democratic approach useful in interpreting policy evolution within means-tested old age pensions or unemployment relief between the two world wars, when unions and social democratic parties were weak. By seeing welfare politics only as an arena for the struggle between the working class and business, social democratic interpretations also assign no independent role to state administrators, professionals, or middle-class reformers other than as potential allies or adversaries of labour or capital.[21] Finally, by positing an inherent tension between welfare and the market, social democratic theorists fail to acknowledge that 'the welfare state may be, but certainly is not invariably or even usually, in opposition to property and market forces.'[22]

Unlike social democratic theorists who see the welfare state as a set of entitlements wrested from capital and the state by an organized working class, many Marxist and neo-Marxist analysts argue that the welfare state is an instrument of social control or that it reflects more contradictory purposes serving the needs of both capital accumulation and state legitimation. As Ian Gough puts it: 'The welfare state ... simultaneously embodies tendencies to enhance social welfare, to develop the powers of individuals, to exert social control over the blind play of market forces; and tendencies to repress and control people, to adapt them to the requirements of the capitalist economy. Each tendency will generate counter-tendencies in the opposite direction; indeed this is precisely why we refer to it as a contradictory process through time.'[23] Rather than reflecting a smooth trajectory towards greater equality and the provision of an ever-expanding range of social rights of citizenship, the welfare state, according to the fourth group of theorists, neo-Marxists, is inevitably balanced on the knife edge of either fiscal or political crisis; it 'can never develop a set of policies truly designed to meet human needs, because these policies will invariably encounter the constraints of the capitalist economic system.'[24]

Of all those writing within the Marxist tradition, no authors have been more influential in interpreting the evolution of means-tested social assistance programs than Frances Fox Piven and Richard Cloward. Their books on American social welfare, particularly *Regulating the Poor: The Functions of Public Welfare* and *Poor People's Movements: Why They Succeed and How They Fail*, remain the starting-point for most discussions concerning the purposes and limits of social welfare.[25]

For Piven and Cloward the function of welfare is social control – the regulation of labour and the enforcement of work incentives within a capitalist labour market, a task that has remained essentially unchanged since the passage of the first English poor laws of the sixteenth century. Within this framework, however, the provision of welfare typically expands and contracts in cyclical fashion in response to economic crisis and waves of social unrest by the poor. In other words, welfare is not simply an ongoing instrument of capitalist control but a potential field for social insurgency within which the poor can exercise agency and power, albeit within sharply constrained limits. 'Relief arrangements are initiated or expanded during the occasional outbreaks of civil disorder produced by mass unemployment, and are then abolished or contracted when political stability is restored. Expansive relief policies are designed to mute civil disorder, and restrictive ones to reinforce work norms. In other words, relief policies are cyclical – liberal or restrictive depending on the problems of regulation in the larger society with which the government must contend.'[26]

Recently, Piven and Cloward have extended their arguments into the 1980s, stating that the current welfare backlash unleashed by the Reagan administration, including the implementation of 'workfare' schemes and the termination of general assistance for able-bodied males by many state governments, 'confirm[s] the cyclical pattern described and analysed in *Regulating the Poor* ... The restrictive phase of the cycle is moving forward.'[27]

The history of welfare in Ontario lends strong support to the arguments of Piven and Cloward and other Marxist theorists concerning the work-maintaining imperatives, cyclical nature, and contradictory moral purposes of welfare policy. Marxist perspectives address centrally, in a way other interpretations do not, why poverty, stigma, and relatively unchanged levels of income inequality persist as enduring features of welfare state development. In this sense they serve as major correctives to liberal or functionalist literature that stresses the role of altruism, humanitarianism, or logic in driving welfare entitlement forward towards ever greater institutional provision for human needs. In contrast to social democratic models, social control theory also incorporates a place for business in the advocacy of welfare reform and helps to account for the controlling and coercive elements of an expanding state welfare bureaucracy.[28] Along with writers within the social democratic model, Piven and Cloward, unlike many Marxist theorists who see welfare only as an arena for domination, also give primacy of place to the poor themselves. They present the poor as historical actors in their own right whose mobilization and insurgency can have significant if episodic impact on the liberalization of the relief system.[29]

However, Marxist theories that stress the dominance of capital often give a coherence and logic to state welfare policy which is difficult to discern in practice. In explaining how the welfare state was formed, they allow little scope for the importance of unintended policy consequences, internal divisions within the state itself, or the ability of workers and their families to influence policy in their favour.[30] Social control perspectives stressing the power of capital are also unable to account for the way many welfare policy initiatives opposed by business interests get created. As Skocpol points out, 'no matter how adaptable American capitalists have proven to be after the fact, the historical evidence is overwhelming that they have regularly opposed the initial establishment of new public policies that (in their perception) would either interfere with managerial prerogatives or in any way raise the cost of doing business.'[31] Within the Canadian context, recent studies of the origins and evolution of unemployment insurance point to the centrality of bureaucracy, regionalism, working-class agency, and professional ideology, and not simply business pressure, in interpreting how this key social policy took shape.[32]

Like social democratic interpretations, social control literature also concentrates on a two-class model of social change that either ignores the role of other key social actors such as women's groups, agrarian interests, politicians, and policy professionals in the shaping of the welfare state, or reduces their influence to mere appendages of labour or capital.[33] In fact, however, women, state officials, municipal politicians, and social work and volunteer agencies all played crucial roles, along with business and labour, in shaping Ontario's response to poverty over the course of the twentieth century.

In recent years, growing attention has been paid to the state itself as an independent actor in the shaping of the welfare state. Variously termed the new institutionalism, bureaucratic autonomy, or structured polity perspective, writers such as Hugh Heclo and Theda Skocpol argue for a state-centred rather than a society-centred approach to understanding the formation of social policy. Simply put, these theorists present a complex model of the state in place of the state as the passive agent of societal forces. Government officials often lead social change, developing welfare measures through a process of political learning from the consequences of previous policy, through the regulatory knowledge and expertise they acquire within government agencies, and through their ongoing dialogue with like-minded policy professionals or advocacy groups outside the structure of government. As Skocpol argues: 'Politicians and administrators must be taken seriously. Not merely as agents of other social interests, they are actors in their own right, enabled and constrained by the political organizations within which they operate ... [S]tates are ... sites of autonomous action, not reducible to the demands or preferences of any social group.'[34]

The state-centred approach to policy analysis brings important new analytical strengths to the study of social policy. By focusing on differential paths of bureaucratic development among industrial nations – the ways in which states develop the administrative capacity to design and deliver welfare programs – state-centred theory is particularly useful for understanding why some nations are leaders and others laggards in creating welfare states. Unlike other approaches, this fifth model is also sensitive to the importance of unintended consequences, the impact of policy feedback from previous legislation, and the importance of incremental change. For this reason it can be particularly useful for analysing the development of specific policies over time. Unlike two-class models of social change, which see all ideas and initiatives emanating from either labour or business, state-centred analysis also creates historical space for the impact of knowledge-based professions on the growth of the welfare state through tracing their linkages with or location within state agencies.[35] Doctors, nutritionists, social workers, economists, and accountants all played important roles in the formation of welfare policy and in mediating responses to poverty within Ontario. Within a federal system like Canada's, state-centred theory is also highly sensitive to the importance of jurisdictional rivalry both within and between competing levels of government.[36]

Despite these strengths, interpretative models that assign primacy of place to bureaucratic actors often overstate the extent to which state officials can develop social policy initiatives independently of societal pressures and constraints. Nowhere is this more evident than with respect to means-tested social assistance. Regardless of the state's enhanced bureaucratic capacity, the impact of policy feedback, and burgeoning social science expertise, over the half century between 1920 and 1970 welfare in Ontario remained grossly inadequate, highly stigmatized, and profoundly influenced by the legacy of the 'less eligibility' principle. As Chambers has argued within an American context, 'in social welfare, resistance and continuity have been the rule, inertia and momentum the law.'[37] Why this should be so is not easily explained by models stressing the importance of political learning and state-centred administrative leadership.

Heclo, Skocpol, and other advocates of the new institutionalism also understate the importance of shared class and administrative perspectives between managers in government and in business in the framing of social policy. Contributory insurance principles, for example, which underpinned the development of key welfare policies and set sharp limits on their ability to redistribute income or combat poverty, were transferred from the private to the public sector across all industrial nations, including Canada, in the early decades of the twentieth century.[38] Between 1920 and 1970, book-keeping and accounting skills, not social work expertise, remained the fastest route to promotion and leadership within Ontario's Department of Public Welfare. In other words, sites of training and socialization for state officials are important for understanding the extent to which they remain insulated from or independent of market paradigms in their deliberations on social policy. Interpretations stressing the importance of bureaucratic leadership, expertise, and the 'autonomy' of state officials also harken back to an older tradition of writing about social reform, one that exalted the altruism and benevolence of an enlightened elite. 'Not all statist reformers were quite so honourable,' Alan Wolfe observes, a theme that will be echoed in the pages ahead.[39] Finally, state-centred theorists, like many social control analysts, fail to provide much scope for the capacity of marginalized social actors outside the structure of the state – women, the unemployed, or the elderly – to shift social policy periodically to their own advantage.

Gender analysis of the welfare state constitutes the sixth and most recent interpretative approach, one so new that, as one of its most recent converts, Theda Skocpol, observes, 'it is difficult to find straight-forward causal propositions.'[40] Yet, in many respects, gender analysis of social policy is the most exciting and original of all the perspectives discussed thus far, one that forces us to re-examine many familiar programs and policies, the division of labour within the welfare state, and the boundaries separating public and private life in completely new ways.

Although there is no single, overarching gender theory of social welfare, there are common areas of agreement. The most important is that welfare state policies in the early decades of the twentieth century were designed to shore up a family-wage model that viewed women and children principally as dependants of male wage-earners. In other words, welfare policies sought both to exclude women from the labour market and to uphold their essential role as mothers and caretakers of the nation's children. As a consequence of this family ethic, new social rights of citizenship, to use T.H. Marshall's well-known phrase, developed along highly gendered and unequal lines. 'Malestream' welfare entitlements, developed for a mostly male, wage-earning labour force, tended to take the form of automatic, actuarially determined payments, delivered without stigma or moral supervision, to replace the lost component of the breadwinner's wage. Women and children within such programs also received economic protection against the ravages of lost family income through accident, illness, or unemployment, but only as dependants of men.[41]

Welfare policies targeted specifically at women were premised on their role as mothers, not as wage-earners or citizens. These programs, such as mothers' pensions, tended to be administered 'not as a citizenship right but as a form of charity,' allowing scope for bureaucratic discretion and ongoing moral regulation of women's private lives in order to determine their eligibility for benefits. Within this two-tiered welfare state, men claimed entitlements by virtue of their public participation in the capitalist labour market, while women received discretionary assistance, contingent on proof of need, by virtue of their private role within the family as deserving mothers.[42]

Apart from differential policies and entitlements flowing from women's position as dependants within a family-wage model, gender analysis of the welfare state also concentrates on women's predominance within the shaping of welfare policy as clients, reformers, and state employees, on the increasing feminization of poverty, and on the overwhelming importance of women's socialization as caregivers 'provid[ing] welfare services gratis, disguised as part of their responsibility for the private sphere.'[43]

Beyond the centrality of the family wage for understanding women's position within the welfare state, consensus on the role of gender in social policy breaks down. For writers who see social policy as the entrenchment of patriarchy, the welfare state represents simply another illustration of gender inequality and male domination over women, with the state increasingly substituting for absent husbands or fathers in regulating and controlling the lives of women. 'By creating the conditions for continued male control of women at home and on the job,' Mimi Abramovitz argues, the welfare state, insofar as it celebrated and reinforced a family ethic, 'muted the challenge that increased employment by women posed to patriarchal norms.'[44]

Increasingly, however, such a one-sided reading of social policy as male domination is being challenged, for reasons similar to earlier criticisms of social control theory. If the welfare state is too complex to be understood simply as an expression of business power, then seeing it purely as an instrument of male power does not represent much of an advance, since this approach neglects the role of women themselves in the making of social policy. As Skocpol argues, 'gender is not just a relation of social domination or social inequality ... Female gender identities ... can also be sources of social solidarity, organization, and moral purpose.'[45] From this perspective, social policies premised on the centrality of women's role as mothers and caregivers can be seen not simply as repressive instruments of male domination, but as cross-class accomplishments of women attempting to build a 'maternalist welfare state' to gain public recognition and support for their labour. From this perspective, according to Linda Gordon, programs such as mothers' allowances represent 'a major victory for women, particularly working-class and other women, and demonstrate ... their ability to influence middle-class women reformers with political clout.'[46] Seeing the welfare state, in part, as the creation of 'social feminism' also expands our capacity to view women, even before they possessed the franchise, as effective political actors capable of mobilization, lobbying, and influencing state policy to their own advantage, in order to enhance the conditions of their own lives and those of their 'poorer sisters.'[47]

While most recent writing on the welfare state acknowledges the importance of bringing women back into our understanding of state social policy, sharp disagreements still remain over how much autonomy they exercised over the programs created, or to what extent gender solidarities based on 'mothering' overcame class or racial inequalities in the forging of a 'maternalist' welfare state. As with state-centred social theorizing, which emphasizes the autonomy of bureaucratic elites, care must be taken in writing a new feminist history of the welfare state, Gordon argues, to avoid 'a kind of female Whiggism: crediting the value of such welfare programs as we have to women's nurturing inclinations, while the limitations of our welfare state are derived from male individualism. This approach is limited by both a romantic view of women's generosity and an overly dichotomized view of gender, which in turn assumes a kind of unity among women that was never present.'[48]

Women, after all, did end up 'design[ing] inferior programs for other women,'[49] as happened in mothers' allowances within Ontario. Through their own detailed analysis of American welfare policy, Piven and Cloward also remain sceptical of arguments that see women as primary agents in the forging of a maternalist welfare state. 'Family concerns and family politics have not determined the shape of the main welfare-state programs,' they insist. 'To the contrary, in the clash with market interests, family interests have consistently given way; and in the clash with market actors, women acting out of family interests have consistently been defeated.'[50] Other commentators have pointed to the inherent limitations of maternalist assumptions in winning full social rights of citizenship for women. 'Women can have protection or rights, but they cannot have both,' Wolfe observes. 'There is simply too great a tension between the notion that women and men act properly in different spheres of life and the notion that public policies can be designed in a universal and egalitarian fashion.'[51] As with other theoretical approaches, gender analysis of the welfare state contains both promise and potential pitfalls.

This book is a history of welfare in Ontario during the half century between 1920 and 1970. It is not a work of social science. My purpose is not to demonstrate the inherent superiority of any single theoretical perspective for understanding the evolution of the welfare state, nor to argue that generalizations derived from a study of welfare can be transferred easily to other, less stigmatizing forms of social policy. Rather, in the pages ahead I will borrow freely from many of the explanatory models described above when, in my judgment, they shed light on interpreting the complex events and issues surrounding the response to poverty and need within Ontario during the years under review. Although some interpretative perspectives are more useful than others, none is without its limitations in understanding how social policy gets made, nor will any single theory suffice for unravelling the complexity of what has come to be known as the modern welfare state. Instead, by examining the evolution of means-tested social assistance within one province over half a century, I wish to show the many factors that come into play in attempting to understand an issue as complex and morally charged as the response to poverty in the midst of affluence.

1

'In the Interests of the Children':
Mothers' Allowances and the Origins of
Income Security in Ontario, 1917–30

The origins of income security in Ontario begin with motherhood. With the creation of mothers' allowances in 1920, women became the first clients of provincial social assistance. In singling out impoverished widows with children as a category deserving special public recognition and entitlement, Ontario was by no means breaking new ground. Between 1911, when the state of Illinois enacted North America's first mothers' pension scheme, and 1920, thirty-nine American states and all four western Canadian provinces set up similar schemes providing pensions or allowances to dependent widows and their children.[1]

Why did the needs of widows with children, rather than those of the unemployed, the disabled, or the elderly, break the mould of local poor relief and private charity that had dominated the response to poverty and dependency in Ontario, as elsewhere in North America, throughout the nineteenth and early twentieth centuries? On what terms did mothers receive assistance from the state, and how did their claims differ from those of men? In what ways did mothers' allowances, as Ontario's first income security program, establish a welfare framework that would shape the provincial response to other forms of poverty in this century? To what extent did the provision of 'pensions' for mothers represent a new departure in thinking about the minimum needs of Ontario families for an adequate and decent social life?

These questions reflect the extent to which mothers' allowances are central to any understanding of the gendered basis of the welfare state both within Ontario and elsewhere in this century. As feminist historian Linda Gordon has argued, 'if the state were a family, it would be assumed that welfare is a woman's affair ... [W]omen constitute most of the recipients and providers of "welfare."'[2] Within Ontario, women were critical in the campaign to bring about mothers' allowances between 1912 and 1920, and they formed the core staff, although not the key administrators, within the program's early bureaucracy. As Theda Skocpol argues within an American context, mothers' allowances represented the most fully realized vision of a maternalist welfare state, built by and for women.[3] Moreover, policies and regulations aimed at the female clients of mothers' allowances serve to illustrate another key element of the welfare state within Ontario. It operated as a powerful reinforcement for existing assumptions about the essential differences in the needs, roles, and responsibilities of women and men within society. If social policies aimed at men were designed principally to foster the ideal of wage-earning independence, 'women's policies turned on motherhood.'[4] Quite simply, women's right to state aid presupposed their reproductive role within the family and their economic dependency upon men. Only women still fulfilling the first role and deprived of the second were considered eligible for state support.

As a consequence, within mothers' allowances, women in Ontario entered into a unique moral relationship with government. On the one hand, state allowances paid on a regular monthly basis to those women who met the eligibility criteria provided a minimal guarantee of income sufficient to allow them to stave off absolute destitution and, most importantly, to keep their families intact and their children free from the orphanage or foster care. On the other hand, the state, through Ontario's Mothers' Allowance Commission and its cadre of investigators and local boards, explicitly took the place of the absent husband. Financial support and the right to retain care of one's children were given only in exchange for strict fidelity to specific moral norms and expectations concerning the proper external behaviour and innate qualities of a 'good mother' and housekeeper. Women received help not as independent citizens in their own right, but as paid caregivers for the state. Mothers' allowances, Ontario officials argued at the scheme's inception, were justified 'primarily in the interests of the child – the future citizen of the country; the mother being only a secondary from the standpoint of the State.'[5] In this respect, provincial social policy alleviated women's need while at the same time it reinforced their social subordination. Within the early years of mothers' allowances, then, can be found many of the essential contours and contradictions of the gendered response to poverty in twentieth-century Ontario.

The campaign for mothers' allowances in Ontario began, as elsewhere in North America, in the decade before the First World War. The centre of activity was Toronto, the city whose social reform, philanthropic network, and large population would be instrumental in provoking much of the province's response to welfare throughout the remainder of the century. As with most concerns affecting Ontario children in this era, the earliest exponent of mothers' allowances was John Joseph Kelso, a former Toronto newspaper reporter who was the driving force behind the creation of Children's Aid Societies across the province in the early 1890s.[6] In 1893 Kelso was appointed Ontario's first superintendent of neglected and dependent children, responsible for overseeing the regulation of child welfare and protection work across the province. Brought into constant contact with needy widows driven to surrender their children to foster care because of poverty alone, Kelso soon became a forceful advocate of some form of regular financial aid for such women, through a partnership between local government and private charity, to prevent the unnecessary breakup of otherwise worthy families. 'It is no real charity or help to a poor mother to close up her home and send her children, one to this institution and one to that, thus robbing both of the ties and influence that are, after all, the only thing worth living for,' Kelso argued on behalf of widows' pensions in his annual reports to the Ontario legislature from 1895 onwards.[7]

Although Kelso and the Children's Aid Society movement were the earliest advocates of the idea, it gained momentum in the years immediately before the First World War when the campaign was taken up by a wider coalition of women's groups, social service professionals, juvenile court magistrates, labour leaders, and child welfare advocates. They came together through an umbrella Committee on Mothers' Allowances led by the Reverend Peter Bryce, a reform-oriented Methodist minister who was instrumental in settlement work among British immigrant families in the Earlscourt or 'shacktown' district of Toronto.[8]

Bryce was one of the leaders in Toronto's social reform movement. A British immigrant and theology graduate who had studied sociology and political economy with Professor James Mavor at the University of Toronto, Bryce was at the centre of a wide network of child welfare activities within the city. Through his Earlscourt church he administered Canada's biggest Sunday school, with more than 2000 children. Along with publisher and fellow Methodist Joseph Atkinson, he was the orginator of the *Toronto Star*'s Santa Claus Fund, and his Earlscourt Children's Home was one of the largest and most energetic Protestant orphanages and day-care facilities within the city. He was also the first president of Toronto's Federation of Community Services, its Child Welfare Council, and the Neighborhood Workers' Association, the city's largest organized charity. He would also become the first director of Ontario's Mothers' Allowance Commission. Bryce's career in social reform in the first two decades of the new century ably captures the transition from evangelism and moral uplift to a growing faith in the redemptive powers of government. 'At one time Child Welfare had its source in the ministering spirit inculcated by religion, then in the natural impulses of human sympathy,' he argued in 1920. 'Now it is part of the defensive foresight of citizens who would protect the future of the state.'[9]

Although Bryce, like Kelso, provided important leadership in the campaign for mothers' allowances, the core constituency of this reform movement, in Toronto as elsewhere throughout North America, came from the growing ranks of middle-class women involved in voluntary, philanthropic activity. As Gwendolyn Mink argues, 'women's policies were the achievement of middle-class women's politics.' Even before they had the vote, women across the continent used the politics of motherhood as a 'wedge into the political community,' attempting to feminize political life through asserting the centrality of motherhood, home, and family life to national efficiency, moral character, and the productivity of the state.[10] Within Toronto, organizations such as the Wimodausis Club (wives, mothers, daughters, sisters) provided the core financing and administrative support for the work of Bryce's Earlscourt Children's Home. Through this volunteer work, middle- and upper-class Toronto women were exposed to the problems that drove widowed, abused, deserted, and unwed women to place their children in residential care; at the same time, they gained an institutional vehicle for the assertion of their own social and political power within the community.[11] As a consequence, improving the conditions of maternal and child welfare became the crucible within which women forged their own political identity in the pre-suffrage years. Pensions for mothers became one of their most important strategic victories.

Within Toronto, the Local Council of Women took the first step in the mothers' allowance campaign. In 1914, three years after the enactment of the first mothers' pension act in Illinois, the council sponsored an 'experiment' by providing a monthly subsidy for one year to six needy widows and their families in order to demonstrate to government the feasibility and necessity of mothers' pensions. The experiment was 'an unqualified success ... [with] absolutely no pauperizing tendency observed,' the council argued, and the unmet need it revealed was immense. When the project received publicity, 'applications for help poured in from all sides, even from men who were out of work and wanted assistance for their families.'[12] The design of the experiment closely prefigured the final shape of Ontario's 1920 mothers' allowance scheme. The women received help only 'after the most thorough investigation as to their worthiness and their necessity,' and only in return for 'direct supervision of the conditions in each home' by a public health nurse who visited each family regularly, 'advising as to the best means of maintaining the health of the children ... and emphasizing at all times the fact that the mother's duty was to remain at home and to care for the children.' The visitor also advised the mothers 'in a friendly manner as to the best outlay of the pension money' and required written monthly statements from each one showing what she had spent for food, clothing, shelter, and fuel.[13] As Mariana Valverde has argued, the creation of the welfare state was as much a project of private philanthropy as it was the result of efforts by politicians and civil servants. This is certainly evident in the campaign for and design of mothers' allowances. As Ontario officials themselves concluded in appraising the Local Council of Women's experiment, 'private philanthropy must always point the way for state legislation in matters pertaining to charities or pensions.'[14]

Lobbying for mothers' pensions received help from other quarters as well. By the second decade of the new century, overcrowding and high death rates within children's institutions created a growing critique of their role as the primary response to the plight of dependent children. Few of the residents of Toronto's so-called orphanages, as elsewhere in North America, were in fact orphans at all. At the Earlscourt Children's Home, for example, 79 per cent of the children receiving residential care were discharged to their own families, and more than one-third came from mother-led households. A 1918 survey of all 1741 children in institutional care within Toronto uncovered only twenty who had lost both parents. Two-thirds of the remainder were there because of the death, illness, or desertion of one parent, a statistic underscoring the financial fragility of most working-class households. These homes functioned most frequently as the last resort for families in financial crisis rather than as refuges for the parentless, and mothers deprived of the earnings of a male breadwinner constituted their most regular clientele.[15]

Within Toronto's public health, child welfare, and social service community the anomaly of orphanages providing care principally to children with living parents who, but for finanical necessity, wished to keep their families intact was a growing mockery of the sanctity of motherhood, home, and family life. Concern reached a climax during the final years of the First World War. Public health officials pointed to high death rates due to contagious disease among infants surrendered to institutions by working mothers. 'One of the most essential things if the babies are to survive is that they should have mother's care; that they should be nursed through the period of infancy,' Toronto's medical health officer told Ontario officials in making the case for a mothers' pension scheme. 'Now, hundreds, probably thousands of children are weaned because the mother has to go to work to earn a living.' Pensions for mothers would also provide an inducement to persuade tubercular fathers to seek sanatorium care, thus reducing the risk of infection to their families. Toronto school officials pointed to the high dropout among fatherless children and noted that sixty-two exemptions from school had been granted in one year to children under fourteen 'because their mothers were wage-earners requiring [their] help.'[16]

As in other North American cities, juvenile court magistrates also played a key role in making the case for mothers' pensions as an antidote to delinquency. Three of the twenty-six members of Bryce's Committee on Mothers' Allowances were from the city's juvenile court system and all made direct linkages between working mothers and youth in trouble with the law. 'Children who carry the key while their mothers work all day are not long in getting beyond their mothers' control,' the commissioner of Toronto's juvenile court argued in support of keeping women at home through a mothers' pension scheme. Others pointed out that public money spent on mothers' allowances would be returned 'in saving our boys from penitentiaries and our girls from houses of ill fame.'

Even those in charge of childrens' institutions confessed to increasing disillusionment with the results of this form of care. 'The insufficiency of institutional life, the stigma later attached to the institutional child, the over-crowding of our institutions, and the increasing cost of their upkeep' were all arguments in favour of launching a publicly funded program of mothers' pensions, child welfare workers maintained. As one of Toronto's leading Catholic refuge directors put it, 'one of the biggest mistakes that can possibly be [made is] to place any child in any institution, if it is possible to keep it out ... [T]he best institution under the best management is not equal to the poorest home, provided that home be morally correct ... Under present conditions we are obliged to put children into institutions who really should not be there.' Mothers' pensions and the 'proper home training' they would provide would produce 'much better citizens of the country.' Other infant home directors complained that overcrowding in their institutions was a 'terrible problem ... Our cities are growing, and war conditions are making things worse.' Mothers' pensions were 'absolutely necessary' and could reduce the number of children in infant homes by 40 per cent, at great savings to the wider community. Institutionalization was a 'most extravagant way of dealing with the children,' Ontario's superintendent of prisons and charities argued in making the case for mothers' pensions. 'The total cost of keeping the individual homes together would be but a small fraction of the sum' spent on maintaining them within orphanages.[17]

Union leaders, anxious to keep working-class families intact and to reduce the threat of low-wage competition from poverty-stricken working women and children, were a final important constituency behind the drive for a provincial mothers' pension scheme. Fresh from their successful campaign to achieve state-administered workmen's compensation in 1914, Ontario labour leaders saw pensions for mothers as a logical next step on the road to protecting the incomes of working-class families. Why should the widow of a man killed through an industrial accident receive 55 per cent of his former earnings, while the widow of a man dying from tuberculosis receive nothing, the *Toronto Star* asked, in making the connection between workmen's compensation and mothers' pensions. 'In both cases there is the personal loss, but the one family has security of social status, while the other falls into the abyss of poverty.' Labour leaders agreed. Three union officials were represented on the Committee on Mothers' Allowances, and resolutions endorsing the concept poured into Queen's Park from local labour councils across the province in the years between 1914 and 1919. Of all advocates of mothers' pensions, unionists were most in favour of an all-inclusive scheme incorporating not just widows, but deserted, divorced, and unwed mothers as well. 'It is up to the Country to see that [these] children get a fair chance for their bringing up and for their education,' Hamilton labour leader Walter Rollo argued before a government inquiry into the subject. 'It is through no fault of the child that such conditions exist. We believe that the Act should be made as wide as possible and should cover every case ... It keeps the family together.' Ironically, as the minister of labour in charge of implementing Ontario's first Mothers' Allowance Act in 1920, Rollo would find himself presiding over a measure far more restrictive than this generous vision.[18]

The First World War provided the political context for mobilizing these diverse arguments and constituencies above the critical threshold for government action. On the one hand the enormity of the slaughter produced by the war itself heightened the already growing prewar concern that the conservation of children was essential to the productivity and social efficiency of the nation. 'Losses on the battlefield,' Veronica Strong-Boag writes, 'could most logically be made up by renewed efforts to reduce infant mortality. Improved care for mothers and their children would also ensure a generation physically and morally fit to inherit the 'brave new world' for which Canada's soldiers had fought.'

Mothers' pensions thus formed a core component of this war-heightened campaign to shore up family life and redeem the colossal sacrifices of the battlefield.[19]

At the same time, the mobilization of voluntary effort through the Canadian Patriotic Fund to care for the needy families of men overseas provided a practical illustration of the benefits and the methods of administering regular allowances for women raising children. The Patriotic Fund in many ways was nothing but a national illustration, enormously expanded in scale, of earlier experiments, such as Toronto's, in the provision of aid to deserving mothers. 'The experience gained from the administration of pensions to soldiers' dependents by the Patriotic Fund,' Ontario officials argued during war, served as 'a guide' to their efforts in designing mothers' allowances for a postwar world.[20]

Three features of the fund's experience with women were particularly important in this regard. The first was the necessity for 'strict supervision' through regular home visiting of the mothers receiving support, given the 'lack of foresight shown by some of the women who receive[d] Patriotic Fund money.' Women getting help needed 'the supervising and personal touch' to enable them to 'do the best with the sum allowed,' while the community needed a 'safeguard [to] prevent ... an unintelligent distribution of public moneys.' As a result of such close moral supervision, 'in a great many cases [the mother] ... has become a very much better woman.'[21]

Second, the work of the Patriotic Fund demonstrated that 'in every locality there are public spirited and socially minded men and women ready and anxious to give their services in the cause of public welfare.' The fund had worked through the close cooperation of central administrators with local committees of volunteers and visitors operating at the municipal and county level. Ontario advocates of mothers' pensions argued that this model could be transferred successfully to the administration of mothers' pensions.[22]

Paradoxically, the third lesson drawn from the Patriotic Fund experience was that there was 'no suggestion of charity' in receiving money from the fund. Given the close moral supervision and the regular involvement of volunteer women visitors in the intimate details of a client's family life, all of which was borrowed directly from the charity organization model, this insistence that the stigma of charity was entirely absent from the Patriotic Fund's operation was somewhat surprising. However, fund officials gave two critical reasons why this should be so. The first was that the money was 'given in recognition of the service of the husband.' Although mothers' pensions would be justified on the basis of a mother's 'service to the state,' this was not the case with the Patriotic Fund. At bottom, it was the man's sacrifice, not his wife's, which dictated the basis of entitlement. By implication, the moral policing of her household was simply the fund's attempt to look after his interests while he was absent overseas.[23] Second, fund officials argued that the taint of charity was eliminated because they 'provided what we thought was sufficient to give a decent living and a decent living was dependent altogether on the cost of living in the locality. We didn't follow out the principle of the English Poor Law, which gives them just enough to keep up an existence. That would have been a very easy matter to do, but we tried to place them on the basis of a decent living in the community in which they did live ... We tried to give them sufficient to keep on their house.'[24]

When asked by Ontario government officials investigating mothers' pensions what such a standard of 'decent living' might be, fund officials did not hesitate to provide explicit answers. 'Based on the [Patriotic Fund] allowance a widow and two children would now get a minimum of ... $65 a month,' a Hamilton representative pointed out. For a mother with seven children the allowance might range up to '$100 a month.'[25] Simply put, the stigma of charity was dispelled by paying women and their children an adequate and decent allowance geared to actual living costs in the community. Although mothers' allowances in Ontario would borrow much from the Patriotic Fund experience in its design and operation, this commitment to basic adequacy as the cost of avoiding stigma and humiliation for its clients was deliberately forgotten.

The war also provided one last tangible benefit to those interested in the design and implementation of a mothers' pension scheme in Ontario. Through National Registration, government officials knew with a fair degree of accuracy both the number and the location of widows with children in the province and could make a reasonable estimate of how much different versions of a mothers' allowance act were likely to cost. When Department of Labour officials were given the go-ahead by Conservative premier William Hearst at the beginning of 1919 to begin work on the design of 'as sound and perfect a scheme as possible,' they had the models of forty-three American and western Canadian schemes to drawn upon as well as a solid database on the target population within Ontario.[26] A sample of more than four hundred widowed women, selected from the National Registration files, were visited by special investigators sent out by the Department of Labour to determine 'in what percentage of cases the Government would be justified in providing funds.'[27] The questions they asked, borrowed from the operation of mothers' pension schemes elsewhere, ulimately shaped the structure of entitlement under Ontario's mothers' allowance program. Government investigators wanted to know

the number and ages of the children; their nationality; the number of children at home; at school; and working; whether the family occupied the whole house or part; kept lodgers or boarders; whether the mother worked or stayed at home with the children; if she worked, for whom and at what wage; what other income the family received, whether from children or otherwise; what other assets were available, whether in property or insurance; how long the family had lived in Canada and in Ontario; and in addition ... some estimate of the general circumstances of the home, and of the ability of the mother as a homemaker.[28]

Behind all these questions lay the core assumptions concerning who was or was not entitled to state support and under what circumstances. On this basis, department officials determined that 80 out of the 400 families visited, or one-fifth of the total, would be eligible for mothers' allowances should such a scheme be implemented within Ontario. Extrapolated to the more than 16,000 widows in the province, this yielded the estimate of a probable caseload of 3200 families at a cost of almost $1 million annually – figures that would be reached within the first two years of the scheme's operation. Unlike old age pensions, which would be launched a decade later with wildly inaccurate estimates of the population initially eligible, mothers' allowances would be based on remarkably accurate forecasts of costs and caseload size.[29]

Of all the key decisions surrounding the inauguration of mothers' allowances in Ontario, none was more critical than which mothers should be entitled to receive the state's support. Once the decision was made by the Hearst administration early in 1919 to launch such a scheme, public hearings were scheduled in Ontario's four largest cities to test public opinion on the issue. In all, ninety-three witnesses testified at these hearings and none of them spoke against the concept. 'It was distinctly evident ... that this idea of the State employing the mother of its future citizens to rear her children according to approved standards, and subsidizing the home for this purpose where need exists, has taken hold of a very large element in the community,' labour department officials observed.[30]

But which mothers? Evidence given at the public hearings gave conflicting points of view. On the one hand, much of the rationale for mothers' pensions came out of their supposed efficacy in a postwar attack on poverty. 'The day is past when thinking men and women could take poverty for granted,' Ontario officials argued in making the case for such a scheme. 'The causes of poverty ... may be to a large extent eradicated,' and, among them all, the absence of a parent through sickness, death, or desertion was the leading source of hardship for most families in need. Of almost 2000 Toronto children removed from their families to institutions in 1918, one-half were there because of the illness or desertion of a parent, one-quarter because of the death of a parent, and less than 10 per cent because of emotional or physical neglect. Only 1 per cent were true orphans.[31] If rescuing innocent children from poverty was the principal rationale for mothers' pensions, statistics such as these made a strong case for making the scheme as comprehensive and all-inclusive as possible.

Much of the evidence presented at the public hearings in 1919 lent weight to this point of view. If mothers' allowances were restricted only to widows, as was the case in most other jurisdictions, 'the majority of the children will remain where they are,' since only 12 per cent of the population of Toronto's orphanages were there because of the death of their fathers. Insofar as infant mortality was an argument for mothers' pensions, this too mitigated in favour of extending the scheme to 'all dependent mothers, whether widowed, or deserted, or unmarried, as only if the mother can nurse her own child, has the child a fair chance to survive,' public health and children's aid workers in London, Ontario, argued. Finally, 'no need was presented more frequently at the Public Hearings' than the plight of deserted wives with children. Many of these were 'worthy women ... deserted by worthless husbands,' and their children would be 'an asset to the State, just the same as children who have lost their fathers by death,' witnesses argued.[32]

While recognizing the legitimacy of these concerns, both government officials and the leaders of most social work and women's organizations lobbying for mothers' pensions came out strongly against including deserted and unmarried women in the scheme. Toronto's powerful Committee on Mothers' Allowances did not even mention the possibility of including any group other than widows in the legislation. Women leaders were the most forceful advocates of a plan restricted to widows only, largely because of moral concerns. Despite paying lip-service to the idea of deserving women deserted by 'worthless' men, a strong aura of suspicion and moral disapprobation hung over the heads of women abandoned by their husbands. Only 16 per cent of their number living in poverty, social workers estimated, would qualify for mothers' allowances 'under an Act strictly administered according to approved home standards,' and even in these cases the 'worthiness of the wife would require special investigation.' Other witnesses, such as Elizabeth Shortt, one of the province's leading advocates of mothers' pensions, argued that 'the present unsettled domestic relations due to the war' militated against any financial inducement being provided by the government for men to abandon their families. In cases of desertion, most women witnesses agreed, the state's core obligation was to 'provide some way for getting after the man and making him provide for his family,' not to take his place as the family's chief source of financial support.[33]

If relieving the plight of deserted wives through mothers' pensions was morally dubious, doing so for unwed mothers was downright dangerous. 'When we open these doors the flood that will appear makes a man sit back and say "Who will foot the bill?"' clerics testified before the inquiry. Most of these mothers were 'not women who could safely be trusted with the upbringing of children,' infant home directors observed. 'In so many instances [they] are feeble-minded or irresponsible' and only 'a small percentage ... have been very worthy.' Although many wanted to keep their children, in most cases it was 'in the better interest of the child if it were adopted into some other family.' Nor were government officials willing to give any estimate of the anticipated cost of including unwed mothers within the legislation. 'What would be the effect in relation to the present Anglo-Saxon regard for marriage as a national institution if the State undertook to support ... the children of unmarried parents?' labour department officials asked. Although some doctors and nurses argued that unwed mothers should be supported for at least nine months while they nursed their children, only union leaders expressed unreserved support for their equal right to mothers' allowances. 'It is not so much a pension for the mother ... as it is looking after the child. The child has no choice as to whether it is born in the home of the unmarried or the married mother,' and many illegitimate children grew up to 'become some of the brightest citizens of this and other countries ... I don't think we should allow sentiment to enter into it,' Trades and Labour Congress president Tom Moore argued. This view remained exceptional, however.[34]

A final but decisive factor governing entitlement to mothers' pensions was the scheme's initial cost. Dr Walter Riddell, superintendent of labour within the Ontario government and architect of the province's first Mothers' Allowance Act, had been warned by Hearst in drafting the legislation to develop 'carefully thought out provisions ... to prevent abuse.' Considerations of cost as well as moral regulation weighed heavily on his mind in designing Ontario's scheme. 'One thing I am trying to get at is some of the limits we would fix ... to get it in such a way that it will not be abused,' Riddell told witnesses at the public hearings. The inability even to estimate the cost of including unwed mothers rendered them ineligible for support for fiscal as much as for moral reasons. Moreover, compared with the certainty of counting widows, the number of deserted wives who might seek aid could only be roughly guessed. In order to limit costs, Riddell went so far as to maintain that widows with only one child should be excluded from coverage. Although nearly 8000 women in Ontario fell into this category, their need was not desperate, the superintendent of labour argued. 'There are ... numerous good homes open to a mother with one child, where she might go in as more or less of a working housekeeper and take her child with her. The influence of that home would probably be excellent ... [I]t might be the best thing in the world not to pension the mother, so that the child would have the added advantage of being in a good home.' More to the point, cutting out this group, comprising half the widows in the province, from coverage 'would make a great difference [to] the cost of the scheme.' In launching mothers' allowances, Riddell wished to keep 'our position ... comparatively conservative ... [A] solid foundation, well-laid, is the best assurance of a really adequate administration and to secure this at the beginning of so new an undertaking, the doors should not be thrown open wide to all classes of applicants.' Similar arguments prevailed in the decision to limit eligibility to women owning less than $2000 in property and with liquid assets of less than $500. Only 'British subjects' who had lived at least three years in Canada and two years in Ontario prior to their application were eligible for support.[35]

Apart from narrowly restricting the scope of entitlement, the other main determinant of the scheme's cost was the amount to be paid to each mother. Without knowing the extent of need within individual families, Riddell's department used only two rough guidelines to calculate cost estimates. The first was the expense of caring for children within institutions in Ontario, which worked out to $10 per child per month. The second was the average monthly payment of $35 made by Manitoba's mothers' allowance scheme, which had been launched in 1916. Both figures yielded initial estimates in the range of $800,000 to $1 million annually for a mothers' allowance scheme in Ontario restricted to widows with two or more children. Although in many other respects the Patriotic Fund provided the most immediate point of comparison for mothers' pensions, this did not prove to be the case in deciding how much was enough for Ontario widows and their children. In designing the Mothers' Allowance Act, government officials, despite arguing that the legislation should 'provide an amount adequate to secure for the child proper home care,' took as their point of departure a monthly level of support roughly half that used by Patriotic Fund administrators as the standard for a 'decent living.' Moreover, in another precedent that would echo throughout the building of Ontario's welfare bureaucracy, Riddell's report, although refusing to specify a minimum level of entitlement, argued that it was 'necessary that a *maximum per family* should be determined, based on a cost of living budget.' Like much else within the province's emerging welfare structure, mothers' allowances would have a ceiling but not a floor.[36]

Given the critical importance placed on ongoing supervision to ensure the 'moral worthiness' of mothers to receive support, women witnesses at the public hearings also argued strongly against the payment of any routine, fixed amounts to families as was done for injured men through workmen's compensation. Within the mothers' allowance program, women's judgment, not any pre-fixed formula, was the best means of determining a mother's level of entitlement. 'Women ... have been dealing with these problems all these years without assistance from the Government,' female charity workers testified at the public hearings, 'and would be thoroughly trained to take each case on its merits ... [I]t would be ill-advised to have hard and fast cast iron rules laid down on this question ... [I]t should be left to the Committee in charge to judge each case.' Local mothers' allowance boards should be composed equally of men and women, and the latter should be left in charge of the details of family investigation and supervision, these women told Riddell.[37]

As a consequence, within Ontario, as in the United States, mothers' allowances emerged as part of what Nelson has called the two-channel welfare state. 'Industrialists set the terms for the male, work-based parts of the welfare state while their wives, through charity organization work, set the terms for the female, motherhood-based segments.' Unlike workmen's compensation, which was 'male, judicial, public and routinized in origin,' mothers' allowances from their inception were 'female, administrative, private, and nonroutinized in origin,' with levels of discretion and moral judgment borrowed directly from the realm of charity organization rather than the insurance industry, the other main administrative model for social reform.[38]

Although Ontario's Mothers' Allowance Act was developed by Hearst's Conservative administration in time for the 1919 provincial election, the first ever in which Ontario women would cast a vote, Hearst did not benefit from its preparation. Instead, victory fell to the insurgent United Farmers of Ontario in tandem with the Independent Labour Party of Ontario. Together these two groups would enter into a coalition government, led by Simcoe County farmer Ernest Drury, which in 1920 would introduce mothers' allowances within the province. However, the details of the legislation were identical to those already worked out by Riddell during his 1919 investigations. Like the Patriotic Fund, mothers' allowances in Ontario would be administered through a central commission, not a department of government, working with ninety-six municipal and county boards to be established throughout the province. A locally administered scheme without 'centralized control,' government officials concluded, would be too 'irresponsible.'[39]

The province would finance half the cost of the scheme and would retain final decision-making authority over who was entitled to receive support. Local governments would finance the other half and, through their mothers' allowance boards, would receive initial applications for support and advise the central commission in Toronto concerning their worthiness. A staff of seventeen paid investigators, employed by the commission, would undertake the initial home investigation and maintain ongoing supervision of the women who qualified for help. Although Riddell's report had recommended that these investigators should be chosen from among the ranks of experienced social workers and should be free from the taint of patronage, such was not the case. More than three hundred people applied for these positions, and those chosen were often women with public health or educational, but not social work training, who owed their appointments to good political connections.[40] They also endured considerable hardship in physically getting to their clients, particularly in remote rural areas. Investigators commented in their reports on enduring 'a drive or horse-back ride of thirty miles ... long walks of twelve to fifteen miles' or occasionally the necessity 'to travel by hand-car back into the mining districts.' Some told of 'travelling ... by stone-boat' or surviving 'drives in the North through snow so deep that it has to be left to the horses to stick to the trail.'[41]

Peter Bryce was chosen first chairman of the five-member Mothers' Allowance Commission. Other representatives included Elizabeth Shortt; Minnie Singer, a nominee of the labour movement; Arthur Reynolds, a dairy farmer; and Major Thomas Murphy, a lawyer. Three years later, however, Bryce would be gone. When the Conservatives returned to power in 1923, Bryce was replaced by veteran Tory backbencher David Jamieson, an elderly doctor from Durham, Ontario. In 1927 Shortt resigned in protest against Jamieson's blatant use of patronage in hiring commission investigators. Local mothers' allowance boards were also required to duplicate the central commission's pattern of reserving two out of five positions for women, although out of ninety-six boards across the province, only twelve were chaired by women. In terms of eligibility, the Mothers' Allowances Act of 1920 was only slightly different from the criteria recommended in Riddell's report. Allowances would be restricted to needy widows with two or more children who were British subjects, owned less than $2500 in property and $350 in liquid assets, and had lived at least three years in Canada and two years in Ontario before applying for support. Women with husbands whose whereabouts had been unknown for seven or more years were also deemed eligible for support, as were wives of men with total and permanent physical incapacitation. This latter group would prove to be a steadily rising percentage of mothers' allowance families, reaching almost one-quarter of the total caseload by the late 1920s, with tuberculosis the leading cause of dependency.[42]

Most importantly, even if these criteria were met, entitlement to state support was by no means automatic. Widowed mothers still had to meet one more key moral requirement. They must be deemed 'fit and proper persons' to rear their own children, a test of character and worthiness familiar to most other mothers' pension schemes throughout North America. 'The Act was framed in the interests of the children,' its administrators pointed out in their first annual report. 'The mother is regarded as an applicant for employment as a guardian of future citizens of the State, and if she does not measure up to the state's standards for such guardians, other arrangements must be sought in the best interests of the children.' The allowance was 'a reward for service, not a form of public relief,' a distinction deemed critical by the scheme's administrators in order to forestall 'any humiliating feeling of "charity."' 'Family pride is ... a valuable asset to the state and one which we cannot afford to break down.' More to the point, this strict insistence on the moral probity and deservedness of mothers receiving help was a necessary corollary to the sanctification of motherhood itself upon which the campaign for mothers' pensions had been constructed. As Mink puts it, 'these policy victories socialized motherhood rather than citizenship,' and women entitled to help had to live up to prevailing Anglo-Saxon standards of the maternal ideal.[43]

Within Ontario's Mothers' Allowance Act, the regulation and enforcement of these standards were left up to the discretion of local mothers' allowance boards and the commission's own corps of investigators, all but one of them women. For the most part their reports on the lives of the women they visited read like a discourse on their own ideals of middle-class, British, Protestant family life. In the homes of deserving mothers, 'cleanliness and neatness await the visitor instead of untidiness,' their rooms had 'clean curtains ... flowering plants ... [and] good bedding' and their tables were set 'with a clean white cloth, a warm bright fire, and the children sitting around a simple, but wholesome meal.' These women kept 'a close track of every penny that comes into the house,' made their purchases 'economically ... sew [instead of] buy ready to wear articles ... cook wholesome dishes ... [and] pay ... a little monthly on their old debts.' They took care to 'watch ... closely [over] the physical development of [their] children,' ensured their regular church and school attendance, and were not 'overworked ... anxious ... or irritable.' They took 'pride in their homes and gardens and [made] ... great efforts to beautify and make them comfortable.' They also paid attention to their own personal grooming, appearing in 'a clean, neatly worn dress, [with] hair nicely arranged,' and where possible wore 'a look of hope and contentment on [their] face[s]' when the investigator came to call. They did not look for full-time work, but in consultation with their investigator, undertook a selected range of approved part-time labour in order to 'adequately supplement the allowance and yet maintain the position of homemaker.' Women living in the countryside grew 'much of their food stuffs,' or sold 'ice cream and home made baking' at the road side. Others made 'plasticine work, women's wool hats, christmas tree decorations, carding buttons, artificial flowers, reedwork ... brushes ... slippers ... canvas shoes, dresses, millinery ... shirts ... [and] flower buttonholes.' They took in boarders, did laundry, or most frequently laboured as part-time domestics or charwomen in other people's homes. Above all, they managed, without complaining, on whatever allowance they were granted by the commission, demonstrating their 'ability ... to maintain a good standard home on a very small income' through a process of 'wonderful thrift' and 'pride in their efforts' that was often 'nothing short of amazing.' In this they provided a 'training ... [for] the children [which] is greatly to the advantage of their future citizenship.' Needless to say, 'fit and proper' mothers did not drink, use bad language, or consort with men.[44]

Unfit mothers failed to meet these standards. They had a 'record of immorality, neglect of [their] children, or of feeblemindedness with its consequent shiftlessness, inefficiency, and dirt.' They would not provide 'necessary information [such as] the names and addresses of relatives' to investigators, claimed they were 'too sick to work but will not go to the doctor,' or 'refuse[d] to move from an unsanitary home or a demoralizing neighborhood.' They could not control their children, failed to keep them regularly attending school or off the streets, were not seen in church, and could not manage on the money they were given. They took single men into their homes. They drank or used bad language. Above all, they were dirty. Untidiness and lack of cleanliness, in fact, is the most common complaint in the early reports of mothers' allowance investigators, testifying to a connection between dirt, vice, and immorality which, as Valverde has argued, was a central metaphor for the moral reform and social purity movements of this era. Within the maternal feminism of the 1920s, she observes, lay a 'parallel between what was known as "political purity" and personal hygiene. Physical and sexual hygiene – which were to a large extent in women's sphere – were the microcosmic foundation of the larger project of building a "clean" nation.'[45]

In this sense, the connection routinely made by mothers' allowance investigators between mothers' 'service to the state' and the physical conditions of their homes is hardly surprising. As one visitor put it, 'marked improvement in cleanliness of both home and children show the awakening of ambition in the mother,' with results that augured well for the future of her offspring. Throughout commission reports of the 1920s, the moral transformation of women's households through cleanliness imposed by mothers' allowance investigators was a dominant and recurring theme. One recounted her initial visit to a home 'dirty beyond description' in which the language of the children and the mother was 'frightful' and 'appalling.' 'This woman was given instructions as to cleanliness, language, and the home education of her children. The change was far more rapid than one could hope for ... On my last visit both she and the home were the acme of neatness and cleanliness, nice curtains covered the windows and the house was nicely arranged and the children were neat and clean.' It was 'one of the most remarkable cases of social regeneration that I have ever met with.' Another described a family 'living in a one room shack and the floor, walls, and tables were very dirty, the room was filled with flies. The mother was far from clean and was of slovenly appearance. [I] gave careful instruction in detail as to scrubbing and cleaning and advised the mother as to looking for more suitable quarters. Six months later the family had moved to a semi-detached frame house ... The home was clean and neatly arranged and the mother and children showed better personal care.'[46] A third investigator recalled a

family ... found housed in an old shack, surrounded by factories and warehouses, and almost destitute of sunshine and fresh air. Dirt and unsanitary conditions abounded. The children were in rags and had no change of clothing, and the furniture was of the scantiest description. The mother ... had no training in caring for a house or children. The visitor made almost daily visits to this home in the early days after the pension was granted, keeping the mother constantly mindful of what was expected of her ... Little by little changes were made, bedding and clothing procured, and the mother has gradually become a better housekeeper. After 15 months of careful watching and regular income, the family is now in a little five room cottage in a much better district. This new home shows many signs, outside of its improved cleanliness and better furnishing, of the family's new spirit.[47]

Other investigators reported similar transformations of their clients 'from a despondent downcast drudge ... [to] a cheerful mother who can take an interest in her home and family, and the home and family show the result of her interest in their greater cleanliness and neatness.' Such clean and tidy homes created within children 'an appreciation of their home and a willingness to work in and for it that indicates they value such home life and their right to it in the interest of future citizenship.' These 'manly boys and tidy girls' soon developed a 'spirit of independence and are ready to insist that they be given equality of opportunity with other children.'[48]

Alone among welfare programs, mothers' allowance during its first decade developed a discourse which, in a complete reversal of the assumptions of organized charity, linked the provision of regular and certain state relief to the building of character and independence in its clients, through the central metaphors of motherhood and better housekeeping. Within the early years of mothers' allowances, welfare was, in theory, uplifting, not degrading. 'We have seen the beneficial results of state aid in improved home conditions, where before was nothing but poverty and distress, the mother untidy and discouraged,' the commission argued. 'All of this has been changed as if by magic. The whole atmosphere of the home breathes happiness and comfort under the wise and always beneficent influence of the Mothers' Allowances Act, replacing private charity, with the limitations of amounts, its demoralizing effects, and its destruction of self-respect among our people.'[49] In this new framework, private charity, not the state, was the agency of demoralization.

Why this should be so pertained exclusively to the scheme's exaltation of motherhood. Unlike other clients of the emerging welfare state, women staying at home to raise their children were at work performing an essential service. It was for this reason, the commission argued, that mothers' allowance was 'regular in its payments, giving a sense of stability. The recipient looks upon it as in some sense a wage for public service rather than as a dole to a pauper. This makes for self-respect ... The whole tone of the home has been raised by the receipt of an allowance. Mothers who have been indifferent housekeepers and home makers, through the efforts of the Investigator and the local Board, become thrifty, cleanly, and painstaking. The children are better clothed, better fed, and even better mannered, and a chance for education and advancement is given them.'[50]

Although the logic was impeccable, during the 1920s it was not expanded beyond the boundaries of a select group of needy widows with more than one child. Other widows, deserted wives, and divorced or unwed mothers attempting to raise children on their own were kept outside the 'magic' of mothers' allowances and remained dependent on irregular earnings and the uncertain support of absent men, families, friends, and private charity.

As the widowed mother's new employer, the state drove a hard bargain. Mothers' allowance, although ostensibly geared to a 'cost of living schedule,' did not pay anything close to the real monthly costs of raising a family, nor did it draw upon already existing levels of entitlement developed through the wartime Patriotic Fund. Initially, the Mothers' Allowance Commission asked each local board to draw up cost-of-living schedules for mothers with two or more children in their own communities. Although some did, their findings were not reflected in the benefit structure developed by the commission in 1920. Lanark County's board, for example, developed a detailed budget schedule in 1921 showing that $65 was the minimum needed for a mother with four children 'to live in Lanark one month,' but the average monthly mothers' allowance payment in that county was only $30, and the commission itself set a maximum payment ceiling of $40 a month for women in this category living in rural areas.[51]

During its first year of operation, the Mothers' Allowance Commission developed a sliding scale for maximum ceilings of monthly aid based on the number of children in a family and its rural or urban location. Within cities, mothers with two children and no other means of support could get up to $40 monthly, while those with five or more children in the same situation received $55. In rural areas the corresponding payments were $10 less. However, these were maximum levels of support. Deductions were routinely made for income from any assets, or the earnings of the widow, her children, or any support from other relatives. Widows with assets such as the insurance policies of their dead husbands were told to invest the amount in the purchase of homes. Unemployment was not considered a legitimate reason for the deferral of such support and, 'where the family could be self-sustaining without an allowance, were all the members employed, it is not considered eligible' unless the reason was incapacitation due to sickness.[52]

During the scheme's early months of operation, monthly payments averaged more than $43, but thereafter dropped steadily so that by the year's end $35 was the normal allowance, a level that remained constant throughout the decade. The processing of neediest families first, and, more importantly, the commission's increasing experience in the investigation of income and assets, accounted for this 18 per cent drop in the average size of monthly allowances. In its first year of operation,

2660 women qualified for aid. By the end of the decade, steady but modest caseload growth would push the number of families dependent on the program to more than 5600, including almost 17,000 children, at an annual cost of almost $2,400,000. Although the criteria for eligibility or the incidence of widowhood did not change markedly, Ontario's growing population and a rapid rise in the applications of physically incapacitated fathers accounted for the largest elements of program expansion.[53]

The commission acknowledged from the start that the allowances it paid were 'insufficient to maintain the family and can only be regarded as supplementary to the mother's own earnings or other source of income.' Mothers were expected to work on a part-time basis to bridge the gap between their allowance and a basic level of adequacy for their families, and about 60 per cent of them derived income from a wide variety of tasks. Charwork, sewing and knitting, and keeping boarders provided the overwhelming source of extra funds for most mothers. Factory work, because it removed the mother from the home and supervision of her children, was explicitly discouraged. Forty per cent of those receiving allowances reported no employment at all.[54]

If these deserving mothers were truly 'servants of the state,' why were they not paid a living wage to support their children, particularly in light of the uplifted conception of motherhood and full-time care of children which underpinned the scheme? Throughout the first decade of its operation, the rationale for this contradiction shifted in revealing ways. In its inaugural year the commission chairman, Peter Bryce, argued that the 'very large number of applications, many more than at first anticipated,' was the primary reason behind the decision to keep maximum payments within the range of $30 to $55 a month.[55] However, since $35 was the average monthly payment on which Riddell's 1919 investigation had based its initial cost estimates of the scheme, it is hardly surprising that this figure soon became the actual average payment made by the commission. Before long the necessity of mothers working part-time in order to make ends meet was heralded as a positive virtue of the legislation. As Bryce put it in his 1924 annual report: 'While the allowance does not cover the full maintenance of the family yet it is just enough to give encouragement to the mother so that, with careful management on her part and by doing a little work to supplement the allowance, she is able to keep herself and family comfortable in every respect. Were the allowance made to cover full maintenance it would create wastefulness and probably laziness ... The encouragement thus given to the mother to be industrious ... has a good deal to do in making her family likewise.'[56]

Apart from this moral reinforcement of thrift and the work ethic, the labour and earnings of mothers were also deemed useful 'so that the children may benefit to the fullest extent from the Mothers' Allowances.' In other words, the monthly payments were principally for the upkeep of the children, not the mother, who was expected to earn the cost of her own maintenance. Most women were allowed a total income of about $55 a month, inclusive of the average $35 mothers' allowance payment, without suffering any financial penalty. In this respect the program was unique in being the first to provide a financial incentive for supplemental earnings without dollar for dollar deductions from the allowance paid.[57]

The commission soon argued that even $35 a month, without any additional income, was sufficient for those women, particularly in rural areas, who were wise and efficient money managers. One mother with three children living on only $36.50 a month who kept 'close track of every penny that comes into the house' was lauded for her 'amazing ability to maintain a good standard home on a very small income.' Her family was 'well and receiving excellent care.' Another woman living in a small village, also with three children, received 'an allowance of $33 per month and is keeping up a ... comfortable home without debt,' with additional monthly earnings of only $2. A third, with two children, received $30, earned another $3.75 a week, and 'on this income maintains a good home where her children have excellent care ... She has no debt and about $50 in savings.'[58] And so on. The subtext of these tales, which appeared constantly in commission reports in the middle and later years of the decade, was clear. Thrifty mothers could manage well on the income paid through mothers' allowances, particularly if they moved out of the city, and local boards constantly exhorted their mothers 'to try to get along more economically.'[59]

Those who could not were judged the authors of their own misfortune. If they ended up in debt, ran out of food near the end of the month, could not pay the rent, or failed to clothe their children properly, the fault lay within themselves, not in any basic inadequacy of mothers' allowances, and such women faced interviews by their local boards 'regarding unpaid accounts.' The penalties for such failure could be severe. Investigators were constantly reminded that one of their chief tasks was to monitor 'the mother's ability to wisely expend the allowance,' and the commission's annual reports noted that 'often the allowance has actually to be administered to insure the family deriving the proper benefit from it, particularly where the mother is of low mentality,' usually through the offices of the local clergyman's wife, the storekeeper, a member of the local mothers' allowance board, or as in one case, 'the wife of the [township] relief officer [who] ... arranged with

Mrs. H. to help her manage her money affairs for a period of 2 months.' In these cases, control over the expenditure of her allowance would only be restored when the mother demonstrated her ability to 'pay the rent regularly, keep out of debt, and buy food of good nutritive value without extravagance.' One widow with five children, deemed 'a good mother but inclined to be easy with her family' by her local board, lost control of her allowance simply because of her inability to compel her two eldest children to earn enough to keep the family out of debt. 'For this reason it was thought advisable that she should have some supervision or guidance in the handling of an Allowance. Her older children would in this way be taught that it is necessary for them to be responsible for themselves.' Her cheque was initially turned over to the wife of the local clergyman and eventually was administered through the local storekeeper and postmistress. Some local board members reported visiting mothers 'twice a week, helping the mother in the spending of her allowance and in the care of her home,' leading one exasperated former board member to complain, 'why any fur-coated investigator should be allowed to go into a widow's home and demand that she give an account to her of every cent of her allowance is more than I could ever swallow for justice or sympathy.' As a final threat, in homes where 'poor conditions' continued to prevail, the local Childrens' Aid Society would be called in to remove the offspring. Faced with the prospect of losing control, first of their allowances and then of their children, through failure to make do on the money paid, few mothers were apt to complain to their local boards or the commission about the adequacy of their entitlement.[60]

Local mothers' allowance boards, during the scheme's early years, played a critical, albeit idiosyncratic role in regulating the lives of the women under their jurisdiction. Decisions of the central Mothers' Allowance Commission were final, but local boards had influence because municipalities and counties were responsible for half the cost of all allowances paid. In addition, they were able to keep a closer scrutiny over women collecting mothers' allowance than the commission's staff of seventeen investigators, spread across the entire province, with caseloads averaging more than 300 clients each.

In making their initial recommendations about mothers who were 'fit and proper persons' under the meaning of the legislation, local boards were apt to be swayed by rumour, gossip, ethnic and racial prejudice, or their own personal judgment of the reputation and often shifting circumstances of the families under their purview. In contrast, the Mothers' Allowance Commission in Toronto placed more emphasis on strict interpretation of the language of the act itself. Whether women benefited from the gaze of their local boards depended on where they fit within a hierarchy of moral deservedness. During the scheme's early years, when the extent of discretionary judgment permitted by the act was not always clear, this idiosyncrasy of local board decisions was particularly pronounced. In some cases recently deserted, rather than widowed wives, or mothers with only one child, would be recommended for an allowance by local boards when their plight seemed particularly deserving. '[She] has only one child but the mother is an invalid,' Lanark County's board pleaded on behalf of one applicant. '[She] is in very poor health. Her husband having been heard of in recent months would make her ineligible, but [it] was decided ... that this application be sent to [the] Commission,' they agreed in another case. Brant County's board, in its early years, also proved willing to recommend applications for clients who 'did not come under the Act' when moved by their plight, as did Lincoln County. 'While the resident clause would apparently bar a pension,' this board argued on behalf of one recently arrived family, 'we are of the opinion there is a moral claim that should not be set aside. The children are not too rugged and unless nourishment is furnished them, there is just a chance of trouble ahead.' Another mother of eight, recently deserted and abused by her husband and who 'lived in terror of him ever since,' was also recommended for an allowance. 'She experienced nothing but hardship all her married life and our Board, several of whom have known the case for sometime, feel that Mrs. J. is MOST DESERVING of help and ... they strongly recommend that allowance be granted.'[61]

Almost always such claims were rejected by the central commission, no matter how tragic the circumstances, on the grounds that only the strict language of the act itself, not hardship or suffering, conferred entitlement. 'We cannot understand anybody ... telling Mrs. J. that her case would be made a "special" one,' commission administrators told Lincoln County board members in a stiff rebuke regarding the case cited above. 'May I point out that the Act does not provide for an allowance unless that applicant is a widow, or the wife of the father of her dependent children if the husband is incapacitated or has disappeared for ... years ... We are sorry for the difficult circumstances in which this woman finds herself ... especially in view of the fact that the Commission is unable to render any assistance.'[62]

More often, however, the closer scrutiny of the local boards was employed as a check upon mothers who, either for reasons of behaviour or additional income, were deemed no longer worthy or in need of government support. In these cases the role of gossip, rumour, and local reputation often proved critical. Even during a time when entitlement was restricted only to the most 'deserving' of mothers – widows with two or more children – a climate of suspicion always coexisted alongside the lofty rhetoric portraying mothers as 'servants to the state.' Lanark County's board, in only its second year of operation, noted 'there is considerable criticism of the many recipients' and argued that 'many ... were now receiving the allowance but ... not living up to their obligations.'[63] As eligibility under the act expanded in the years to come, the scope for doubt within the community concerning the moral deservedness of its clients would widen even further.

Four areas of women's lives were particular subjects of attention by local boards. The first was sex. On the one hand, widowed mothers were expected to remarry. '[T]his return to the normal home where the man is the wage earner and the mother is the home-maker constitut[es] the best solution of the problem of the support and care of these dependent children,' the commission argued.[64] On the other hand, women seen fraternizing too closely with men risked being viewed as unfit mothers under the meaning of the act. In the case of one Brant County mother, the local board, while 'recogniz[ing] the great financial need of [the] family,' refused to recommend an allowance 'on account of the reputation of the mother which does not seem to be all that could be desired.' A Lanark County mother was terminated because her 'conduct was the occasion of a great deal of talk.' In Lincoln County 'rumours of the conduct' of another mother led to an 'investigation' and suspension of her allowance. A neighbour's letter sent to this same board in another case triggered the suspension of a woman's allowance and the recommendation that her 'home [be] kept under observation for two months.' Her crime was to have been seen going with a man 'to a doctor's office and later to a beverage room and from a reliable source [we were] told this was a common occurrence in Grimsby on Saturday night.' She, too, lost her allowance. In her wide-ranging research into mothers' allowances in this era, Margaret Little has also uncovered numerous instances of women cut off from support on the grounds of alleged sexual impropriety. 'These women were supposed to donate all their time and attention to their children and to never show another interest in a man as long as they received the MA cheque,' she argues. 'Just as their husband had financially supported them in return for sexual monogamy, the state struck the same bargain.'[65]

Mothers also had to live up to strict standards of housekeeping in the eyes of their local boards, but even here there was a fine line to be drawn between keeping their physical surroundings 'neat and tidy' and spending too much on their homes. Reports to London's board that a mother was living in 'quarters unsuitable for the bringing up of children' was sufficient reason for denying her a pension. Lincoln County's board accused a St Catharines mother of 'living ... in such a condition of filth and degradation as to remove her entirely from our Branch of the work.' Her allowance was suspended. 'Untidy conditions' in another home were taken as evidence that the mother 'was not a good housekeeper.' A third mother was told bluntly that her 'living conditions ... were brought to the attention of our Board at their last meeting and at that time I was instructed to warn you that unless these conditions are improved immediately, your allowance will be cut off.' Yet when another woman 'bought ... new furniture, had a new bathroom put in, new linoleum on floors, new curtains etc, since her husband died,' these actions were considered sufficient grounds for why 'our Board could NOT recommend this case.' Only recognition by the central commission that the mother was using her husband's estate correctly to improve living conditions for her children succeeded in winning a pension for this widow, against the wishes of her local community.[66]

The capacity of other family members to come to the aid of widows in need was the third area in which local boards were given free rein to exercise discretionary moral judgments. Since local taxpayers were responsible for 50 per cent of the cost of mothers' allowances, this was a particularly sensitive issue within counties and municipalities across Ontario, and local gossip and monitoring by neighbours provided local boards with a critical conduit of information on the shifting financial circumstances and earnings of family members. 'A lady called me up over the 'phone this morning respecting [a] mother's pension beneficiary – Mrs. H.,' London's city clerk told the local board. 'She claims that the man is going around dressed in white flannels like a well-to-do merchant prince. A daughter is working in the Bell Telephone Co., and the brother is an insurance agent making big money. The woman is working regularly, and generally they are living in opulence and wealth. She claims that they are not deserving a mother's pension and that it is a crime against the general taxpayer.'[67] In Brant County, grandparents were considered, in another case, to have 'some responsibility in the care of [a widow's] children and ... are financially able to look after them without public assistance.' A similar view prevailed with respect to a Lincoln County mother. 'While the applicant appears to have no assets,' the local board argued, 'we feel that the ability of the parent to assist should be considered in deciding the amount of allowance to be granted.' More commonly, other widows had their pensions reduced or suspended altogether because of the expectation, as Lanark County's board put it, that 'so many adult children should maintain the mother and child,' or because 'wage earners should contribute more to the house.' 'The applicant should have some help,' Brant County's board argued in a typical case, 'but [we] took into consideration that there were children 16 & 17 yrs who should be helping the [mother].' As would become the rule with Old Age Pensions in the 1930s, this anticipated income from siblings, children, and parents was counted against a woman's monthly entitlement whether or not it was actually received.[68]

Finally, regular school attendance and the appearance, language, and behaviour of their children within the community were a constant measurement of how well mothers were living up to their role as 'servants to the state.' As the commission gained experience in administering the program, new methods were sought to 'get better results ... for the allowance granted.'[69] One of the most effective was demanding the monthly return of school attendance cards by mothers to the central commission offices in Toronto, and 'if the card is not in by the 20th of the month, the beneficiary knows that her cheque will be withheld,' officials pointed out. In cases where attendance was deemed unsatisfactory, a financial penalty would be deducted from the family's monthly allowance. Here, for example, are typical entries appearing in the Lanark County board minutes between July and November 1929. 'Mrs. L, Perth, decreased from $35 to $30. Arnold not at school. Mrs. S. decreased $35 to $30. Bonnie not at school. J.D., Maberly, cancelled, only 1 at school ... M.L., decreased $30 to $25. Laura not at school. A.D, decreased $45 to $40. Jonathan not at school.'[70] And so on. Through these bureaucratic devices not only mothers but children themselves were made directly aware of the strict relationship between behaviour and entitlement. As the commission put it: 'The mother knows at once that her children must have her first care ... she is told her children must not keep bad company, must not be out late at night, in addition the children as they grow older know the income into their home depends largely on how they conduct themselves, they know that periodical school reports are sent to Head Office, and so the boys and girls are under this steadying influence all the time, and especially at that critical age of fourteen to sixteen when so many ... make a wrong turn.'[71]

Local police appreciated this extra control mechanism on children's behaviour. 'A chief of police of one city ... says he has little or no trouble with children of beneficiaries,' the commission reported. 'If he meets one with a tendency to misbehaviour he has only to threaten to report to the Investigator, it has the desired effect.' Cooperation of mothers with doctors and local public health officials in seeking treatment for themselves or their children was also essential in their retention of a monthly allowance; investigators armed with the threat of witholding monthly income 'succeeded where others have failed in persuading a mother to have her child admitted to a hospital, or taken to a doctor.' In short, through developing new channels of information with other agencies of the state such as school officials, public health nurses, and the police, the Mothers' Allowance Commission and its local boards by the later 1920s were able not only to 'merely collect information in order [to] ... decide on the eligibility of an applicant,' [but] rather [to become] vitally interested in every phase of the family life.' In this way its moral gaze into the lives of its clients became ever more penetrating.[72]

The race and ethnicity of clients also influenced the way local boards judged their deservedness in the program's formative years. The requirement that applicants be British subjects, along with the scheme's strict residence requirements, acted as an arbitrary bureaucratic filter for excluding many immigrant widows and their children from coverage. Throughout the 1920s the ethnic origins of over 90 per cent of mothers getting aid through the program were either Canadian, British, English, Scottish, or Irish, compared with only 9 per cent born elsewhere, at a time when almost 15 per cent of Ontario's population was of non-British or French ancestry.[73] Apart from this formal stipulation, other barriers of ethnocentrism and racism excluded mothers of non-Anglo-Celtic origin from equal treatment. Some local boards, Little discovered, disqualified ethnic minority women 'because they could not read or write English.' Inability to produce the necessary legal documentation proving marriage, widowhood, or the birth of their children operated as a further bureaucratic obstacle excluding many immigrant women of non-English ancestry from eligibility. It is also clear, as Little argues, that 'families from ethnic minority backgrounds underwent more intense investigation than their WASP counterparts' and that 'neighbours were more likely to spy and complain about minority families.' In Lincoln County's surviving case files, the claims of some mothers with non-British names, no assets, and debts sometimes totalling over $750 were dismissed simply on the grounds that 'we think she can manage' or because 'she lives in a fruit section where both she and her family can obtain almost steady employment.' In other cases a mother was 'cut off ... because of her anti-British sympathies' or because of 'evidence of disloyalty.' In contrast, other applicants, as Little notes, could be congratulated for coming from 'a beautiful Scotch family' or being 'very worthy, reticent, Scotch people.' In this way local boards, by reflecting existing community patterns of ethnocentrism, prejudice, and discrimination in their recommendations, cut off many otherwise eligible and deserving mothers and children from the support available through the program.[74]

Despite the powerful role of moral judgment, community scrutiny, rumour, and prejudice in the administration of mothers' allowances, which undercut the program's continual claim that it was free from any 'stigma or taint of charity,' and regardless of the inadequate benefits it paid, there is no doubt that the program's arrival in Ontario during the 1920s was a blessing to the thousands of women who qualified for its support. That this was the case can be seen from the letters they sent to the commission itself, from the conditions they faced prior to applying for help, and from the desperate pleas of thousands more deserted, divorced, or unwed mothers who could not qualify for support under its terms. 'I wish I could tell you the joy it is for me to be able to stay at home and make our home bright and comfortable for my children,' one mother wrote on receipt of her allowance. 'My own health was failing and I do not like to think of how we would have lived this winter without help.' 'What a blessing your pension is,' wrote another in a letter typical of many others sent to the commission. 'Now we poor widows and orphans can live like other people and have some pleasure. Before we had this pension our poor kids were certainly to be pitied, but now they can pass with the others and be safe from hardships.' 'Without your help I don't know what would have become of my children and myself,' a third simply stated.[75]

For the mother who had 'lost her home and her furniture was set out on the road'; for the woman who occupied 'the most needy home I was ever in, positively bare, some boxes for table and boxes to sit on'; for the family 'depending on whatever their brothers give them'; for the mother with three children living entirely on 'two dollars per week for the last two years from North Grimsby Township Council'; or the mother of three getting '$10 per month as a domestic' – the regularity of a $35 or $40 monthly mothers' allowance cheque made an extraordinary difference in their lives and those of their children.[76] If it was not, to be sure, an adequate and decent standard of living, it was nonetheless the difference in many cases between keeping a family intact on the death of the husband and surrendering children to the uncertain fate of institutional or foster care. In many cases it represented the first regular income such women had ever seen. However, it was also an allowance paid for the care of the children, not the mother. When they turned sixteen, she was left to the care of her own children or, failing that, to relief or to private charity. Yet as a woman too young for the means-tested old age pension, she was often too old or too ill for paid employment. 'I have been a widow for the past three years and have two children, a girl sixteen in December and a boy twelve years,' one mother wrote Premier Howard Ferguson in despair on learning that her allowance was to be cancelled. 'By the help of the Mothers' Allowance so far I have been able to manage ... Mrs. Preston ... who visits me on official business concerning the Mothers' Allowance on her last visit spoke as though I would be without this support as soon as my girl was sixteen. I am at a loss to know what to do to meet expenses from now until such times as my boy is able to take a man's place on the farm.' Ferguson's reply was short and to the point. 'There frequently arises cases similar to yours ... but there are no monies available ... I am very sorry that this should be the case.' Mothers' allowance, Ferguson responded to all such queries, 'was not a pension scheme. It is merely intended as an aid to mothers to enable them to provide a home and properly rear their children.' When their reproductive work was finished, so too was their claim upon the state for support.[77]

Mothering was a central metaphor for the development of Ontario's welfare state. The claims of motherhood as a service to the state provided the first compelling arguments for breaking down the tradition of exclusive local responsibility for the care of the poor. Within Ontario's mothers' allowance program, moreover, lay the seeds of a new basis for thinking about welfare as entitlement rather than as charity. The rationale employed by women's groups and other social reform constituencies for legitimizing mothers' allowances, and in the reports of the commission itself during the first formative decade of its operation, was always that state support to mothers was a reward for service, that it did not stigmatize, that it fostered independence, and that it uplifted the character of both the women and the children who received it. Simply put, mothers' allowance during the 1920s was the first means-tested social program based on the premise that steady and certain state assistance was not demoralizing, and that the reproductive work of women merited some degree of social entitlement.

However, both the level and the scope of this entitlement remained highly ambiguous. Although better than the uncertain support of relatives, neighbours, local relief, or private charity, mothers' allowances never came close to providing a sufficient income in itself for a decent standard of living even as defined within the context of the 1920s.[78] Nor was it meant to. Even the most deserving of the poor – worthy widows of British stock with two or more children – were still expected to need an 'incentive to effort' in the form of part-time work, in order to underwrite the cost of their own care, to motivate their children towards self-reliance, and to bridge the gap to a minimally adequate living standard. By failing to come close to adequacy despite recognizing entitlement and need, mothers allowances thus became an ominous indicator of contradictions that would soon bedevil other welfare programs to emerge within Ontario.

Despite its claim of fostering independence, moreover, the program did not leave mothers on their own. Commission investigators, local boards, other agents of the state such as school officials or public health nurses, and neighbours subjected the lives of mothers in the program to an unrelenting moral scrutiny and supervision. Widows on mothers' allowance may not have been stigmatized, but as women living on their own at the expense of taxpayers they were always morally suspect and the conditions of their entitlement required unremitting attention to their standards of character, homemaking, sexual behaviour, thrift, and industry. Deviations from these standards, or simply inability to cope, could and did result in loss of control over their allowance or, in extreme cases, in loss of their own children. As the program was expanded to include deserted wives and, ultimately, unwed mothers in the decades to come, the grounds for suspicion of moral worthiness would expand even further.

Finally, mothers' allowances were justified 'in the interests of the children.' Although paid to mothers, the allowances were intended for their children. Thus an unresolved contradiction between the needs of women and children was embedded in the program from its inception. Were mothers' allowances truly a payment to women in reward for service to the state, or were they instead a sum entrusted to mothers for the care of their children? In the former concept there was a sense of earned entitlement; in the latter, only stewardship. As the plight of mothers whose children turned sixteen clearly revealed, it was stewardship, not entitlement or a reward for effort, which underpinned mothers' allowances in Ontario. When their nurturing task was done, women were cut off from the program's support at an age and often in a state of health which made paid employment uncertain at best. From their ranks, as well as others, would emerge a new category of aged women living in poverty.

Regulating the Elderly: Houses of Refuge, Old Age Pensions, and the Politics of Aging in Ontario, 1900–45

Old age in early twentieth-century Ontario was for many of the province's elderly a time of poverty, physical and economic insecurity, and social marginalization. Private pensions were few, public pensions non-existent, and the scant institutional accommodation for the indigent aged in county and city houses of refuge sparked feelings of terror in those facing uncertain prospects in their final years. One retired London, Ontario, schoolteacher, pleading for an old age pension scheme, wrote to the federal government in 1925:

What an awful thing it is for some of us, who, through illness, losses, etc arrived at old age WITHOUT ANYTHING to live on and no one to show the least concern as to what becomes of us! ... Thousands have no children – nor anyone else to look after them. I am one of the thousands ... I am seventy-three, not in good health ... but struggling for existence daily. SEVENTY-FIVE cents is the amount that stands between me and starvation ... I do not want to beg ... Often the only resource for men who have lived useful lives ... is to go to one of ... those horrible, abominable institutions, the county poor houses, most of them run in a way that is shocking and a crying disgrace to a civilized and supposedly Christian community – those PLAGUESPOTS of the universe as someone has called them. They may do for some of the feeble minded and for sots, but certainly are not places for decent citizens.[1]

This man's predicament and fears were shared by thousands of aged men and women across Ontario as the province emerged from the crisis of the First World War and entered into a decade in which 'youthfulness was celebrated to an unprecedented degree in print, on film, and on radio.'[2] Growing old in Ontario, or in any other part of Canada in the previous century, had certainly not been an easier, more pleasant experience. There had never been a 'golden age' for the elderly in

North America's past. Grinding physical labour, primitive medical knowledge, dangerous machinery, and the strain of frequent childbirth condemned the third of the population that survived beyond sixty to only a few, often painful years between the end of a working life and the grave.[3]

Nonetheless, by the early twentieth century some important changes had occurred in the circumstances and attitudes surrounding the elderly. Most importantly, old age itself was becoming a more prolonged phase of life. Improvements in diet and public health produced an increasing number of the elderly relative to the whole population and an extended period of time between the end of physical labour and death. Old age, in short, was becoming a common rather than an exceptional part of life, and the years of economic and physical dependency it produced were also lengthening.

One direct consequence was an increasing association between poverty and old age. By the late nineteenth century, growing numbers of elderly, unable to look after themselves, were joining the poorhouse, refuge, asylum, and even jail populations across North America.[4] York County's House of Refuge in 1883, a visiting delegation from Oshawa noted, although containing 'men, women and children from three to 112 years of age [was] composed chiefly of old people.' The province's jail system as a whole, an 1891 Ontario Royal Commission on the Prison and Reformatory system complained, was filling up with 'large numbers of homeless elderly charged with vagrancy because they had no place else to go.' In Whitby at the turn of the century over half of all committals to the county jail between January and May of each year were for vagrancy. In pleading for the erection of an old age refuge in Ontario County, prominent local citizens lamented that 'the halt, the maimed, the blind and the aged friendless' were being 'compelled to herd with criminals' for the simple offence of 'begging for the necessaries of life.'[5] Twenty-eight years later Toronto workers pointed out to another royal commission that many of their poverty-stricken elderly comrades with no pensions or savings for old age were still being sent 'up before the Police Court for vagrancy and the sentence they give them is to carry them over the winter at the jail farm.'[6]

As its frequency and duration expanded, old age was often perceived as a pathological medical problem. 'Geriatrics,' as the specialized medical study of old age, first entered the lexicon in 1909. By the late nineteenth century, however, doctors armed with a new 'anatomical view of disease,' which stressed the internal degeneration of vital organs, increasingly viewed the elderly as a population whose 'normal physical condition had become one of disease' and for whom 'separation from society was both necessary and desirable.'[7] Medical labelling of old age as synonymous with infirmity and sickness was critical to the creation of overwhelmingly negative public attitudes towards old age and the elderly. Simultaneously, the intensification of pace and work discipline within North American industry promoted the view that the old, even before the age of sixty-five, were unemployable and of little economic or productive use. Such attitudes fuelled the movement for mandatory retirement as part of a wider drive for industrial efficiency. Advancements in science and education, at the same time, discounted the value of traditional knowledge and experience so that, ironically, 'as education improved ... the relative condition of [the] elderly ... grew steadily worse.'[8] In short, by the first two decades of this century, although the life expectancy of the elderly had advanced, in other respects their cultural and material position had worsened. Increasingly, old age was viewed as a stage of life synonymous with poverty, disease, uselessness, and dependency, and the elderly were seen as a group whose best interests were served by their 'remov[al] ... from industrialized society.'[9]

In nineteenth-century rural Ontario the old lived with their children, most often their unmarried children, or other relatives.[10] Not simply ties of sentiment and obligation, but ownership of farm property provided the elderly in rural society with the rudiments of security near the end of their lives. Farms transferred from fathers to sons typically contained guarantees for the continued support of parents by their offspring, either on the farm itself or on land severed from or adjacent to it. Unmarried daughters, who often became the caregivers to their parents, were included in these legal arrangements.[11] In rural society, not only was the productive power of the elderly more evident and prolonged, but farm communities could also serve as moral watchdogs over the care of the old by their children.

As Ontarians abandoned rural life for towns and cities, these traditional social mechanisms for providing care to the aged slowly disappeared. By 1911 almost half of all Ontarians were living in urban areas, compared with only one-fifth forty years earlier. In 1921 the proportion would be over 58 per cent. By 1931 10.2 per cent of the province's population was over sixty years of age, compared with only 8.4 per cent in 1901.[12] Within cities the elderly found themselves far more vulnerable to poverty and dependency than in the countryside. On farms the old could continue to eke out an existence on their own or live with children or relatives. But in the cities the end of wage employment for many meant sudden impoverishment and isolation. As Toronto's medical officer of health complained to the city's mayor in 1924: 'Under existing industrial conditions many men and women, especially married couples who have reared a family, have found it impossible to provide for their old age. Each year it becomes more difficult for these old people to find employment of any kind ... High rents and over-crowding in houses make it difficult for the poor to provide for their aged parents.' Increasingly, Toronto social agencies were discovering 'that many of the old men and women in their districts are suffering for the lack of the necessities of life.'[13] In short, not only was the number of elderly in the province growing in the early twentieth century, but the social provisions for their care were deteriorating dramatically.

Before the early 1920s the Ontario government had not singled out the aged, as it had neglected children, widows, and injured workers, as a class entitled to or in need of special legislative protection or consideration. The indigent elderly, without friends or family to help them, were at the mercy of private charity, local jails, or the poorhouse. Poverty, not age, was their only claim to support from the community. In the second half of the nineteenth century the elderly were identified as a 'progressively degenerating underclass,' and aged people's homes or refuges were built in the larger cities, such as Toronto's Belmont Homes begun in 1853 and accommodating 180 elderly by 1908, or Ottawa's Protestant Home for the Aged constructed in 1887. These institutions represented the first recognition of the old as a unique category of the 'deserving poor' who merited, in the words of one Ottawa charity, 'a quiet place in which to die.'[14] They also expressed a desire to control emerging social problems by physically segregating the population in question from society at large and by creating a surrogate institutional family structure. With the elderly, however, unlike orphans, the delinquent, or the mentally ill, no hope was held out for their recovery or rehabilitation.[15]

By the 1920s there were forty-six private refuges for the aged in Ontario caring for about 3400 people at an average daily cost of eighty-nine cents for each resident. All received subsidies from the provincial and municipal governments in recognition of their role in relieving public authorities of responsibility for the care of indigents. More than one-third of this institutionalized population was in Toronto. Accommodation in buildings such as Toronto's House of Providence could range as high as four hundred, although most old age homes provided beds for between thirty and sixty inhabitants.[16]

What kind of care did they receive? Standards varied widely according to the size, sex, and composition of the institutional population or its philanthropic backing. Charitable houses of refuge or shelters for the aged could be segregated according to sex, income, religion, ethnicity, or degree of disability. Others such as Toronto's House of Providence, run by the Roman Catholic Sisters of St Joseph, were congregate dwellings with a large, catch-all population that included many who were indigent and physically or mentally disabled but not elderly. In Ottawa, Sharon Cook argues, gender did 'appear to have made some differences in the care of [the] aged poor.' The Protestant Home for the Aged, which catered exclusively to men, dealt with a more transient population that moved frequently in response to the availability of work opportunities. Here the atmosphere was spartan, with emphasis on discipline and the maintenance of a sober, obedient, and pious population. Aged women, in contrast, cared for through the Refuge Branch of the Protestant Orphan's Home, tended to remain permanently in the home once admitted. Although subject to strict rules, on pain of expulsion, they received more entertainment, personal contact, and a more deliberate attempt by the women in charge to create a 'disciplined family environment.'[17] In both institutions the resident population was exclusively lower working class.

In Toronto, where nine private charitable institutions served the aged, a wide diversity in care existed. In the House of Providence, the city's largest shelter for the elderly, dormitories slept from eighteen to fifty residents. Women were given a locker, a chest of drawers, a screen for privacy, a small table, two chairs, and a bed. Men made do with a locker, table, and bed. Within the House of Industry, old people sleeping eighteen to a room had only a bed, from which they were exiled during the day while the heat was turned off and the windows were opened to circulate air. Two nurses cared for 164 aged poor. At the Jewish Old Folks Home built in 1916, in contrast, dormitories held at most four to a room; the 105 residents had a medical doctor, four nurses, and an orderly to care for their needs; occupational therapy was provided; married couples could live together in private rooms; and the building was equipped with a synagogue, library, and 'large recreation room.' No discipline was enforced, and the elderly, if they wished, could remain in their beds all day.[18]

Care such as this, however, was the exception rather than the rule. Within most charitable refuges, as one government report observed, the intention was simply 'to see that they are kept clean and warm; that the residents are well clothed and fed, and that the food is wholesome and plentiful.' Annual reports from these refuges reveal that little was provided for or expected from the elderly beyond waiting out their time. 'Generally speaking the days pass quickly and pleasantly as each one is free to follow her own desires,' the directors of Toronto's Aged Women's Home observed of their 117 clients in the mid-1930s. 'Sewing, reading, visiting friends in the Home, having a cup of tea with one another, or when the weather is fine, going for walks ... all these pleasant diversions fill the days and make the quietness of the evening hours even more enjoyable.' Down the street at the Aged Men's Home the scene was equally quiescent. 'To look in at the old men as they sit in all sorts of attitudes in their sitting room makes one think of a hazy day in Indian Summer,' the 1935 annual report commented sentimentally. 'The men are comfortable and for the most part very content for to them has come a bright and happy time in the eventide of life. The many gifts of tobacco help the Superintendent to keep "that contented look" in the old faces.' In short, the elderly were expected to rest, not cause trouble for the matrons or superintendents, and prepare for death. Some homes possessed radios, playing cards, and newspapers, and others had organized sewing circles as well as gardens. For the most part, though, few provided much in the way of recreation or entertainment. It was gratifying enough, directors commented paternalistically, 'to know that their last days have been made comfortable and their pathway smoothed in the decline of life, and to hear, from their own lips, as we often do, expressions of gratitude for the care bestowed on them.'[19]

At the bottom of the scale in the care of the aged, apart from jails themselves, were Ontario's forty county houses of refuge or county homes. Throughout the interwar years they cared annually for between two and three thousand indigent old people, or about seventy-five per institution, at about half the cost of their urban counterparts.[20] Essentially these were poorhouses, or more accurately poorfarms, since almost all were located in the countryside and were required by the province to devote at least forty-five and preferably one hundred acres of land to cultivation, both as a 'work test' for their inhabitants and as a means of defraying part of their cost of operation. In the late nineteenth century some county councils had built such refuges voluntarily, with the encouragement of the province, in response to the growing numbers of indigent poor flooding their jails. In 1903, however, their construction was made mandatory for all counties in response to the sharp rise in 'tramping,' vagrancy, and homelessness. Some parsimonious rural reeves would have preferred to have continued shipping the indigent and the helpless to the nearest city.[21]

County refuges were not constructed specifically for the elderly, although almost from their inception the aged became their principal clients. Unlike city refuges where women made up fifty-five per cent of the inmates, two-thirds of the county refuge population were men, reflecting the more transient nature of the rural male labour force.[22] These homes were congregate institutions, dwellings of last resort for all forms of social wretchedness and dependency, whatever its cause. Like poor-houses everywhere, their role as institutional repositories embedded them from the beginning in a hopeless contradiction. As Michael Katz argues, 'the almshouse was to be at once a refuge for the helpless and a deterrent to the ablebodied; it was supposed to care for the poor humanely and to discourage them from applying for relief ... In essence, social policy advocated shutting up the old and sick away from their friends and relatives to deter the working class from seeking poor relief.'[23]

County houses of refuge in Ontario fit this description exactly. In the York County Home, in the 1880s, where children as young as three mixed with a population composed mostly of old people, all the inmates, visitors noted, 'who are able to work are ... employed in making clothing, mending, scrubbing, knitting, and ... taking care of those inmates not able to care for themselves. Those who are able to perform manual labor on the farm do such work as they are able to do.' In Ontario County's refuge, inmates who disobeyed work orders from the matron and the superintendent in principle 'forfeit[ed] all right to return to the Home again.' At the Stormont, Dundas, & Glengarry County poorfarm, elderly women who were 'quite able to knit or patch as commanded by the Matron' and refused to do so were threatened with expulsion. Male inmates who were capable of labour were required to milk cows, pile stone, paint and renovate the buildings, and 'be in readiness for farm work by 7:30 a.m. daily,' and these requirements for farm work remained in place until the late 1940s. Board of management minutes from this refuge during the interwar years also note the occasional male inmate receiving a 'peg leg' or a new set of false teeth from the refuge directors *as a reward* for doing 'considerable work around the institution.' Although work requirements were a feature of all county houses of refuge, how strictly they were enforced remains unclear. As a detailed study of the Wellington County House of Industry points out, because of the aged and infirm nature of its population, the attempt to offset costs through work by inmates was 'spectacularly unsuccessful.' As inspectors' reports lamented, 'Many do nothing and others do so very little.'[24]

Deterrence operated as the dominant motif in these homes in other ways as well. Although the most common rationalization for their construction, as one 1899 grand jury argued, was to empty county jails of the indigent 'who have committed no crime,' county refuges in many ways mirrored the jails they replaced. Many were built with punishment cells in their basements to enforce discipline. Here troublesome inmates could, on the order of the matron or the superintendent, be subjected to solitary confinement and their diets limited to bread and water. Given the elderly and usually frail composition of the refuge population, these cells soon fell into disuse on a regular basis for punishment purposes, although the superintendent of Ontario County's Refuge noted in the 1940s that the 'barred cell which was built into the basement ... may still be used ... for brief periods when a resident became gravely disturbed mentally.' At the Stormont, Dundas, & Glengarry poorfarm, instructions to the superintendent from the board in the late 1930s noted that 'no inmates [could] be kept in the cells *except for discipline*' and none could be incarcerated 'over night.'[25]

Houses of refuge resembled prisons in other ways as well. Most notably, residents could not come and go as they pleased, no matter what the reason for their committal. At the Stormont, Dundas, & Glengarry poorfarm, the board of management made it clear that 'no person be allowed to leave the home until applications are received in writing from responsible persons.' Those who tried were ordered to be picked up and arrested by the provincial police. In the early 1930s, when the board realized that 'several of the male inmates would escape if given a chance,' they ordered the 'erection of an enclosure to hold [them].' Permission to leave became a powerful tool for controlling behaviour or assessing moral deservedness. Some were allowed to depart on condition that they never return to the county; others were allowed out temporarily to 'get some clothes and see what things were like'; while many others were simply told, like the wife of one impoverished Glengarry farmer during the Depression, that she must remain an inmate 'until such time as [your husband] can show the Board that he has sufficient funds to support himself, wife, and children.' At the Middlesex County House of Refuge in the 1920s one elderly resident, promised a home and a small wage in return for chores on the farm of 'old time friends,' was informed that it would be a 'very great mistake at your time of life' if he thought of departing since he would soon be applying to get back in. 'As far as we are concerned *we could not entertain the idea* of your leaving the institution under the present conditions.'[26] Against arbitrary decisions such as these there was no appeal, nor even the prisoner's slight comfort of a fixed sentence.

Consigned to these refuges and poorfarms, the elderly, like convicts, were also subject to the stringent discipline of matrons and superintendents (usually married couples) who lacked any medical or dietary training, or expertise in working with the elderly or disabled, and whose authority was only mildly held in check by occasional visits from boards of management or provincial inspectors. Often ruling these institutions for decades at a time, these poorly paid couples were concerned with maintaining order and strict behaviour among the inmates, managing the farm in return for their own room and board, and remaining on good terms with parsimonious local councils. According to the board of management at the Ontario County Refuge, the 'greatest characteristic, [the] outstanding characteristic' of that institution's administrator 'was his control over men and women. Discipline, always discipline, without undue stricture. He was the one man on the job and they all knew it.'[27]

Within such homes, elderly inmates enjoyed little privacy or personal freedom. Superintendents were given 'full authority to search and open all parcels, trunks, etc of all inmates entering the institutions,' and boards of management, Ontario government officials pointed out as late as the 1940s, were 'making a practice of interfering with the mail of inmates.' Even marriages could be forbidden. At the Stormont, Dundas, & Glengarry refuge, when one elderly couple wished to wed, the man was 'discharged from the Home at once,' so infuriating other residents that in their one recorded act of spontaneous rebellion over a twenty-year period they subjected board members to 'yelling and hooting' when they drove away from the farm. An outraged board 'cancelled all leave of all inmates ... until further notice.'[28] Privacy within buildings such as the Ontario County Refuge, where overcrowding, by the early 1940s, pushed sixty-six inmates to sleeping in the attic, nine in the hallways, and sixteen more in the basement, was simply an impossibility. Fire was a constant danger.[29]

Although visitors to the Stormont, Dundas, & Glengarry poorfarm in the 1930s noted that 'the cattle were found to be in good condition, clean and comfortable,' the same could not be said for the inmates. Board of management minutes in this decade describe an institution ridden with vermin, where garbage and animal manure was piled high in the yard and bird droppings covered the buildings. Dietary guidelines emerging for the first time from the provincial Department of Public Welfare were routinely ignored. Since the government did 'not contribute anything towards the cost of [maintaining] ... the inmates,' its board of management protested, they were 'stretching a point in suggesting a menu.' Meanwhile, residents complained of 'scraps left on plates being mixed together and served again.' The appearance of the men was a source of 'so much disrespectful criticism' that the board finally ordered them to be 'shaved at least twice a week' and to be given new suits for weekends and holidays. For the bedridden, adequate daily nursing care was non-existent. The body of one elderly woman arrived at a Cornwall funeral home so covered in bedsores that outraged undertakers accused the refuge staff of negligence. The home itself, board members confessed in 1940, had 'fallen into a state of disrepair.'[30]

As is clearly evident from the surviving minute books of this and other county refuges throughout the province, farm operations, not the lives of the inmates, consumed the principal attention of county councils and refuge superintendents. Far more time is devoted in the pages of these journals to the condition of cows, crops, or equipment than to the humans under their care. While county councils were willing to authorize capital expenditures for the purchase of expensive agricultural machinery for their poorfarms, refuge doctors lamented the 'almost ... complete lack of accommodation for hobbies, handicrafts, etc with which the inmates might amuse themselves.' Nor do the minute books contain any reference to recreational activities. The Stormont, Dundas, & Glengarry refuge did hold an annual field day, but this was to display the care of the animals, not the people. The Ontario County Home was run for over twenty-seven years by a veterinarian.[31]

Refuges became places dreaded by the elderly not only because they punished the poor, but also because they housed the senile, the mentally handicapped, and the insane. Apart from already overcrowded hospitals, Ontario before the 1950s lacked private nursing homes, municipal convalescent homes, or adequate institutional accommodation for its mentally ill or handicapped population. As a result, county and city houses of refuge became 'a "catch all," the home of the sick, the simple, the crippled, the aged, the blind, and the mentally ill, all those ... who for some reason were unacceptable to other institutions.' At any one time probably about one-third of the refuge population was 'either mentally ill or mentally defective,' and there was no attempt to segregate these people from the remaining institutional population. As Toronto's medical officer of health pointed out in the 1920s, most elderly people would 'practically starve in preference to entering [a refuge].'[32]

What circumstances, then, drove them there? During the interwar years total permanent accommodation in Ontario's city and county refuges remained fairly stable at about 6000 people. Two-thirds in 1931 were over the age of sixty.[33] Despite the spartan conditions in these institutions and the onset of a means-tested old age pension scheme in the province after 1929, most of these homes, particularly the private refuges, had long waiting lists for admission, often equal to half their resident population.[34] An examination of letters requesting admission to London's Aged People's Home in the three decades before the coming of means-tested old age pensions in 1929 graphically reveals the circumstances pushing the elderly into such dwellings.

Widowhood, desertion, or simply failure to marry was one fast track to pauperism for elderly females, as the predominance of women in the urban refuges indicates. Older women faced grim prospects in a labour market in which less than 5 per cent of their gender over the age of sixty-five found employment. 'I cannot work, at my age, 75 yrs. Broken. Think I am not able for it. I am a widow, no home of my own,' one woman told the directors of a London old age home. 'She is 76 ... and has been earning her own living selling crochet work but is not able to maintain herself any longer. Her husband took her two children away to Scotland when they were very small ... She has no means whatever,' a neighbour wrote on behalf of another applicant seeking asylum. 'I was a dressmaker,' wrote a third woman. 'I helped my sister at that business before she married ... [H]er husband does not care to keep me, and I cannot get work to do on account of being deaf.' And so on. County refuges and most old age homes were not desirable places to eke out the remaining years of one's life, yet in the absence of any alternatives, many of Ontario's aged had little choice but to plead to get in.[35]

Old age pension applications sent to local boards, such as Lincoln County's, when the scheme was first established, provide further insight into the plight of Ontario's elderly prior to the onset of pensions. The most overwhelming evidence from these files is the extent to which ill-health drove the aged into poverty. Surviving case files of this local board show that 42 per cent of pension applicants were either sick or chronically disabled and unable to work at the time of their application; 28 per cent had exhausted all their financial resources and were completely indigent, possessing no income, property, or savings of any kind. Although another third owned their own homes, most often these were farms they were no longer capable of working. Many, no longer able to pay taxes, had turned these properties over to their children in return for guarantees of care. Most male applicants with some income earned only sporadically, either through casual farm labour or through small businesses such as barbering, sales, or repair work that had dwindled almost to nothing. Women did housekeeping, took in washing, or most commonly rented out rooms to boarders when they had homes. Indeed, since home ownership was the asset most widely available to the elderly, income from boarders or from their own adult children boarding with them provided the most frequent form of earnings reported. During the Depression, unemployed children, no longer able to provide their elderly parents with financial help, often moved in with them and paid rent or provided caregiving in return for shelter.[36]

Whether widowed, unemployed, senile, or disabled, all the elderly who ended up in Ontario's refuges ultimately got there because no one else was willing or able to look after them. As Ontario County's refuge superintendent put it, 'there is nothing surprising in the fact that the inmates are content to stay. Most of them are so helpless, physically or mentally, so lacking in friends or relatives ... that they naturally cling to the ... home ... as a place of refuge for their declining years.'[37] In virtually all the applications to London's Aged People's Home before the onset of old age pensions, the absence, poverty, or unwillingness of family members to care for their parents left the elderly at the doors of the refuge. 'I am writing to ask ... if you can do something about my mother and father in law. I want to put them in the Home,' one man wrote to city council in 1913. 'I have kept them nearly two years now. I am not able to keep them any longer as my family is too large. I have eight children home. I can't do justice to my family and support the old people.' 'My wife died and I am left with her mother, an old lady of 78 years of age not able to look after herself ... I am not able to support her and ... will have to put her in the home,' wrote another.[38] Or as a son explained to London's relief authorities in refusing to pay for his father's support within the home, 'My Father threatened to kill my Mother ... I know that he is in need of help, [but] I don't think he deserves it.'[39]

In response to this growing reluctance of children to provide financial support for their aged parents, the United Farmers of Ontario administration in 1921 passed the Parents' Maintenance Act, giving the dependent elderly the legal right to summon their children before a magistrate who, in turn, could order 'support payments of up to $20 weekly, having due regard for the children's means and other obligations.'[40] Similar legislation had already been enacted by a number of American states in the early years of the twentieth century, and its emergence in Ontario was the first symbolic recognition within Canada that a crisis in the care of the aged had arrived.[41] 'What had once been more or less taken for granted,' the biographer of UFO premier E.C. Drury writes, 'would now ... have to be insisted upon by the state.'[42] Maintenance agreements, according to James Snell, 'had deep historical roots in the culture of the family.' In rural societies the elderly commonly used the bargaining power they derived from the ownership and transfer of property to their children to extract, in return, lifetime guarantees for food, clothing, fuel, and shelter.[43] Although Canadian data are lacking, estimates from the United States show that in 1900, more than 60 per cent of the elderly age sixty-five and over lived with their children, and that well into the 1920s between 30 and 50 per cent of the aged were dependent on the support of their offspring. The existence of 'this very heavy burden for many adults gave proposals for new public old age protection some of their political appeal.'[44] By the early decades of the twentieth century, as the plight of those sent to London's Aged People's Home demonstrates, families in urban, industrial Ontario were quite often physically fragmented, financially overburdened with the care of children, particularly during periods of recurrent unemployment, and increasingly unable to cope with the medical disabilities of the elderly.

Above all, as recent studies of working-class incomes in Ontario before 1921 reveal, too many were simply living in grinding poverty to assume the added costs of their parents' old age. Legislating the obligations of family members to one another could no more ensure decent care for the aged than it could for the children of deserted wives or unwed mothers, also subjects of similar familial legislation by the UFO administration.[45] The Parents' Maintenance Act was a lament for a fading social order, not a remedy for the poverty of elderly Ontarians. In the end it was of more symbolic than practical importance. Although having it on the statute books was a useful club for local governments to hold over the heads of some children, in practice it was seldom enforced.[46]

Ultimately it was Ottawa, not Queen's Park, that came to the rescue of Ontario's aged poor. In what has now become a classic story in the history of Canadian social democracy, the elderly received an alternative to the poor house when Canada's first national old age pension scheme was inaugurated by the King administration in 1927 in return for the strategic support, in a hung Parliament, of two independent labour MPs, J.S. Woodsworth and A.A. Heaps.[47] Although the launching of old age pensions, as with much else in Canadian social policy history, has received considerable analysis at the national level, almost nothing has been written about how this means-tested scheme was actually developed and administered by provinces and local governments in its formative years.

A close examination of the launching of public pensions in Ontario between 1929, when the province began participating in the plan, and the early 1940s provides a fascinating case study in social policy for a variety of reasons. In the first place, old age pensions were our first major cost-shared federal-provincial program in the social policy field and one that had a number of peculiar wrinkles. In Ontario, municipalities and county councils were partners in pension financing, administration, and investigation during the scheme's early years. Thus, like unemployment relief during the Great Depression, old age pensions in Ontario began as a three-way partnership among the federal, provincial, and local governments. Unlike relief, pensions became an area where any real local autonomy was effectively terminated within four years of the scheme's inauguration. Moreover, old age pensions represented the only cost-shared program in which Ottawa, after 1931, paid 75 per cent of the costs, but had relatively little say in how the program was administered – a discrepancy that became the source of much frustration within the federal Department of Finance.

Second, old age pensions also represented Ontario's first major acceptance of responsibility for the aged, but both the legislation and its administration embodied contradictory ideals. On the one hand, pensions were justified as a 'reward' or 'right' of citizenship for elderly citizens in need, age seventy and over, who had served their country. At the same time, pensions also incorporated and increasingly refined the concept of parental maintenance, enshrined in Ontario's earlier Parents' Maintenance Act, that children were financially and legally responsible for the support of their aged mothers and fathers.

Third, although old age pensions were initiated by Ottawa at the peak of late 1920s' prosperity, in Ontario the scheme was launched and administered during the first year of the Great Depression. In other words, the idea of a new social right for the elderly enjoyed its baptism during the worst economic crisis in our history, and throughout the 1930s, the exigencies of fiscal crisis profoundly shaped the administrative bureaucracy that took shape within Ontario's pension scheme.

Fourth, pensions were also Ontario's and Canada's first 'gender inclusive' social program. Unlike mothers' allowance legislation, which paid monthly pensions to widows in need, beginning in 1920, or unemployment relief which, in the early years of the 1930s, excluded most women from eligibility, old age pensions were paid from the start to both men and women. However, as with the concept of parental maintenance, the gender politics of pensions were inextricably entangled with the ideal of a family income and the reality of women's more irregular attachment to and earlier withdrawal from the labour market. In other words, gender played an important role in limiting and constraining the entitlement of women to state support in their old age.

Finally, old age pensions in Ontario were launched with extreme reluctance and scant political support by a provincial government that possessed little administrative competence, bureaucratic preparation, or knowledge in the field. This was clearly a policy initiative forced upon Ontario by Ottawa. Almost immediately the provincial government was overwhelmed by the magnitude of need pensions revealed among its elderly and by the administrative and fiscal demands this new program placed on the provincial and local state structure.

The early history of old age pensions in Ontario, then, is highly revealing of the difficulties and the conflicting priorities involved in building an administrative state in the social policy field. Old age pensions started out with a significant degree of local control and a remarkable amount of diversity and experimentation at the local level in interpreting the meaning of social entitlement for the elderly. Very quickly, however, local autonomy in dealing with the aged was first constrained and then eliminated through a process of administrative centralization that had little to do with improving or protecting the rights of Ontario's aged poor.

About 3.5 per cent of Ontario's population, or approximately 100,000 people, were age seventy or over when the province's old age pension scheme began in 1929. Before its advent, no more than 10,000 exerted any claim on the provincial or local state for support. About 3500 residents filled up county and municipal houses of refuge, and almost an equal number received provincial subsidies for their care in charitable homes for the aged. Another 700 senile elderly resided in Ontario's mental institutions, and an indeterminate number of elderly poor men enjoyed the hospitality of local jails as indigent vagrants during the coldest winter months. Police magistrates were among Ontario's most vigorous lobbyists for old age pensions in the 1920s, pleading with Premier Howard Ferguson to be relieved from the 'depressing duty of committing friendless, penniless, offenceless, and homeless old men to Gaol.'[48]

Throughout almost the entire history of Ontario's means-tested old age pension scheme, benefits were limited by federal regulations to a maximum ceiling of $20 a month, although recipients were allowed an additional $125 a year in annual income before becoming ineligible for pension entitlement. Those earning more than $365 a year, including the maximum pension of $20 a month, were excluded from eligibility. In order to qualify, applicants also had to be British subjects who had lived at least twenty consecutive years in Canada and five in Ontario. Anyone transferring property within five years of applying for a pension was also ineligible. Like mothers' allowances, the other major income security program launched in Ontario during the 1920s, old age pensions began at a level of living far below basic adequacy. Although the benefits were meagre, even labour witnesses testifying before the 1924 federal parliamentary committee that designed the scheme agreed it would be politically expedient to begin on a modest basis, providing 'relief' rather than an 'adequate amount.' 'Half a loaf is better than no loaf at all,' union representatives conceded, 'and the experience gained may point the way to a full loaf.' As with the British, Australian, and New Zealand schemes on which it was modelled, Canada's old age pension legislation was designed to supplement and encourage private saving, not provide a real subsistence income for the elderly.[49]

Although $20 a month did not even come close to a living income for anyone with no other resources, old age pensions nonetheless appeared as a godsend to many of Ontario's aged poor. 'I cannot express my gratitude enough,' one elderly widow wrote to Queen's Park on first receiving her pension. 'I must tell you I was not able to get enough to eat last year and so you can guess how grateful I am for it.' This letter is typical of many more sent to the Ontario government during the first year of the scheme's operation.[50]

Thanking Ferguson for old age pensions was somewhat ironic. The premier detested the scheme, was furious with Ottawa for introducing it, and delayed its implementation within Ontario for as long he could despite letters of pathetic desperation sent to him from the elderly in need throughout the 1920s pleading for help. 'If I live to July I will be 82 years of age and my wife ... will be 73 ... and neither of us are able to do much work. We have a little home ... but no money to live on,' one man wrote. 'I am ... seventy years old and ... had my back hurt awful bad this summer ... Can't you do something for me?' asked another. 'I am now 75 years old. I found it impossible to get any work to keep a shelter over my head and I go around now for a man just off the Danforth, selling shoelaces, soap, pine, etc,' wrote a third. 'I am badly ruptured and badly crippled up with rheumatism and the ... weather makes it very hard for me. If the Old Age Pension Act would only come into force it would be a Godsend.' To all such entreaties Ferguson suggested applying for admission to the county poorhouse, if they were in real need, or replied that an old age pension scheme would be too expensive given his government's more pressing budgetary priorities.[51] As his biographer points out, the Ontario premier 'showed for pensions all the enthusiasm of a man swallowing a distasteful medicine.'[52] Ferguson believed care of the aged belonged on the shoulders of their own children, Ottawa, or local governments – anywhere but at Queen's Park.

Only the fact that Ontario taxpayers were subsidizing the cost of federal old age pensions launched in the four western provinces finally drove him to bring in a similar pension bill for Ontario. Moreover, despite more than two years of grace between the inauguration of Ottawa's cost-shared pension scheme and its implementation in Ontario in 1929, Ferguson's administration did little advance preparation or planning, and did not even ascertain how many people would need it. His government's best guess was that perhaps 20,000 Ontarians might apply. In fact, almost 40,000 were receiving a pension within the scheme's first year of operation.[53] It truly was Ontario's first great welfare program for the aged, greater by far than anyone in the government had dared to imagine.

Elderly Ontarians, Ferguson told the legislature in March 1929 on introducing the scheme, would henceforth be 'getting a pension as a matter of right.' Pensions were 'in no sense a charity or gratuity,' he argued, 'but a recognition of *the obligation of the state to give a comfortable, decent, old age to the needy, elderly citizen* who had put his best efforts into making his contribution to the upbuilding of the country.'[54] For a politician who had denied any provincial responsibility for pensions when the federal scheme was introduced, these were uplifting words that mirrored the arguments used by the Asquith government in Great Britain when a similar non-contributory old age pension scheme was introduced in 1908. But this rhetoric was also paradoxical given the meagre $20 monthly maximum set by the pension scheme, a maximum that relatively few of Ontario's elderly actually received. Not only did the pension act continue to hold children with 'sufficient means' responsible for the support of their parents, but Ferguson chose to administer the plan by a cumbersome method. A central Old Age Pension Commission located in Toronto would make the final decision on pension entitlement and would issue the cheques; but the initial applications, the investigation of eligibility, and the key recommendations would be made by local pension boards established by each county and municipal government within Ontario.[55]

Ferguson's decision to entrust local communities with the core elements of pension administration was consistent with Ontario's tradition of local government responsibility for relief, but it also reflected the absence of a provincial structure for assessing need and, above all, his desire to limit the potential costs of old age pensions. Local governments were to be held responsible for financing 20 per cent of the burden. 'You know your own people best,' the premier told the legislature in introducing the bill. 'Every move towards pensions should come from local sources where [the applicant's] circumstances are known, where they have all the machinery for investigating conditions ... So we will have the cooperation of the neighbors, the local people who know all about the situation, furnishing the central board with the necessary information to enable them to come to a wise conclusion as to the payment of a pension.'[56]

Ferguson's insistence on local control of pensions saddled the pension scheme with severe administrative weaknesses and a major political contradiction. On the one hand, the benefits provided were explicitly characterized as a 'right,' not as state charity. On the other hand, this right was constrained not only by stringent federal eligibility criteria which, in effect, made near pauperism the precondition for application, but also by the requirement that these criteria be interpreted and applied by almost a hundred different local county and municipal boards according to their judgment of individual circumstances. How were these myriad local bodies, with no previous experience in social administration on such a vast scale and no common yardsticks or staff for such investigation, to apply comparable standards to the determination of need and eligibility among Ontario's aged poor?

As it turned out they could not. Within Toronto, for example, where both labour representatives and women's groups had lobbied vociferously for old age pensions throughout the 1920s and had exerted a strong influence on the local pension board, the idea that pensions were a social right or a reward for those who had built up the country was taken at face value. In its first year of operation, Toronto's pension board granted a pension to 82 per cent of all those applying, and in 94 per cent of these cases the full $20 maximum was recommended. In almost every case the board ignored the income of children in making its decisions. Pensions were 'a reward earned through [the elderly's] contributions to the progress of our country,' board members argued, money that would restore to the aged a 'certain degree of independence' and 'lighten the financial burden of many a married son or daughter.'[57]

Other communities, particularly in rural Ontario, did not share Toronto's liberal view of pension entitlement, as a perusal of local pension board minutes reveals. In Stratford, pensions were denied to men 'considered ... still able to maintain [themselves] by working at [their] trade,' no matter what their age. A woman in Deseronto lost her pension for 'allowing drunks in her home.' In Middlesex County, married couples saw their pensions cut back to $15 a month in 1931 on the grounds that a $30 monthly income for those able to 'grow their own vegetables and ... keep a few hens or a cow' was more than enough to keep any rural couple 'quite comfortable and independent,' a practice quickly adopted by most county boards across the province as a Depression austerity measure. Within other boards, federal auditors discovered that 'where a man and his wife were both applicants, one would be granted the pension and the other refused, or ... both pensions would be reduced to $10 each.' Elderly women in Lanark County earning room and board as housekeepers were judged to have sufficient means not to need pensions.[58] Men, regardless of their age, were expected to keep working until physically unable to do so, since most rural pension board members had difficulty accepting the concept of unemployment when room and board, in return for labour, were available to some of the elderly. Urban pension boards such as London's, in contrast, appeared more willing to accept advanced old age as a legitimate reason for unemployment and pension eligibility.[59]

How much support children owed to their parents became the most controversial aspect of the means test. During the 1920s, when legal action before a police magistrate was needed to bring the Parents' Maintenance Act into effect, it was seldom used.[60] With the creation of old age pensions, however, the issue of parental maintenance became a matter of discretionary administrative judgment by old age pension boards, not the courts. Toronto's board, which investigated 20 per cent of all pension applications within Ontario (a caseload larger than in any other single Canadian province), did not consider the act in making its recommendations. Most other boards did, however, and in rural Ontario it was a critical factor in determining pension entitlement. Applicants who met all other age, residence, and personal income and property criteria routinely had their pensions reduced or denied, as board minutes put it, 'on the ground that your immediate relatives are amply able to support their parents for some time yet.' 'You have two single sons living at home, and although temporarily out of employment, they should certainly be expected to contribute liberally for their board at least,' one elderly man was told in a typical letter when his pension was cut early in the Depression. Where parents were living with their children, federal officials discovered, many local boards simply deducted 'an arbitrary amount of $5 or $10 per month' from their benefits. Within Lincoln County, surviving case records reveal that almost one out of every four applicants with children had the pension reduced or denied altogether on the grounds that offspring were capable of providing financial support, even if such help was not forthcoming. In most cases, however, the board conceded that the children 'have all they can do to keep themselves.' [61]

Despite the impact of the Depression and a pension caseload accelerating in 1931 beyond 40,000, far above the estimated peak of 20,000 when the bill was introduced, decisions such as these kept Ontario's pension burden well below that of other provinces. Although 3.5 per cent of Ontario's population was over the age of seventy, compared with an average of only 1.5 per cent in the other provinces with pension schemes, only one out of every three Ontarians of pensionable age was able to qualify for assistance, compared with more than one out of two in Alberta, British Columbia, and Manitoba and two out of three in Saskatchewan. Of those who did, most received less than the maximum pension of $20 per month. Ontario officials attributed this result to the greater degree of wealth and savings in their own province. Although this was undoubtedly a factor, so too was the parsimony of local boards. This was certainly Ottawa's viewpoint. Rural pension boards, some federal auditors complained, were 'actually defeating the will of both Provincial and Federal parliaments' because 'in not one single solitary instance of the cases examined in some of these counties [was] the maximum pension of $20 per month ... paid.' Although local boards did have discretionary powers to conduct a means test, 'it was never intended they should decrease the maximum allowance from twenty dollars to fifteen dollars.'[62] Unlike the aged in western Canada, moreover, Ontario's elderly failed to develop any lasting associations or pressure groups of their own comparable with British Columbia's Old Age Pensioners' Organization, formed in 1932, to lobby for a more liberal interpretation of pension regulations and entitlement throughout the entire era of means-tested old age pensions. As a consequence, although the average pension paid in Ontario was about the same as in western Canada, a conservative senior pension bureaucracy, tight-fisted local boards, and a succession of provincial governments bent on retrenchment were able to keep the percentage of those qualifying for assistance lower than in any other province except Prince Edward Island.[63]

Senior pension administrators at both the federal and provincial level turned a deaf ear to protests from their staff concerning the parsimony of local boards. It was doubtful whether Ottawa had 'any moral or legal right to question the matter of under payments,' nor was it 'good policy for the federal authorities to take any action,' field staff were told by their superiors. Within the provincial pension bureaucracy, employees were instructed 'not to concern themselves with under payments but to watch carefully for over payments.' For those elderly getting less than they deserved from local boards, 'the remedy lies in the hands of the pensioner himself.' Since few pensioners understood how their pensions were calculated, and there was no formal appeal process or any uniformity of pension decisions across the province, this was small comfort to Ontario's aged poor.[64]

As the number of pension cases continued to soar above initial expectations, reaching almost 60,000 by 1936, or 36 per cent of the population age seventy or over, the Ontario government became increasingly suspicious of the competence and impartiality of local pension boards. Why were so many more of the aged applying for a pension? Much of the answer was provided by the Depression itself, which thrust the elderly more quickly into the ranks of the unemployed and deprived their children of the income needed to assist them.[65] However, while acknowledging the Depression's impact, provincial and federal officials continued to insist, much as they did with respect to local administration of unemployment relief, that favouritism, lax investigation, and sheer incompetence within local pension boards lay behind much of the soaring pension caseload. Beginning in 1933, then, senior levels of government moved to centralize pension decision-making and to eliminate local autonomy in order to place a cap on the inexorably rising costs of the non-contributory scheme.

By then, Ontario's Department of Public Welfare, first organized in 1930 in response to the report of a provincial commission on public welfare, was beginning to put into place a more centralized structure for coordinating and regulating Ontario's diverse and haphazard provincial social policy framework, a task soon underscored by the burgeoning crisis of unemployment relief. The department's first minister, William Martin, was a newly elected former Methodist clergyman from Brantford. His deputy minister, Milton Sorsoleil, was nearing the end of a long civil service career devoted mostly to developing technical and vocational education throughout the province. Both men remained deeply involved in the United Church and shared a common interest in juvenile delinquency. Neither had much experience in or aptitude for dealing with the problems of the aged or the unemployed.[66]

Old age pension policy remained in the hands of Dr David Jamieson, the elderly chairman of Ontario's Mothers' Allowance and Old Age Pension commissions. Although trained as a doctor, Jamieson was in fact a veteran Tory politician first elected to the provincial legislature in 1898. A former rural reeve and gentleman farmer from Durham, Ontario, he had served faithfully in the caucus of James Whitney and William Hearst, and had been Speaker of the legislature during the First World War. After the Conservatives returned to power under Howard Ferguson in 1923, Jamieson was rewarded for his years of party service by being appointed chairman of the Mothers' Allowance Commission the following year. He was also a minister without portfolio in the Ferguson cabinet. Throughout the remainder of the 1920s Jamieson resolutely guarded against any movement for liberalizing entitlement under mothers' allowances to include widows with only one child or deserted wives, and, as noted in chapter 1, his blatant use of patronage in appointing loyal Conservatives as commission investigators so offended commission vice-chairman Elizabeth Shortt that she resigned her position in disgust in 1927. When he assumed the chairmanship of Ontario's Old Age Pension Commission in 1929, Jamieson was already three years past the age of eligibility for collecting the pension himself, and he would retire five years later at the age of seventy-eight. A product of late Victorian Ontario as well as a loyal and partisan Conservative, he was ill-disposed to act as an advocate for Ontario's elderly poor. When pension applications mushroomed beyond all expectations in the early years of the Depression, he moved quickly to find a means of bringing costs under control.[67]

In 1932 his welfare minister, William Martin, 'declared war upon

abuses of the Old Age Pension Act,' transferring the power of investigating and approving all old age pension applications to a new staff of
eleven provincial inspectors working directly for the provincial Old
Age Pension Commission.[68] The new core of inspectors quickly got
down to work by cancelling or reducing 80 per cent of the almost one
thousand pensions they investigated within Toronto's caseload. Once
Queen's Park took over pension investigation in that city, the proportion of applicants getting a full pension plunged from 94 to 32 per cent.
Pension inspectors began to search local records to detect the transfer
of property from parents to children within five years of a pension
application, required applicants to sign permission forms giving them
access to their bank records, and launched a crackdown on 'base in-
grates' – children who forced their parents onto the pension when they
could contribute to their support. After 1932 the ability of children to
help their parents financially, Martin announced, would be 'regarded as
income so far as [pension] applications are concerned,' whether or not
the money was actually received. The maximum pension of all married
pensioners or those living with their children was reduced to $15 a
month. In the same year, local pension boards lost the power even to
recommend a specific amount applicants should receive.[69]

With the election of the Hepburn government in 1934, this attempt
by Queen's Park to centralize and refine the bureaucratic efficiency of
pension admnistration temporarily ground to a halt. As a cost-cutting
measure the incoming welfare minister, thirty-four-year-old David Croll,
who had gained the reputation as a progressive Liberal during his tenure as mayor of Windsor since 1930, simply sacked the entire team of
provincial pension inspectors on the grounds they were 'no damn good
and nothing but a bill of expense.' Croll also abolished local pension
boards across Ontario except in the province's four largest cities. Henceforth, to save money and speed up the process, pension applications
were to be dealt with by municipal and township clerks throughout Ontario and forwarded to the Pension Commission accompanied
by sworn affidavits as to their veracity, without independent local
investigation.[70]

Federal officials, who had never been impressed with pension administration in Ontario, were appalled at this turn of events, especially
since Ottawa, after 1931, was paying for 75 per cent of the cost of each
pension. Between 1935, when the federal Department of Finance took
control of pension administration away from the Department of Labour
in order to contain its rising costs, and Croll's departure from the Hepburn
administration in 1937 over the Oshawa General Motors strike, open
warfare took place between federal Finance officials and Croll over the
slipshod quality of evidence and utter absence of verification in Ontario

pension applications compiled by overworked local clerks. As one harassed local official complained to Queen's Park, 'if we are only going to take everyone's word for everything then we might as well hand out $20 to every one who applies.' In 1937, when Ontario abolished all remaining local contributions to pension costs, Ottawa delivered its ultimatum to Hepburn. It would refuse to contribute its share for pensions until their administration was reformed and proper inspection of applications was reinstituted.[71]

Hepburn and his deputy provincial treasurer, Chester Walters, formerly chief tax collector for the federal government, were also alarmed at a pension caseload more than three times the peak size anticipated when the scheme was launched in 1929. In close cooperation with federal finance department officials, pension regulations and administration in Ontario were completely overhauled. Control of pension administration was placed firmly in the hands of the Ontario Pension Commission, now headed by an official from the premier's office, and a new squad of fifty-six pension investigators was appointed. All 60,000 of Ontario's pension cases were reinvestigated to weed out past abuses and, beginning in April 1938, all pension cases were scrutinized at least once each year.[72]

In a further effort to slow the rate of expansion in Ontario's pension caseloads, both federal and Ontario officials mounted an aggressive campaign in the late 1930s to force children to assume a greater share of the cost of parent care. Beginning in that year, Ontario formally required all children of pensioners to obtain a 'certified statement of earnings' from their employers for the perusal of pension investigators, although in practice this regulation was only irregularly enforced. In addition, the Pension Commission adopted, for the first time, a formal table of earnings, based on sliding scales geared to income, marital status, family size, and co-residence with parents, for calculating arbitrarily how much children were expected to contribute to the cost of parent care. A single child, for example, living with a parent and earning $1500 a year, was expected to pay at least $125 annually towards that parent's income, and this amount was deducted from the annual ceiling of $365 the elderly were entitled to receive, inclusive of pensions, in order to qualify for aid. Pension officials implemented these scales of support knowing full well that 'the children seldom make a direct contribution and the pensioners do without.' Nonetheless, the expected support was calculated as part of a pensioner's real income whether or not it was actually received.[73] 'Scores of pensions were reduced or suspended' in Ontario on the basis of this sliding scale, the federal finance department noted with approval in 1941. By that year, in fact, Ontario's pension caseload finally peaked, after which it began a modest decline to 56,000 by 1944, at which point only 29 per cent of those seventy and over were getting a pension, compared with 36 per cent only five years earlier.[74]

While the number of pensioners was going down, the province's staff of pension investigators was going up, almost doubling to ninety-five by 1943, thus cutting the size of the average investigator's caseload in half. More investigators with smaller caseloads meant a more stringent enforcement of pension entitlement, particularly given the increased earnings of the elderly and their children as a result of wartime employment and dependant's allowances. In other words, wartime prosperity did not necessarily bring about an increased standard of living for old age pensioners as the growing earnings of themselves and their children were simply deducted from their monthly entitlement. In this way, thousands of pensions across the province were either reduced or eliminated altogether through a combination of economic growth and more efficient bureaucratic regulation. In 1939 the average monthly pension in Ontario was still only $18, the same amount as in 1932, and more than a quarter of all those eligible received less than the maximum allowed.[75]

Ironically, while the state developed increasingly uniform standards for measuring the assets and means of the elderly and their children during the 1930s, it did not develop or impose any corresponding standard for assessing their minimum needs. Indeed, such a role was expressly ruled out by the federal Department of Finance. 'There is in the [Pension] Act no attempt to define a minimum pension,' department officials were told. In order to avoid 'strained relations between the Provinces and the Dominion,' federal officials 'never attempted to check rejected claims, nor have we followed the practice of insisting that pensions should be increased or reinstated where, in our opinion, the pension authority has been too severe.' Ottawa's role was 'limited to dollars and cents,' according to accountant J.W. MacFarlane, the civil servant in charge of supervising the pension scheme. Any attempt to define or enforce minimum needs, he argued, would 'draw ... [the dominion] into social welfare work which comes under the jurisdiction of the province.'[76]

For Ontario's aged poor, this failure by the early 1940s to inquire into the adequacy of pensions meant a life of growing hardship, particularly in lieu of a worsening wartime housing crisis. 'I have a little room to myself, 9 x 9, poorly heated, partly furnished,' one eighty-eight-year-old told Premier Gordon Conant in 1942. 'I take the cheque to the landlord, he hands me back $8. With the mounting cost of living

I find it hard to exist ... Where I was able to go out I could distinguish every old age pensioner by the haggard expression on his face.' 'We old fellows have a hard time getting along on $20,' another wrote. 'Most of us pay $18 for board, and count the pennies to buy smokes and other details with the $2. It is just enough to make things miserable.'[77] Their complaints were confirmed by a Toronto welfare department study in 1943, which revealed that even without pricing the cost of special diets, household necessities, medical care, or drugs, the $20 maximum pension fell anywhere from $3.52 to $9.62 per month short of minimum requirements, depending upon whether the elderly lived alone or with relatives. Rent alone averaged $12 a month for old people living by themselves, leaving only $2 a week to meet food, clothing, and any other expenses. Many of the elderly surveyed reported living only on bread, butter, and tea for the last week of every month.[78]

Once the federal government acknowledged the reality of inflation for wartime workers by providing their regulated wages with a cost-of-living bonus early in 1942, and Toronto's municipal government brought relief allowances in Ontario's largest city up to a minimum standard of nutritional health the following year, the pressure on Ottawa and Queen's Park to do something for the plight of the aged poor, still eking out an existence on the $20 a month pension ceiling set in 1927, became impossible to ignore. From 1941 onwards, letters and resolutions flooded into Queen's Park from the elderly and city councils across the province urging that some comparable cost-of-living adjustment be made to old age pensions. Within Ottawa, researchers for the federal government's Advisory Committee on Reconstruction condemned the finance department's obsession with 'mathematical slide rule calculations from the top down' and an 'almost exclusive [emphasis] on audit and financial control' for creating a 'repressive influence on provincial [pension] administration.' Pensions should be placed on a 'social' basis related 'to the living needs of the applicant,' committee researchers advised.[79]

Within the federal Department of Finance, opinion over the merits of boosting old age pensions remained divided. Officials such as Robert Bryce argued that 'consideration for a minimum standard of health and decency for these people would fit in well with a general policy of more progressive attitudes in respect to post-war times.' Senior administrators such as Deputy Minister W.C. Clark, however, continued to insist on the 'fundamental distinction' between indexing 'contractual payments' such as wages and salaries to the cost of living, in order to 'induce persons to perform services,' and bonusing old age pensions, which were, in his view, 'really a compassionate payment made ... to assist aged persons who have not made provision for their later life to take care of themselves.' Although sympathetic to their plight, Clark insisted 'we must have some realism in these matters.'[80]

Finally, in July 1943, in response to growing public pressure over the inadequacy of pensions and requests from all nine provinces for a cost-of-living pension increase in the face of wartime inflation, Ottawa reluctantly raised its maximum shareable pension ceiling to $25 a month. Finance department officials, facing a $3 billion federal wartime deficit, continued to grumble about the cost, particularly since Ottawa's share was 75 per cent at a time when most provinces were running budgetary surpluses. In making this announcement, federal finance minister J.L. Ilsley also signalled, for the first time, a radical shift in Ottawa's thinking about the whole issue of non-contributory, means-tested pensions administered by provinces but financed largely through federal tax dollars. 'I, myself, am in favour of old age pensions being within the jurisdiction of the dominion parliament,' Ilsley told Parliament, 'and I look forward to the day when there will be in force in Canada a system of contributory old age pensions, along the lines recommended by the Beveridge report, or something of that kind, and administered on a nation-wide scale by this Parliament.'[81] Two years later these sentiments would be imbedded within Ottawa's Green Book Proposals for postwar reconstruction.

A month before the upcoming provincial election, Ontario also implemented an additional $3 monthly increase for its pensioners. In a remarkable display of parsimony, however, Ontario's Pension Commission revealed that instead of granting the increase across the board, all its 59,000 pension cases would be individually reviewed and the bonus paid on a case-by-case basis to those who could prove real need. As one outraged Anglican minister aptly commented on hearing the news, through this action Ontario had clearly earned the 'label of the stingiest province.'[82] Certainly this cheese-paring gesture did little to forestall the electoral rout of the Liberals by the Conservatives and CCF one month later in a campaign fought largely over the issue of social security. Here pension entitlement would remain until the entire scheme was made universal for all those age seventy and over in 1951.

During the first two decades of old age pensions in Ontario, the aged poor paid the price of depending on a scheme that was launched at the beginning of the Great Depression by governments unprepared for a spending program of such magnitude. Against a background of weak political commitment, administrative incompetence, and economic crisis, it is hardly surprising that old age pensions soon lost all semblance of providing a new social right or a 'comfortable, decent old age' for

Ontario's elderly. By the mid-1930s pensions had degenerated, in the words of one federal finance department official, into nothing more than 'state charity ... designed to provide for bare subsistence ... hardly anything but a form of relief granted to the aged poor by a benevolent state,' complete with means-testing almost as parsimonious and degrading as that experienced by the unemployed dependent on the dole.[83]

Had the scheme been administered in the liberal spirit of Toronto's Pension Board between 1929 and 1932, non-contributory old age pensions might well have attained the promise of an earned social right of citizenship – a reward, free of stigma, for years of labour in building up the nation. However, Toronto's resistance to the concept of parental maintenance and its willingness to grant the full $20 pension in almost every eligible case was quickly targeted by provincial pension officials as evidence of fiscal abuse. Rural boards, in contrast, which cut down pension entitlement for married couples, often forced the able-bodied elderly over seventy to keep working, and vigorously upheld the responsibility of children to pay for parent care, became progenitors of policies ultimately adopted and enforced by provincial and federal pension authorities in the name of economy.

Ironically, old age pension administration by local boards in Ontario during the scheme's early years provided divergent models for how non-contributory pensions could be developed, either as an earned right or as charity. In the end, charity prevailed. Centralization of decision-making away from the local level came about in 1933 to restrict, not enhance, pension entitlement; it made the means test, applied with greater precision not only to the elderly but to their children as well, more effective through the superior investigatory power of senior levels of government. With considerable prodding from Ottawa, pension administration in Ontario became more administratively competent and uniform in the interests of cost control, not social fairness or adequacy. As the provincial state gained administrative experience in the pension field and enhanced its capacity to measure the poverty of the aged, old age pensions came to resemble charity from a benevolent state rather than an earned social right. In all these developments, the background of the Great Depression, in which Ontario's first old age pension scheme was launched, figured largely as both Ottawa and Queen's Park struggled unsuccessfully throughout the 1930s to place a cap on ever-rising pension expenditures.

How Much Is Enough? Creating a Social Minimum in Ontario, 1930–44

The creation of mothers' allowances and old age pensions in the 1920s represented Ontario's first foray into the realm of income maintenance. Although both schemes represented important building blocks in the development of a bureaucratic welfare state and were significant departures from a traditional reliance on private charity and local responsibility for the indigent, neither the scope nor the caseload of either program prepared the province for the magnitude of need unleashed by economic collapse after 1930. Only three years after the government's reluctant launch of old age pensions, more than 400,000 Ontarians would be dependent upon state relief for survival. Out of this economic and social catastrophe emerged the administrative structure of Ontario's welfare state.

Spawned by the Depression, the province's public welfare bureaucracy was shaped as much by fiscal crisis as by the massive dimensions of need revealed within the population. On the one hand, it was an immense administrative challenge to put a structure in place, administered through 900 municipalities, to keep so many families alive. On the other hand, it drew government into a realm of contested needs never before imagined by policy-makers during the 1920s. What were the limits of society's obligations to the able-bodied on relief? How much was enough to keep a family alive and healthy over long periods of idleness? How should such minimum standards be defined and whose measurements were authoritative? What relationship should be maintained between the income available through relief and the income available through work at a time when one out of three wage-earners within the province could not find employment? What was the linkage between the cost of relief and the cost of living for those dependent on the dole? Throughout the 1930s successive Ontario governments led by George Henry and Mitch Hepburn grappled with these questions in the face of falling revenues, soaring expenditures, and the emergence of powerful definitions of minimum needs put forward by organizations of the unemployed, social workers, health-care professionals, and women community activists. Although the fiscal crisis of the Depression provided a bleak climate for welfare reform, it sparked a wide-ranging debate within the province on human need, social obligation, and the imperatives of a market economy. By the end of the Second World War, although some of these questions would be resolved, most would remain unanswered and forgotten until poverty was 'rediscovered' in the 1960s.

When the Great Depression began in 1930, Ontario for the most part lacked a provincial public welfare structure for assessing or alleviating need. Only impoverished widows with two or more children and the indigent elderly over the age of seventy enjoyed a public welfare entitlement through provincial mothers' allowance and old age pension programs created in the 1920s. A provincial Department of Public Welfare had been established in 1930 in response to the recommendations of a Royal Commission on Public Welfare, appointed the previous year, but its task was to coordinate the work of Ontario's existing institutional structure for the care of the sick, the elderly, the insane, and orphans and neglected children, not to cope with the emerging unemployment crisis.[1]

Ontario also lacked a poor law. Unlike the Maritime provinces, there was 'no legal obligation upon ... local authorities to provide work or maintenance for the able-bodied poor and their families,'[2] although in practice a number of Ontario communities had established relief departments in the 1920s to dole out aid sporadically to the unemployed. In others, including Toronto, relief was provided through private or semi-private welfare organizations, supplemented in varying degrees from public funds. Relief and casework to needy families in Toronto, for example, was dispensed through eight separate agencies: the Neighborhood Workers' Association, which dealt with Protestants; the Catholic Welfare Bureau; the Jewish Family Welfare Bureau; the Home Service Association, a separate organization for blacks; the Poppy Fund, which aided indigent veterans; the Samaritan Club, which relieved the tubercular in distress; the city's Division of Social Welfare, which offered casework only to the chronically indigent; and the House of Industry, which was the refuge of last resort. Even experienced social workers found the situation 'most bewildering and complicated.' In smaller towns and cities relief could be dispensed through a variety of means including the municipal clerk, the sanitary inspector, mayors, reeves, aldermen, or the police. In the case of unemployed single men and women, it was not given at all. Only Ottawa and Hamilton in the years before the Depression possessed municipal public welfare departments that coordinated the distribution of all forms of social aid.[3]

Not surprisingly, the onset of the Depression threw this disorganized and haphazard welfare structure into crisis. No one knew how many were unemployed, who should be given help, how much they should receive, or in what way they should get assistance. During the first two years of the crisis, municipalities scrambled to put in place structures for dispensing aid on a mass scale, with only the vaguest guidance from the province or the federal government.[4] Until the spring of 1932, municipal relief work or job creation schemes, funded with federal and provincial aid under the Unemployment Relief Acts of 1930 and 1931, provided the principal response to the unemployment crisis.[5] Provincial orders-in-council channelling relief aid to the municipalities gave only broad outlines for its expenditure. 'Work should be provided ... before direct relief,' the province specified, and it should be 'distributed as widely as possible amongst the unemployed ... to give them all work for some time.' Direct relief, if given, should be for food, fuel, clothing, and shelter only. The province also asked municipalities, 'if possible,' to show 'the number of persons out of employment.'[6] Yet Queen's Park provided no definition of the term 'unemployed,' no financial support for developing a relief administration structure, and no guidance on who was eligible to receive aid or how much it should be.

With little guidance from either Ottawa or Queen's Park, Ontario cities during the first two years of the Depression groped for their own standards of determining how much relief should be given, how it should be distributed, and who was eligible to get it. As the largest centre of relief activity in the province, Toronto provides a good case study of how a welfare bureaucracy was created at the local level. Three problems in relief administration confronted that city during the early years of the Depression. The first was the transient crisis as thousands of single men poured into the city looking for work, food, or a bed for the night. The second was sorting out who among the thousands of unemployed in need was entitled to get the scarce supply of relief work funded by all three levels of government. The third was coping with almost 23,000 families who, by late 1932, were solely dependent upon outdoor relief from the city's House of Industry for their survival.

In early October 1930, in response to the sight of 'hundreds ... sleeping in parks ... brick yards' and the 'benches and floors' of rest rooms, the proliferation of door-to-door begging, and bread lines of more than a thousand men lining up for hours to receive 'wrapped lunches' prepared by the city's philanthropic women, Toronto's Board of Control appointed a Civic Unemployment Relief Committee, under the leadership of F.D. Tolchard, general manager of the Board of Trade, to deal with the crisis.[7] Tolchard's committee worked quickly to provide food, shelter, and some system for sorting out eligibility for relief. Its first step was to register, investigate, and categorize the transient unemployed. By the end of December it had established the Central Bureau to register all homeless men and women, particularly for the purpose of separating residents and non-residents and to prevent single men from applying for scarce municipal relief work. A meal ticket system was put in place providing sixty cents a day for food in return for sawing wood in the municipal woodyard. Single women were placed as domestics in private homes, and additional emergency shelters and soup kitchens were established through donations from individuals and businesses. Almost 8100 homeless men and women were registered that winter through the bureau. On average, about 1400 beds and 4400 meals were provided each day.[8]

By the following year Toronto had organized a system of hostels for single men, with the help of private charities, and was placing women 'in a quiet and effective manner' in 'suitable homes' of the unemployed so that the benefits of their relief might be maximized. Thanks to the effective work by Tolchard's committee the transient problem, from the city's point of view, seemed under control. 'Panhandling ... and graver still the criminal possibilities of the situation could easily be imagined,' Toronto's first welfare commissioner, A.W. (Bert) Laver, appointed in 1931, later reflected. 'The protective measures taken at the outset prevent[ed] the spread of these things and provide[d] some kind of local control over a situation which could easily get out of hand in a metropolitan area.'[9]

Tolchard's committee also registered more than 15,000 men applying for relief work, investigated their circumstances, and rationed out the scarce supply of jobs. Almost 9400 got some work and another 5000 were weeded out either because they were not married, not British subjects, or had not lived in Toronto for at least twelve months before applying. But even the lucky who survived this screening got only one week's wages, or $28.80, every two months. Given these meagre earnings, about half the men and their families were also dependent for survival on outdoor relief from the House of Industry.[10]

This venerable institution, although almost totally dependent on civic grants, was an independent charitable organization supervised by its own board of trustees, chosen mostly from Toronto's business community. First established in 1837, the House of Industry was Toronto's only centre for publicly funded direct relief to families until 1933.

During the 1920s, private family agencies had provided most Toronto families in need with casework and relief. Overwhelmed by the Depression, however, they quickly realized they had no choice but to send their clients to 'line up with the old timers at the House of Industry.'[11] In 1931 more than 11,000 Toronto families survived on House of Industry supplies. The following year the number doubled to almost 23,000, and by early 1933 it would reach almost 27,000. By 1932 the House of Industry was issuing more supplies each day than it had doled out each year in the 1920s. Every morning that year, 4000 people travelled from all across the city to the building at 87 Elm Street to wait in line for their family's weekly bag of groceries.[12]

What did they get? The House of Industry diet for the poor remained unchanged from the 1920s. Indeed, it never varied from week to week. Grocery bags came in two forms, the small and large order: the first for families under five members, the second for families over five. Families receiving the large order got the same amount of food whether there were five or ten mouths to feed. Other families might have to make the order stretch for ten days rather than one week, depending on their size. Inside the bag the relief recipient found oatmeal, rice, flour, cornstarch, cream of wheat, sugar, syrup, beans, potatoes, carrots, onions, turnips, cabbage, tomatoes, prunes, cocoa, butter, dripping, cheese, along with a little tea, salt, and baking powder, for a total of about $2.50 in groceries. By 1932 tickets for ten loaves of bread a week and one to two quarts of milk a day were also issued which could be redeemed at local stores. In addition, the House of Industry delivered four pounds of meat a week to the homes of its clients.[13]

The diet was starchy and monotonous: heavy on carbohydrates and low on protein, fresh fruit or vegetables, and vitamins. Above all, it was simply not enough. According to Alice Laird of the Department of Household Science at the University of Toronto, a House of Industry large order in 1931 provided a family with 7389 calories per day. Yet the average adult man alone required 3300 calories, almost half of the total order. For a family of five this was serious; for larger families it was clear the House of Industry grocery bag could 'not possibly serve' to sustain health. To make matters worse, much of this meagre supply of starchy foods was often '[un]used and ... stored on the shelves' because families lacked the milk or the fuel for cooking it.[14]

Despite these criticisms and the fact that almost half the families dependent on the House of Industry also had to rely on private social agencies for supplementary aid, City of Toronto officials remained convinced that relief families were getting enough to eat. 'In fairness to the taxpayers,' the Department of Health told its visiting public health nurses in 1931, 'the standard supplies [from the House of Industry] are the cheapest which will meet the minimum requirements,' and they were capable of making 'palatable meals of considerable variety.' If the mother 'who does the cooking is not resourceful,' the department conceded, there could be 'ill-considered ... complaints' and 'unrest' directed against House of Industry investigators. Nurses were advised to 'discourage' such 'destructive criticism.'[15]

Belatedly, in the spring of 1932, the Ontario government took its first steps towards developing some provincial standards and uniformity in relief administration. The need for such action in the third year of worsening depression was long overdue. According to the only authoritative study of relief policy in Ontario, written in 1932 by Harry Cassidy, a University of Toronto social scientist, the province's laissez-faire approach to municipal relief administration had produced a social catastrophe. Food vouchers for a family of five in the eleven cities he studied 'varied from $3.50 to $8.50 weekly,' and in most of the communities there was 'no attempt ... to determine scientifically the least amount of food and the smallest possible order necessary to maintain a family in health ... [T]he size of the orders was determined by the municipal councils or by the relief officer more or less arbitrarily on the basis of what they considered reasonable.' Cassidy estimated from nutritional evidence that in most Ontario cities in 1932, 'the minimum retail cost of adequate food orders' for a family of five could 'scarcely be lower than $6.00 to $7.00 a week,' figures confirmed a year later by the Ontario Medical Association in its own publication, 'Relief Diets.' In eight of the communities he studied, relief officers themselves conceded 'they did not consider the food allowances adequate for the maintenance of health.'[16]

Ontario's Conservative government, led by Premier George Henry, was not motivated by these concerns when it embarked on its first attempt to formulate provincial relief standards. A devout Methodist and rich dairy owner from North Toronto, Henry was a dour, efficiency-conscious premier whose 'disposition was to "plough the straight furrow" and pursue the path of moderation.' Henry was also an ardent devotee of Pelmanism, a 'gospel of efficiency' popular during the Progressive era, which taught that prosperity and happiness could be achieved through the pursuit of mental discipline, efficiency, and hard work. As minister of public works throughout the Ferguson administration in the 1920s, Henry had sought to bring 'uniformity and standardization to Ontario's highways.' Beginning in 1932, he began to apply the same principles of efficiency and a quest for standardization to the province's unemployment relief expenditures, which seemed to be ballooning out of control.[17]

Between 1931 and 1932 the cost of relief spending to the province jumped from $4,300,000 to more than $13,500,000, and the numbers on the dole soared from 60,000 to more than 203,000.[18] Within Ottawa, the federal government of R.B. Bennett, in response to soaring relief costs and the threat to its own credit rating caused by Britain's departure from the gold standard in the autumn of 1931, abandoned the $50 million originally budgeted for funding public works as an unemployment strategy across Canada. At the federal-provincial conference of April 1932, Queen's Park, along with Ottawa, agreed instead to contribute one-third each to the cost of local expenditures on direct relief.[19] At the same time, Henry's government began sending its own relief inspectors across the province throughout the spring and summer of 1932 to examine how the municipalities were spending its money. Their reports painted a vivid contrast of relief practices in Ontario cities, and reinforced Queen's Park's desire to gain better control over the process.

On the one hand there were cities like Hamilton where Sam Lawrence, 'a labour man ... even a "Red"' according to provincial inspector James Malcolm, was supervisor of relief. Here, 'the relief department ... trust too much to the honesty of the people they are dealing with.' There was no home investigation and 'no hard and fast schedule of relief allowance.' Instead, the department took 'the man's word for too much with regard to the possession of radio, car, telephone, boarders, liquor etc' and the relief allowance was 'arranged according to individual circumstances.' Lawrence's 'foreign friends were well stocked with all they asked for,' the inspector reported. Indeed, 'foreigners' in Hamilton were getting allowances for family members 'probably living in Central Europe.' Relief rents 'appeared to be handled by a secret society,' and Hamilton officials refused to tell the provincial inspector what procedures they followed in giving it. There were 'too many local organizations ... "getting their hooks" into the relief treasury,' including Lawrence himself who, Malcolm argued, encouraged relief spending in order to gain popularity for his anticipated campaign for mayor. It was impossible to estimate per capita costs.[20]

At the opposite end of the spectrum was East Windsor, home of the Ford Motor Company and a city with 39 per cent of its population on relief in April 1932. This community was 'very fortunate,' Malcolm reported, because 'some of Ford's Departmental Managers control the relief operation and ... in a very thorough and methodical manner.' The office itself was 'the most orderly I have visited,' as a 'police officer is in attendance at all times.' The Ford managers in charge of relief had a 'great advantage over the men,' since '90% of them have been and hope again to be employed in Fords Works.' Malcolm described the relief investigation system they administered with relish:

No relief is granted before a careful personal enquiry is conducted and the home conditions are investigated. These officers work on the theory that ... most men squeal before they are actually hurt. Every month a fresh investigation takes place but not necessarily of the home. They give the indigents what they term the 'Third Degree.' I would call it the 'Three Table Investigation.' The method is – their investigators are seated at three tables placed in a row. The indigent approaches table No. 1 where the previous application is reviewed ... [and] an oath form is then ... completed ... The indigent is then passed to table no. 2. If [the] investigator is suspicious an X is marked on the questionnaire ... The indigent if he survives passes to table No. 3 which is occupied by the Employment Agent and Notary for the Ford Plant ... [who] ... warns that prosecution will follow if falsehood is discovered. In this way every man is re-examined each month. And on every occasion from 50 to 100 men funk [sic] on taking the oath and are thus cut off and never reappear at the relief office. Both [the employment agent] and his investigation officer are experts along this line. They exercise many detective tricks one of which is they spring a sudden question out of order such as 'Let me see your [liquor] permit.' If the man's hands move before his lips, in 95 cases out of 100 he possesses one. [The agent and his officer] are capable of teaching most of our relief officers a great deal on investigation.[21]

Malcolm's travels across the province convinced him, as it had Harry Cassidy, that Ontario had to move towards 'more uniform methods and [a] uniform scale of relief,' but for reasons far removed from those of Cassidy's study. Where the professor found need, Malcolm discovered only fraud – either local politicians catering to the relief vote or families 'falsifying their ... circumstances' to get the dole. Rigorous standards of home investigation and vigilant provincial supervision of municipal relief administration were essential to root out abuse. As Malcolm concluded, it was 'much easier to refuse them at the beginning than to cut them off later on.'[22]

In response to these internal reports as well as to the necessity for relying totally on the dole as its only unemployment policy, Henry's Conservative government appointed an Advisory Committee on Direct Relief that spring to 'assist the Government in dealing with the problems arising out of unemployment, including the distribution of relief to the needy.' As chairman of the committee, the premier picked Wallace Campbell, general manager of the Ford Motor Company of Canada in East Windsor, the one Ontario community where Queen's Park knew relief was well under control.[23] Of the other seven committee members, six were businessmen and only one – D.B. Harkness – was from the social welfare community. No doctors, public health nurses, nutritionists, women, or anyone familiar with questions of diet or food preparation were included.

The Campbell Committee set to work on 29 June and produced its twenty-four page report exactly one month later. The document was a landmark in Ontario social policy. It provided the first rationale for the standardization of welfare policy and practice at the provincial level. Moreover, the standards it recommended for food, shelter, and clothing became the benchmark for social assistance rates across Ontario until 1944. The Campbell Report thus provides important insights into the assumptions built into Ontario's provincial welfare bureaucracy as it first took shape in the early 1930s.

'Up to the present,' the committee told Henry, 'your Government [has left] ... the municipalities almost complete jurisdiction in respect of ... welfare policy.' The result was a 'notable lack of uniformity in [their] ideas ... as to what constitutes adequate relief' as well as a 'great diversity in [their] standards and methods' of administration. In the interests of 'efficiency and economy' Queen's Park had to step in and 'exercise [its] authority.'[24]

The core message of the Campbell Report thus became the need for standardization. However, the standards it called for were maximum ceilings, not minimum floors on municipal welfare expenditure. Food provides the best example. The report acknowledged that these essential supplies should be 'suitable as to quality, quantity, and dietary variety so as to adequately safeguard the health of all recipients,' but refused to provide a standard list of what such a *minimum* food allowance might look like. Instead, attacking the 'indefensible spread in [food relief] costs among Ontario communities,' the report published a *maximum* schedule of weekly food costs for families of varying size on relief beyond which the province should refuse to contribute. For the typical family of five, the Campbell Report set the food allowance ceiling at $5.00 per week. For a family of ten it was $8.25, the absolute ceiling provided in the schedule (see appendix, table 1). No nutritional evidence was provided on how the committee arrived at this figure, nor was any variation allowed for differing ages of family members. Correspondence in the Henry Papers reveals that the food ceiling estimates came from H.L. McNally, sales manager of National Grocers, via Allan Ross, president of the William Wrigley Co, who was one of the business members of the committee.[25]

The report also argued for standardization in other areas of relief administration in order to cut costs. Shelter allowance payments should never exceed $15.00 monthly 'for any type of family'; electricity payments should be limited to $1.00 a month; cash relief should be prohibited; and in no case should the 'total charges for all relief services other than food ... constitute more than 40 per cent of the total expended for relief' by any municipality. The report called for standardized relief investigation and voucher forms, standardized residency requirements, and a 'planned policy' towards transients to eliminate the 'begging,' 'panhandling,' and 'anxiety caused by the presence of unknown and unattached men in the community.'

The report also asked the province to prepare a standard plan for the creation of Public Welfare Boards in each Ontario community; these boards should be composed of members appointed by the provincial government in order to 'remove the administration of relief and public welfare services ... from the more immediate influences of municipal politics.' The key theme of the Campbell Report was that Queen's Park had to develop a 'permanent structure' through which it could exercise 'continuous supervision ... of municipal administrative methods and standards in order to ensure reasonable uniformity in policy and practice in all parts of the Province.' The standardized relief forms, investigation procedures, and maximum ceilings on provincial contributions it called for were essential to 'assist ... the Province in its inspection and supervision of municipal methods and policies.'[26]

Nowhere did the need for such scrutiny seem more apparent than in those Ontario municipalities facing bankruptcy from soaring relief costs. Sturgeon Falls provides a good illustration. This northern Ontario company town of about 5000 people found itself in a hopeless position after Abitibi Pulp and Paper, its only major employer, closed down operations near the end of 1930. Two years later the town was saddled with $350,000 in debentured debt, three out of every four members of its population on relief, and a growing mountain of almost $56,000 each year in unpaid tax levies. Beginning in July 1932, to stave off municipal default, the provincial and federal governments agreed to pay 85 per cent of the town's relief bills, but Ontario officials soon became horrified at how the community was spending the province's money. As a provincially appointed judicial inquiry revealed, relief had become the town's biggest business. Food, clothing, and rent vouchers were distributed through a committee of town council, supervised by the mayor, without investigation. Orders were often issued in blank to be filled in by local merchants as they saw fit. Landlords got all their unpaid rent back-dated to November 1930, when the mill first closed. School children were invited to the town hall to receive clothing vouchers. Town council members appropriated wood cut by relief recipients 'as a gift' in return for food vouchers. Most of the town's routine maintenance expenditures were charged to its relief account in order to receive 85 per cent federal and provincial funding. Local organizations, such as the Knights of Columbus, cooperated with the town council in a fraudulent scheme to recycle some municipal relief funds as 'donations' in order to gain matching federal and provincial contributions to charitable aid. When confronted with these revelations, town officials 'openly and frankly admitted that they were all anxious "to save the Town from any relief expenditures, and get as much as possible for the people,"' investigating Judge James Hall reported to Queen's Park. As Sturgeon Falls' most prominent merchant put it, 'the Town had to have the money and there did not appear to be any other way to get it.'[27]

Another 1933 judicial inquiry into relief administration within York Township revealed similar irregularities. With almost a third of its population on relief and facing more than $2 million in unpaid taxes, township officials, according to Judge Hall, improperly charged $121,548 in routine maintenance expenditures to the province's direct relief account in order to 'assist the unemployed and secure as large a payment as possible from the [federal and provincial] governments.'[28] Cash-starved municipalities on the verge of default, it seemed to provincial authorities, were more interested in maximizing federal and provincial relief payments than in paring relief expenditure to the bone. In response, the Henry administration placed the supervision of relief in these bankrupt communities under the control of the Ontario Municipal Board. By 1935, thirty-two Ontario municipalities, mostly company towns where the single industry had closed, or suburban townships saddled with horrendous fixed debenture costs from rapid growth in the 1920s, found themselves under the stewardship of the Department of Municipal Affairs.[29]

Armed with the Campbell Report recommendations, the province also moved quickly, after 1933, to impose the report's recommended ceilings on its relief contributions to all municipalities, although Ontario cities and towns could continue to pay the jobless as little as they wished. Standard relief investigation and food voucher forms were issued to all the municipalities by December 1932.[30] The province established a network of district relief inspectors, who began to subject municipalities to regular visits in order to supervise municipal standards of home investigation of relief families and to determine that no community was charging Queen's Park more than the Campbell Report ceilings for food, shelter, and other necessities.

Beginning in 1932, then, the framework for a provincial welfare bureaucracy took shape in Ontario. Neither its origins nor its ongoing concerns had anything to do with ensuring nutritional adequacy or meeting minimum standards of need for the poor. Indeed, the Campbell Report food allowance *ceilings* were themselves inadequate to protect the health of the unemployed. As the Ontario Medical Association publication 'Relief Diets' pointed out one year later, only a family of five in which all the children were under five years of age could receive a minimum adequate food ration under the Campbell Report. For families with older children, $6.59 to $7.00 a week was the minimum amount needed to purchase the bare essentials for health, a sum 25 to 30 per cent more than the provincial ceiling allowed.[31] As one *Toronto Star* reporter caustically pointed out, '$5.00 a week ... works out to 4 3/4 cents per meal per person for a family of five ... Even a schoolchild knows that for a nickle one can't buy a meal to "safeguard health."'[32] However, the OMA's study was ignored by Queen's Park.

Cities across Ontario, under increasing supervision and pressure from the Ontario government and from the soaring numbers of their citizens dependent on relief, also began to reform their relief operations and to develop permanent bureaucracies for dispensing public welfare. In Toronto, for example, 1933 marked the year in which the House of Industry, after almost a century of operation, finally went out of the relief business. In 1931 the city had established a Department of Public Welfare, in response to the recommendations of the Tolchard Committee, to coordinate its diverse grants to the city's myriad collection of social welfare organizations and institutions, including the House of Industry. The Tolchard Committee had recommended that the new department be led by a 'man of capacity, broad vision, sound judgment, marked organizing and executive ability ... a knowledge of social service work, and a personality which will command respect.' Toronto's Board of Control chose Bert Laver, the city's chief tax collector, for the position.[33]

For the next two years Laver struggled to wrest control of relief away from the House of Industry, which continued to take the city's money to provide outdoor relief yet jealously fought any attempts at interference by Laver, City Council, or the Board of Control over its domain. In the spring of 1933, when Toronto's relief load reached almost 27,000 families dependent on House of Industry supplies, Laver succeeded.[34] Three arguments carried the day. One was the sheer impracticality of forcing 5000 people a day to trek from all over the city to a downtown location to pick up groceries. The second was the city's lack of financial control over the $3.5 million a year the House of Industry was spending on its behalf, a sum the city was only able to carry, along with its other relief expenses, by borrowing on the private market.[35] Finally, like the good accountant he was, Laver promised that a new relief system run by his department, with decentralized food depots, closed vouchers, and 'rigid [home] investigation' to root out fraud, could 'cut ... down the number now on relief' and save the taxpayers thousands of dollars.[36]

On 17 April Laver's department took over relief. He established a network of food depots across the city, staffed by the white-collar unemployed working out their relief rent; hired a new army of relief investigators, also recruited from the unemployed, to conduct an investigation and 'rigid supervision' of families on relief; instituted a closed voucher system for food allowances, which allowed local merchants a piece of the action to bid for relief supplies; and instituted a new procedure for taking 'sworn affidavits' from those on relief to provide an additional check upon their veracity. About the only aspect of Toronto's relief operation that remained unchanged was the level of food, fuel, and shelter allowances actually supplied to families on the dole. These remained fixed at the Campbell Report ceilings. Although city relief caseloads continued to soar upwards to more than 27,000 families by the year's end, Laver nonetheless wrote with pride to Queen's Park, six months after his new system had gone into effect, that he had succeeded in cutting 8300 families off the dole for a saving of $314,000. 'Use of this affidavit form, coupled with thorough investigation and energetic fraud prosecution in the Courts has had a moral and deterring effect on would-be imposers,' the welfare commissioner pointed out.[37]

Hamilton adopted similar reforms to its welfare system. Beginning in the fall of 1934 the loose administrative structure presided over by Sam Lawrence was subjected to 'drastic changes.' All cases were reregistered and reinvestigated; Campbell Report allowance scales for food, fuel, light, rent, and clothing were rigidly enforced. Most importantly, relief vouchers issued to the unemployed at the central relief office, with only 'occasional investigation,' were replaced by systematic home visits every two weeks by a new squad of forty-two relief investigators equipped with 'ledger sheets' and 'daily report forms' listing every item of relief supplied to and every cent of income earned by families on the dole. As A.P. Kappele, the city's new commissioner of public welfare, observed with pride, 'in three months time after we established the visitors, over 1200 cases voluntarily withdrew from assistance as the visitor proceeded with the investigations ... The cutting off of 1200 families at 5 to a family – 6000 individuals at an annual cost of $100 per person made a saving of $600,000 in relief.' After these reforms, Hamilton's relief load remained among 'the lowest proportionately of any city in the province.'[38]

With the defeat of the Henry administration by Mitch Hepburn and the Liberal party in the 1934 provincial election, the movement to reform relief administration in Ontario received a powerful boost. Although a farmer from St Thomas, the exuberant and populist Hepburn made frequent statements while in opposition that gave hope for real change to the unemployed. 'I swing well to the left where some Grits do not tread,' he told one meeting in Long Branch, a suburban community outside Toronto where over 40 per cent of the population was on relief. 'One of the first things I will do if I form a government in this province will be to call together the best men of Labor, Progressives and Liberals and seek their advice. I hope to see a realignment of political thought in this country.'[39] Over the next two years, however, the real catalyst for change in welfare policy was David Croll, minister of both public welfare and municipal affairs. Described by Hepburn as 'the immigrant boy who made good,' the youthful and energetic Croll was Canada's first Jewish cabinet minister and one of the most influential members of Hepburn's first administration. Elected mayor of Windsor at the age of thirty on a labour platform, Croll had earned the reputation of a sympathetic, progressive, and conscientious administrator during his four years as leader of one of the Ontario cities hardest hit by the Depression. As one of the province's leading social workers in the 1930s later recalled, 'we thought he was perhaps God's messenger of salvation.' On taking office, he vowed to 'humanize' his departments and 'serve the little men and the little women of this province.'[40] Relief in Ontario under the Henry administration, Croll charged, was 'haywire,' a 'hodge-podge of baffled municipalities, each one separately groping its way blindly, dizzily, without direction or set purpose' and in which 'uniformity was unknown.' In some communities 'living standards had been ruthlessly cut to the famine point'; in others 'it seemed to be a case of the loudest howl getting the best results.' His first task, Croll argued, was 'to establish ... uniform standards throughout Ontario ... [and] gradually remove ... unfair differentials between relief rates in similar communities.'[41]

Both Croll's election rhetoric and some of his first actions promised a new deal for the unemployed. His department issued regulations requiring municipalities to provide food and shelter relief for jobless single men and women. Women social workers were brought into the department as senior investigators and one, Nell Wark, was promoted to assistant deputy minister. Some outlying rural communities were cajoled by the welfare minister into paying more adequate levels of relief. Croll also announced a plan by which the unemployed could earn one-third above Campbell Report schedules through working one or two days a week on municipal relief projects in participating Ontario municipalities.[42]

Despite these initiatives, Croll's attempt to reform relief administration soon embroiled the welfare minister in pitched battles with the jobless in supervised municipalities across Ontario, including his home town of Windsor. At issue in these struggles was his concept of 'uniform standards.' As soon became apparent, Croll was more concerned with controlling expenditure through systematic procedures for the administration of relief than with raising inadequate allowances.

Whereas the previous government had implemented maximum ceilings on how much it would pay towards the dole, Croll was determined to develop minimum standards in the way local governments decided who could get it. Impressed by the results achieved through regular home investigation of relief recipients in Toronto and Hamilton, Croll wanted to see similar reforms occur in communities throughout the province.[43] 'Cheating is rampant in respect to direct relief,' he declared, both on the part of families failing to disclose income and by municipal politicians 'try[ing] to turn the giving of relief to their personal political benefit.' Croll also told the legislature of his 'disquiet and fear that able-bodied men were being given rations, shelter and clothing and other commodities without being required to make any return. Who will seriously attempt to deny that this was detrimental to anyone's morale. Something for nothing is a dangerous creed.' Henceforth, the motto of his department would be 'Relief for Workers, Nothing for Shirkers.'[44]

During the winter of 1935 Croll moved quickly to implement his reforms. The province's Unemployment Relief Branch, 'loaded with political heelers, nearly all of them ... utterly incompetent,' according to Croll, was thoroughly purged and a new school for relief inspectors established to create a 'field staff of thoroughly competent men who will receive decent salaries.' 'Politics must never again enter the administration of relief in this Province,' the welfare minister vowed.[45] A minimum one-year municipal residency requirement for relief was imposed across the province to stop the migration of families to cities that paid more generous unemployment assistance. All relief recipients were forced to reregister for the dole and to make sworn affadavits that they were totally destitute. The welfare department dispatched expert advisers like Nell Wark to Brantford, St Thomas, Sarnia, London, and Windsor, where the department believed routine home visiting of relief recipients was haphazard or non-existent, to establish proper investigative procedures along lines similar to those in place within Toronto and Hamilton.[46]

Croll's principal attention, though, was reserved for reforming relief administration in Ontario's 'pampered, inefficient, and political crybaby municipalities' – the thirty-two bankrupt communities where the province was paying the total cost of the dole. 'By achieving a marked degree of success in the 100 per cent municipalities,' one Toronto newspaper observed, 'the government hopes that ... the other municipalities will eventually adopt similar systems and thus create uniformity.'[47] The relief problem in these communities, according to Queen's Park, was city and town councils paying too much, not too little to the unemployed. In cities like Niagara Falls and Windsor, company towns like Pembroke and Hawkesbury, or the suburbs surrounding Toronto – Mimico, Etobicoke, New Toronto, Leaside, Long Branch, York, East York, and Scarborough – the numbers on relief ranged anywhere from 33 to 45 per cent of the population. As John Taylor has pointed out, with misery geographically concentrated on such a scale, under certain circumstances 'the poor could win. They had the vote, they had propinquity ... they had a common grievance or threat; and they had organizations in place.'[48] In York Township, Long Branch, and three wards within Toronto, Communists were elected to city council. In Hamilton, Windsor, Niagara Falls, and Crowland, left-wing candidates were also voted in as aldermen and city councillors. Arthur Williams, a left-wing CCFer and prominent leader of the unemployed in East York, became reeve.[49] Through political action and direct pressure exerted by increasingly militant local organizations of the unemployed, the jobless succeeded in pushing relief rates in these bankrupt municipalities 14 per cent above the provincial government's maximum ceiling, established before the 1934 election, of the Campbell Report plus 25 per cent. Since Queen's Park was already paying the total cost of the dole up to this scale in the supervised municipalities, the political will on the part of local officials to resist pressure for further increases by the jobless was weak (see appendix, table 2).[50] 'Meetings, demonstrations, pickets, petitions, delegations, parades, hunger marches – every means was used to press upon government,' one former participant in the struggles of the unemployed within Hamilton recalled. 'The agitation was rewarded by the pressure developed and by the individual cases won: the four-dollar voucher which secured food for a hungry family; the shoes or coat won for a child unable to go to school for want of clothing; the bag of coal for a family freezing in mid-winter; the medicine for someone ill; the removal of a welfare official for insulting relief recipients; the interpreter supplied for some damn foreigner.'[51]

Although the leadership of most of these organizations outside East York was Communist, 'most of those...active in unemployed ... struggles were not.' The East York Workers' Association, which by 1933 claimed more than 1600 fee-paying members, originated 'through people – men especially – meeting at the welfare office to pick up their welfare vouchers.' Those who joined such organizations were attracted not by ideology, but by the chance to express their anger and frustration at the humiliation and abject inadequacy that surrounded life on relief at the Campbell Report ceilings. 'How many people who at first lost their jobs, then their homes, then their pride, found this was a way of fighting back?' ex-organizer Peter Hunter points out. 'It was much healthier to transfer criticism of the family head who could not provide for his family to criticism of the government heads who could not provide work or hope for the people.' Or as Nell Binns, a former member of the East York Workers' Association, remembered about the meetings she attended, 'it was tremendous really for people to let go to people who understood.'[52]

The province's welfare minister, however, had little sympathy or understanding for the desperation and anger that fuelled increasing demonstrations by the unemployed against his policies. Despite medical and nutritional evidence to the contrary, Croll remained convinced that the province's maximum relief scales – 'the highest in the Dominion of Canada,' as he inaccurately informed his fellow MPPs – were adequate, particularly in light of the declining living standards of the working poor.[53] 'With wages at their present level,' two veteran women social workers in his department warned, 'we are already at a point where our relief allowances are so close to the amount that can be earned by laborers on full time work that the wage earners' point of view becomes important. What incentive is there for them to work?'[54] Uniformity in relief, from Croll's perspective, primarily meant rolling back the gains achieved by the jobless in the bankrupt municipalities to the provincially imposed ceilings. To do this, Queen's Park took over direct control of relief administration in these communities. Over the winter of 1935 a field staff of 140 administrators was sent out to manage the dole in supervised municipalities and townships where the welfare department was convinced relief was excessive. All the elements of administrative reform developed in Toronto and Hamilton were implemented by Queen's Park officials, including systematic home investigation to detect undisclosed assets and income, work requirements for relief, detailed case files on families, and rigid adherence to Campbell Report ceilings.

The result was an explosion of unrest by the unemployed, who fiercely resented cutbacks in their relief allowances; the necessity to cut wood, rake leaves, or shovel snow to prove their entitlement; or the invasion of their homes by provincial inspectors searching for evidence of concealed income. Over the winter and summer of 1935 relief strikes broke out in Markham, Crowland, Windsor, and London Township, as the unemployed demanded higher payments for or an outright end to the work required for their direct relief. In Lakeview and York Township, delegations of the jobless occupied relief offices in protest against the relief allowance cutbacks. In East York 2700 families, led by Workers' Association leader Arthur Williams, participated in a November strike against provincially imposed work requirements and reductions of relief allowances in that community to Campbell Report ceilings. When local councillors refused to meet with them, the strikers took over the township's council chambers, provoking a riot when forty provincial police were called to remove them.[55] In these and other supervised communities, raucous demonstrations at municipal council meetings or 'hunger marches' to Queen's Park became well-publicized tactics to denounce the decline in relief living standards. As one pamphlet distributed by the protesters during a hunger march to the legislature put it: 'Under the heading of "levelling up" relief schedules, the Government has reduced the amount of relief given to certain municipalities, who had only gained the higher schedule by militant struggle. While doing this they consistently refused to raise the amount given where the standards were low. At the same time ... they loudly shouted about ... promises of "uniform relief" schedules for the province. The obvious conclusion to draw is that all schedules must be "uniformly" low.'[56]

Instead of winning a restoration of higher relief allowances, however, these protests succeeded only in contributing to a backlash against the dole within the Hepburn administration. Croll dismissed the 'parades and make-believe sieges' as the result of a 'carefully planned ... [and] covertly organized [campaign] by two cent revolutionaries, who visualize themselves as Lenins.'[57] Hepburn was even more enraged. In late July, following the end of the On-to-Ottawa Trek and the collapse of a bitter two-day woodyard strike in Windsor by 1500 relief recipients protesting against the new provincial requirement of compulsory labour for the dole, the premier unveiled three radical changes in Ontario's relief policy. While Croll was away in England studying British unemployment administration, Hepburn suddenly announced that on 1 August all single men across Ontario would be cut off the dole; that a month later responsibility for administering relief would be returned to all of Ontario's supervised municipalities; and that from that date onwards the province would replace percentage contributions to relief with lump-sum payments on a fixed per capita basis according to Queen's Park's determination of a municipality's 'need.' Croll's welfare department would be gutted, as the 140 investigators and twenty-four accountants hired to administer the dole in supervised municipalities were laid off. 'Our objective is to reduce the welfare department to a mere shell,' Hepburn said in announcing the changes. 'The per capita cost of relief is lower in many of the municipalities which handle their own relief. Our system has been too expensive.'[58]

Hepburn cited a number of reasons for the drastic reversal in policy: a cut in federal support for relief to only 20 per cent of Ontario's costs; soaring provincial expenditure on the dole to more than $3 million a month in spite of a decline in the numbers dependent upon it; farmers complaining they could not get harvest help; and his own 'disgust ... with the attitude taken by the agitators.' Above all, the premier pointed to a taxpayers' backlash 'against agitated strikes, treks, and similar antics contrived to extort an endless series of costly concessions from the overburdened taxpayer ... There's a growing impression among the taxpayers of this Province that they are being drained of their money to provide a living for idlers. There's a growing demand for a halt on rising relief costs. The agitators are to blame ... Their demands for "idle relief" are stirring up a revolt, but it's a revolt among the taxpayers.' Municipalities coddling the unemployed with provincial and federal funds could expect no extra help from Queen's Park. 'We [will] pay the municipalities a lump sum every month,' Hepburn declared. 'In other words, we will say to them: "Here's the alimony, you raise the children."'[59]

When Croll returned from England in mid-August, Hepburn's much-heralded taxpayers' backlash faded into insignificance as the premier quickly reversed or postponed two of his three changes in relief policy. Single men, within days, were returned to the municipal hostels from which they had been evicted once farm jobs in sufficient numbers failed to materialize. The shift to block funding for municipal relief was first postponed to January and then to 1 April 1936 after the newly elected Liberal administration of Mackenzie King, at the December 1935 dominion-provincial conference, boosted federal relief payments to the provinces by 75 per cent.[60] But the policy of handing relief administration back to the supervised municipalities, along with the massive cutbacks in Croll's welfare department and the shift to block-grant funding for local relief, ultimately remained intact. After April 1936, the province indirectly capped municipal relief spending through a system of 'double controls.' Provincial contributions to relief were limited to the Campbell Report ceilings for each family, and to its own estimates, compiled by welfare department inspectors, of the percentage of 'legitimate unemployed' on the dole in each municipality, rather than the numbers actually registered on relief. Communities spending above these amounts, either through setting too generous allowances or allowing too many people on welfare, paid the remainder themselves. If they refused, as was the case in some previously supervised muncipalities such as East York, Scarborough, York Township, Windsor, North Bay, and Hawkesbury, Croll's department imposed a special property tax levy of five to six and a half mills on local taxpayers to fund the difference.[61]

Queen's Park also insisted that all muncipalities conduct a 'purge of exploiters and cheaters' from their relief rolls between January and April 1936, when the new funding system came into effect.[62] 'For months squads of relief inspectors have been examining the situation in every part of Ontario. We know the extent of real need in the municipalities,' Croll claimed. 'If a municipality does not purge its lists, then the maximum will not cover its relief costs. It must look elsewhere for funds and it can only look to its own taxpayers. Our new policy is ... a matter of purge or pay.' To drive home the point, Croll's department also compelled all municipal tax bills to list separately the cost of direct relief to each individual household. All employable relief recipients were required to register regularly with the Employment Service. By the following year all employers would be required to forward their paylists to local relief departments in order to improve detection of unreported income. Through this 'great housecleaning,' as Croll termed it, almost 31,000 people were dropped from the dole during the normally peak winter months.[63] Faced with a property tax increase because of the Queen's Park cutbacks, the City of Ottawa took matters one step further by 'purging' its own relief department of forty women social workers and replacing them with eleven male 'detectives' to root out 'chisellers.' The women were 'good for social service work,' the mayor claimed, but 'the men investigators did better work than women; they were not interested in social service but in seeing that those on relief gave the city the right information and reported their earnings.'[64]

By the end of 1936 Croll's overhaul of relief administration in the province was complete and the unemployed movement for higher allowances had been broken. In Toronto, CCF mayor and labour statesman Jimmy Simpson, one of the few civic leaders to criticize Queen's Park's relief policies vigorously during the summer of protest in 1935, had been driven from office by the end of that year. Although a scathing critic of Hepburn, the populist mayor, as the only CCF member in an otherwise conservative council and Board of Control, was unable to implement cash relief in his own city or to push Toronto's relief scales to the provincial maximum ceiling. Elected by only a slim plurality in the January 1935 contest, Simpson became an easy victim to taxpayers' anger the following year when the city swallowed the largest mill-rate in its history during his term of office. In East York, CCF relief strike leader Arthur Williams, although elected reeve in 1936, proved unable to survive the mill-rate levy imposed on local ratepayers by Queen's Park to fund that community's higher scale of relief allowances. Attempts to organize tax strikes in that community and in York Township against the special mill-rate levies ordered by Croll's department soon collapsed.[65]

By any standard, the response of David Croll and Mitch Hepburn to reforming relief administration in Ontario was bitterly disappointing both to the unemployed and to social welfare activists desperate to see food, clothing, and shelter allowances raised to a level of basic adequacy. Despite his reformist credentials as a labour mayor and his attempts to improve the administrative efficiency of the welfare department, Croll's tenure as minister of public welfare was characterized primarily by an unremitting campaign to perfect techniques of relief investigation, auditing, and inspection in order to weed out fraud and chiselling on the dole, both on the part of uncooperative municipalities and the unemployed. As he told one group of London welfare officials whom he accused of slipshod administration, 'persons on relief are entitled to a decent subsistence but not to a higher standard of living than employed persons ... [T]here is only so much relief money to go around, and whatever fakers get on the relief lists represents that much less which is available for those who are legitimately on relief.' Toronto had achieved excellent results through a 'squad of special investigators' to purge its relief rolls. London should 'borrow an efficiency man from private business' to obtain similar results.[66]

Most of Croll's political energy in the area of unemployment policy was consumed in a two-year battle, in the name of this kind of uniformity, to roll back relief allowances and spending levels in the supervised municipalities to provincially imposed ceilings and to neutralize the strength of unemployed organizations that had fought for these higher standards. To accomplish this objective, Croll's policy fluctuated from direct administration of the dole by Queen's Park, to indirect control of municipal spending through tightly enforced caps on local spending, to provincial authority to impose mill-rate increases on communities where allowances were too high. By the time of Croll's dismissal from the cabinet in 1937, in protest against Hepburn's labour policies, Queen's Park had developed a far greater capacity to regulate, audit, investigate, and inspect municipal relief administration and, indirectly, the lives and actions of the unemployed. While maximum relief scales remained unchanged from the standards set by the previous administration, the welfare department's capacity to enforce these ceilings had improved enormously.[67]

As a result, the political efficacy of the jobless declined. During the Henry administration an unemployed movement had flourished in communities where the percentage and concentration of families on the dole was large, where the bureaucratic capacity and political will of local governments to regulate and limit relief was weak, and where the local contribution to the dole was minimal. In these supervised municipalities, pressure from the jobless had succeeded in pushing relief allowances substantially above standards prevailing anywhere else in the province. As Croll conceded in 1936, when he took office 'the unemployed were ... very strong ... and more militant than they are today ... Concessions were a safety-valve for this potential danger.'[68] After 1934, drastic cutbacks in federal relief spending, growing taxpayer and agrarian anger against the unemployed, increased employment, and the greater regulatory capacity of Croll's department to control access to and spending on relief broke the momentum of the unemployed movement.[69] As Queen's Park expanded its bureaucratic efficiency and control over relief policy during Croll's tenure of office, in order to limit expenditure, the capacity of the jobless to push for higher standards on the dole receded. Levelling down, not up, became the welfare minister's chief legacy.[70]

Mothers' allowances represented the only exception to Hepburn's campaign for retrenchment in welfare spending during the 1930s. The Depression exposed in dramatic form the plight of thousands of needy mothers and their children who had been excluded from assistance by the rigid eligibility requirements of the scheme. Widows with only one child were denied aid as an economy measure during the plan's early years. As time went by their continued exclusion from help was justified on the grounds that they did not really need assistance. Such a woman 'often had a little insurance or found a home for herself and child with her parents, or managed to get along somehow,' the commission argued. Moreover, a 'majority ... were comparatively young and would be able to re-establish themselves without state assistance.'[71]

The economic devastation of the 1930s shattered these illusions. As unemployment soared, the ability of widows with one child to find work of any kind or men willing to support them eroded rapidly. So too did the ability of their children to earn money and contribute to the family's support once they turned sixteen and were cut off from assistance under the legislation. By the early 1930s the commission reported a 'steady increase in the request for allowances,' owing to 'the inability of the husband and father to provide insurance, the difficulty of the widowed mother in finding remunerative occupation, and closer health supervision leading to the discovery of greater numbers of totally and permanently unemployable men.' As a consequence, beginning in 1933, letters, resolutions, and petitions began pouring into Queen's Park from increasingly desperate mothers and from local governments responsible for their support, pleading that the scope of eligiblity under the act be widened. 'Children over sixteen ... in this time of depression are a greater problem to their mothers than they are while under that age owing to their inability to secure employment,' municipalities argued in pressing the province to extend the age of eligibility to at least eighteen.[72]

Mothers living in desperate poverty also made their pleas directly to Ontario's premier. 'I am a widow for seven years with one child and no support or a home, no money to buy milk or bread, and in need of clothing to keep warm,' one woman wrote to Hepburn. 'I wish to mercy I could get the mothers' allowance as my child and I will starve. I have to get help right soon ... I am so sick I can't get around to hunt work.' As another widow with a sick nine-year-old son explained, 'the last few months I have become an invalid through asthma and angina and have been unable to take a position, consequently, hav[e] used up all my available cash ... and am rooming with my parents who are also on relief ... There must be many other widows in the same position and I speak for them as well as myself. Please try to obtain a pension for us ... [T]o raise a future Canadian in the way he should be raised is an important and full time job, enough responsibility for any woman however strong, without the added burden of trying to find a job and keeping it, but it is an impossible task for a delicate woman.'[73]

Beginning in 1934, in response to municipal as well as trade union pressure, the Henry administration began the process of liberalizing eligibility for mothers' allowances by allowing children up to the age of eighteen to receive support through mothers' allowance provided they remained in school. The major changes in mothers' allowances, however, occurred under Hepburn's leadership between 1935 and 1937. During the 1934 election campaign the Liberal leader promised to extend the program to include widows with only one child, a pledge he redeemed the following year. As a result, the commission soon bemoaned that it was 'literally swamped with applications,' as its caseload grew by 40 per cent, from 7517 to 10,413 women, between 1935 and 1936 at an extra cost of more than $80,000 per month. Although expensive, the change was justified, the commission argued, because many widows with two or more children 'had not had time to become re-established when the second youngest child reach[ed] the age of six-teen.' In fairness to the life chances of the remaining child, there was no longer any justifiable reason for denying such families the benefits of a regular monthly allowance.[74]

Another significant change that same year was the reduction of the 'unknown whereabouts' of a deserting husband from five to three years before a mother could apply for an allowance. This, too, was in direct response to the unemployment crisis. As men increasingly left their families in search of work or in frustration at the shame of prolonged joblessness, the plight of the mothers and children they left behind became ever more desperate and a mounting fiscal burden on hard-pressed municipalities, county councils, and townships. The five-year waiting period, difficult in the best of times, 'became impossible to bear during the early 1930s,' Margaret Little argues. Through this change, the proportion of deserted mothers on the mothers' allowance caseload rose modestly from 7 to almost 9 per cent of a program which, by 1939, supported over 12,000 families, four times more than in the early 1920s.[75]

In a final dramatic change, the Hepburn government, as with old age pensions, assumed the total cost of the program in 1937, relieving Ontario's local governments, already staggering under an immense re-lief burden, of their 50 per cent share at a cost of more than $2 million. Again, the fiscal exigencies of the Depression explain the change. Since Ottawa and Queen's Park were contributing 75 per cent of the cost of local relief in most Ontario communities by the late 1930s, it made little sense to hold municipalities responsible for paying half the cost of mothers' allowances. Under these circumstances, local officials strove to keep needy families on the relief caseload rather than the more regular mothers' allowance program in order to save money.[76]

Despite a major broadening in its terms of eligibility, however, the Mothers' Allowance Commission strove mightily to keep program costs under control through a rigid application of its new criteria and a steadfast refusal to enhance benefit levels, which dropped on average to only $28 a month per family by the mid-1930s, an amount the commis-sion openly conceded was 'not, in itself ... adequate to supply all the families' needs.' Many widows with one child applying for help after the 1935 changes were refused aid because they had 'become re-estab-lished in employment and were living with relatives who cared for the children while the mothers were at work.' These circumstances 'did not reveal the need for an allowance.' Others with older children in the home were told to look to their earnings in order to be self-supporting. Women deserted by their husbands found even the three-year waiting period seldom led to the granting of an allowance, since any hint that the man's whereabouts were known by someone became grounds for the refusal of support. 'This is a cruel situation and very difficult to handle,' the commission chairman conceded in 1936.[77]

As with old age pensions, the province by the later 1930s also developed a much larger and more thoroughly trained staff of fifty-seven investigators who were far more capable than harassed municipal clerks and local allowance boards to provide detailed information on the lives of women under the program in order to determine their eligibility. 'As a result of this intensive work,' the commission boasted by 1939, 'it has been possible to secure more regularly the yearly financial status of each family thus enabling [us] to regulate more thoroughly the amount of the allowance that should be paid, and also to decide as to whether or not the families can carry on without further assistance, and thus keep the cost to a minimum.' More than 43 per cent of new applications that year were refused, the commission noted with pride, and more than a thousand mothers were cut off from support 'due to the careful supervision and ... efficient work of our Investigators.' The program's goal, according to its annual report, was to 'administer the act in order that need, not greed, is adequately met; that a spirit of independence, coupled with incentive, is developed.'[78]

Judged by these standards of fiscal regulation, mothers' allowance was the province's most successful social program during the 1930s. Both overall expenditure and caseload size only doubled during a decade of general economic collapse, and the average benefit paid per family actually declined. Compared with the explosion of provincial expenditure on unemployment relief and old age pensions, the $5 million annual cost of mothers' allowances in Ontario by 1939 was modest indeed.[79]

Over the next decade, leadership in the struggle to secure an adequate social minimum in Ontario shifted from the unemployed in the province's bankrupt municipalities to Toronto. Laver's welfare department in particular became the battleground for reform as the leadership in the fight for a decent standard of relief shifted to social welfare and community activists determined to build some concept of a decent social minimum into both the city's and the province's relief standards. It was a campaign led, for the most part, by women working through a variety of organizations, including the Child Welfare Council, the Federation for Community Service, the Visiting Homemakers' Association, the Toronto Welfare Council, and the Women Electors of Toronto. Nutrition became their rallying point, an area in which women felt enough confidence in their knowledge and authority to challenge a male-dominated system of relief administration built on accounting principles.

A key organization in the struggle for relief reform became the Visiting Homemakers' Association, a division of the Red Cross which sent dieticians and mothers' helpers into the homes of the poor to aid women struggling to cope with too many children and not enough money. As the one organization that combined nutritional expertise with daily contact inside working-class households, the VHA was well placed to document the inadequacy of relief food allowances. By 1934 VHA workers were becoming fed up with their role of helping mothers on relief stretch fundamentally inadequate food allowances past the breaking point. 'Most people believe that if the mothers could buy and cook to advantage ... an adequate diet could be obtained from the most meagre allowance,' Margaret McCready, a VHA supervisor, told a 1934 national meeting of Canadian social workers, 'but this help will not solve the problem of an inadequate food allowance.' Throughout Ontario her organization had found 'everything from excessively inadequate to moderately inadequate relief food allowances, with only a few that could be called adequate.' Something had to be done to 'rectify ... the situation,' McCready argued, and the place to start was in 'local women's organizations. A public opinion on the subject needs to be aroused and ... the greatest interest would be in women's groups.'[80]

The first stirrings of such a campaign in Toronto began two years later in the fall of 1936. Its initial trigger, however, was not relief, but low wages. In November the Federation for Community Service, the central organization for coordinating charitable fundraising and its allocation within the city's Protestant community, appointed a committee to study low incomes. Too many families, where the father was fully employed but earning as little as $11.00 a week, were coming to private charities for financial help, since they were ineligible for city relief. Although these families lacked enough for the 'merest necessities,' they were not properly a private agency responsibility either. Where should they go for help? The FCS subcommittee on low incomes ultimately decided this was a business responsibility. It recommended that the Toronto Board of Trade take up the problem through establishing a fair-wage committee. To assist the work of the board, however, the FCS Social Policy Committee also recommended that Marjorie Bell, of the Visiting Homemakers' Association, be hired to prepare a minimum standard budget that might form the basis of 'defin[ing] an adequate wage ... for Toronto.' 'Wide publicity through the press [and] through women's organizations' was also urged.[81]

Toronto's Board of Trade, predictably, did nothing with this suggestion, but in January 1937 Bell did deliver her report on 'what it costs a family to live in Toronto' to the Social Policy Committee. The minimum budget for a family of five (children ages six, eleven, and fourteen) Bell pointed out, was $25.30 per week, of which at least $8.00 had to go towards food. Yet the average weekly wage of 243 VHA families of five in 1936 was $17.85. Toronto's relief allowance for food was only $6.04 per week for this same size family. 'Children are not getting enough to eat,' Bell concluded.[82]

Shocked by these figures, the Social Policy Committee agreed to raise the question of inadequate income with the Federation Council and to attempt to secure private funding for a 'complete survey of living conditions among families in the low income group.' Lois Fraser, president of the Child Welfare Council and one of the most dynamic philanthropic women involved in Toronto's charity scene in the 1930s and 1940s, was put in charge of raising the money. Fraser wrote to five of the city's wealthiest families asking for support. The wife of prominent Toronto lawyer Kaspar Fraser, who worked closely with E.P. Taylor, Fraser was both a dedicated and forceful advocate of welfare reform and someone well connected to Toronto's business elite.[83] 'The plan is to make a detailed study of the amount and kind of food actually eaten by the members of typical families living on very low wages or on relief,' Fraser told them. 'In spite of the number of studies on nutrition which have been made recently, this one, on individual food intake has not yet been done. One is accustomed to hearing that people on low income "get along somehow." It would be important to know exactly what this means in the feeding of the people concerned. Do they spend their money wisely? Have they enough to buy the right kind of food? If not, what food do they eat? If there is any deficiency does all the family share in it, or are some well fed at the expense of others? Is it the mother who goes short?' The proposal involved sending VHA staff directly into one hundred selected families for a week, to 'observe and measure the food actually eaten at each meal by each member of the family.' In this way exact and scientific knowledge, not simply of the nutritional needs but of the actual food consumption of low-income families, could be gained to establish the extent to which it met or fell short of existing minimum guidelines for protecting health.[84]

While Fraser attempted to raise money for the nutrition study, the Social Policy Committee, composed mostly of social workers, lobbied the Federation Council, dominated by businessmen, to launch a publicity campaign for the city council to begin a full-scale independent inquiry into Toronto's relief policy, particularly the food allowance ration that was 20 per cent below the Ontario Medical Association minimum nutritional guidelines.[85] By the summer, however, it was clear that businessmen and some of Toronto's more conservative social work executives on the council, such as Frank Stapleford of the Neighbor-hood Workers' Association, wanted no part of such overtly political action. Fears of losing wealthy donor support and antagonizing City Hall outweighed the anger of some FCS members at the inadequacies of Toronto's relief policy. Much more could be accomplished 'by work-ing through officials of the Department of Public Welfare' than by making relief a public issue, Stapleford cautioned. After months of doing nothing, the FCS handed the whole issue over to its newly formed social planning body, the Toronto Welfare Council, in September 1937.[86]

The Toronto Welfare Council, unlike the Federation for Community Service, was strictly a social planning body and was dominated by social workers, not donors and fundraisers. Consequently, it was poten-tially less inhibited about tackling the inadequacies of Toronto's relief allowances head on. One of its first actions was to appoint a Committee on Relief Standards, chaired by Lois Fraser, to take up the work Fraser and Bell had begun the previous year – the detailed investigation by the Visiting Homemakers' Association of food consumption among low-income families. This time the TWC found the money for the study through a $2000 grant from the London Life Insurance Company; 110 volunteer families who agreed to keep detailed records of their indi-vidual daily food consumption and expenses for one year were se-lected; and a blue-ribbon committee of leading nutritional and medical experts was established to evaluate the results scientifically.[87]

In the meantime, Toronto City Council wrestled with the decision of whether or not to spend $390,000 to increase its relief allowance by 15 per cent in 1938. Even Bert Laver, the city relief commissioner, con-ceded the existing food allowance was 'not adequate,' although the recipients, he argued, were 'supposed to make an attempt to earn,' in order to bridge the gap. In fact the food allowance, according to Dr Harold Wastenays, chairman of the TWC's committee of nutritional experts, had to be boosted by 26 per cent to bring it up to the lowest minimal standard for health put forward by the Canadian Council on Nutrition.[88]

Toronto City Council ultimately decided it would raise the relief allowance 15 per cent if the province would provide matching funding. Queen's Park refused. In private, Hepburn's deputy minister of welfare had told the premier that Toronto relief costs were already too high because the city did not employ enough relief investigators to cut down the numbers on the dole. The whole city relief operation needed a thorough investigation and audit by the province before any increase in grants could be considered. Publicly Eric Cross, provincial minister of welfare, echoing identical arguments by David Croll three years earlier, told a delegation from the Toronto Welfare Council that Toronto's relief scales were already dangerously close to lower wage levels. 'If the relief allowance were raised, more people would demand relief instead of trying to find jobs,' he argued. In any case, relief was 'not intended to cover the complete needs of a family. Relief recipients are encouraged to find odd jobs,' or to turn to 'assistance from relatives.' Nor was there any convincing evidence that children of relief recipients were 'any more malnourished than other children.' Although Cross was undoubtedly right in describing how many poverty-stricken families actually survived on the province's inadequate relief allowances during the 1930s, this was hardly a justifiable argument for keeping welfare below minimum nutritional levels. Nonetheless, as long as these views remained entrenched within Queen's Park, Toronto could expect no help from the Hepburn administration.[89]

Without provincial support, Toronto refused to go ahead with any increase. Marjorie Bell, architect of the TWC's study of food consumption among relief families, urged the council to keep pressuring City Hall through a publicity campaign. 'If the Welfare Council cannot act on this matter, by comparison, there is nothing at all that it can feel justified in doing.' For the moment, however, the meeting with Ontario's welfare minister had taken the wind out of its sails. The TWC would continue its research on nutrition throughout 1938, but further public action on the relief question was ruled out.[90]

In the spring of 1939 the inadequacy of relief diets exploded once again. Two issues precipitated the outbreak of public concern. The first was the publication of the Toronto Welfare Council's long-awaited study of nutrition among low-income families, ironically titled *The Cost of Living*. Although the report appeared in July, its key nutritional findings were first published in April by Dr E.W. McHenry, director of the University of Toronto's School of Hygiene. McHenry was one of the experts on the TWC subcommittee that produced the study and a leading authority on nutritional studies in Canada.

The one hundred families who participated in the study over the course of the year were low income, but not on relief. On average they earned $19.64 per week and had 4.2 children. According to McHenry, they also were only 'secur[ing] about three-quarters of the total amount of food which they needed to satisfy their energy requirements.' Only three families, the nutritionist reported, 'received an adequate supply of food.' Half the total group got less than three-quarters of this minimum satisfactory supply of calories.[91]

Inside these families the burden of undernourishment was starkly skewed according to gender and age. 'The fathers were best cared for, younger children next, then the older children and finally the mothers. This is what would be expected,' McHenry observed, 'since a common characteristic of mothers the world over is an unselfish desire to do the best possible for the family.' Mothers were getting only 73 per cent of the protein, 82 per cent of the calcium, and 53 per cent of the iron they needed to stay healthy. Young children were also suffering with only one-half the amount of iron and calcium they needed. Pregnant and nursing mothers suffered from the most acute diet deficiencies. As McHenry put it, 'on the whole the men did reasonably well but one is forced to conclude that the women and children were inadequately nourished.'[92]

Both the Toronto Welfare Council and the press gave the study maximum publicity, with headlines such as 'Not Enough Food for Toronto Poor' and 'Only 3 of 100 Homes Getting Enough to Eat.'[93] Unnoticed at the time were the different interpretations which the council and McHenry placed on these findings. For the TWC, the *Cost of Living* study represented conclusive proof that poor families were 'slowly starving.' As the document put it, the argument was 'frequently made that some families "get along very well" on a low wage, and that the ability to manage is the most important factor.' The findings of the report, however, demonstrated that 'the ability to manage well, while valuable, is not sufficient.' Instead, it provided 'evidence of harm resulting from the low standard of living made necessary by inadequate income.'[94]

McHenry did not draw this conclusion. For him the evidence of the effect of low income on diet was inconclusive, since food consumption among higher income families had not been studied. In any case, 'under present conditions,' he argued, 'little can be done to overcome the economic factor causing malnutrition.' Instead, the University of Toronto nutritionist was more inclined to blame the mother for her own and her family's undernourishment. Families with similar incomes achieved widely divergent levels of nutritional adequacy because some mothers 'wasted money in the purchase of food.' The same was true with families on relief. Here allowances could provide a diet 80 per cent to 85 per cent adequate 'provided the vouchers are carefully spent.' As the TWC study showed, the diets of low-income *working* families in Toronto were only 75 per cent adequate. In other words, relief diets, McHenry argued, could furnish 'nutrition more adequate than is being secured by working families,' principally because of vouchers for milk and eggs which could not be spent for anything else. The diets of many low-income families, including those on relief, 'could be improved without increasing the allowance by training mothers how to buy food,' McHenry concluded in almost direct contradiction of the TWC study.[95]

The Hepburn government signalled its response to the arguments of the *Cost of Living* by slashing relief allowances in the suburbs surrounding Toronto by 10 per cent. East York, York Township, New Toronto, and Mimico were once again paying their unemployed families 35 per cent above the Campbell Report ceilings, yet by 1939 the provincial maximum for relief contributions was still only the Campbell Report plus 25 per cent. Ontario wished to bring all its municipalities within a uniform relief scale, Welfare Minister Eric Cross told the press in justifying the move, and the Campbell Report schedule plus 25 per cent was 'fair.'[96]

The government's decision produced an explosion of outrage. The Toronto Welfare Council organized a public forum attended by 250 people to protest the cutback. More than 700 relief recipients in the affected townships staged a day of parades and demonstrations culminating in a long march to Queen's Park to confront the welfare minister directly. Labour unions across the province deluged the welfare department with resolutions deploring the decision and arguing that relief allowances needed to be boosted at least 50 per cent above the Campbell Report schedule to conform with revised nutritional guidelines published by the Ontario Medical Association in 1937. 'The mothers are really desperate,' Eva O'Rourke, a York Township relief recipient told Deputy Welfare Minister E.A. Horton when the demonstration reached Queen's Park. 'I have seven children and they have suffered through this reduction, as I know other children have too. My children went all day yesterday on a cup of cocoa and a slice of dry bread each. I sent five of them to school this morning without food because I couldn't get my voucher until noon.'[97]

Both Horton, a former investment analyst, and his minister Eric Cross remained unmoved by the protests. Relief allowances in York Township for some large families, Cross told the demonstrators, were as high as $84.00 a month. 'That is a lot more than some people can earn in that area, the people who must help to pay the cost of relief. It forces people on relief. My problem,' he told the delegation, 'is to give relief in some proportion to what people can earn.' Relief allowances were adequate, the welfare minister insisted. 'Many of the children on relief are in better health than many who are children of low-wage earners.' Charges of malnutrition were 'absolutely unfounded.'[98]

Apart from their fears that relief in the suburbs was already exceeding wage rates for the unskilled, Horton and Cross also remained convinced by their own internal investigation of Toronto's relief department that administration of the dole in that city was too lax. By 1939 Toronto was absorbing one-third of all provincial relief expenditure, compared with only 19 per cent in 1933, yet relief loads in the city were declining at only two-thirds the average of surrounding municipalities. A team of provincial relief inspectors sent in to reinvestigate 939 relief cases picked at random in 1939 found that only one-third had no irregularities. Of these clients, 20 per cent had their allowances cancelled, reduced, or suspended for a variety of offences ranging from possession of a telephone to unreported income. Until Toronto reformed its own relief administration to bring about substantial savings and a reduction in caseload similar to trends throughout the province, it could expect no increased help from the province.[99]

Canada's entry into the Second World War in September 1939 fundamentally changed the terms of the debate surrounding the adequacy of relief in Ontario in at least three ways. Most importantly, the war dramatically began to shrink the size and to restructure the composition of the relief caseload. Recruitment and war production provided alternatives to life on relief for thousands of the unemployed for the first time in more than a decade. This process was speeded along by provincial government orders-in-council in the summer of 1940 which cut off funding for employable single men and married men on relief under the age of forty-five with up to two dependants.[100]

Between 1939 and 1941 Ontario's monthly average number of relief recipients dropped from 133,971, or 9.8 per cent of the population, to only 27,713, or 1.9 per cent of the population. By the end of 1943 only 15,216 Ontarians were still on the dole. Three out of four were over fifty years old; 60 per cent were women, and 88 per cent were sick. Neither in size nor in composition did the relief caseload bear much resemblance to the 1930s. These were the unemployable poor who, for one technicality or another, could not qualify for the province's other categorical programs such as mothers' allowances or old age pensions. With no work ethic left to protect, as one internal provincial government memorandum put it, there was 'no longer any justifiable argument that the relief schedule should not be on an adequate minimum total maintenance basis' for this group.[101]

The war also provided a tremendous impetus to the public climate of concern over nutrition and health. The 40 per cent rejection rate due to medical reasons for the first recruits in 1939 drove home dramatically the extent to which Depression diets had taken their toll on working-class health. Wartime food rationing for the entire population, combined with nutritionally adequate dependants' allowances for the families of soldiers fighting overseas, also highlighted, by contrast, the stark inadequacies of families still dependent on relief food allowances. As Bessie Touzel, executive director of the Toronto Welfare Council put it in lobbying City Hall for a boost in food vouchers in 1942, 'the children growing up in these families should be well enough fed to enable them to undertake their fair share of the burden when their time comes, whether in war or peace.'[102]

The war also raised the issue of reconstruction and the possible threat of a return to Depression conditions of unemployment. Improving relief allowances for the ten thousand still on relief in Toronto was important, the Welfare Council argued in 1942, but of far greater importance was its potential influence on postwar conditions. Should the unemployed of the Depression years who were now 'offering their lives for our safety' be told, if thrown out of work once the war ended, 'thank you very much. We regret that the best reward for your services that our system can afford is to provide a standard of subsistence on which we know you and your wives and children will not be able to have enough food to keep you well. You and your dependants will be humiliated by being obliged to wear clothes which mark you as public dependants and which label your children as being inferior to their fellows. You will have so little money for rent that you will be obliged to live in bug-infested slums.' Providing a relief scale sufficient to maintain health and self-respect, the council argued, was essential to 'improve morale among those who are fighting and working for the country.'[103]

Despite the favourable climate for reform created by the war, it took the specific initiative of a core group of women activists to push Toronto and ultimately the province into abandoning the Campbell Report relief schedule. The key individuals in this campaign were Bessie Touzel and Lois Fraser of the Toronto Welfare Council; Marjorie Bell, head of the Visiting Homemakers' Association; Dr Alice Willard, a professor of nutrition at the University of Toronto; Theresa Falkner, president of the Women Electors of Toronto; and Adelaide Plumptre, ex-chair of the city's Board of Education and since 1936 a prominent member of city council.

The push began in the fall of 1940 when Plumptre and other reformist municipal politicians, such as Controller Lewis Duncan, joined with the Women Electors and the Welfare Council to urge the creation of a Public Welfare Advisory Committee at City Hall to supervise Laver's Department of Public Welfare and to plan for reconstruction. Plumptre and Duncan attempted to make the committee a major issue in the January 1941 municipal election otherwise overshadowed by the war.[104] Representatives of the Women Electors and the Welfare Council spoke widely throughout the community on the question, and the campaign was effective. In June 1941 City Hall established the committee. The TWC had finally 'gain[ed] a foothold in City Council,' as one of its members put it. It was 'a golden opportunity ... [that] might not last,' and the social planning body was determined to make the most of it.[105]

A month after the Public Welfare Committee began its operations, the six women planned their strategy for persuading it to endorse an adequate relief allowance. The first step was to prepare a brief for the committee demonstrating the gap between the Campbell Report schedule and what families actually needed to survive in Toronto. 'I have no high opinion of the intelligence of the men to whom this document is to be presented,' Plumptre warned the group at the outset. 'We are dealing with men who like and are prepared to believe anything put out by the official authorities, while they are often anxious to criticize and reject anything which they find different and off their usual channels of thought.'[106] As a consequence, the women determined to line up their own authorities in order to overwhelm the committee with scientific evidence.

The first step was to refute the common impression, reinforced by the recent articles by E.W. McHenry, that if only mothers on the dole could be taught to shop and cook intelligently the deficiency in relief diets would go away. To eliminate this argument, Bell and Willard spent a week attempting to shop and cook nutritionally adequate meals for a family of five on relief. They could not do it. Out of a city relief allowance totalling $9.20, their budget fell $1.30 short of what they needed to buy. Their results were presented to the Committee on Public Welfare in a joint brief by the Women Electors, the TWC, and the Visiting Homemakers' Association in early July. The shopping habits of welfare mothers were not the problem, the Welfare Council argued conclusively, since 'in this case the buying has been guided by two people whose nutritional education far surpasses any that might be contemplated for the average housewife.'[107]

The strategy paid off. The Willard-Bell experiment was 'so striking that it was very telling in its effect on committee thinking,' Touzel recounted. The Public Welfare Committee asked the Welfare Council to prepare a further brief that would provide scientific evidence for what a nutritionally adequate relief allowance should be.[108] In the interim, the Public Welfare Committee recommended a 30 per cent increase in Toronto's food allowance. The Toronto City Council ultimately agreed to a 20 per cent cost-of-living adjustment, but Premier Hepburn, claiming he would 'pay no more towards Toronto's relief bill,' refused to provide matching provincial funding. The increase cost Toronto $128,000.[109]

In the meantime, the Welfare Council hired Dr Frederick Tisdall, director of the Research Laboratories Department at the Hospital for Sick Children and author of the 1933 Ontario Medical Association study 'Relief Diets,' to work with Willard and Bell in the formulation of a new Toronto relief schedule, as requested by the city council. In November 1941 the Tisdall-Willard-Bell Report, 'the first scientific report of its kind for Canadian welfare administration,' was presented to the Public Welfare Committee. The report contained a complete schedule for nutritionally adequate diets for families of varying size, age levels, and gender composition calculated at 1941 prices. For the typical family of five with three children aged four to twelve years, a rock-bottom minimum of $10.00 a week for food was necessary. Toronto's food relief voucher, even with the new 20 per cent increase, paid this same family only $7.13, a shortfall of $2.87 per week. In other words, Toronto's food relief allowance for such a family needed to be boosted by more than 40 per cent to reach the minimum standard necessary for health.[110]

To continue 'a diet inadequate for health is a policy [we] reject on grounds of economy, good government and humanity,' the Public Welfare Committee concluded. Laver, the city's welfare commissioner, was instructed to prepare and cost a new city relief schedule based on the Tisdall-Willard-Bell Report findings. In February 1942 Laver presented his results. To meet the report's dietary standards would require increases ranging from 20 per cent to 70 per cent, depending on the age of family members, for Toronto's 10,000 people on relief. It would cost the city another $193,000 a year over existing expenditure, Laver concluded. Had such a recommendation been adopted three years earlier in 1939, when an average of 67,599 were on relief, it would have cost Toronto an extra $1,351,000 per year.[111]

For the next six months, and for perhaps the only time in its history, the adequacy of welfare allowances became a major issue in Toronto politics. A confusing struggle ensued over whether the city would place relief on a 'scientific' basis by implementing the Tisdall-Willard-Bell Report. On one side, pushing hard for the report, were the Welfare Council, the Women Electors, the Local Council of Women, the Toronto Trades and Labour Council, the CCF and Communist Party members, as well as the mayor himself, Fred Conboy. This broad coalition was organized and led by the Toronto Welfare Council, primarily through the reformist activism of a young group of social welfare professionals like Bessie Touzel, the TWC's executive director, who had been radicalized by the Depression. On the other side was the Board of Trade, led by F.D. Tolchard, the Property Owners Association, and the Bureau of Municipal Research. Their opposition was fuelled, not so much by the actual cost of the proposal, as by its potential effect on low-wage earners, who, as one controller put it, were 'often getting starvation wages [and] ... were also taxpayers ... [Why] should they have to pay towards the upkeep of people receiving higher food allowances than ... themselves?' Probably more significant was the fear of postwar unemployment and a 'possible large increase in dependency' thrown once again upon the limited tax resources funding municipal direct relief.[112]

The critical opposition to Tisdall-Willard-Bell, however, came from the Hepburn administration at Queen's Park. In March 1942 both the Public Welfare Committee by a large margin, and the Board of Control by a narrow three-to-two vote, approved the adoption of the report and the upward revision of Toronto's relief schedules. Almost immediately, Queen's Park announced not only that it refused to match the increase, but that it was cutting back its own contribution to relief from 75 per cent to 50 per cent, effective 1 April. 'Toronto was definitely out of line with the other municipalities in Ontario,' welfare minister Farquhar Oliver maintained. With only 17.5 per cent of the provincial population, it contained 43.5 per cent of the relief load. The city had 'too many straw bosses ... clamouring for publicity.' Hepburn himself was even blunter. Unless some city council members 'quit making a political football of relief, the province will step in and handle the situation,' he warned. 'Certain members of the Council are putting a premium on idleness ... The rates Toronto proposes to put into effect would seriously interfere with the people who work every week and would compete with wage practices throughout the province.' For precisely this reason, organized labour in Toronto vigorously endorsed both the *The Cost of Living* and the Tisdall-Willard-Bell Report and would soon be buying up hundreds of reprints of the former document – nicknamed 'The Redbook' after its bright cover – to back up its own claims at the bargaining table for a living wage.[113]

News of the provincial hard line weakened the city's resolve. Both the Board of Control and the Public Welfare Committee withdrew their approval of the Tisdall-Willard-Bell Report relief schedule and instead appointed a new umbrella advisory committee composed of representatives from the Toronto Welfare Council, the Labour Council, the Women Electors, the Property Owners Association, and the Board of Trade to reconsider the report and its recommendations. Unlike its vacillation in response to business pressure during the 1930s, the Toronto Welfare Council this time decided to stand firm. Tisdall-Willard-Bell was a 'scientific report,' council members argued. 'It would be inconsistent ... to suggest that less than that described in the report would at any time be adequate.' If the council reached an 'impasse ... with the Board of Trade' on the advisory committee, the board of directors agreed, it would take a 'non-compromise attitude as to the necessary standard.'[114]

When the new advisory committee handed down its report in May 1942, however, the TWC had won over the critical support of L.F. Winchell, vice-chairman of the Board of Trade, who was also on its own board of directors. With the dissent only of the Property Owners Association representative, the advisory committee reaffirmed support for the Tisdall-Willard-Bell Report and recommended that even if the province withheld further funding, Toronto 'had a responsibility to give leadership' and should fund the entire increased cost of bringing welfare up to an acceptable minimum nutritional standard on its own. City council received the committee's report and, after a few months delay, implemented a new schedule of relief allowances based on the Tisdall-Willard-Bell Report on 16 March 1943, at an extra cost, unshared by the province, of $108,000 a year.[115]

The nutritional impetus provided by the controversy over the Tisdall-Willard-Bell Report, rapid shrinkage and the changing composition of the provincial relief caseload, and concerns about postwar reconstruction on the part of a new Conservative administration led by George Drew pushed Ontario slowly towards an abandonment of its commitment to the 1932 Campbell Report relief schedule. In January 1943, in an obvious response to the Tisdall-Willard-Bell Report, Queen's Park appointed its favourite nutritionist, Dr E.W. McHenry, to conduct a fact-finding investigation into the 'dietary budget of relief recipients ... in the light of present and possible future food rationing.' McHenry had previously been appointed honorary consultant in nutrition to the provincial Department of Health. The aim of his study was to 'determin[e] a proper diet which can be built on those foods which can be purchased under the rationing program.'[116]

Six months later McHenry delivered his *Report on Food Allowances for Relief Recipients in the Province of Ontario*. Like the Campbell Report, which it soon replaced as the basis for calculating food allowances for welfare recipients in postwar Ontario, the McHenry Report was a key document in the formation of the provincial welfare state. In some respects, it followed closely along the lines of the Tisdall-Willard-Bell Report in Toronto. Like that document and unlike the Campbell Report, McHenry's relief schedule was based on scientific nutritional data and varied its food allowance recommendations according to the sex and age composition of the family as well as the number of children. Compared with the prevailing provincial ceiling of $8.00 a week for the typical family of five (the Campbell Report plus 60 per cent), McHenry's recommended maximum in a city such as Toronto was

$11.16. This was a significant increase, although below the $13.32 called for by the Toronto Welfare Council in the update of *The Cost of Living* published at the same time.[117]

Unlike Tisdall-Willard-Bell and the *The Cost of Living*, however, McHenry continued to place the principal blame for nutritional inadequacy on welfare mothers, not the state. 'In the final analysis,' he argued, 'the nutritional value of the food consumed by a family will depend as much, if not more, upon the wisdom with which the allowance is spent and upon cooking methods used as upon the money supplied. A liberal cash allowance can not, in itself, guarantee an adequate diet.' Since the poor could not be trusted to spend their money wisely, McHenry suggested that establishing 'restaurants at which nutritious meals could be economically provided' might be preferable to cash relief. At the very least, relief recipients should receive cookbooks and continuing nutritional advice with their monthly cheques. McHenry also refused to recommend a single provincial nutritional standard. Instead, he argued for a zonal system in which food allowances varied depending upon the relationship of local prices to those in Toronto.[118]

Ironically, the typical family of five, for which the McHenry Report was aimed, had largely disappeared from the provincial relief rolls by the time the report was published in 1944. By that point 60 per cent of the province's relief load were single, mostly old, sick, unemployable women living alone who could not qualify for any other categorical program. For them the McHenry Report schedule represented a cut in relief food allowances from $2.40 to $2.22 a week. Cookbooks, tips on shopping, and the nutritional education McHenry argued was urgently needed were unlikely to make a significant impact on their lives.[119]

On 22 September 1944 newspapers announced that the 'underfeeding of relief recipients' in Ontario was coming to an end. The old Campbell Report food allowances, in place since 1932, were to be scrapped in favour of a new scientific schedule based on individual needs devised by Dr McHenry. After twelve years of debate, Queen's Park finally conceded what welfare organizations had been arguing since 1932. The province's relief allowances could 'not enable an individual or a family to procure sufficient nutritious food to provide even a basic minimum adequate diet.'[120]

How much was enough for families on relief? Between the beginning of the Depression and the end of the Second World War this question sparked a convoluted search for standards to define and regulate the contested needs of Ontario's poor. The debate began with the Campbell Report's attempt, in the context of fiscal crisis, to place checks and ceilings on provincial contributions to local welfare expenditure. By the mid-1940s the grounds of the debate, at least insofar as food was concerned, had shifted from principles of accounting to those of nutrition. Unquestionably, this change represented a major and permanent gain for those dependent on the dole, one in which local welfare councils, nutritionists, labour unions, the unemployed, and especially women community activists played a critical role.[121]

More important as well was the changing context of the war itself. War heightened the consciousness of Canadians about questions of diet and nutrition, whether they examined the inadequate health of army recruits, the standards of support necessary for the families of those fighting overseas, or their own ration books. War also raised concerns about reconstructing society. When Ontarians thought about social security in a postwar world, their principal memory from the 1930s was most often one of avoiding hunger. Reforming public assistance to prevent the recurrence of such abject want became a principal component of plans for building a provincial welfare state to assuage these fears and improve wartime morale. Above all, though, war changed the composition and scale of the relief caseload in ways that made nutritional adequacy a more attainable political objective for reformers. Quite simply, the financial implication of placing the diets of 10,000 Torontonians on a nutritionally adequate basis in 1944 bore no relation to the cost of doing the same thing for 120,000 relief recipients in 1934. By the 1940s the social implication of such a shift had changed as well. The relief load after 1940 were *unemployables*. All the able-bodied had been cut from the rolls. The work ethic of these old, sick, mostly single women was no longer a cause for concern as it had been for those shaping relief policy towards employable men in the 1930s.

Even with the nutritional standards of the McHenry Report in place, Ontario officials did not fear a major escalation of relief costs or a loss of financial control over municipal expenditures in the postwar world. As with the Campbell Report, the province was only establishing maximum ceilings towards which it would contribute, not minimum floors which muncipalities had to meet in developing their relief allowances. As one provincial Department of Welfare memo put it in arguing for the McHenry Report schedule:

If it were necessary to provide all the assistance required to fulfill this scientific schedule, it would probably increase the cost to the province by approximately thirty-five percent. However, the local municipality only grants assistance on the basis of need. In this connection, the schedule *merely becomes a guide* enabling a maximum contribution which will be shared by the province and the municipality and limited to what assistance is granted by the local municipality which, in many cases, would only be a proportion of this proposed schedule. The safeguarding of expenditure rests at the local level. Since a local municipality is concerned with fifty percent of the cost, no better safeguard could be found.[122]

The McHenry Report also represented, in some ways, a limitation as well as a gain for those interested in welfare reform within Ontario. Inadequacy of food allowances, although compelling and serious, was only *one* cause of inadequate diet among Ontario's poor in the 1930s and 1940s. The other major cause was not lack of nutritional education among welfare mothers, as McHenry believed, but rather the *total* inadequacy of relief in meeting the diversified needs of the poor, in particular for shelter, clothing, and household necessities. As the Toronto Welfare Council publication *The Cost of Living* recognized, families needed more besides food for survival. Glaring inadequacies in other areas of relief budgets, especially rent, ate into the all too scarce resources available to buy food. Yet the overhaul of welfare contained in the McHenry Report singled out only food for reform, an arena of need in which mothers as well as the state could continue to share the blame for unmet wants. In postwar Ontario, as in the 1930s, mothers would continue to bear the brunt of their own unselfishness by depriving themselves of food needed for nutrition in order to buy clothes or pay the rent.

Placing food on a scientific basis of nutrition nonetheless had a compelling attraction for welfare reform. As one Department of Welfare memo put it, with the adoption of the McHenry food schedule, Ontario's 'forgotten residue' could now be assured that the province had 'an interest in their well-being.'[123] Unlike other dimensions of poverty, the calculation of food needs possessed a scientific and biological certainty that lent itself to the formulation of provincial standards and reform, much as the mystique and finality of actuarial science underpinned Canada's acceptance of unemployment insurance in the same time period.[124] With the McHenry Report schedules in place, Ontarians could feel comfortable, after the war, knowing that the needs of the poor were now calculated according to the best scientific advice their money could buy. When they asked themselves 'how much is enough' in meeting the claims of those on welfare, the answer was apparent. As much food as it took to keep a family alive and healthy. In this sense, at least, nutrition became not only a lever but also a blinder in the creation of Ontario's postwar welfare state.

4

Reconstructing Welfare, 1944–50

As the Second World War drew to a close, Ontarians, like other Canadians, envisaged a 'reconstructed' nation in which the catastrophic levels of mass poverty and insecurity that scarred their memories of the 1930s would be forever banished from public life. The critical importance of this demand became embodied in the phrase 'social security,' which shaped political discourse both in Canada and throughout the Western industrial world over the next five years. Depression-based fears of 'relief-mongering' and subsidized idleness, which dominated much political discussion of welfare in the 1930s, had disappeared by the early 1940s in the context of the full employment brought on by the Second World War and the removal of the able-bodied from welfare caseloads.[1] Instead, the language of Leonard Marsh's 1943 *Report on Social Security for Canada* more accurately captured the new public mood. 'Social security payments are not money lost,' the report argued. 'They are investments in morale and health, in greater family stability, and from both material and psychological viewpoints, in human productive efficiency ... It has yet to be proved that any democracy which underwrites the social minimum for its citizens is any weaker or less wealthy for doing so.'[2]

The first downpayment on the promise of postwar reconstruction arrived in 1940 with the passage of national unemployment insurance legislation just prior to that year's federal election. The political momentum for more sweeping social reforms, however, continued to accelerate over the next four years with the appearance of a flurry of reports, books and articles on postwar social security.[3] There was also a dramatic upsurge in public support for the collectivism embodied in both the industrial unionism of the Canadian Congress of Labour and the democratic socialism of the Co-operative Commonwealth Federation. Seeking to forestall a further drift to the left, Prime Minister

Mackenzie King committed the federal government to underwriting a 'national minimum of health and decency' for postwar Canadians in the January 1944 Speech from the Throne. As his first instalment on this promise, he introduced a sweeping new program of universal family allowances, payable monthly to every Canadian mother for each of her children, later that same year. Additional proposals for national health insurance, contributory old age pensions, subsidized housing, equalization grants among provinces, and comprehensive unemployment assistance soon appeared in the federal government's Green Book proposals on social security as a prelude to the upcoming Dominion-Provincial Conference on Reconstruction in August 1945. Within Canada, as in other Western industial nations, welfare policy entered into an 'era of consolidation' in which 'the question was not whether some extensive, permanent system of state activity called the welfare state was necessary. The question was how to bring it all together.'[4]

Ottawa was not alone in putting forward new ideas and proposals for a more secure postwar social life. Within Ontario, George Drew led the Conservative Party back into power in the August 1943 Ontario election, defeating by a margin of only four seats the socialist CCF on a twenty-two point platform that promised the creation of a 'sound basis of social security, health insurance and protection in their old age for all our people.'[5] Social security and social welfare reform were never more central to political discourse at all three levels of government than in the waning years of the Second World War, as a 'sense of common danger and vulnerability ... made the security-equality-liberty aims of the new welfare state seem consistent and integral to the functioning of both society and the economy.'[6]

But this seeming consensus on the need to create a 'welfare' state out of the ashes of a 'warfare' state within postwar Canada was deceptive. Promises of cradle-to-grave social security and an adequate and decent 'national minimum' disguised deep and enduring divisions at all levels of government and society over the relationships between work and welfare, taxation and the constitution, social entitlements and charity, bureaucratic power and clients' rights. Although the haunting memory of the Great Depression united Canadians in their search for a future free from want and poverty, they soon discovered there was no clearcut or non-partisan blueprint for such a 'reconstructed' nation or province.

Women dependent on Ontario's mothers' allowance program became the first clients of the provincial welfare state to experience both the effects and the limits of a new wartime climate of reform. War changed the lives of mothers within the program in at least three ways. First, it significantly enhanced the employment prospects for themselves and their children, a point the Mothers' Allowance Commission lost no time in stressing. Between 1939 and 1943 the program caseload plummeted dramatically from a peak of more than 12,000 families to fewer than 8000, a decline that would continue until 1947, when the number of mothers in the program bottomed out at 6300.[7]

The movement of mothers, unemployable fathers, and children into the workforce and off the caseload was by no means an automatic process in response to changing labour market conditions. Unlike unemployment relief, which was simply terminated for all employable males after 1941, mothers' allowances remained an ongoing program. Finding out who was working and what kind of money was now coming into client households became a task that 'require[d] continued vigilance,' the commission noted. A 'very fluid' wartime labour market, the increased 'earning power of the children,' and the movement of widows into industry 'necessitate[d] more frequent investigations of the homes.' Although its caseload was shrinking rapidly, the commission almost doubled its investigators to ninety-five by 1943 and, to keep track of rapidly changing household income, insisted that 'four calls each year on the recipients of Mothers' Allowances [were] now necessary.' As a consequence, the average investigator's workload had 'increased in order that a competent check of the earning powers of a family might be afforded.' By the early 1940s, fiscal rather than moral regulation of mothers' allowance families was becoming the principal component of the commission's work.[8]

A rapid 15 per cent rise in the wartime cost of living between 1939 and 1942 also exacerbated the basic inadequacy of mothers' allowance benefits which had plagued clients dependent on the program since its inception. The average Ontario allowance of only $29 per family in 1942 was far below the $39 average paid in British Columbia or $36 in Manitoba, and was only pennies more than in Nova Scotia. Although eligibility under the program had widened during the 1930s, and a winter fuel allowance was added in 1941, the maximum level of benefits ($45 monthly for a mother with three children) had remained unchanged from the program's inception in 1920, despite more than two decades of development. Quite simply, mothers' allowances in Ontario by 1943, as the Canadian Welfare Council put it, were 'hopelessly inadequate' and wartime price inflation was quickly eroding whatever gains accrued to family budgets from the prospect of increased earnings. Nowhere was this crisis more acute than in Toronto, where the cost and limited availability of housing was becoming critical. As Mayor Fred Conboy warned Hepburn late in 1941, 'families formerly able to manage on the amount of mothers' allowances paid, along with some asssistance from other sources, are finding it impossible to maintain themselves with the increased cost of living that has already taken place,' and the city was more frequently being forced to 'supplement ... by public relief the assistance rendered under the Mothers' Allowance Act.'[9]

In partial recognition of the impact of wartime inflation, Ontario's outgoing Liberal administration granted a 20 per cent scale increase in mothers' allowance rates beginning in April 1943, the first such across-the-board hike in the program's history. It was a move that pushed the maximum monthly benefit for a mother with three children to $54. This jump paralleled similar federal and provincial increases in maximum rates for old age pensions from $20 to $28, which also occurred just prior to the upcoming provincial election. But as with the pension increase, the boost in mothers' allowance rates was quickly and widely denounced as grossly inadequate in comparison with similar cost-of-living budgets being allocated for other wartime families.

The case was made most forcefully by the Toronto Welfare Council, which pioneered the development of cost-of-living studies in 1939. 'No family groups who receive Mothers' Allowances are able to live on them in health and decency if the allowance is their sole source of income ... [and] even the new scale of allowances will not be enough to maintain them and their families properly,' the council warned the Liberal government's welfare minister Harold Kirby when the 20 per cent increase was announced. 'No woman can pay for proper food, clothing, and shelter and all the other small essentials for four people with as little as $12.50 a week.' Mothers who were in poor health, who had several young children, or who had to care for invalid husbands were simply unable to find employment to supplement this basic inadequacy. Allowances under the program had to be 'varied according to the circumstances and needs of families,' the council argued. A good starting point was 'the allowance of $89.00 per month that is paid to the wife and three children of a man in the Armed Forces. [This] ... is more nearly in line with a [minimum adequacy] budget.'[10]

Toronto's city council, which used the welfare council's cost-of-living research as the basis for the development of its own nutritionally adequate food allowances for families on urban relief, made identical arguments in a 1943 brief submitted to George Drew's newly elected Conservative government. Conboy pointed out that even with the recent 20 per cent scale increase, mothers' allowance rates were far below established minimum living standards for families seen by most welfare organizations and agencies. According to the Visiting Homemakers' Association of the Red Cross, Conboy observed, the minimum monthly budget needed to sustain adequacy for a mother with three children in Toronto was $113.32. The Toronto Welfare Council's estimate was $86.60. The Dependants' Allowance Board in Ottawa actually paid needy soldiers' families of this size $91.00. The city's own welfare department paid the same family $64.50, and in addition provided assistance for household remedies, cleaning materials, and other special services. In contrast, the maximum monthly benefit payable through mothers' allowance was only $54.00, and unlike Toronto's welfare budget, this did not include any additional help for household remedies or other items of special need.[11]

These comparative figures 'indicate such a disparity between allowances for mothers, and families, that the differences are unexplainable,' Conboy argued, especially to the 1600 mothers in Toronto who were currently attempting to scrape by on the 'meagre budgets' provided through the provincial program. Mothers' allowances were 'fall[ing] far short of adequacy' and the argument that women should supplement the amount through part-time work was simply an unacceptable double standard.

It has become increasingly recognized that a mother's place is in her home caring for her children. Only in cases where there are relatives or others capable of assuming responsibility for children can mothers satisfactorily augment their allowance by employment. Furthermore, mothers receiving military allowances are not generally expected to augment same by self employment, rather they expect the state to increase the allowances for adequate living ... [T]here would appear to be no reason why Mothers' Allowances beneficiaries should be discriminated against and expected to leave a crippled or otherwise incapacitated husband or children and go out to work to augment their allowances.[12]

Within Queen's Park, Burne Heise, the newly appointed deputy minister of welfare, agreed with Toronto's assessment. In fact, his department's own calculations showed that the minimum monthly budget a mother with three children needed to live decently at the beginning of 1943 was $117.57.[13] 'There is ... an unanswerable case for the consideration of Mothers' Allowances on the basis of actual need and individual treatment of each case, especially those with large groups of young children, and in homes with an incapacitated father,' Heise informed his welfare minister early the following year. 'The present Ontario system is neither based on a strictly flat-rate schedule nor is it on a complete basis of need ... [T]he Act provides that it be based on need but in practice a definite ceiling has been placed on the amount that can

be granted. It is, therefore, a bastard system.' Yet to switch to a completely needs-based approach would be a massive undertaking, Heise
acknowledged. At present his department had ninety-nine investigators to cope with a combined old age pension, blind persons, and mothers' allowance caseload of more than 65,000 clients. A change to a
'system which operates on a basis of need' with the 'complete supervi-
sory service' necessary to 'keep the Commission properly informed of
the status of each beneficiary and family' would require seventy-five
investigators for the 7449 mothers' allowance cases alone.[14]

As a compromise, Heise put forward an interim solution to meet
the 'agitation that the amount granted to beneficiaries be increased.'
Late in 1943 the commission's investigators were asked to sample 'a
fair cross-section of beneficiaries across the province' to determine
how much of an increase would be necessary to bring their clients up to
the cost-of-living budget developed by the province's nutritional consultant, Dr E.W. McHenry, and to measure 'the budgetary deficiency
necessary to assure decent, minimum provisions in each case.' An analysis of 1400 cases indicated that, on average, allowances needed to be
boosted by at least another 14 per cent. Based on the total caseload as
of December 1943, it would cost the province an additional $1,217,464
to bring all families up to McHenry's minimum budgetary basis of
adequacy, or almost a one-third increase in provincial spending on the
program. Moreover, 'trends ... indicate an increased case load in 1944–
45,' the commission's vice-chairman, Harold Bentley, warned.[15]

Coming close on the heels of the previous year's 20 per cent increase, this was far too big a hike to sell to cabinet. Instead, Heise put
forward a more modest proposal to his minister, Dr R. Percy Vivian, as
a means of redeeming 'pre-election pledges.' A $10 monthly increase,
based on need, and limited to no more than $50 annually for any one
family, would be made available. Heise estimated that no more than
2000 to 3000 cases at the most would be eligible, for a maximum one-
year cost of only $150,000. This was 'merely a stop-gap,' he argued,
and was no alternative to the 'vital importance' of placing the entire
program 'on [the] basis of need determined by a budget ... which would
give a clear consideration of measurement in these cases.' However,
Heise also noted that the impact of federal proposals for a universal
system of family allowances on Ontario's mothers' allowance families
was as yet uncertain. Moreover, the provincial scheme, he argued, should
in any case eventually be merged into a single, unified system of social
assistance, administered at the county level, in which 'impersonal ...
rule of thumb and mathematical calculation[s]' would be replaced by
an approach that 'treat[ed] case[s] as human problem[s] on a basis of
need.'[16]

The $10 monthly supplement was duly implemented in 1944 for cases of 'extreme necessity' at an eventual cost of $180,000, but apart from enhancing the means-tested component of the program, its impact on the lives of women clients was arguably modest. Average monthly benefits paid under mothers' allowances rose by only $1.35 to $41.68 over the course of the year, hardly enough to merit the government's public claim that Ontario had now 'adopt[ed] the principle of aiding necessitous mothers and children on basis of budgetary need.' Instead, the commission continued to point to a wartime labour market as the principal avenue of relief for women within the program. Because 'the mother is allowed and in fact encouraged to work,' both her satisfaction and the overall 'morale of the family' was raised. Through their own part-time work, children also took 'great pride in helping their widowed mother to bear her heavy responsibilities,' a factor that undoubtedly explained 'why juvenile delinquency is a negligent quantity in the families of our beneficiaries.' In fact, major relief for the morale and the glaring need of Ontario women on mothers' allowances came from Ottawa, not Queen's Park, in 1944. With the launching of universal family allowances that year, a typical mother with three children in the program saw her monthly income jump by almost 40 per cent overnight once the scheme was up and running by 1945. Federal, not provincial, policy thus was largely responsible for the significant inroads against child poverty which were achieved during the 1940s. Moreover, the economic impact of family allowances had the further effect of dulling whatever sense of urgency existed within Queen's Park on issues of welfare reform.[17]

After the launching of family allowances, the next major step towards postwar reconstruction for Ontarians began in 1945. In August of that year, Ottawa and the provinces met to discuss the federal government's comprehensive Green Book proposals on social security. Ontario, it quickly emerged, wanted no part of the federal government's vision of a reconstructed Canada which centralized fiscal and economic power within Ottawa. Since 1943, the Drew administration had watched the King administration's growing ambitions within the fields of postwar health and social security with a mounting sense of unease and distrust. Although promising 'consultation and close co-operation with the provinces' in the area of welfare and social security in its 1944 Throne Speech, the federal government at the same time moved unilaterally to introduce family allowance legislation that same year, created its own new Department of National Health and Welfare, and unveiled a scheme for a shared-cost health insurance program, again without provincial consultation. In the eyes of the Ontario government, these initiatives taken in advance of a dominion-provincial conference on postwar reconstruction represented not only a direct federal government invasion of provincial rights, but an ominous foretaste of Ottawa's determination to hold on to the lucrative income tax revenues needed to finance such schemes which were temporarily surrendered by the provinces during wartime tax rental agreements.[18]

Half the $200 million budgeted by Ottawa for family allowances would come from Ontario taxpayers, deputy provincial treasurer Chester Walters warned his minister, Leslie Frost. 'The outlook for the provinces to get back the taxing rights temporarily suspended by the Dominion-Provincial Tax Agreement of 1942 is bleak indeed. Yes, you have guessed it: – the result will be as stated in the words of [federal finance minister] Mr. Ilsley himself – the province will be driven out of the Income Tax field (also the Succession Duty field) by the Dominion's policy of attrition.'[19] Ottawa's unilateral action in this area quickly pushed Ontario premier George Drew on the offensive through a vigorous defence of provincial rights. Family allowances, he told the Ontario legislature early in 1945, were 'within the exclusive constitutional jurisdiction of the provinces.' Postwar welfare security could 'not be done on a bits and pieces basis. It has to be unified and its administration rests with the provinces unless the whole basis of confederation is to be destroyed.'[20]

But Ontario's vigorous defence of provincial rights in the area of postwar social security was deceptive. In warning Drew that Ottawa's Green Book proposals would 'destroy the Federal system and certainly ... prevent the Province from doing those things which, by the Constitution it is our job to do,' Frost made it explicitly clear he was referring to economic development, not social policy. 'My reference is *not so much to social services* as it is to the great development projects which must be carried out by Ontario if we are to maintain our position.' 'The representatives of every other province, except perhaps Quebec, will be looking for Ontario to walk into the Conference and empty its horn of plenty,' he warned the provincial premier. Frost made the same point in private conversations with the province's most important potential ally at the conference, Quebec premier Maurice Duplessis. 'A continuation of the present trend at Ottawa in concentrating power there would certainly not "Make Ontario Strong" but actually make us weak and impotent, lower our standard of living, reduce the sums of money which our people should rightly have for the development of our province, and in the end ... it would kill the goose that lays the golden egg because we are contributing about one-half of all Dominion revenues.'[21]

Drew agreed. 'Having established the principle that they can impose any tax structure upon the provinces, they will follow as a matter of course with the occupation of legislative and administrative fields as well on the ground that their over-all tax powers demand over-all administrative powers,' he warned his treasurer. 'Either we accept this situation and all that it implies or we don't. If we don't then we must devote all the thought and energy at our disposal ... to defeat their invasion of our position ... [I]t is a showdown fight.'[22]

Despite this blunt rhetoric, neither Drew nor Frost was particularly concerned about developing any alternative provincial proposals on social security even though, in the public mind, this was the principal objective of the conference, the Green Book proposals, and the myriad political promises made since 1943 by all levels of government for a 'reconstructed' Canada.[23] Instead, their energies remained focused on defeating Ottawa's plans for fiscal centralization. Despite Drew's 1943 election promise to bring about health insurance for Ontarians, Ottawa's own health insurance plan, when presented to the provinces, was quickly dismissed by Frost once the conference began on the grounds that 'Ontario could not undertake the financial burden of the health security scheme as the province had assumed heavy obligations as to roads, assistance to municipalities, etc.' The province also argued that because of the huge costs of family allowances and payments to veterans, and given the 'limits of hospital accommodation,' it was 'financially undesirable to add the cost of health insurance at the present time.'[24] In virtually every other social policy area, Ontario officials were more than happy to transfer almost the entire responsibility to Ottawa. In stunning contrast to his tenacious defence of Ontario's taxing authority, Frost was eager to suggest that

all Welfare services of the Provinces be transferred to the Dominion. The small Social Services, such as Children's Aid, Refuges, Orphanages, etc., could be continued as part of the Provincial administration, but ... approximately 70% of the cost be assumed by the Dominion Government. It is suggested that the Dominion assume, in addition to Old Age Pensions, the responsibility for Mothers' Allowances and the unemployed unemployables ... In these proposals, the Province would provide the necessary administrative machinery if desired, to conform to a Dominion plan and direction, and would be subject at all times to Dominion inspection.[25]

Four months later, Ontario modified this proposal somewhat. Since Ottawa was paying the total cost of its own family allowance scheme, the province suggested, it should also be willing to assume 75 per cent of the cost 'in all provincial welfare services,' as it was currently doing with old age pensions. As for pensions, they should be paid for completely by Ottawa, Ontario's deputy treasurer argued, because 'immigration policies [are] largely determined by the central government' and it was certain the province would soon be inundated by 'a great influx of immigrants from Europe, many of whom will be almost past the earning period of life and are almost certain after twenty years' residence to become eligible for Old Age Pensions.' Given the federal government's disgust with Ontario pension administration throughout most of the 1930s and its constant bickering with the province during the Depression over unemployment relief, these alternative Ontario proposals could hardly be taken seriously, particularly given the province's unwillingness to budge on the issue of surrendering taxing authority to Ottawa as a *quid pro quo*. Nor was it consistent with Ontario's vigorous defence of provincial rights in matters of fiscal policy throughout the conference. As national health and welfare minister Brooke Claxton pointed out to Frost, 'the Ontario proposals in respect of welfare services would place the Dominion in control of them all.'[26]

In April 1946 the Conference on Reconstruction finally broke up without agreement, largely due to the unwillingness of Ontario, allied with Quebec, to concede the taxing authority demanded by Ottawa to finance its Green Book proposals on social security, public investment, and fiscal equalization. Ontario, which went into these discussions determined to restore and defend its fiscal autonomy, but lacking a coherent social policy agenda beyond off-loading as many of its costs as possible onto the federal treasury and preventing raids by weaker provinces on its wealth, emerged with all its prewar powers of taxation intact. As the most perceptive student of the province's role in these negotiations has concluded, Ontario's resistance to the federal government's reconstruction proposals was rooted both in its 'tradition of responsibility for its own development' and in its 'traditional fiscal conservatism,' which remained deeply hostile towards and suspicious of the new Keynesian economic thinking within Ottawa.[27] Although Ontario's autonomy emerged victorious, it was not without some bitter costs, most of them paid for by the aged, the sick, the poor, and the unemployed, who would continue to wait more than two decades for the unfinished agenda of 1945 to be fulfilled in the areas of old age pensions, health care, housing, and social assistance.

Despite Ontario's rigidity during the 1945–6 reconstruction conference negotiations, the province was not unaware that within its own jurisdiction the reform and overhaul of its social welfare structure was long overdue. Within Ontario, plans to rethink and reorganize the province's welfare services had been under study since 1943, beginning with the McHenry *Report on Food Allowances*. By that year, 85 per cent of all those on relief were getting assistance because they were too sick to work; 54 per cent were over the age of sixty. With employable men finally cut from the relief rolls, the province was now willing to consider a liberalization of basic welfare entitlement. As Heise put it, the 'fixed policy' of providing relief 'for unemployables only has enabled improved standards of ... assistance on a ... nutritionally adequate [basis].'[28] Over the next two years a number of studies, both within and outside the provincial government, subjected public welfare administration in Ontario to searching scrutiny. During the 1930s, under the auspices of crisis-driven relief spending, a welfare system responsible for the expenditure of more than $230 million had emerged on an ad hoc basis, not only within the provincial bureaucracy but throughout Ontario's more than nine hundred municipalities. Compared with the almost 450,000 people, or one out of every eight Ontarians, on relief in 1936, the province's welfare caseload had plummeted seven years later to fewer than 19,000 of its citizens, a majority of them old, sick, and unemployable women ineligible for a means-tested pension.[29] With major new social security initiatives such as unemployment insurance and family allowances in place at the national level, and with the numbers on relief at less than 1 per cent of the Ontario population, now was the time, social policy experts argued, to take stock of provincial social administration and place it on a firm foundation for the anticipated social security needs of the postwar world.[30]

Within Ontario there was no more perceptive or knowledgeable critic of provincial social policy than Harry M. Cassidy, the acerbic and ambitious director of the School of Social Work at the University of Toronto. During the 1930s Cassidy had written the only definitive study of Ontario's relief system, before going on to reorganize British Columbia's social welfare administration and pioneer an ultimately unsuccessful health insurance scheme as director of social welfare for that province. A former member of both the League for Social Reconstruction and the CCF, and Canada's most prolific and incisive writer on social policy during the 1930s and 1940s, this 'Canadian Fabian' was rivalled only by Leonard Marsh as the country's leading authority on social welfare.[31]

In 1945 Cassidy subjected Ontario's welfare structure to comprehensive analysis through an exhaustive privately commissioned study for the provincial Department of Public Welfare[32] and his more widely read definitive text on provincial social welfare administration, *Public Health and Welfare Reorganization in Canada*. Cassidy's appraisal of Ontario's social welfare setup was characteristically blunt. The province's 'complicated system' of public welfare administration possessed 'little rhyme or reason.' Some programs, such as mothers' allowances and old age pensions, were administered by provincial commissions; others such as direct relief were run by the province's hundreds of municipalities, with widely differing fiscal and administrative resources; and child welfare was the responsibility of privately organized Children's Aid Societies, which received the bulk of their funding from local governments and the province. Care of the aged and the disabled occurred through a confusing mixture of grossly overcrowded county houses of refuge and private charitable institutions, each subsidized differently by Queen's Park. Much of this welfare structure was regressively financed on a local property tax base whose fiscal capacity varied enormously.[33]

Cassidy also echoed criticisms shared widely throughout his profession that Ontario's welfare structure at the provincial and local level was shot through with politically appointed incompetents who gained their positions during the Depression and lacked the social work training or administrative experience required to run a modern public welfare system. During the 1930s the province had made 'no serious effort to recruit trained social workers for relief administration.' Nor did it set any personnel standards for municipal welfare agencies. As a consequence, complaints about the 'baneful effects of a patronage system' that produced 'discouragement and poor morale among the more competent civil servants' were widespread, particularly 'in the field of public assistance ... where the political authorities saw no need for technically trained staff as they did in the fields of public health and mental hygiene.' Ontario's welfare system, Cassidy argued, needed a 'reorganized and revitalized provincial welfare department'; a much simpler basis for provincial-municipal financial relationships, including 'a system of grants that recognizes the great differences in municipal needs for assistance'; reorganized local health and welfare units; and, above all, 'a positive personnel policy designed to attract trained and competent persons into provincial and local services.'[34]

As the title of his book implied, the most pressing welfare problem for Cassidy in the mid-1940s was 'reorganization' – not the launching of new programs but the creation of a rational, coherent, and efficient structure for the delivery of already existing social services and income, on a professional basis, to those in need. His principal recommendation to the Ontario government was to consolidate, over a ten-year period, the delivery of all forms of social assistance, including old age pensions, mothers' allowances, and local relief, into sixty-five new 'welfare units' – in effect regional welfare agencies – run by professional social workers and supervised by committees composed of members from both municipal councils and the provincial government. The main advantages of 'unified administration,' Cassidy argued, were that these welfare units could dispense and coordinate social assistance to Ontario families on a far more efficient basis, and through a broader tax base, than could 960 municipalities of widely varying degrees of size and wealth. Regional welfare units could also afford to employ more trained and qualified social work personnel and could more easily develop 'a general budgetary standard [for assessing need] which would be applicable to all programs.' Over time, through the welfare unit delivery model, social assistance in Ontario could become more professionalized, more uniform in standards of service and assistance, and more equitable.[35]

Given the full employment produced by the war and the collapse of social assistance caseloads to almost negligible proportions by 1945, it is not surprising that Cassidy's reform agenda focused principally on bureaucratic and administrative reorganization, not an attack on poverty per se, particularly given the ad hoc growth of public welfare within Ontario since 1930. His confidence in the welfare unit model reflected recent developments in American social welfare administration at the state level, gleaned from his tenure as dean of social welfare at the University of California in Berkeley, as well as his own personal experience in placing British Columbia's welfare services on a sound administrative footing in the 1930s. Doubtless, his disgust at the incompetence and patronage that proliferated throughout Ontario's provincial and local welfare structure played an important role as well. Ultimately, Cassidy's faith in the powers of administrative reorganization also reflected the professional vision of most social workers as well as the emerging science of public administration in the 1940s – that problems of need could best be resolved by placing qualified professionals in charge of an efficient and responsive welfare structure.

Ontario's other equally renowned but more conservative voice of social work, Charlotte Whitton, former director and guiding force behind the Canadian Welfare Council during the interwar years, made almost identical proposals in her massive 1944 survey, 'The Administration of Welfare Services in Ontario,' also commissioned by the province's new welfare minister, Dr Vivian.[36] Like Cassidy, Whitton found the province's present welfare structure 'bewildering,' and she also argued that 'reorganization' and 'coordination' of the entire system was the most pressing priority. In conclusions almost identical to his, Whitton argued that all provincial and local welfare schemes should be merged into one general assistance program administered through a system of forty-nine welfare units.[37] Aid should be based on a standard-ized family needs test in order to guarantee 'minimum adequacy in nutrition, shelter, clothing, fuel and health care.' To finance this reor-ganized system, Whitton called for a 'standard welfare levy' on local property, topped up by the province for less prosperous regions, and like Cassidy she placed special emphasis on the need for putting trained social work professionals in charge of the system. These recommenda-tions were also echoed by the Canadian Association of Social Workers in their brief to the province's legislative committee on postwar social security.[38]

Calls by social workers for an end to patronage and the professional-ization of public welfare administration were not new. They had been a longstanding part of the profession's critique of mothers' allowance, old age pension, and child welfare administration since the late 1920s, and the enormous explosion of unemployment relief during the Depres-sion only underscored their arguments for the critical urgency of ad-ministrative reform. What had changed, by the early 1940s, was a radi-cal shift in the size, composition, and cost of the province's welfare caseload, as well as the promotion for the first time of a professionally trained social worker to the position of deputy minister of Ontario's Department of Public Welfare in 1944. Burne Wismer Heise, one of the first male graduates of the University of Toronto's School of Social Work in the 1920s and former director of Hamilton's Children's Aid Society, was one of the few professional social workers to find and keep employment within the Department of Public Welfare as its super-intendent of neglected children and director of child welfare beginning in 1934.

In the 1920s Heise had worked closely with Robert Mills, the first trained social worker to direct Toronto's Children's Aid Society. Under Mills's reforming aegis, the Toronto CAS underwent rapid profes-sionalization in staffing and casework techniques. Heise duplicated Mills's reforms on becoming director of the Hamilton CAS. When he replaced J.J. Kelso as Ontario's chief civil servant in charge of child welfare, Heise lost no time in devising the first attempt to raise profes-sional standards in Ontario child welfare by implementing a grading system for Children's Aid Societies. Those societies that hired trained social workers and met other administrative standards received higher subsidies from the province. During the early 1940s Heise was the guiding force behind the resettlement in Ontario of almost eight hun-dred British 'Child Guests' seeking shelter from bombing raids, a serv-ice for which he received an OBE.[39] His promotion to deputy minister in 1944, along with the comprehensive studies of the department by

Whitton and Cassidy, represented the most tangible evidence that the newly elected Drew administration was indeed serious about the reorganization and reform of Ontario's social welfare structure.

Heise's appointment was greeted with acclaim within Ontario's social work community. Like the hiring of former Canadian Welfare Council director George Davidson as Canada's first deputy minister of national health and welfare, Heise's promotion was viewed by social workers as concrete evidence that at last their professional advice and knowledge was to be utilized in the making of Canada's postwar welfare state. Heise, like Davidson, was a good friend of Cassidy's and, like his Ottawa counterpart, he looked to the University of Toronto social work professor for ideas and advice on the directions his department should take in the reform of public welfare. Cassidy's 'A Proposed Public Welfare Plan for Ontario' became his principal guide in shaping departmental policy recommendations over the next five years.[40]

Almost as soon as he took over as deputy minister, Heise began signalling his intention to effect major changes in provincial welfare administration, much as he had previously done in child welfare. He found a sympathetic ear in his minister, Dr Percy Vivian. Vivian, a novice in politics, was first elected in 1943 from Durham County, where he had gained the reputation as a progressive physician with an active interest in public health. Heise's first objective, long advocated by Cassidy, was to replace the province's Unemployment Relief Act with a 'general assistance' program. 'Unemployment as a cause for granting of aid does not presently exist,' Heise argued in 1944, and 'the time has arrived when [our] administrative house should be put in order.' The 'aimless policies ... guided by local whims or fancies, or financial expediency' had to be brought to an end, to be replaced by a social assistance system that provided 'remaining social care cases with proper standards of aid.'[41]

Closely following the recommendations of Cassidy and Whitton, Heise stated that Ontario's present categorical aid programs for mothers, the blind, the elderly, and unemployables should be replaced by a single general assistance program administered through regional welfare units 'organized on a county, city or district basis' and staffed by professionals. This reform would 'assure equal standards of assistance for all persons, regardless of where they live within the Province.' Such a plan had been 'tried and found satisfactory ... in the United States' and allowed 'local administration, under Provincial supervision.'[42]

In terms of providing a more standardized and equitable level of services and allowances to those in need, the advantages of one general assistance program delivered through regional welfare units seemed obvious. But what attraction did such a proposal hold for the provincial government, or for Ontario's nine hundred municipalities that were, after all, the elected bodies that would have to agree to such a radical change in welfare practice? For municipalities, Heise argued, the principal gain would be property tax relief. In addition to its current 50 per cent subsidy of local relief, Heise recommended that Queen's Park pay an extra ten cents per capita of assessed population to those areas covered by a welfare unit and also subsidize their welfare administration costs on a sliding scale ranging from 25 per cent in big cities to 75 per cent in counties. In order to receive these extra subsidies, however, local welfare units would have to be 'administered and staffed according to standards set out in regulations prescribed by the province.' Although the welfare unit model would 'keep the direct administration as close to the people as possible,' Queen's Park for the first time would be monitoring and enforcing not only shareable costs charged by municipalities against the relief budget, but the actual administration and delivery of welfare services at the local level.

For the province, a welfare unit system promised an end to 'the more or less hodge podge system of welfare administration across the Province,' especially growing pressures 'for provincial assumption on a piecemeal basis of the cost of specific services.' His welfare unit scheme, Heise estimated, could be implemented 'for approximately the same expenditure as would be necessary to pay 50% of Children's Aid costs,' the municipalities' current key welfare demand. More importantly, through one general assistance program delivered by regional welfare units regulated by Queen's Park, 'provincial controls could be maintained over the whole system.'[43]

After the collapse of the Dominion-Provincial Conference on Reconstruction, Heise was given the green light to develop a Welfare Units Act, a process completed in 1948. But even as the legislation was being prepared, strong signals were emerging that the idea of professionalizing and reorganizing Ontario's welfare structure on a decentralized, general assistance model – so widely shared throughout the social work community – was not greeted with equal enthusiasm either by municipalities or by powerful members of the government, most notably provincial treasurer Leslie Frost. In a private memo to Premier Drew, Frost conveyed his lack of enthusiasm for social assistance reform. Non-contributory social welfare programs had 'an undermining effect on public morals,' Frost argued. 'One could not say this too openly for fear of being misunderstood, but ... through non-contributory old age pensions, mothers' allowances, unemployment relief etc. we have tended to instill into our people the feeling that the country owes them a living.'[44] Heise would not find much sympathy in the Treasury Department for his ambitious welfare reform agenda, a problem compounded when Frost replaced Drew as Ontario's premier in 1949.

Heise was equally mistaken in his belief that since problems in social administration were 'well recognized by municipal authorities ... the development of County Welfare Units would be received favourably.'[45] Once smaller municipalities got wind of what his department was planning, their opposition to the scheme built quickly and was communicated immediately to the provincial cabinet. Orillia's city council, for example, where Frost grew up, wrote Drew immediately to 'vigorously oppose any plan' for a unified county welfare board. In an impassioned attack on the very idea of regional centralization or professionalization of social service administration sent to all members of the cabinet, the town councillors objected both to the potential cost of the scheme and to the loss of local control over welfare spending it implied.

> The Councils of local municipalities ... would have no voice with respect to the actions of the Board and would no doubt in the long run be compelled to raise by taxation such amounts the County Welfare Board demanded from the County ... Appointed Boards, which have no statutory limit to their spending, unfortunately have not the incentive to handle the taxpayers' money with the same care as elected Council members ... Through his ... franchise, the local taxpayer is a definite brake on unwise spending, waste and inefficiency ... [I]f they are not careful ... the Councils will soon become mere rubber stamps elected to set a tax rate and then retire for the rest of the year to let innumerable centralized Boards spend the taxpayers' money.

If Queen's Park wished to centralize the administration of welfare, Orillia argued, 'it should pay 100% of the cost.'[46]

During the summer of 1947 these conflicting visions of welfare reform clashed head on at the Ontario Conference on Social Welfare, a major gathering of provincial and federal politicians, social workers, and municipal representatives sponsored by the Community Welfare Council of Ontario to debate the future of social assistance in the province. By this point it was clear even to Cassidy, the principal originator of the welfare unit idea, that the concept was in deep political trouble and in desperate need of the 'development of favourable public opinion ... [T]here is a good deal of resistance from people in the rural districts, who either do not like the idea or do not understand it ... The provincial Department of Public Welfare,' he told the conference, 'appears to be ahead of public opinion.'

His profession's vision of an integrated, coherent, and progressive public welfare structure, staffed by trained personnel and dedicated to the prevention, not merely the alleviation of poverty, had 'ample precedent ... [in] the development by Ontario of public health units on a county basis,' Cassidy argued in a passionate defence of the welfare unit proposal. A similar rationalization of social assistance could 'only emerge if there is vigorous provincial leadership ... [and] money is in large measure the key to the solution of this problem.' Local politicians 'talk about money all the time when they discuss welfare questions and appear to many of us to be oblivious to the issues of human well-being which are involved.' Reforming Ontario's outdated social welfare structure might cost 'millions, probably tens of millions of dollars ... annually,' he conceded, but compared with the 'hidden costs of social neglect' such spending would still be 'thoroughly economical.'[47]

Grant Crawford, secretary-treasurer of the Ontario Municipal Association, took dead aim at these arguments in his address to the conference, outlining with considerable insight some of the sources of rural and municipal opposition to welfare reform. 'Municipal councils in general have a healthy skepticism of experts and of promises,' Crawford told the province's assembled social workers. When ideas for reform were advanced, there was some need 'to satisfy the elected representatives with factual evidence that the proposals advanced will meet the need and that there is some reasonable limit to the apparently limitless expansion of welfare services.' Doubtless with Cassidy in mind, Crawford argued that too often social workers lost sight of the fact that 'the primary responsibility of the elected representatives, as such, is *to those whom they represent and not to the underprivileged* or those in need of assistance ... [T]axpayers may be unwilling to sacrifice their present resources for unprovable benefit in an undetermined future.' More than other levels of government, local councillors 'still cling to the old-fashioned idea that the interests of those who pay the costs are entitled to serious consideration.'[48]

These points were not lost within the Ontario cabinet, where support for the welfare unit concept was eroding quickly as its political and financial implications were more thoroughly understood. With his medical and public health background, Vivian had been sympathetic to Heise's reform agenda, which seemed to parallel the earlier consolidation and professionalization of the province's public health system. In 1946, however, Vivian retired from politics, to be replaced as welfare minister by William Goodfellow, a farmer and MPP from the rural riding of Northumberland, whose previous political experience had been as councillor, reeve, assessor, and tax collector for Durham and Northumberland counties. Goodfellow, much more closely attuned than Vivian to the rural and small-town perspective on welfare matters, was frankly hostile to the social work agenda for an expansive welfare state. The growth in health and welfare spending within his own department during the 1940s gave him cause for alarm. 'As a boy brought up on a farm, [it] worries me,' he told one northern Ontario audience. 'I think people are losing their spirit of independence, their sense of responsibility, of thrift, and the will to do for themselves ... These people are only kidding themselves if they think they can get something for nothing ... They are depending too much on government and not enough on themselves.'[49] Throughout his tenure as welfare minister between 1946 and 1956, Goodfellow resisted arguments that Queen's Park assume a greater part of the cost of welfare services. 'As soon as the Government takes over the cost,' he told one Perth County audience, 'control of the service is going to pass out of local hands ... We don't want all welfare services centralized at the higher levels of Government because that would create a welfare state sooner or later.'[50]

Although willing to steer the Welfare Units Act through the legislature in 1948, Goodfellow was frankly unsympathetic to the professional social work vision that originally animated the idea, and the final version of his bill bore little resemblance to the earlier and more sweeping proposals of Cassidy, Whitton, and Heise. In the first place, there was no mention of replacing existing categorical programs, such as mothers' allowances, unemployment relief, or old age pensions, with a general assistance scheme, nor did the Welfare Units Act provide any attempt to equalize the burden of welfare costs on local property tax throughout Ontario, another critical objective of reformers anxious to ensure minimally adequate standards of assistance. Most importantly, the bill contained no mention of nor mechanism for establishing a consolidated and rationalized system of county welfare units – the heart of all earlier recommendations of those interested in the idea.

Instead, the bill was an entirely permissive and vaguely drafted piece of legislation. It promised that the province would subsidize 50 per cent of welfare administration costs for any municipality which passed a bylaw indicating that, within its boundaries, it wished to establish a welfare unit. Such a unit would then be established by Queen's Park to handle local relief, the investigation of all applications for mothers' allowances and old age pensions, as well as municipal contributions to Children's Aid Societies, admission to charitable homes, day nurseries, and any other local welfare matters. At the insistence of some cabinet members concerned about controlling administrative costs, the bill also stipulated that, 'with the consent of the council of the municipality,' the provincial cabinet 'may appoint an administrator ...

and such staff as the administrator may require for the due carrying out of his duties.'[51]

Almost as soon as it was passed, the Welfare Units Act became a political embarrassment. By the end of 1949 three Ontario municipalities – Toronto, Hamilton, and Windsor – created the requisite by-laws indicating they wished to establish welfare units within their boundaries in order to qualify for a 50 per cent provincial subsidy of their welfare administration costs. At this point, almost everyone connected with the legislation within the Ontario government began to have second thoughts. In a remarkable about-face, Heise, at the end of 1949, told Goodfellow and Frost that he no longer supported the principle of local welfare administration. 'Since the passing of this Act I have become more convinced that the general trend over the years has been away from municipal administration of welfare services. Notwithstanding my belief at the time the Act was passed that administration should be localized, I have gradually come to the conclusion that, in all probability, it will be necessary for the province to assume a greater measure of responsibility in welfare administration matters.'

Consequently, Heise now questioned whether the Welfare Units Act was either 'feasible' or a step in the right direction. The deputy minister's disillusionment was fuelled by his difficulties in negotiating the merger of provincial mothers' allowance and old age pension staff within unionized local welfare departments such as Toronto's, as well as his belated discovery that the municipalities seeking a 50 per cent provincial subsidy of their welfare administration costs had 'taken a grudging attitude to the principle of dual control.' 'The whole program would be exceedingly difficult to supervise,' Heise concluded.[52]

His minister, Goodfellow, was even more critical, proposing early in 1950 that the entire bill be removed from the provincial statutes. 'It is a foregone conclusion that the Province under this Act will not have any definite means of curtailing expenditures for administration and as a result considerable conflict appears inevitable between Provincial and municipal authorities,' Goodfellow warned the new premier, Leslie Frost. As presently drafted, the Welfare Units Act gave neither the province nor the municipality 'clear-cut authority to direct or control staff.' Looking at the higher salaries, better benefits, and lower caseloads of Toronto's unionized welfare department, Goodfellow also concluded that 'the Provincial staff presently treating Mothers' Allowances and Old Age cases can more effectively do the job and will require fewer persons for this purpose than would be necessary under the Units programme.' Rather than enduring the political embarrassment that a formal repeal of the legislation entailed, Frost decided instead 'simply to ignore it.'[53]

The Welfare Units Act remained on the provincial statute books, but was never proclaimed. Toronto, Hamilton, and Windsor, meanwhile, were quietly refunded almost a quarter of a million dollars by the province for the inconvenience of setting their 1949 welfare budgets in anticipation of a 50 per cent provincial subsidy for administrative costs that never materialized.[54]

Within Ontario's welfare department the fiasco surrounding the Welfare Units Act ultimately cost Heise his job. The deputy minister's social work approach to welfare issues was simply too far removed from the perspectives of his own minister, municipal politicians across the province, and the premier. Since 1946, Goodfellow had been relying increasingly for policy advice on the department's director of unemployment relief, James Band. In 1950 Goodfellow made Band acting deputy minister and, two years later, Heise resigned in bitterness. Band held the position uninterruptedly until his own retirement in 1969. Over the next two decades, 'Jimmy' Band, as he was known to his contemporaries, would dominate social policy in Ontario as no other civil servant has before or since.[55]

Band shared none of his predecessor's political liabilities. Unlike Heise, he had no social work or university training whatsoever, a source of great dismay and even alarm to leaders in the profession across the province when he replaced Heise as acting deputy minister in 1950.[56] Instead, the dapper and diminutive deputy minister, after working in accounting during the 1920s, started his civil service career at the age of thirty as a relief inspector for the province during the depth of the Depression in 1933. As a roving trouble-shooter in the unemployment relief division, Band reorganized municipal welfare departments whose costs were soaring out of control, developed elaborate systems of home visiting, and supervised the distribution of relief in numerous bankrupt communities across Ontario, particularly in the north.

In contrast to Heise, Band was 'well connected' to the provincial Conservative Party through his wife's family. More importantly, he was a shrewd and highly competent administrator whose extensive travels across the province during the 1930s gave him an exceptional knowledge of municipal politics and local conditions as well as a finely honed political sense of what welfare initiatives the cabinet, backbench MPPs, and local councillors were likely to support – a skill that undoubtedly ensured his survival during the long Liberal tenure of the Hepburn administration. Alternatively described as 'both smooth and tough,' 'competent,' 'neurotic,' 'charming,' and a 'manipulator' by those who knew him, Band was in complete mastery of his department, his ministers, the cabinet, and the legislature on most welfare matters throughout his long tenure as deputy minister.[57] 'It's as if he was very fine-tuned to public approval, public expectations. What society saw as reasonable and appropriate,' one of his close colleagues in the department remembered. As another put it, 'with the cabinet he was able to fix just about anything they brought him. And his attitude was, "the member wants it, get it." And that was very hard for all of us to resist ... His power over members of the Legislature was very strong.'[58] Throughout his two decades as deputy welfare minister, Band 'kept the chief initiative and control firmly in his own hands. Policy and project making was, in that regime, very much a "top down" affair,' and his 'response ... to the aspirations of social workers ... was not very favourable.'[59] With the departure of Burne Heise, the bright hopes of welfare professionals since 1943 of a fundamental 'reconstruction' of Ontario's social assistance framework came to a bitter and pathetic end.

The collapse of welfare reform at Queen's Park was mirrored by similar developments within Toronto, the city whose activist social planning council had pushed first city council and ultimately the province into placing relief allowances on a nutritionally adequate basis in 1944. Once again at the heart of welfare politics in Toronto was *The Cost of Living*, the Toronto Welfare Council's impressively researched analysis of minimum living costs in the province's largest city. First published in 1939 and revised and updated in 1944, the Red Book, as it came to be known from its deep scarlet cover, had become the bible of all social welfare professionals advocating the need for 'minimum standards of health and decency' in assistance programs across Canada. As the only study of its kind in Canada, *The Cost of Living* had provided Leonard Marsh with his basic data for estimating the minimum social benefits recommended in his *Report on Social Security for Canada*, and had also been used by the federal government in establishing benefit levels for its wartime dependants' allowance and family allowance programs (see appendix, table 3).[60]

By 1947, however, both the Red Book and its sponsor were embroiled in a political controversy that starkly underlined the worsening prospects for social welfare reform across Ontario. The revised 1944 edition of the Red Book had become a national bestseller as more than 5000 copies, ten times as many as the original 1939 version, were printed and sold. The biggest customer was Ontario's burgeoning trade union movement, which found the detailed analysis of price increases and their effect on family budgets an invaluable tool for collective bargaining with employers in an era of postwar price increases. By 1947 unions began pressing the Toronto Welfare Council for yet another update of the popular study, to take postwar inflation into account. At the same time, employers were becoming increasingly angered by encountering the council study across the bargaining table. Ironically, a study originally undertaken to boost welfare allowances was now in danger of being sideswiped by the growing polarization between business and organized labour over wage increases and post-war inflation. The issue came to a head when the president of Simpsons, Edgar Burton, discovered employees on strike against his own com-pany distributing information outside his downtown store comparing their own wages against the minimum budget guidelines from *The Cost of Living*. Burton was also chairman of Toronto's Community Chest, the fundraising arm of organized private philanthropy in the city which, since a merger with the Toronto Welfare Council in 1943, also exer-cised ultimate control over the social planning body. Burton ordered the council to withdraw the booklet immediately from circulation.

At the time of the merger between the Toronto Welfare Council and the Community Chest, some council members had warned against 'hav-ing the financial side of the chest dominate the planning side.'[61] Now these earlier fears proved all too prophetic. In the autumn of 1947 a bitter battle erupted within the council over whether the *The Cost of Living* should be killed. Burton argued that 'the information contained in the report was being used by labour organizations to support their case for increased wages,' and he was 'unable to understand why the Welfare Council should interest itself in a study of this question at all.' Research of this kind was really a government responsibility. In response, the Red Book's defenders argued that 'the fundamental question of Council autonomy' was at stake. The study provided 'the only material of its kind in Canada,' and its minimum living cost estimates were carefully researched and quite modest. 'The budget as reported in the Red Book is a maintenance budget and does not provide for the creation of a home or the development of adequate retirement plans,' council direc-tor Bessie Touzel argued in defending the study. Other members pointed out that 'the mystery prevailing in regard to the whole matter was the worst possible publicity and was likely to cause difficulty with the newspapers.' In an attempt at compromise, the Welfare Council agreed that updating *The Cost of Living* was 'essential,' but that nothing should be done until there was further discussion with members of the Com-munity Chest.[62]

A month later, 'tired of the constant criticism and underlying conflict that lay between the Chest and the Council,' Touzel resigned as execu-tive director to take up a position with the Canadian Welfare Council in Ottawa. With her departure, Toronto's welfare community lost one of its most capable and knowledgeable social policy activists. Almost a year later, after nothing had been done, angry council members demanded to know when the *The Cost of Living* would reappear. A chagrined executive explained that a close review of their constitution revealed that 'no authority was left with the Welfare Council Board.' The Toronto Welfare Council, after its merger in 1943, had simply become 'the social planning body of the Chest.' And on this issue, the Chest's will would prevail. There would be no reissue or updating of *The Cost of Living*. Instead, the Canadian Welfare Council would be asked to take on the project. Toronto council president Margaret Kirkpatrick summed up for other board members the reason why. 'Some of the members of the Chest Executive still consider that the publication of the Red Book with up to date figures would be a serious threat to the collection of funds because, while there is no mention of income in the Red Book, the figures of cost are being quoted and used by employees to increase wages in business, some of whom are large contributors to the Chest.' For the previous two years, the Community Chest had been unable to meet its fundraising objectives and 'it was recognized that certain actions of the Council ... do jeopardize the collection of funds ... and that the agencies do need as much money as can possibly be raised to carry out their services.' Community Chest executives did not foresee any other difficulties with the Welfare Council, Kirkpatrick reported. 'The only repression ever considered was in the matter of the Red Book.'[63]

If the Toronto council hoped the issue was dead, it was badly mistaken. Once organized labour realized that corporate pressure, exercised through business control over the Community Chest, had killed its favourite research tool, a deluge of criticism was unleashed within the local press as union leaders argued, quite accurately, that the Red Book 'was being suppressed by the financial interests in the Community Chest.' The labour movement demanded that the council reconsider its decision not to reissue its popular study. 'This was no time to withdraw the figures when the information was needed now, more than it had ever been,' Steelworker president Charles Millard pleaded.[64]

By the autumn of 1948 the Canadian Welfare Council had indicated it had neither the time nor the research expertise to take over *The Cost of Living* project. With the ball now back in its court and facing increasing anger from the labour movement, the Toronto Welfare Council finally agreed to reissue an updated study, provided its figures were reviewed by 'a group of neutral citizens representing many groups in the community ... from the standpoint of formal and general acceptability.' The committee would include two representatives each from labour and the Community Chest.[65] In the spring of 1949, eighteen months after its suppression, the revised study, retitled *A Guide to Family Spending in Toronto*, was released. The name change was significant. As Jacquelyn Gale Wills points out, 'Rather than a measure to help determine a community standard that would "maintain health and self-respect," it was now a guideline for individual and family responsibility ... [and] depended more on the view that incompetency on the part of the homemaker was the problem to be addressed than any income policy of the wider community.'[66]

Significantly, whereas *The Cost of Living* had been a bestseller among Ontario's trade unions, its successor generated interest 'particularly in the Personnel Departments of industrial firms.'[67] The shift in interest was symbolic. Instead of a critical union tool for collective bargaining, the *Guide* would now be used by employers to encourage their workers, like welfare mothers, to manage their limited resources more efficiently in the name of economy.

Across the province, throughout the late 1940s, a combination of unanticipated prosperity, the deepening impact of the Cold War, and the resulting collapse of a wartime political climate favourable to social democracy eroded support for further experimentation with social planning and social security as an 'era of austerity' gave way to an era of unprecedented affluence 'corrosive of the social solidarity that had inspired the austerity welfare state.'[68] By the decade's end, according to one analyst of this era, 'most Ontarians were in no mood ... to create a socialist heaven on earth, especially one directed by bureaucrats. They wished only to drive their new cars down one of Ontario's many new expressways, or mow their suburban lawns.' Or as CCF leader Donald MacDonald put it, 'Everybody just wanted to relax. The normal apathy of the electorate vis-à-vis politics became even more pronounced with relatively good times.'[69] Over the next decade, public interest in the reform of Ontario's welfare system would prove sporadic at best.

5

Poverty in Progress: Welfare in Ontario, 1950–8

The 1950s is now remembered as a time of affluence. Through large-scale immigration and an explosive birth rate, Ontario's population grew by more than one third. Unemployment until the decade's end ranged between 2 and 3 per cent of the workforce, and real per capita income grew by 28 per cent.[1] If ever a minimum standard of health and decency seemed both affordable and feasible, it was during these years. For Ontarians dependent on welfare or living at or near the poverty line, however, the decade was no golden age. Male workers lacked a minimum wage, and more than a third of the labour force was ineligible for unemployment insurance and had no entitlement to local relief if workers lost their jobs. Large families and the elderly saw the value of family allowances and old age security eroded by inflation. Those living on welfare lost the advantages gained by nutritionally adequate food allowances to exploding shelter costs during a decade in which little new social housing was built. Although rising state revenues and rapid growth provided governments with the economic tools to fight poverty, the political will to use them remained absent. As a result, standards of living for Ontario's poor slipped even further behind the rising prosperity of the general population. By the decade's end, bold reconstruction promises of an adequate and decent minimum of social security seemed as distant as ever.

As wartime price controls were lifted gradually from the Canadian economy after 1947, the need for putting in place definitions of adequate minimum living standards mounted daily within Ontario's larger cities. Between 1947 and the end of 1948 a 25 per cent jump in the cost of living rapidly ate away at the important gains achieved by the poor through family allowances and the McHenry Report revisions to welfare food allowances in 1944.[2] After examining the shopping lists of a selected group of welfare families across the city, the nutritionist for Toronto's welfare department pointed out that 'families were purchasing a rather high percentage of bread, macaroni, and other starchy foods, while their consumption of fruits, vegetables, and meat was in most cases very low.' The single person on relief was making do by 'limiting himself to two meals per day and not getting up until late in the morning.' Welfare visitors from across the city reported that 'family allowances were being used almost entirely for food whereas previously ... they had been used for clothing and other household needs.' Once again, as in the hungry 1930s, 'mothers were often doing without to allow younger members of their families to have more.'[3]

A delegation composed of members from Hamilton's city council, board of control, Public Welfare Board, veterans, Council of Social Agencies, and the legislature made identical points to provincial welfare minister W.A. Goodfellow. A cross-section poll of 169 welfare families in that city turned up 158 cases in which 'it was necessary to secure outside help or use the family allowance to maintain the family. In only 11 cases was the [food] allowance considered adequate.' Food costs in that city had risen 'to the point that the health and morale of the families ... is being threatened.'[4]

In response to such criticisms and the rapid rise in the postwar cost of living, food allowances for relief families were increased 25 per cent by the province between 1946 and 1948. Even with these changes, however, families on relief in Toronto were still unable 'to purchase more than a small quantity of butter, and meat only two or three times in the half month period' and found it impossible to buy eggs, the city's welfare officials reported. 'They are ... having a very difficult time ... Their diet would now fall considerably below the minimum standard of requirements recommended to maintain health.' Despite these limitations, throughout the remainder of the 1950s food allowances remained the only item in welfare budgets that stayed in rough alignment with the rising cost of living, rising by 38 per cent over the course of the decade. By 1960, however, they would still be almost 8 per cent below the minimum amount recommended by the Toronto Welfare Council to maintain adequate health.[5]

Soaring rents were principally responsible for playing havoc with the budgets of welfare families and cut deeply into the increases passed on by the government to buy more food. Even before the war's end, Ontario welfare officials recognized that the Depression-based formula for shelter allowances which gave families 200 per cent of property taxes to a maximum of $20.00 a month fell 'short of actual requirements ... by over 50%.' Designed simply to give landlords enough income to pay their taxes and do minimal repairs, the shelter allowance bore no relationship to market rents, nor did it give them any incentive to take on welfare clients, whom most did not want in any case. The hardship was worst for large families that needed the most room, yet could only afford to live in those areas of cities with the lowest assessment rates, and hence the lowest allowances according to this tax-based rental formula. To house them, welfare departments in cities like Toronto coped 'by placing more than one family in large houses where ... the total of the several payments for these families equals the normal rental.'[6]

Although a wartime increase bumped the maximum shelter allowance up to $27.00 per month, Ontario officials acknowledged by 1946 that the formula itself was simply 'inadequate.' A spot check into family rentals in medium-sized cities such as Ottawa, Hamilton, Windsor, London, and York Township revealed that, on average, shelter allowances covered only 65 per cent of the normal rent. In Toronto the gap was much worse. In that city 'the average normal rental was $21.02. Based on taxes, the monthly allowance was $9.29.' Nor were welfare clients within rural municipalities better off. In these communities, department officials noted, it was 'not uncommon to note monthly shelter allowances of $1.61, $3.21, $3.35, $4.75 etc. ... when the normal rental is from $15.00 to $20.00 monthly.'[7]

To help bridge this gap, the province adopted a new method of calculating shelter costs at the end of 1946. In large cities it agreed to pay up to $10.00 a month for the first room rented by a family or individual and $2.00 for each additional room, to a maximum of $30.00 in cities over 500,000 and $24.00 elsewhere. The formula was a simple one, provincial officials admitted. Although more flexible than previous formulas geared to property tax assessments, the adoption of a new standard for shelter costs, compared with the extensive research and agitation over nutritionally adequate food allowances in the 1940s, was hasty, arbitrary, and underpinned by little discernible research. Unlike revised food allowances, moreover, this new formula for calculating shelter costs bore no relationship to real market costs, a structural deficiency that would play havoc with budgeting the needs of families and individuals on welfare for years to come. In fact, since the relief caseload when the new rental allowance ceilings were adopted in 1946 was composed mainly of aged persons, the formula seems to have been designed principally to keep total welfare allowances for single elderly people in line with the existing federal government ceilings for old age pensions. As one provincial welfare official later recalled, 'for a single person, [relief] never exceeded ... a pension paid by Ottawa.'[8]

Once rents were decontrolled at war's end, the gap between shelter allowances and Toronto's real housing costs escalated so quickly that the city could only find shelter for its welfare caseload through topping up the province's maximum rental payments with supplemental allowances, financed totally out of its own funds. By 1949 more than two-thirds of that city's relief tenants were receiving supplementary municipal rental aid at a cost to Toronto of $174,000 a year. Despite this additional help and a boost in the provincial rental allowance ceiling to $40.00 a month in 1952 and to $50.00 in 1956, in response to pressure from the Ontario Municipal Association and the City of Toronto, welfare tenants were the victims of a chronically inadequate housing supply and a welfare shelter policy that actively fostered slum conditions. 'A family on relief is not considered a desirable tenant,' Toronto's housing officer noted in the early 1950s. 'It is only rooming house keepers in the downtown districts that will accept families with several children, and consequently [they] demand a high rent.' If tenants objected, they were told 'if you don't like it, get out.'[9]

Frustrated by its inability to get realistic cost-shared rental allowances approved by the province, Toronto's welfare department conceded they did 'everything possible to hold shelter allowances to $40.00 or less' throughout the 1950s. Relief tenants who complained about inadequate shelter allowances were told 'it is up to them to contact the rent control where the rent appears to be excessive. However, they all agree that when a tenant does contact the rent control and they in turn contact the landlord, there is a tendency on the part of the landlord to make conditions so uncomfortable that the tenant has to move and possibly pay more rent, if and when they locate other accommodation.' Single people on relief found it equally difficult to find accommodation on shelter allowances ranging from $6.00 to $10.00 a month. 'The majority ... are either aged or infirm and landlords do not want tenants who require care and quiet.' By the end of the 1950s conditions for these people had not improved. 'The single allowance granted according to relief regulations is $48.36 per month. In no case is this considered sufficient by the recipient,' a provincial welfare supervisor informed James Band in 1958. 'Rents [in Toronto] range from $6.00 to $7.50 *weekly* for single, drab, unattractive, ill-furnished rooms. Recipients pay the rent first, then try to feed and clothe themselves and provide basic necessities, with the remaining $5.00 per week. Diets in many cases are not adequately balanced ... [P]eople were obviously undernourished.'[10]

Throughout the 1950s, although more than half the province's total relief caseload lived in Toronto, a proportion rising to two-thirds by the decade's end, the province refused to make any special concession to higher rent costs in that city in setting its provincial shelter allowance ceilings. In response, the city drastically pared down its own supplemental rental payments over and above the provincial maximum. In the early 1950s Toronto also abandoned the practice of paying rent directly to the landlords of welfare clients, ostensibly in order to restore dignity and freedom of choice to clients on relief. But as welfare officials conceded privately, 'the Department's rental allowances are, *in the majority of cases, less than the actual rent being paid by the recipient* and our requiring a statement from the landlord might put us in the position of being expected to meet the full rent.'[11]

Despite average rentals of over $100 a month for one bedroom apartments by 1962, the city was still determined 'that in so far as possible rental allowances be held to $40.00 a month for families of two, three, and four, and $50.00 a month for larger families.' Knowledge that its own rental allowances were grossly inadequate to meet real shelter costs did not stop city officials from denying any responsibility for the slum conditions endured by those trying to live on public assistance. 'Families and individuals on relief generally assume full responsibility for maintaining themselves on the relief allowances,' welfare commissioner H.S. Rupert told staff members of his department. 'They choose their own food and fuel supplies and where they will live ... Therefore, the Department has no more control over whether they live in substandard housing or not than it has over other citizens generally.' In fact, by consciously cutting back rent supplements for inadequate provincial shelter allowances, the city left its welfare clients little choice but to endure squalid housing. By the end of the 1950s, despite a 42 per cent rise in average shelter costs and a major expansion in welfare caseloads, Toronto was spending 40 per cent less on rent supplements than it had in 1949.[12] Quite simply, welfare clients in the postwar era, unable to find accommodation in the severely restricted supply of public housing, bore the brunt of increased shelter costs by paying market rents out of money supposedly budgeted for food, clothing, and household necessities. In return, they received the worst accommodation cities had to offer and remained at the mercy of landlords who did not want them as tenants and were only too happy to see them move.[13]

By the end of the decade, a major study of Toronto's welfare caseload by the city's Social Planning Council revealed the extent to which provincial ceilings on welfare allowances fell short of meeting actual need. More than 2500 families in the city were receiving supplements for basic budgetary items such as food, clothing, and shelter from United Appeal agencies. For every dollar of public welfare assistance, these families were getting forty-one cents from private charities. In 70 per cent of the cases, housing costs ate up half the total monthly income. Despite a provincial shelter allowance ceiling fixed at $50 a month, more than half the families studied were spending over $60 a month on housing. Four out of five cases needed help from private agencies to buy food, while almost two-thirds required assistance for clothing or housing costs. Although monthly allowances for clothing and household necessities, which had remained virtually unchanged since the 1940s, were singled out for criticism, it was the structural gap between shelter allowances and real housing costs which was principally responsible for creating hunger among Toronto's poor.

Basic material needs, the Social Planning Council concluded, should be 'met by governments in sufficient amounts to enable families to maintain a minimum standard of health and decency.' Private agencies had no business being called upon to subsidize inadequate provisions by the state for food, shelter, and clothing. Toronto's United Appeal agreed. In 1960, in response to the findings of the council report, it abolished any funding for the supplementation of basic needs under public assistance allowances.[14] Director Harold Lawson concisely summed up the dilemma of welfare clients and welfare agencies, trapped within a set of provincial regulations which paid shelter, clothing, and household allowances that bore no relation to real living costs and which, even at their maximum ceilings, had not kept pace with the growth of Ontario's economy.[15]

The regulations ... do not ... provide any guidance to municipalities with regard to the MINIMUM ALLOWANCES they should provide ... Except for food, the amounts allowed for budgetted items appear to have been either arbitrarily set without relation to any standard of need or are based on surveys done many years ago ... [A]llowances being paid by municipalities are not sufficient to meet minimal living costs [and] *the major reason for this is in the shelter item and the way in which it must be computed* ... The absence of any recognized standard against which to test the adequacy or otherwise of all items except ... food ... handicaps the department of public welfare in its attempt to set realistic or logical minimum or maximum levels of assistance whether for rent, fuel, clothing, household sundries, or [the] total allowance.[16]

Stung by this criticism, Ontario welfare officials dismissed the council report as 'irresponsible' and 'misleading,' claiming it was based on 'hearsay evidence.' In how many of these cases 'where there was supplementation of food, clothing, and shelter was the assistance provided ... by the City used to pay debts and other items for which it was never intended?' The Social Planning Council's revelation that 80 per cent of welfare clients never received the maximum allowances permitted was 'true, but meaningless' because the amount cost shared by the province was 'determined by the budget for each case and may be any amount up to the maximum.'[17]

The province's response, however, missed the essential point of the study that extensive private agency supplementation was necessary because the provincial maxima themselves were clearly inadequate, causing families on welfare to plunge quickly into debt and to use food allowances for paying back-owed rent or buying clothing. As the Canadian Welfare Council argued in its influential 1958 publication *Social Security for Canada*, public assistance programs needed to be 'based upon sound and clearly defined standards' that included 'a definition of what constitutes a minimum level of health and decency' as well as a 'schedule of minimum requirements based upon this definition.'[18] Apart from food costs, such a clearly articulated minimum standard still remained absent within Ontario's assistance schemes.

Privately, however, some city and provincial officials were willing to concede the basic inadequacy of provincial welfare allowances. Statistical comparisons with the rest of Canada, the province's chief provincial economist pointed out in 1955, reflected 'the better than average conditions of employment and income in Ontario and ... also suggest that Ontario's system of poor relief and assistance has been more restricted than in other provinces,' a point underscored by another internal government memorandum which revealed that almost a third of Ontario's 900 plus municipalities, mostly rural small towns, did not pay any relief assistance to their citizens whatsoever in the early 1950s.[19]

Within Toronto, Robena Morris, the city's assistant welfare commissioner, acknowledged to those attending a 1957 conference on nutrition that it was difficult helping relief families 'to plan meals wisely when ... a portion of the food allowance was used to pay rent or other necessary expenses.' However, unlike Toronto's Social Planning Council, Morris remained convinced that little more could be done without throwing out of balance the necessary and delicate relationship between welfare allowances and wage rates for the working poor, particularly in a province lacking an effective minimum wage for men.

The schedules set up by the province for relief allowances ... bear a relationship to the incomes of low-income wage earners ... [T]hese low wage earners have other obligations such as high rent, transportation, medical expenses, etc. ... which would possibly also have to be met from money otherwise designated for food. The problem of spreading the relief allowance to cover rent and other needs was essentially the same as that encountered by the low-wage earning group and therefore their situations could be considered to be more or less comparable.[20]

Provincial officials also echoed Morris's analysis of the work/welfare tradeoff. The maximum welfare allowance for men with families 'of approximately $40.00 per week plus medical benefits, together with family allowances and other exempt income (not to mention the possibility of undisclosed day to day casual earnings),' was already above what many low-wage earners could make, and most men were 'reluctant to accept employment unless it would afford a higher income than Public Assistance.'[21]

Since only unemployables could qualify for relief between 1941 and 1958, enforcing the incentive to work, although by no means absent, did not play the dominant role it had during the Depression in the discourse surrounding welfare policy. Instead, the 'rehabilitation' of those on relief became the ostensible goal of Ontario's public welfare system. If ever there was a time when the effectiveness of social casework within public welfare offices could be demonstrated, the 1940s and 1950s was surely it. Those who simply lacked work were gone from welfare caseloads, which were now less than 10 per cent of their size during the 1930s. Eight out of ten clients on general assistance throughout this period were women and children. The women were either deserted, sick, or unmarried mothers. The remainder of the caseload were sick or elderly men and women.[22] The resort to welfare, in short, was the result of physical, family, or personal breakdown, rather than the generalized economic collapse of the 1930s when Ontario's public welfare system began to take shape.

'Very few, if any cases, have no health or social problems,' social workers reported, the roots of which were often 'obscure and elusive ... frequently having origin in the individual's own personality and being displayed in his behaviour and attitudes.' These problems 'must first be scientifically diagnosed before they can be treated and helped,' Morris told members of city council. Professionals skilled in the 'art of interviewing' were 'deeply aware of the depths of human emotions and suffering which sometimes must be explored in order to assist clients to express and reveal the true nature of their social and economic maladjustments.' During the Depression, 'deprivation and humiliation were thought to be the incentives' that would stimulate clients to get off relief, Eleanore Songhurst, chief casework supervisor for Toronto's Welfare Department, told her staff in the mid-1950s.

Due to our increased understanding of human motivation and behaviour we now know this is not so ... [T]he best way to help a person become independent is to provide assistance in a way that preserves his self-respect and dignity ... The need for public assistance should not impose any social stigma ... nor should it be

used as a lever to attempt to force [clients] to conform to social standards which
have no bearing on their eligibility ... An unrestricted, reasonably adequate cash
allowance ... permits them to live normally in the community ... [T]he most
important principle underlying public assistance is that the client is entitled to
prompt, efficient, and humane service from a Welfare Department.

Rehabilitation, then, was the application of social casework techniques designed to 'help families and individuals towards the solution
of their own social difficulties,' all the while allowing them 'to retain
their self-respect, personal dignity, and morale.'[23] This, at least, was the
theory.

The reality of how welfare actually functioned was rather removed from
these lofty ideals even within Toronto, the city with Ontario's largest
concentration of welfare professionals and over half its relief caseload.
At the Depression's end, the department employed a staff of 311 serv-
icing a monthly caseload of more than 77,000. By the late 1940s, as the
city's relief rolls dropped to only 6300, employment in the department
was pared back to slightly more than two hundred, a figure city council
always complained was too high given the collapse in numbers on
relief. Welfare staff responded that modern public welfare techniques
required that 'welfare visitors must have time' to rehabilitate the
unemployables now dominating relief rolls, an argument city council
never really accepted. Although caseloads would rise over 70 per cent
between 1949 and 1956, the size of the department remained unchanged.[24]

Only a small minority, almost all women, were trained social workers. Given the minute output of Ontario's two schools of social work,
most of whom were hired by child welfare and private social agencies,
and the vast dimensions of need produced by the Depression, Toronto's
welfare department during the 1930s, like those everywhere across
Canada, had hired welfare visitors where they could from a diverse
range of occupations, including 'women trained as teachers, nurses,
business or with other qualifying experience.' During the Depression,
Morris pointed out, 'it was the policy of the Department to employ [as]
investigational staff chiefly married men, with general experience of a
practical or business nature, with mature judgement and an interest in
people ... [but] with no initial training in social work.' For almost all
this group, 'in the absence of any tradition or precedent to service as a
guide, public welfare work could only be learned by doing it.'[25] This
was also true of the city's first two commissioners of public welfare,
who presided over the department from the 1930s until the early 1960s.
A.W. Laver, who built the department during the Depression and died

in 1946, was an accountant. His successor, H.S. Rupert, was a city engineer. Although Rupert and his assistant, Robena Morris, made an effort to recruit social work graduates in the 1940s and 1950s, and to institute in-service training, they were hampered by poor working conditions and low salaries compared with child welfare and private social agencies or even other City of Toronto departments.[26]

The result was a staff with little professional training, constant high turnover, and chronic morale problems as welfare visitors quickly 'burnt-out' confronting both their clients' problems and the department's own bureaucracy.[27] Within the job a fear of disorder prevailed. Just as welfare visitors frequently commented in their case reports on families who were 'very dirty in appearance' and premises that were 'very untidy ... very dark and dingy, with clothing scattered on every chair,' so their supervisors castigated them for 'sloppy housekeeping' in district offices where 'desks were not in alignment' and 'empty boxes, old file covers, and all manner of used material' were spread around the room. 'There should be a place for everything and everything kept in its proper place,' caseworkers were reminded. 'The tidiness of Offices is to be watched closely ... Walls should be kept free of flamboyant posters and calendars, etc.'[28]

More demoralizing to those staff with some social work training was the realization that despite the lip-service paid to rehabilitation through casework, there was little time, opportunity, or commitment by the department or the city to working intensively with clients. A monthly caseload of seventy-five was considered the maximum optimal size for effective social work by members of the department. In fact, caseloads averaged 135 in 1949 and rose to 200 by 1956.[29] 'How long may a worker spend to get at the real problem?' supervisors asked. 'One hour was the average time required to complete a first interview,' welfare visitors were told. After this initial interview, caseworkers reported they had time for a twenty-minute home visit every month, rising to once every three or four months by the late 1950s, in a workload expected to average at least eight home visits per day. 'In actual practice I feel there is very little [social improvement] in most cases ... [T]he welfare visitor within the Department has little opportunity of making his influence felt,' one caseworker reported to her supervisor in frustration. The province's regional welfare administrator for Toronto concurred. Because of the 'drastic shortage' of experienced staff in the city's welfare department, it was impossible for welfare visitors to meet more than 'routine requirements in granting assistance ... [and] even this is not always possible. Service seldom goes beyond this minimal point ... [T]here is a very strong feeling that workers' time and service are very limited and they "only scratch the surface." The complexities ... in these family cases are rarely dealt with and more often not understood by workers handling them ... Supervision is very spotty with the result that many opportunities to help the recipient cannot be explained, or are completely overlooked by unexperienced workers.' Even the Department's chief casework supervisor, Eleanore Songhurst, confessed despair by the mid-1950s. Because of 'larger caseloads than they can adequately handle, there is the tendency for ... work to become just a routine matter of getting an investigation form completed. Everything else tends to be handled on an emergency basis. This can be ... demoralizing for the client, and frustrating to both the welfare visitor and supervisor.' Staff working under her were 'resentful ... and fear that if they do not make up the required number of visits per day they will be considered inefficient.'[30]

High caseloads and insufficient staff were a problem not only for Toronto but for welfare departments across the country, a crisis only aggravated by declining enrolment within schools of social work throughout the 1950s. Within Ontario's Department of Public Welfare, few trained professionals found employment. 'Our field workers are largely recruited from the teaching and nursing professions, and of course from the business world,' welfare minister Louis Cecile, who replaced W.A. Goodfellow in the portfolio in 1956, told the legislature in 1956. Senior officials were recruited 'from the ranks' and 'largely received [their] training on the job.' Written examinations for those wishing to enter the department were implemented only in 1955, but these served merely as a 'screening process,' not a competition, Cecile pointed out. Individuals could still apply directly to the department for work, bypassing the Civil Service Commission, 'while other prospects are sponsored by Members of the Legislature.' Within Ontario's welfare department, in other words, patronage, not professional training, was the surest route to employment throughout the 1950s. Despite acknowledging that in Toronto there was a 'reluctance on the part of the City ... to provide adequate staff,' Cecile, along with his powerful deputy minister James Band, remained 'very much opposed' to suggestions that the province subsidize municipal costs of welfare adminstration in order to upgrade staff and the delivery of social services. 'We are dangerously close to what might be considered "safe" in assisting municipalities to bear their just share of welfare expenditures,' Cecile advised Frost in 1958. 'I am afraid if we extended financial aid beyond our present share ... to the point where we also assumed a share in the administrative costs, it would be far better for the Province "to take over" the entire responsibility for all services ... [W]elfare is primarily the concern of the municipality.'[31]

Since high caseloads and poor training ensured that rehabilitation of unemployables was not the actual function of welfare visitors, what did they do? In fact, social work rhetoric notwithstanding, the fundamentals of the job had not changed significantly since the 1930s. As a Toronto Personnel Department report on the subject put it in the mid-1950s, 'determining eligibility for public assistance ... is the very core of the Welfare Visitor's job.' This was by no means a routine task, given the complexity of provincial welfare regulations and the wide variety of individual financial and personal circumstances encountered by welfare visitors. It involved 'detailed knowledge of eligibility requirements, the ability to obtain accurate information quickly, to assess the person's situation in terms of the eligibility requirements and sound judgment in the application of the general eligibility requirements to individual cases.' It was not, however, either rehabilitation or social casework, particularly given the fact, frequently stressed by welfare administrators, that the 'client should take as much responsibility for himself as possible in substantiating his own eligibility for relief.'[32]

What had changed significantly since the 1930s, however, was a welfare caseload of so-called unemployables, mostly women with children, the sick or disabled, and the elderly. Apart from establishing their right to assistance, welfare visitors and administrators were principally involved with the moral regulation of these families and individuals.[33] The task demanded not enforcement of the work ethic, as in the 1930s, but rather the regulation of family life. This intervention could take a variety of forms. Some, such as strictures against drinking, were as old as the origins of organized charity itself in the nineteenth century. Welfare visitors in Toronto during the 1950s were reminded that their department 'does not condone drinking on the part of relief recipients' and were told to 'be on guard against the use of relief funds for other than the real necessities of life. This excludes liquor, telephone, automobiles, radios, and appliances purchased on the installment plan.' Clients discovered with such items either had their relief cancelled or, where children were involved, administered directly by the department. Welfare recipients were also told by the department that rent allowances were 'only given to them in trust for the landlord' and were instructed to 'pay the amount ... promptly' as well as to keep their accommodation 'clean and tidy.' Those with children were reminded that it was 'necessary ... to do laundry frequently and avoid any accumulation of soiled clothes or household linen.'[34]

Clients with health problems were prodded to get back into the labour market. 'Mrs. G. had been ill, but was certified by the doctor as now employable, however she refused to work as she said she did not feel sufficiently well to do so,' one caseworker reported. 'Eligibility was interpreted to her, and her relief was cut off ... Mrs. G. finally went to work, saying that she was very glad she had been given the push to get out on her own.' In another family of four, where the man had a 'minor physical disability ... [and] a history of mental illness,' the 'problem' was defined as 'developing a desire in the man to support his family ... [I]t is his irresponsibility which prevents him from working,' the caseworker reported. 'Relief was cancelled temporarily ... in an attempt to force him to find work.' When this failed, the family was put back on welfare, but their money was administered by the caseworker 'since they were not able to manage cash relief efficiently.' Although both physical disability and a diagnosis of 'severe neurosis' were acknowledged, the family's plight was essentially interpreted in moral terms as a 'lack of responsibility ... for both the man and the woman seem perfectly satisfied to remain on relief for the rest of their lives.' In this instance, the caseworker concluded that the 'solution is, of course, to remove him from the house for a course of intensive treatment and not to return him until it has proven successful.'[35]

Removal of problem men was a recurring theme in the discussion of family casework during the 1950s. When reports of disorderly, drunken conduct were received from one emergency housing project, 'welfare visitors in this department ... suggested that if the husband got out of the home, the department would be in a better position to help the family,' Commissioner Rupert was told. Another female 'applicant for assistance was advised that the only way to obtain relief was for the husband to desert the family.' Although this advice was obviously against departmental policy, recurring complaints about such statements by welfare visitors caused Rupert to warn his staff continually about 'exercising great care' in what they said to their clients.[36]

Both control over the interviewing process and interpretation of complex welfare regulations could also be used creatively by welfare staff to control their clients' behaviour and assess their 'deservedness.' Applicants for relief in Toronto were subjected first to an 'oral investigation' at the district welfare office, usually lasting one hour, following which they were given a detailed application form, a wage letter to be completed by their previous employer, and a medical certificate to be completed by their doctor testifying to their unemployability. 'These forms ... should have a stimulating and moral effect upon the recipient,' welfare visitors were told. 'When properly made out [they] are recognized by courts and may be required as evidence.' Clients were 'psychologically ... ready at the time of application to give information' and if 'not obtained at this point it is difficult and sometimes impossible to

obtain it later,' Morris advised her staff. If immediate aid was necessary, it was up to the 'interviewer's judgement as to the honesty and
integrity of the applicant ... in determining the urgency of the need.' Welfare staff were also urged to keep clients on emergency rather than
regular relief for as long as possible. 'The psychological effects of giving emergency assistance are good on the whole, as applicants are
made to feel that continued effort on their part is expected ... [It] also
acts as a safeguard, as the applicant must come to the office each time he
needs further help, and his circumstances are kept in constant review.'[37]

Since most welfare families in this era were headed by women, the
major component of moral regulation was directed at their relationships
with men. 'Where the man is absent from the home, various emotional
and social problems accompany the economic one and the case worker
can be of value here,' staff supervisors pointed out. The unwed mother
was 'by far the most penalized by society' and could anticipate only 'a
wretched existence if she doesn't want to give up her child,' an option
caseworkers tried to discourage. Despite the thin veil of casework objectivity, such women were viewed through a gaze of moral disap-
proval throughout the 1950s. Visitors described them as 'difficult to
work with,' 'likely to be unstable,' and 'quite defiant at times.' 'Some
are mentally below average,' while others have 'never worked, [are]
extremely dependent, and afraid to face the competitive hostile world.'
Regardless of how their clients felt, caseworkers were told to 'use
every means possible to have unmarried mothers make a declaration of
paternity at the Parliament Buildings when they first make application
for assistance ... [in order to] obtain support from the putative father.' If
determined to keep their babies, young mothers were discouraged from
staying at home, living on public assistance, and raising the child themselves, but instead were told to seek day care. 'By going to work she
can adjust more quickly, meet other people, and possibly marry.'[38]

Women in abusive relationships, whose husbands had deserted them,
were counselled that reconciliation, where possible, was a preferable
alternative to dependency on public assistance. The following case summary is typical:

A more advanced type of psychotherapy was done with Mrs. R. The family,
composed of Mr. R., aged 29, his wife 23, and two children of one and two, felt
that there was no hope of reconciliation. Mr. R. ... possesses a violent temper, and
last fall after beating his wife, he deserted her ... His wife was a somewhat
immature girl who might have made a success of a marriage ... but was unable
to help her husband adjust to his situation ... [The caseworker] helped Mrs. R. to

talk out all her hard feelings against her husband and to think of them more calmly. Then she suddenly recognized that his actions were those of a little boy who had not grown up ... Much discussion followed this point in regard to *how important the marriage was to her, as to whether she wanted to continue bringing up two children by herself, with only the prospect of living on public assistance for several years, or whether she could herself make some concessions* and be the strong person in her marriage, attempting to bring her husband out of his emotional difficulties and making allowances for his immaturity. At first she continually returned to the unfairness of having a 'little boy husband,' but eventually she began to feel that the latter course would be preferable ... Mrs R., fully cognizant of what her choice would entail, decided that she would make the effort at reconciliation.

Another woman, in similar circumstances, was told 'she would have to do much of the adjusting to her husband if he were to come back, that this would not be easy, and that there would be many times when she would probably feel that she was better off on relief, but that *she would have to feel that their marriage was more important than her own individual feelings.*' Two months later she called 'to request that her assistance be discontinued, as her husband was now back in the home.'[39]

Women whose husbands simply deserted without any hope of reconciliation, Band argued, were 'responsible for more complications in the administration of public assistance than any other type of case.' Their problems were 'bedevilling' and a 'source of constant irritation' to welfare authorities. Desertion was a 'cowardly and almost unforgivable offence,' which should be covered under the criminal code, the deputy minister maintained. Not only did children suffer financial hardship in its wake, but 'more than that, however, the deserter foists his own responsibilities on neighbours and other taxpayers of the community at large.'[40]

Although in principle the mother was not morally to blame for being deserted, she and her children were the ones left behind whom welfare authorities had to support. Consequently, welfare mothers found their lives subjected to close moral scrutiny in order to monitor their continuing entitlement to public assistance. The main ground of confrontation between mothers and the state became their relationship with other men, specifically whether men who were not the fathers of their children were living in their homes. On this issue, establishing welfare eligibility and regulating morality became one and the same thing, as the state used social policy explicitly to reinforce patriarchal family relationships and to limit entitlement to public assistance. Welfare regulations throughout the 1940s and 1950s were quite explicit on this point. 'Couples applying for assistance where there are children who are not the children of this union should not be recognized for relief purposes unless the union has been of long duration and the man has shown evidence of having assumed responsibility for the support of the family while employed,' caseworkers were told. 'In other cases, eligibility for assistance is conditional on the man securing accommodation apart from the family.' If a woman on relief admitted living with an unemployed man, it was 'assumed that the woman established this relationship expecting him to assume responsibility for support of the family and she should be advised that further assistance will be withheld as long as the man is in the home.'[41]

This was the infamous 'man in the house' rule that drove welfare visitors to perverse extremes of invading personal privacy in the quest to deny deserted mothers with children public assistance. In enforcing the regulation, welfare officers were reminded that entitlement could not be revoked 'on the grounds of suspicion only.' Positive evidence of cohabitation had to be established. As a consequence, visitors were advised to make unexpected 'home visits ... at supper time or early in the morning in an effort to clarify the situation.'[42] The report of such a visit to the home of a mother of two children by one provincial welfare investigator in 1958 leaves an enduring image of just how humiliating and degrading such practices were:

Recipient ... denied that she lived with Mr. U. ... On a Saturday morning ... at 9 a.m. I visited the recipient who had been still in bed. She repeated the denials noted above. On the recipient's permission, I looked into her bedroom. The closet contained male clothing which the recipient said belonged to a relative. On further scrutiny of the room there was revealed a dark skinned man, apparently naked, crouched on the floor behind the bed, mostly covered with bed clothes ... She admitted that this person was the Mr. U. of our enquiry. He has been living with the recipient ... Mrs. H. and Mr. U. being disinclined to further questioning, the interview came to an end.[43]

Caught within such circumstances, mothers who argued that men living with them were either unable or unwilling to provide support for their children faced a stark threat. 'Such situations are to be referred to the appropriate Children's Aid Society,' welfare visitors were told.[44] Even sympathetic caseworkers could not escape the imperatives or the ironies of their role in these situations. 'A woman with a couple of children, separated or deserted for years by a man who can absolutely not assume his responsibility, is more or less forced to live on public assistance,' one Toronto welfare visitor pointed out:

Even if she finds another man who would be willing to assume the responsibility of providing for her and her children ... the ... woman, afraid of losing her children, sometimes resorts to a way of life which has all the aspects of a common-law union without anyone being able to call it that, if she shares or rents a couple of rooms to him. *Your casework skill must be good indeed, for her to admit it when she knows the disclosure will cut her off public assistance* and force her to depend on the mercy of a man with whom she has to live and upon whom she has no legal claim.[45]

Welfare mothers not under suspicion through the 'man in the house' rule could be morally dangerous for their children on other grounds. With their 'limited income,' some were 'tempted to do a little work without declaring the income or ... rent a room ... without stating so and through this dishonesty provide an environment which will not be conducive for the children to learn what our society considers right and wrong. This could ... ultimately lead [the children] into conflict with society.' In other cases, simply living on relief was enough to contaminate the next generation. Such a woman 'with a young family and little hope of marital reconciliation is apt to become more dependent upon public assistance as the years go by and in doing so train her children always to expect this assistance as their right.'[46]

Through this unrelenting inspection and regulation of the lives of women and other so-called unemployables on welfare, Ontario's public assistance system, throughout the 1940s and 1950s, made a mockery of the notion, upheld by public welfare officials, that social assistance was designed to 'preserve ... self-respect and dignity,' did 'not impose any social stigma,' and allowed families and individuals 'to live normally in the community.' In fact, although the size and composition of the welfare caseload had changed dramatically since the Depression, the underlying purposes of the system had scarcely altered. Relief remained inadequate, demeaning, and was administered by staff who were poorly trained and able to do little more than enforce restrictive eligibility requirements. Despite pretensions of 'scientific' casework objectivity, welfare, after the war, continued to be suffused with moralizing assumptions about the worthiness, responsibility, sobriety, and honesty of its clients. Within this system, women were the principal targets of moral regulation, as they and their children remained trapped within a set of regulations that reinforced their dependency on either abusive or deserting husbands, common-law partners, or intrusive state agencies. Those deemed suspect risked losing their assistance or their children. In 1947 Toronto's Community Chest observed that the city's welfare department had 'not yet succeeded in throwing off all or most of its depression characteristics.' Ten years later, little had changed.[47]

Within Ontario's mothers' allowance program, however, significant changes were occurring in the 1950s which would dramatically alter both the caseload, administrative structure, and nature of the program. In 1956 unwed mothers became eligible for benefits for the first time. Although eligibility under mothers' allowances had been undergoing a gradual process of liberalization since the 1930s, including the admission of mothers deserted for only one year in 1946 and divorced mothers in 1951, the decision to include unwed mothers was a dramatic break with the moralizing assumptions that had traditionally underpinned the program. From the scheme's inception in 1920, some advocates, particularly within the labour movement, had always denounced the hypocrisy of legislation ostensibly intended 'in the interests of the children' which denied support to those born out of wedlock. But the program's rationale that only women who were 'fit and proper persons' should be deserving of financial assistance made this a minority viewpoint throughout the scheme's first three decades.

During the 1940s Toronto's city council once again took up the campaign that unwed mothers should be included within the program, arguing from a position that combined social justice with fiscal expediency. 'We cannot consider the interests of a mother apart from her child, or the interests of the child apart from the natural love and care of the mother,' Mayor Conboy told the provincial government in a 1943 brief. 'Although the condition of illegitimacy is unfortunate the social stigma should no longer rest on the children who should be entitled to the same protection and care as those born in wedlock.' Social investigation by his city's welfare department revealed 'many unmarried mothers [who] would be capable and desirous of giving their children good care if assistance were provided.' To include them within mothers' allowances would 'reduce the placements of illegitimate children in foster homes, and the numbers made wards of Children's Aid Societies at heavy costs to the municipality.'[48]

Until the early 1950s, however, even Toronto's Social Planning Council remained sceptical about these arguments. 'Pressure ... exerted by ... municipal authorities to have unmarried mothers keep their unadoptable babies and thereby have the province pay for the babies rather than the municipality through wardship costs' was not a legitimate reason for 'plac[ing] the unmarried mother in the same status as the married or widowed mother,' the council maintained. This would 'tend ... to lower standards rather than raise them.'[49] As these comments reveal, the moral condemnation of unmarried parenthood had by no means disappeared even within the ranks of professional social work by the 1950s. Increasingly, however, the language of psychiatric social work replaced earlier moralistic calls for 'expiation' and 'sacrifice' in the profession's discourse on illegitimacy.[50] 'The day is past for self-righteous condemnation, of punitive attitudes, ... of forcing [the mother] to atone for her wrong-doing,' social workers declared. Each case should be viewed through the lens of casework, 'not ... merely as a sex experience and a violation of the moral code of the community, but as a symptom of behaviour expressing the needs of the individual.'[51]

But while arguments rooted in psychology seemed to suggest a more tolerant or at least morally detached view of unwed mothers, this did not mean that social workers were more inclined to view such women as fit parents. Instead, their behaviour was now viewed as pathological, not immoral, the result of deep-seated psychological conflicts rooted 'in infancy and early childhood,' not feeble-mindedness or depravity. 'Her pregnancy is a symptom, not the cause of her condition,' postwar social work literature on the subject argued. 'Her illness might be of a neurotic, psychotic, or pre-psychotic origin ... Her opinion of herself is inferior, morbid in nature.' Most of these women were 'usually emotionally immature [and] ... have come from families that have given them little affection and security ... [O]ften there is neurosis present, or at least, neurotic trends.' Sex education, according to Dr Marion Hilliard, chief of obstetrics and gynecology at Women's College Hospital, had 'nothing whatever to do with the problem,' which really derived from deficiencies in early childhood. 'We must go back to a primary set of values and the discipline that starts with the very small child.'[52]

Although the cause of her condition was now viewed differently, the unwed mother's right to raise her own children still remained suspect. The best solution was usually adoption, social workers insisted. 'She must be helped to answer the question ... "Where will the child find mother and father figures which he can use to strengthen his own weak ego and with whom he can experience early social relationships? Where has he the best chance of being loved and of giving love?"'[53] Seldom was the answer the child's own home. 'The more healthy, normal unmarried mother ... usually has faced her situation realistically, has a plan in mind, usually adoption ... She can see her child as a human being, with needs, growing and developing, and she is willing to make the best plan for him. Every unmarried mother really needs a great deal of help in deciding to give up her child.'[54]

By the mid-1950s, however, a growing number of voices both within and outside of social work were beginning to criticize the bias towards and motivations behind adoption as the best solution to the problem of unwed parenthood. To what extent were prevailing social work theories that such a woman was abnormal and therefore 'not a fit person to raise her own child' rooted in the self-interest of child welfare agencies, one Ottawa social worker asked? 'Since illegitimate children are today practically the sole source of children for adoption by people unrelated to them, the coincidence of the rise of this latest theory with the Hollywood-inspired demand for children is disturbing. The attitude of one well-known Canadian child welfare "expert" was revealed not long ago in her statement that, "Adoption calls for a steady supply of children, preferably very young infants, from somewhere."'[55]

Even the evidence associating illegitimacy with abnormality was suspect. Most of these studies were based on 'young, poor, undereducated, or psychologically disturbed' women who were the usual clients of psychiatric clinics, social agencies, or charities. This was hardly a typical profile of unwed mothers, who came from all social classes and walks of life. Moreover, although less than 4 per cent of Canadian births occurred outside wedlock, statistics from Europe and Australia indicated that as many as one in four pregnancies occurred prior to marriage. 'So if we are to say with conviction that mothers of illegitimate children are psychologically abnormal and therefore unfit to raise their children we must extend the charge to about a quarter of the married mothers of families. Who would be prepared to do this?' sceptics within the profession asked. Since social workers were also mostly unmarried women, they should be especially cautious about perpetuating harmful moral stereotypes. 'In our culture the unmarried woman is herself still a long way from throwing off her unwelcome tag of frustrated spinster. Let us not be guilty of helping to build the caricature of the unmarried mother.'[56]

Increasingly, social work organizations, by the middle of the decade, agreed with the Canadian Welfare Council that 'where an unmarried mother is able and anxious to provide a satisfactory home and care for her child or children, she should have available to her the same sources of assistance as are provided for families in the community.'[57] This shift in professional opinion, ongoing complaints from municipalities about the growing costs of children in the care of Children's Aid Societies, a sharp decrease in the illegitimacy rate after 1945, and a 6 per cent decline in the overall mothers' allowance caseload between 1952 and 1956 finally combined to persuade the Ontario government to extend eligibility for mothers' allowances, under certain restricted conditions, to unwed parents in 1956.[58] Such mothers had to have previously cared for their children for up to two years prior to their applications for assistance and would automatically be cut off from support if they conceived any more children out of wedlock. 'They must prove themselves first,' welfare minister Louis Cecile argued in explaining the change in policy. 'We have to go slowly in the beginning. We don't want to encourage this kind of conduct, but we ought to encourage a mother to bring up her own child. I believe a mother can do a better job than any other well-meaning group in society.'[59]

Typically, Cecile's department also made the child, not the mother, the principal focus of its concern. Since Ontario was already making payments to foster mothers for the care of illegitimate children deserted by their natural parents, 'there seemed no logical reason why one group of children should benefit as a result of the mother's desertion and the other group be deprived of benefits simply because their mother tried to provide a home for them ... [S]ince we are interested primarily in the child's welfare, the emphasis should not be placed on the marital status of the child's parents,' provincial welfare officials argued. Granting unwed mothers financial support for keeping their children would also reduce the incidence of abortion, welfare agencies hoped. 'The subject is so abhorrent that two of Canada's leading obstetricians will not even discuss it ... It is one more reason why the unwed mother must be given every possible opportunity to have her child under good conditions, and that that child receive every consideration when it faces the world.'[60]

Given these restrictive conditions, the extension of mothers' allowances to unwed mothers did not result in any dramatic immediate change in the program's caseload. The following year only 133 women were getting benefits under the new provisions. But by 1959, after the two-year waiting period had been reduced to only six months, unwed mothers made up more than 8 per cent of a mothers' allowance caseload that itself had increased by almost 25 per cent in only three years. Moreover, for the first time in the program's history, widows and their children were no longer a majority of the program's clientele, which was now dominated by deserted, divorced, and unwed women along with totally disabled fathers.[61]

The second major change to the program took place in 1957, when flat-rate benefits that paid roughly fixed amounts to mothers according to their number of children were replaced by new procedures that ostensibly calculated income according to each family's 'budgetary need.'

This was 'one of the biggest changes in administrative procedure since the Welfare Department was formed,' officials boasted in heralding an increase which, as in 1943, boosted the average monthly benefit paid by almost 20 per cent from $86.61 to $104.38 per family between 1957 and 1958. Given the province's small mothers' allowance caseload of 8000 families, however, the total cost was only $1 million for the first fiscal year of operation under the changeover.[62]

Much of the pressure for this policy shift came from the province's municipalities which, as in the 1940s, were increasingly being forced to top up inadequate mothers' allowances payments with supplemental relief. As Oshawa's welfare department complained to provincial officials in a typical case, a mother with two children in that city receiving a mothers' allowance of $93.75 needed to be supplemented an additional $27.31 each month by the city's welfare department to meet her minimum subsistence needs. 'The Basic Rate for Mothers' Allowance is too low ... [I]t is far less than the Relief Allowance,' the city's welfare officer pointed out. 'Where need exists, [the program should] provide means comparable to Relief Allowances.' Women in the program were becoming 'quite frustrated and anxious about their outlook,' defeating the whole purpose of 'encourag[ing] young mothers to stay with their children and to make a good home for them.' Field workers within the program agreed, reporting to Queen's Park that 'beneficiaries are finding it increasingly difficult to manage on Mothers' Allowances assistance.'[63]

With a reasonably stable caseload and ballooning provincial revenues, the Frost administration by 1957 was persuaded by these and other long-standing social work arguments to put the entire program on a more adequate basis of need. Under the new system of 'needs-testing,' standard cost-of-living budget schedules for families of varying sizes were drawn up with the help of the province's nutritional consultant, Dr E.W. McHenry. Each family's resources, including any earned income, were compared against the relevant schedule for its size, and the government paid the difference between these standard estimated requirements and actual family income up to a fixed ceiling of $180 a month for a family of seven or more beneficiaries. As a result of this change, the program lost any lingering resemblance to a 'pension' in return for 'service to the state.' After the switch to needs-testing in 1957, the calculation of income under mothers' allowances became as complex and bewildering to clients as in any other welfare program. Moreover, as department officials later conceded, the idea of meeting the actual budgetary needs of clients was more rhetoric than reality. 'The method of calculation matters little in welfare allowances, what matters is the sum the government is prepared to spend,' Clifford Williams, the official historian of the department and a former director of its General Welfare Assistance Branch, pointed out in regard to this change. 'Equity and practicality require that each item be based on some average need for some average person, in other words, on a flat rate sum. The needs-test total allowance was little more than a selection of flat rates added together.'[64]

Nor was the switch to needs-testing intended to reduce the necessity for women in the program to earn supplemental income to make ends meet. In order to maintain 'some built-in incentives encouraging women to work part-time,' the department exempted 25 per cent of the standard allowance as income for women working up to half a week or less. In other words, a woman getting a monthly benefit of $100 and earning an additional $60 could keep $25 of this extra income before seeing an equivalent amount deducted from her monthly allowance cheque. Even so, as a scrutiny of case files reveals, the impact of this 75 per cent clawback on part-time wages was still severe. A woman with three children earning $106 a month in 1960 saw $80 of this income deducted from her monthly entitlement, leaving her with a benefit of only $77 to meet a total monthly 'budgetary need' of $157. Under these circumstances, it remained impossible for women remaining within the program to break out of poverty.[65]

Despite these limitations, the province's welfare minister, Louis Cecile, remained convinced that the 'budgetary formula ... on which the allowance is based is on the whole quite generous.' Ontario's average monthly benefit of $102.88 for women in the program now compared favourably with 'the average payment in the United States of America ... which ... was about $102.00 a case.' More importantly, Cecile argued that a woman with two children assessed with a 'budgetary need of about $30.00 weekly ... is not [in] an unfavourable [position] in relation to the general wage structure, particularly when a portion of earnings is exempt from her calculation of income.'[66] Although about 75 per cent of all families on mothers' allowances received increases because of the switch to needs-testing, the remaining 25 per cent, particularly those with 'substantial income from earnings, boarders, etc. or where the living expenses of the family are low,' saw their benefits reduced by the change.[67]

Despite the adoption of a budgetary formula ostensibly geared to meeting 'the actual financial requirements of families who qualify,' mothers' allowances in Ontario, by the end of the 1950s, failed to approximate more than three-quarters of the minimum monthly standard of need for families of varying sizes as calculated by the Toronto Social

Planning Council's *Guide for Family Budgeting*. After 1961, allowances within the program would soon begin to fall away even from this restricted approach to adequacy. The program's failure to meet such a target, as Lorna Hurl has pointed out, 'was in part a reflection of the limited definition of "need" in the newly devised schedules,' in particular the decision to keep maximum budgetary standards closely in line with similar programs elsewhere and in rough relation to earnings available in the private labour market. For mothers with six or more children, the shortfall between the program's limited definition of need and actual requirements could be catastrophic. In these situations, itemized case record assessments of a family's 'budgetary need' at $230.55 for a mother with six children or $305.70 for a mother of ten become simply bizarre, given the program's overall maximum ceiling of $180.00 for families of seven or more people. In situations where mothers' allowances could fall 40 per cent short of meeting even the department's internal assessment of a family's minimum basic requirements, any semblance that the program responded to 'actual need' was perverse.[68]

Nonetheless, by the decade's end welfare minister Louis Cecile remained convinced that mothers' allowances were doing all that could be expected. Suggestions, even from the Premier's Office, that allowances for totally dependent widows might be increased were rebuffed. 'An overall increase would be costly,' Cecile told Leslie Frost. 'There is no great evidence that the allowances presently available are failing to meet the needs in a majority of cases ... [W]e now take into account the reasonable minimum household expenses in maintaining a family.'[69] As far as the province's welfare department was concerned, all the legitimate needs of women and children within the program, by the end of the 1950s, were now being met.

Throughout the 1940s and most of the 1950s one group – the unemployed – stood entirely outside the gates of Ontario's public welfare system. Ironically, it was their plight during the 1930s which had initiated the creation of a provincial welfare bureaucracy in the first place. No other social policy issue proved as controversial for federal-provincial relations during the two decades following the Depression's end as the care of the jobless not covered through unemployment insurance.[70] Between 1941 and 1957 Ottawa, the province, and its municipalities refused to provide any financial aid to the employable jobless who were either ineligible for or had exhausted their entitlement to unemployment insurance benefits. Throughout these years one-third of Ontario's labour force was not covered under this scheme, first initiated by the federal government in 1941. Mostly these were young, immigrant, or seasonal workers who could not accumulate the necessary thirty weeks of employment over two years to qualify for benefits or those who worked in industries such as agriculture or domestic service which remained outside its coverage. Other victims of this jurisdictional battle also included the aging jobless or workers in depressed industries or areas who had exhausted their maximum thirty-four weeks of benefit entitlement. These destitute people and their families, whose numbers Ontario officials estimated at perhaps 26,000 by the mid-1950s, became the innocent scapegoats in a cynical political power-play between Ottawa, Queen's Park, and Ontario's municipalities over which level of government was primarily responsible for unemployment.[71] Until this fundamental question, left over from the 1930s, could be resolved, the development of a truly comprehensive system of public assistance covering all the population in times of need was impossible.

The origins of this struggle lay in the Depression. Throughout this decade, Canada's provinces and municipalities absorbed 70 per cent of the cost of providing almost $1 billion in unemployment relief. The crippling weight of this burden bankrupted four provinces and hundreds of municipalities, including more than thirty in Ontario. During the worst year of the 1930s, Queen's Park paid out more than $21 million in unemployment relief, and thereafter provincial officials vowed that the government 'would not put themselves in a position where they might be called upon to spend such sums again.'[72]

Escape from this burden appeared to come in 1940. In that year, through a unique constitutional amendment that received unanimous consent and, for the first and only time in Canadian history, transferred complete authority over a jurisdiction from the provinces to Ottawa, the federal government gained exclusive control over unemployment insurance. To provincial governments across Canada, this transfer of authority, and the new social insurance scheme that came into effect the following year, appeared to confirm the view put forward by the National Employment Commission in 1938 and the Rowell-Sirois Report in 1940 that, because of its potential cost, the care of the unemployed was or should be a national responsibility.

Had Ottawa's 1940 unemployment insurance scheme covered all the labour force and provided an extensive period of benefits, the issue might have been resolved at this point. Such was not the case. In order to guarantee its actuarial soundness, the 1940 plan was, in fact, a cautious piece of legislation that initially covered slightly more than 40 per cent of Canada's total civilian labour force and provided an inadequate benefit ceiling of $62.40 a month for a maximum of thirty-six weeks. It was at best a scheme designed to tide wage-earners over temporary and short-term spells of joblessness, not a prolonged or deep depression.

Who would care for the remainder of the uninsured unemployed, especially if severe unemployment returned once again? Once Ottawa terminated all contributions to unemployment relief in 1941, this issue loomed large in planning for postwar reconstruction, especially as federal officials privately predicted that unemployment, following postwar demobilization, 'threatens to develop on a colossal scale ... suddenly and unexpectedly.' Without adequate advance preparation, civil servants within Ottawa's powerful Economic Advisory Committee warned, 'the country will run grave risks of facing mass unemployment, social unrest, and a chaotic industrial situation which no ad hoc improvisations will be able to master.'[73] It would 'unquestionably be considered a national responsibility to reduce this unemployment as much as possible ... and to provide an adequate and certain subsistence for the casualties of the process,' committee members advised. 'The most urgent [need] is some plan of unemployment assistance to provide for the unemployed who have exhausted insurance benefits or who are not covered by insurance.'[74]

Accordingly, over the next two years Department of Labour officials were put to work designing a national unemployment assistance scheme as a companion to unemployment insurance, which was eventually contained in Ottawa's Green Book Proposals on Reconstruction presented to the provinces in August 1945. From the start it was assumed such a plan should be financed and administered exclusively by Ottawa. Because of its vast wartime economic powers, the creation of unemployment insurance, and the legacy of the 1930s, the federal government would have to 'assume full responsibility' for unemployment, the King administration realized. Moreover, no one in Ottawa wished to resume participation in the fractious and demoralizing haggling that had characterized federal-provincial negotiations over unemployment relief throughout the 1930s. Beyond these considerations, an unemployment assistance scheme run completely by the national government possessed one further strategic advantage. Ottawa's major objective in reconstruction negotiations with the provinces following the war's end was to retain exclusive control over the lucrative personal income and corporation tax fields it had monopolized since the early 1940s. If the provinces agreed to rent these revenues to Ottawa, the federal government's 'assumption of responsibility for unemployment assistance,' the Green Book argued, 'would relieve provincial and municipal governments of a potential burden which in the past has constituted the most important single threat to real provincial autonomy.' On the other hand, if such an agreement was not forthcoming, King warned the premiers, they could expect no federal aid for unemployment assistance unless they were willing to submit their own governments 'to a means test.' In short, Ottawa's willingness to assume full responsibility for unemployment, including unemployment assistance for those not covered by its insurance scheme, was made directly contingent upon provincial agreement to its tax rental proposals.[75]

Ontario wanted no part of such a fiscal surrender. Provincial officials were in total accord with Ottawa's assumption of complete financial responsibility for the unemployed, but they did not like the unemployment assistance scheme contained in the Green Book proposals, which they characterized as 'confusing,' 'uncertain,' and 'piecemeal.' Ontario's principal objection was that because of its loose definition of 'unemployability,' its low level of benefits, particularly for those with children, and its exclusion of the self-employed from coverage, Ottawa's unemployment assistance scheme would still leave a large proportion of the 'able-bodied' to the care of provincial and municipal taxpayers. Ontario officials also argued that Ottawa lacked the administrative ability or machinery to operate a means-tested unemployment assistance plan across Canada. The scheme 'would be best handled through local City and County Welfare Units,' even though it should remain 'the financial responsibility of the Dominion.'[76] This idea was clearly of no interest to federal officials, who designed an exclusive federal unemployment assistance scheme principally to avoid the fiscal haggling that seemed endemic to joint federal-provincial programs such as unemployment relief and old age pensions during the 1930s. Given Ontario's vehement refusal to surrender the taxation fields sought by Ottawa, however, such technical disagreements over unemployment assistance were beside the point. The entire scheme became a casualty of the collapse of the Reconstruction Conference negotiations in the spring of 1946.

When both the anticipated postwar depression and a tax-rental agreement with Canada's two largest provinces failed to materialize, Ottawa quickly lost interest in unemployment assistance. 'It is obvious that the dominion cannot ... assume responsibility for unemployed employable persons in [some] provinces but not in others,' federal finance minister J.L. Ilsley told Parliament later that year. Although some federal officials conceded privately that the constitutional amendment giving Ottawa authority over unemployment insurance provided 'a basis in fact for an argument that the federal government is fully responsible for assistance to unemployed employables,' this was an obligation that neither the King administration nor that of his successor, Louis St Laurent, was anxious to assume. With Canada's economy booming throughout the 1940s and early 1950s, the plight of the jobless stranded outside its unemployment insurance system seemed remote. 'As long as defence expenditures absorb 50 percent of the national budget and incidentally maintain virtually full employment,' Jack Pickersgill, chairman of the Privy Council Office Committee on Unemployment, told the prime minister in 1952, '[I do not think] there is any justification for a demand from local and provincial governments for assistance.' St Laurent agreed. Apart from unemployment insurance, 'constitutional responsibility for relief and assistance of the unemployed ... rested with the local authorities,' he told a delegation of Ontario mayors that same year. Ottawa would provide aid 'only when the problem reached emergency proportions.'[77]

Provincial premiers, including Leslie Frost, were not willing to let the federal government slide away so easily from its commitment to the unemployed embodied in national unemployment insurance and in the Green Book proposals. When Ottawa terminated its unemployment relief contributions in 1941, Ontario had quickly changed its own regulations to restrict cost-sharing for relief only to unemployables. This remained the basis of postwar provincial welfare policy. The able-bodied jobless were a federal responsibility, Ontario officials insisted, a fact Ottawa itself had acknowledged publicly both in 1941 and in 1945, and which it was now equipped to handle through its network of employment service and unemployment insurance offices across Canada. Failure to reach agreement on a tax-rental formula in 1945 was a separate issue entirely. Care of all the unemployed belonged in Ottawa's hands, and the province would not reimburse municipalities a penny for its cost.[78] Since neither the federal government nor the province would contribute anything towards the care of the uninsured jobless, Ontario municipalities simply followed suit. Those unlucky enough to be without unemployment insurance were denied eligibility for relief by local governments across the province. A signed doctor's certificate documenting unemployability became a key requirement for anyone, besides mothers with children, wishing access to public assistance.

Within large Ontario cities this political deadlock over the care of the jobless became a nightmare for public welfare agencies and private charities, especially as winter unemployment rates crept steadily upwards during the early 1950s. Within Toronto, during the winter of 1952, the crisis was particularly acute. Staff within the Department of Welfare complained of 'emotional strain,' arguing it was 'very difficult ... to have to refuse assistance to people who appear to be destitute.' In many families where men 'cannot secure employment and there is no provision for the family as long as he is in the home ... fathers recognizing this ... have left the home in order to place their families in an advantageous position of securing financial help,' welfare visitors reported. Delegations to city council pointed out that many single men 'were sleeping on floors of buildings.' The department reported that private agencies 'such as the Red Cross, Neighborhood Workers, Salvation Army stated that their resources had been exhausted and they could not continue to give assistance to families.' In response to these pleas, city officials agreed that 'the present rigidity in granting assistance to this group might be slackened a little ... but must be kept under control.' Help would be granted only in 'cases of real need,' which was defined as 'serious illness in the family, an expectant mother, a large number of children, a very young baby or where there is an emergent situation with dire needs.' A total of only $35,000, however, was budgeted for these cases. In some other cities, authorities turned a blind eye to dubious medical certificates of unemployability for men with families in need, reimbursed private agencies who helped such families, or simply paid indigent employables half of regular assistance rates. However, 'most [Ontario] municipalities,' the Canadian Welfare Council pointed out, 'try to avoid assistance to employable persons.'[79]

Senior federal officials acknowledged privately, throughout the early 1950s, that the 'man on the street' assumed that responsibility for all the jobless belonged in Ottawa's hands and that the denial of assistance by provinces and municipalities to wage earners uncovered by unemployment insurance was 'a very human problem which is the source of considerable suffering to many unemployed and their families.' They also estimated that, given present unemployment rates, the cost to Ottawa of launching a joint federal-provincial assistance scheme would run in the neighbourhood of only $4 million a year. Nonetheless, as long as unemployment remained low and there was 'no incentive nor agitation on the part of the provinces' to deal with the problem, they advised against federal action. Any unilateral initiative on Ottawa's part, federal officials warned cabinet, would 'tend to lessen the future bargaining area with the provinces and ... weaken the government's hand ... when the need was great.' Above all, any concession by Ottawa 'that assistance to unemployed employables was a federal responsibility in the first instance would probably lead to pressure for it to assume the whole cost. The possible financial burden might be extremely heavy.'[80] Exactly the same logic, however, prevented provinces from filling the breach. 'The real problem which these governments face, and the one which deters them from taking the first step,' one senior federal official accurately observed in the summer of 1954, 'concerns the implications for them in times of serious unemployment.' If they provided aid to employables 'in times of normal unemployment ... this would commit [them] to financial obligation without apparent limits, if unemployment should become serious and prolonged.' For this reason, he argued, 'it seems probable that no reasonable offer by the Federal Government at this juncture would be sufficient to induce many provinces (if any) to initiate a new provincial-municipal cost-sharing plan of unemployment assistance.'[81] In short, in the event of a serious recession, neither level of government wished to be held primarily responsible for unemployment relief. Consequently, neither was willing to make the first move in prosperous times to resolve the impasse.

Forced to carry the burden of relief for employables in need who had been abandoned by governments, private charities attempted to mediate a compromise through the Public Welfare Division of the Canadian Welfare Council. Early in 1953, after two years of meetings and correspondence with both levels of government, the council released a major policy document, 'Public Assistance and the Unemployed,' which called for extended unemployment insurance benefits and federal cost-sharing of local and provincial welfare payments to employables in need on a sliding scale linked to the level of unemployment. Neither Ottawa nor Queen's Park was interested. The federal government had only a residual responsibility for the jobless outside of unemployment insurance which depended on the fiscal need of the provinces, not the number of employables on relief, deputy national health and welfare minister George Davidson told the council. His Queen's Park counterpart, James Band, was equally unenthusiastic. Ontario 'prefer[red] to have nothing to do with unemployment relief,' the deputy welfare minister told a council official. If Queen's Park agreed to participate in such a scheme 'and the federal government at a later date decided to withdraw from the plan, the province would be stuck with the full cost.' His government also balked at the administrative implications of the proposal. Of Ontario's 960 municipalities, 'only something like fourteen have welfare departments,' Band pointed out. 'If this scheme would be administered by all municipalities, it would mean those who do not have welfare departments would be forced to set up some form of administration.' With the memory of the disastrous Welfare Units Act fresh in his mind, Band observed that 'the province would hesitate in committing themselves' to such a wholesale reform of local government.[82] Members of the University of Toronto's School of Social Work who had worked hard to bridge the gap between the two levels of government were disheartened by the curt dismissal of their efforts over the past two years and were particularly outraged by the intransigence of Ontario officials. 'In effect [Goodfellow] says "I won't do it for one set of reasons; and I can't really let YOU do it for quite another set of reasons. So let'em starve and I'll see you get the blame,"' John Morgan sarcastically commented. 'It MAY be good politics (I doubt it) but it's awful poor social policy.'[83]

Such stubbornness was only possible while unemployment remained low. By the summer of 1954, however, federal officials were willing to concede that 'the postwar boom has ended'; within Ottawa debate resumed over whether the federal government should take some initiative on unemployment assistance. Davidson lobbied hard for the immediate launching of a federally cost-shared unemployment assistance scheme. If an agreement were negotiated now, 'the provinces might be prepared to come in at an early stage and do more for the unemployed than they were now doing and in the long run reduce the financial load on the federal government.' On the other hand, if Ottawa delayed action until a serious unemployment crisis emerged, it 'could not, at that late date, disentangle itself from the 1945 position' of assuming complete responsibility for the jobless.[84] His views were overridden by the Department of Finance, which continued to insist that Ottawa's only obligation was to assist the provinces during an emergency. Providing federal money for unemployment assistance now, finance officials argued, would only deter the provinces from launching their own public works schemes to relieve unemployment. Moreover, the political timing was wrong. 'Because the tax-rental negotiations were going to be tough,' deputy minister of finance Ken Taylor wished to 'hold any federal concession in reserve for the 1955 [federal-provincial] conference ... using unemployment assistance as a sweetener.'[85] As a result, apart from a modest liberalization of unemployment insurance benefits financed out of the fund's huge $1 billion surplus, Ottawa refused to assume any further responsibility for the jobless.

For the unemployed, along with public and private welfare agencies across Ontario, this decision was disastrous. During the winter of 1955 Canada's jobless rate jumped to 7 per cent, the 'highest level in our postwar experience,' federal trade and commerce minister C.D. Howe conceded, due to a 'levelling off in the defence build-up in North America.' In Toronto alone, five thousand jobless were without unemployment insurance benefits, the local manager of the National Employment Service office reported. Queen's Park continued to refuse any money for relieving the families of employables, 'claiming that it was a matter of federal jurisdiction.' The city's welfare department, Commissioner H.S. Rupert told members of the federal cabinet, would provide 'food and necessities only to cases which were in dire need.' Out of a total welfare budget of over $1.6 million, however, Toronto spent less than $26,000 on aid to employables. 'Many married men [were] deserting their families so that the women and children could go on straight relief,' a city controller pointed out. As in the Depression, soup kitchens had reopened, hostels were full to overflowing, and the city was once again 'buy[ing] one-way tickets ... [to] ship ... the unemployed to their former homes.'[86]

The Neighbourhood Workers' Association, Toronto's largest private welfare agency, compiled a grim report from its case files of just what it meant to be jobless and refused aid in the city that winter. The family of one casual labourer out of work for three months 'had no possessions except clothes and they sold some of these ... They were evicted and for three weeks the father stayed at the Salvation Army hostel, the mother with a friend and the child with a relative ... Instead of 2 quarts of milk a day they have evaporated milk. They have no meat, eggs, or fruit. Their main food consists of canned goods and potatoes. They have sought help from five different agencies and from relatives and friends. One agency gave them $4 and another gave canned goods.' Another family with seven children had 'sought assistance from three agencies and got $12 from one.' They were living on 'soups ... pork and beans and ... had not had meat since Christmas. Because of lack of heat the children have had constant colds. The parents and four children have been sleeping in the one room which contains a stove.' A family with two children 'lived on macaroni or potatoes and bread ... [and] moved from one rooming house to another as they were evicted ... The children had continual colds ... The father ... appealed to the Red Cross, the Salvation Army, the Neighbourhood Workers, Dept of Veterans Affairs, the Dept of Public Welfare, [and the] Scott Mission. As a result he [got] ... the following help: tinned food, a suit and a coat, an order of groceries and $14.' These people were 'very bitter,' the association reported, and 'cannot understand why they should not have either work or assistance.' Many were also recent immigrants and their 'greatest burden is ... [a] frantic fear of deportation.'[87]

Despite the obvious hardship suffered by such families during the difficult winter of 1955, neither Ottawa nor the province was willing to budge from its position. 'The responsibility ... must be met by the Government of Canada,' Goodfellow told Ontario's municipalities demanding aid. Ottawa, for its part, continued to insist that since unemployment was mostly 'seasonal,' the relief burden was 'not ... beyond the capacity of [local] communities.' In desperation, Ontario's private welfare agencies urged that 'something had to be done immediately in bringing pressure to bear on the different levels of Government for action.' Otherwise, there was the danger of 'falling into the same pitfall as in previous years,' the Ontario Welfare Council argued. 'The problem ... will be tossed from one level of Government to the other until the spring when the community pressure comes off because of the seasonal drop in unemployment.'[88]

As a result, the Canadian Welfare Council seized the initiative by planning its own national conference on unemployment to be held on 1 April and inviting provincial governments to attend. When most replied they would be delighted to come, St Laurent finally acted to avoid a major political embarrassment. Meeting privately with council president Lawrence Freiman, the prime minister promised to place the issue of unemployment assistance on the agenda of a preliminary meeting of federal and provincial officials later in April if the council agreed to call off its conference. It was a critical victory for Canadian social work. Through adroit publicity capitalizing on the worst winter of hardship and discontent since the 1930s, the Canadian Welfare Council finally manoeuvred Ottawa into taking the first critical step towards a national unemployment assistance scheme.[89]

Federal officials approached these negotiations warily. If the provinces continued to insist on the Green Book proposal for a 'purely federal scheme,' they advised St Laurent to argue 'there was nothing more for the Federal government to discuss.' For its part, Ottawa put forward the most minimal commitment possible, offering contributions to unemployment assistance on a sliding scale ranging from 30 to 50 per cent of costs when welfare caseloads rose above 1 per cent of a province's total population. Assistance on a sliding scale related to need preserved Ottawa's argument that its responsibility was 'residual' rather than primary. The 1 per cent threshold for federal payments provided a statistical means of excluding 'unemployables' from coverage, on the assumption this represented the normal provincial relief burden. Finance officials conceded there was a 'real problem of whether enough provinces would support [such a scheme],' but the main point was to 'show ... a willingness of the Federal government to do something about unemployment. The ideological burden would be shifted to the provinces and the Federal government would be in a stronger position.'[90]

Ottawa's doubts about provincial support for their proposal proved correct when negotiations began in earnest late in June. None of the provinces was happy with the complicated sliding scale for federal aid, which would only be a recipe for endless statistical bickering, or with the 1 per cent relief threshold, which would exclude all but four provinces from any immediate federal aid. Under Ottawa's complicated proposal, Ontario's relief load, the province's chief economist pointed out, would have to double beyond its 1955 level before the province received even a 40 per cent federal contribution. This was a long way from the Green Book proposal. As a result of these objections, St Laurent agreed to lower the threshold from 1 per cent to 0.45 per cent of a province's population, which represented the average caseload of unemployables in Ontario. Under further pressure, he also abandoned the sliding scale formula, agreeing ultimately to a straight 50 per cent subsidy for all relief cases above 0.45 per cent of the provincial population. There he drew the line. The 0.45 threshold was essential to preserve the constitutional distinction that Ottawa shared a responsibility only for 'employables.' Under no circumstances did St Laurent wish to see a limited and reluctant commitment to the able-bodied become an open-ended responsibility for all those in need.[91]

While these concessions proved sufficient to entice six provinces into signing unemployment assistance agreements with Ottawa, they did not satisfy the rest led by the vehement opposition of Ontario premier Leslie Frost. During the June 1955 negotiations, Frost tore into the federal proposal with a savagery which belied his previous willingness to seek harmonious relations with Ottawa, and which undoubtedly reflected his mounting frustration, on a different front, to achieve a more equitable tax-sharing formula with the St Laurent administration. Frost deplored Ottawa's unemployment assistance proposal. It was a 'lamentable retreat' from the Green Book and represented a 'throwback to a system ... in operation in the 1930s.' It would force his government to 'take on a new burden, namely direct relief for able-bodied workers – which they had every reason to believe was not theirs.' The Green Book offer of full federal administrative and financial responsibility for the unemployed was a far more 'sound and logical plan,' which Ottawa could well administer through its existing network of employment offices. However, if the federal government continued to insist that unemployment relief could be 'better administered on the local level,' then it should be willing to 'bear ... a more realistic level' of the cost.[92]

As a minimum, Frost demanded that Ottawa abolish the 0.45 threshold and agree to 'split on a fifty-fifty basis the cost of providing relief to employables and unemployables without distinction.' This was something St Laurent was not prepared to do. The existing offer remained on a 'take it or leave it' basis. As a last ditch effort to get a deal, and as a sign of his own distaste for shared-cost programs supervised by Ottawa, Frost made an entirely different offer later that autumn. On a short-term basis, in return for a straight grant of fifty cents per capita or $2.5 million 'without additional strings,' Ontario would assume total responsibility for dealing with the jobless not covered by unemployment insurance. This money would be matched by the province and passed on to municipalities 'for the financing of local ... "make work projects" as an alternative to the provision of able-bodied relief.'[93]

This sudden, out-of-the-blue proposal reflected the extraordinary unwillingness of Frost's administration to get back into the business of providing direct relief to the unemployed, or, as Goodfellow put it, 'revert[ing] to the dole system of the thirties.' The creation of a cost-shared program for unemployment assistance, Frost's advisers estimated, even in a time of 'virtually full employment,' would at least double the existing size of the province's welfare caseload and push provincial and municipal spending on relief from $5.3 million to 'approximately $10.6 million towards which the Federal Government would have contributed approximately $2.6 million.' It was 'another case of Ontario having to spend money to get Federal money,' George Gathercole complained. This sharp boost in relief costs would also 'saddle the province and the muncipalities with ... the problem of administration,' requiring permanent and unshared administrative expenditures, on a substantial basis, as both levels of government would 'inevitably require additional [welfare] staff to assure proper spending.' Since the job of aiding the unemployed could already be handled through the National Employment Service or the Unemployment Insurance Commission, Ontario believed, these costs were all the more irritating and unnecessary. Finally, the 'main objection' to Ottawa's proposal was that 'it does nothing to provide work.' At a time when Ontario needed revenue for 'the development of essential provincial and municipal services' such as roads, schools, hospitals, water, and sewage systems, Ottawa wished to have money 'diverted to relief payments.' This was a 'step in the wrong direction.' A more preferable program would allow municipalities 'to put a person on relief work rather than on relief and still qualify for Federal aid.'[94]

Having already secured the agreement of six provinces to its unemployment assistance proposal, St Laurent's government had no interest in negotiating a new and entirely different deal with Ontario at the eleventh hour. As a final sweetener, Ottawa offered in December 1955 to include the cost of unemployables in old age or nursing homes as part of its cost-sharing formula. Ontario remained uninterested. Throughout the winter of 1956 federal officials still believed that 'Ontario would wind up by signing a draft agreement' in the summer. They were wrong. When the Unemployment Assistance Act passed through Parliament in July 1956, Ontario, along with Quebec, Alberta, and Nova Scotia, remained outside the agreement. Throughout the protracted negotiations on unemployment assistance, these other provinces looked to Frost for leadership in extracting a better cost-sharing formula out of Ottawa. Facing a provincial unemployment rate of only 2.3 per cent in the summer of 1956 and knowing he could always opt into the existing legislation if conditions deteriorated, Frost was under no immediate political pressure to act. Press coverage of his battle with Ottawa, even on the part of newspapers unsympathetic to his government, was quite favourable, generally accepting the premier's argument that St Laurent's administration was attempting to 'welsh' on Ottawa's Green Book offer and preferred a policy of relief rather than work for the jobless.[95]

In the absence of an unemployment assistance agreement, Frost's government provided municipalities with a special unconditional grant for initiating 'make work' projects late in the following winter, and in April 1957 boosted the provincial share of local relief costs from 50 to 60 per cent. Although such help was welcome, it did not induce any municipal government into assuming responsibility for the able-bodied, leaving the uninsured jobless in Ontario still without any right to public assistance. As Frost conceded during the summer of 1957, his government was 'fortunate' in avoiding 'any sizeable unemployment which might have placed us in the position of having to accept with little or no amendment, the [unemployment assistance] proposal.'[96]

By this point, however, both the political and the economic situation had altered. During the spring of 1957, his chief economic adviser, George Gathercole, pointed out that 'economic conditions [were] now changing for the worse.' Unemployment was higher than in the previous year, and Gathercole predicted it would jump even further in the upcoming winter. More dramatically, the St Laurent administration was no longer in power, defeated that spring by a rejuvenated federal Conservative party led by John Diefenbaker. During the 1957 national election, Frost had campaigned tirelessly for Diefenbaker and now said he was 'in a position to make a new and decent deal with the new administration at Ottawa.' Welfare minister Louis Cecile was told to 'lose no time in getting it taped out.' Given the worsening economic climate, 'some type of agreement' on unemployment assistance was required 'as quickly as possible.'[97]

The key objective, the premier instructed deputy minister James Band, was to get Ottawa to abolish the 0.45 threshold and simply split all relief costs straight down the middle on a fifty-fifty basis. 'Unemployables were our problem. The unemployed employables were the problem of the Federal Government. It has seemed to me to be objectionable that the Federal Government should ask us to look after our share ... and on the other hand ask us to share 50-50 with them in taking care of their share ... [I]f we were to take care of 50 per cent of their load, they should take care of 50 per cent of ours.'[98]

Although federal finance minister Donald Fleming did not 'show ... much enthusiasm about the prospect of having to put up another $11 million to have the threshold abolished,' in the end the deal with Ottawa was struck that December, after some haggling, along the lines Frost wanted. Diefenbaker's government also removed the hated 0.45 threshold from the Unemployment Assistance Act, agreeing to split all costs with the provinces, without a ceiling, on a simple fifty-fifty basis. On 1 January 1958 Ontario came under the terms of the act, providing its employables in need with a right to public assistance for the first time since 1941. 'With relief, Ontario got its way,' Frost observed when the agreement was signed. 'That result is satisfactory. [It] is a reasonable sort of 50-50 deal if unemployment is not too great. If unemployment [is] too high, [the] province may be swamped.'[99]

For Ontario's labour force – a third of which, provincial officials estimated, enjoyed no protection under unemployment insurance – the agreement could not have come too soon, as the province's economy, along with the rest of Canada's, began a steep slide into recession and worsening unemployment which would last until the early 1960s. Thanks to new terms provided to municipalities under the General Welfare Assistance Act of 1958, Queen's Park passed on the benefits of 50 per cent federal financing by reducing the local share of relief costs to only 20 per cent. Apart from this, no other changes were made. Local governments were given no help from either Ottawa or the province in hiring new staff to service the vastly expanded welfare caseload.[100]

Nor did the arrival of federal money result in more adequate scales of assistance or the definition of a decent social minimum. The Unemployment Assistance Act was an extremely flexible and open-ended document which, federal officials acknowledged, 'lays down no restrictions as to amounts or conditions of eligibility: it offers to share fifty per cent of the costs of assistance provided to individuals under *whatever scales or conditions of assistance are considered valid by provincial and municipal authorities.*' In Ontario, these conditions did not change. The new General Welfare Assistance Act simply operated under the regulations and allowance scales of the revised 1957 Unemployment Relief Act. They were kept in place, provincial officials acknowledged, 'as part of the "hold the line" financial policy of the government' in response to a worsening economic climate, and would remain unaltered until 1961 (see appendix, table 4).[101]

During the 1940s a flurry of federal, provincial, and local planning for postwar social security held out bright hopes of a 'decent social minimum' for those Ontarians who were most in need: those who, ineligible for any other social entitlement, were dependent upon relief. Against the backdrop of a hastily contrived and crisis-built relief system, whose glaring inadequacies by the Depression's end were widely acknowledged, a social policy reform agenda emerged which viewed the reorganization of the province's welfare system as the principal objective of postwar social planning and the necessary foundation for true social security. Critical to such reorganization was the creation of one general assistance program, supervised and administered by trained professionals, and consolidated within a system of county welfare units. Such a program should allow for adequate and well-defined standards of food, clothing, shelter, and other basic necessities to those in need without stigma or degradation, and offer casework services designed to rehabilitate public assistance clients, where possible, towards self-reliance.

At no time did the realization of these objectives appear more likely than in the mid-1940s. Full employment during the war reduced welfare caseloads to the barest minimum of unemployables – mostly women, children, the sick, and the elderly who could not work. Their basic needs were easily defined, and were certainly affordable to a provincial economy that had more than doubled in size and had shed the burden of Depression levels of dependency in less than five years. With the memory of mass poverty still fresh in the minds of most Ontarians, the goal of eliminating the indignity of 'the dole' enjoyed wide public support. If the concept of a 'decent and adequate social minimum' upheld by all political parties endorsing 'reconstruction' meant anything, it implied fundamental change in the delivery of services and social entitlement owing to those on relief.

Despite the hopes embodied in social policy blueprints developed for the Ontario government by Harry Cassidy, Charlotte Whitton, and Burne Heise, these goals remained mostly unfulfilled by the end of the 1950s. The collapse of welfare reform in Ontario happened quickly between 1945 and 1950 and left obvious signposts. The breakup of the Reconstruction Conference in 1946, the cynical denial of responsibility for the uninsured jobless by all levels of government, the suppression of the Toronto Welfare Council's *Cost of Living* study by business pressure the following year, the repudiation of a watered-down Welfare Units Act by the Frost administration in 1950, and the resignation of Burne Heise as deputy minister of welfare all testified to the disappearance of a public commitment to providing Ontarians most in need with an adequate and decent social minimum.

Less obvious but equally devastating to the poor was the failure of all levels of governments to continue the effort, begun by the Toronto Welfare Council, the Marsh Report, and McHenry's *Report on Food Allowances for Relief Recipients*, to define adequate minimum standards against which a meaningful poverty line could be measured as a target for social welfare reform. The willingness of governments to allow the gains achieved by universal social entitlements such as family allowances and old age security to be eaten up by grossly inadequate or unaltered shelter, heating, and clothing allowances not only eroded the value of these initiatives for the fight against poverty, but also nullified the marginal gains achieved after 1944 by the provision of nutritionally adequate food allowances. Quite simply, in postwar Ontario the poor went hungry to pay the rent (see appendix, table 5).

Even within the province's best-staffed welfare department, the rehabilitation of those on relief through professional casework, although often stated at public welfare conferences and in social work journals, was an illusory goal. Within Toronto, as elsewhere throughout Ontario during the 1950s, the moral regulation of welfare clients to ensure their eligibility for relief remained the most tangible function of welfare visitors. In turn, these visitors lacked the training, time, and motivation to do more than exercise a cursory and disciplinary influence on the lives of their mostly female clients.

Why did the 1940s movement for welfare reform collapse? As British social historian Pat Thane has argued in a different context: 'If we assume that the chief motivation behind the development of state social action has been the aspirations of the reformers, the removal or minimization of gross disparities in the distribution of material resources and of power over them, the results have been grossly disappointing. Perhaps, then, this assumption is wrong ... In no other area of policy does one expect governments to give primacy to the interests of the weak or to be motivated by single or simple pressures or principles.'[102]

This is certainly the case with welfare policy in Ontario during the 1940s and 1950s. The small numbers and unemployability of those on welfare during this era ensured their political powerlessness and social marginality. Unlike the elderly, the disabled, and the blind, who enjoyed some form of categorical social entitlement (although not adequate allowances), most of those on relief lacked the political power of families otherwise obliged to provide them with care. Both their need for and their right to a decent social minimum was discernible to social welfare professionals, but not to mainstream politicians or most members of the general public. To the extent social security was enacted in this era, it took the form of universal or insurance-based social entitlements such as unemployment and hospital insurance, family allowances, and old age security, delivered to the general population over the heads of or only incidentally to those most in need.

In Ontario, welfare reform was sideswiped by the province's postwar drive for fiscal autonomy from Ottawa, business fears of a socially defined minimum within the context of postwar collective bargaining, federal-provincial bickering over tax-rentals and responsibility for unemployment, and municipal resistance to loss of local control over taxation and welfare administration. Within the governing Conservative Party, welfare policy enjoyed little sympathy or support from George Drew, Leslie Frost, William Goodfellow, or Louis Cecile; with the departure of Burne Heise, the reform cause lost its most effective champion within the civil service. Quite clearly, the movement to reorganize public assistance also suffered from the changing political climate of the late 1940s, as social welfare issues waned in importance in the context of full employment, the Cold War, the rapid erosion of support for social democratic parties such as the CCF, and the priorities of economic growth. With only social workers to speak on their behalf, Ontario's poor were left to a profession itself in crisis from chronic understaffing, low salaries, and weak public esteem.

What endured for Ontario's poor after the Second World War was not a rationalized and reformed public welfare system but, essentially, the old relief structure put together in the 1930s, with its inadequate allowances, incompetent municipal administration, and stigmatizing practices of moral regulation still intact. When poverty was 'rediscovered' in Ontario during the 1960s, most of what a new generation of reformers found had been well known since the 1930s.

6

'Work for Relief,' Unemployment Assistance, and the Poor: The Welfare Crisis of the Early 1960s

Beginning in 1958 Ontario, like the rest of Canada, slid into a deepening recession whose effects would linger on until the summer of 1962. Throughout these four difficult years the average annual unemployment level remained at almost 5.5 per cent, more than twice the level of the previous eleven years and the highest rate of joblessness since the early 1940s. Although modest by today's standards, unemployment of this magnitude would not hit the province again until the mid-1970s.[1] Moreover, the recession struck at a time when one-third of the workforce remained unprotected by unemployment insurance, and job training and apprenticeship programs were almost non-existent. Municipalities, under the impetus of federal cost-sharing for unemployment assistance funnelled through the province's new General Welfare Assistance Act of 1958, had only just begun to extend eligibility for relief assistance to the able-bodied unemployed, and did not have the staff or the structures needed for coping with such an expanded caseload.

During these same four years, federal and provincial spending on unemployment assistance exploded to levels that stunned government officials both in Ottawa and Queen's Park. When the Unemployment Assistance Act was first contemplated in 1954, its designers believed that the program 'would remain a small one'; they estimated a maximum federal expenditure of perhaps $13.5 million per year. In its first three years of operation, in fact, Ottawa never spent more than $8.2 million under its terms.[2] Between 1958 and 1962, however, unemployment assistance was transformed from a relatively minor federal program aimed at the needs of the residual jobless not covered through unemployment insurance into Canada's largest single shared-cost program of social assistance. In the space of these four years, federal spending on the program soared from $8.2 million to more than $92 million annually, and the caseload almost quadrupled from 182,000 to more than 700,000 people. Within Ontario, the cost of General Welfare Assistance, through which unemployment assistance payments were channelled, jumped from $16.7 to over $40 million annually, or by 144 per cent over the same time period, making it by far the province's most costly social assistance program.[3]

The juxtaposition of a deteriorating economy and this sudden explosion in welfare caseloads provoked the beginning of a wide-ranging debate over welfare policy, both across Canada and within Ontario. Why were the numbers on relief spiralling upwards at a rate unseen since the early 1930s? How adequate were existing programs for meeting the needs of the poor? Were there better ways, apart from simply relief-giving, for dealing with the re-emergence of substantial and prolonged unemployment? In Ottawa the Canadian Welfare Council, fresh from its recent success in helping to push Ottawa towards a reluctant commitment to funding unemployment assistance, quickly turned its attention towards the wider issue of an integrated, comprehensive, and adequate program of social security that had been left in abeyance since the collapse of the 1946 Reconstruction Conference. In a widely publicized 1958 study entitled *Social Security for Canada*, the council, in addition to calling for more adequate protection through social insurance for the sick, the elderly, and the unemployed, also revived its earlier 1952 recommendation for a national Public Assistance Act that would provide all those in need, from whatever cause, with 'an assured minimum income below which no one should be allowed to fall' at a level 'sufficient to maintain a reasonable minimum standard of health and decency.' A Royal Commission on Social Security, the council argued, should be established to begin this process of redesigning the country's welfare state.[4]

Within Ontario, the council's manifesto was sharply dismissed. A royal commission would 'serve little purpose at this time,' deputy welfare minister James Band advised Leslie Frost and would only 'open the way for all sorts of pressure groups and others with "axes to grind."' Band was even less sympathetic towards the idea of developing any comprehensive national standards for those in need. 'The standardization of approach towards every aspect or hazard of life, and the assumption of financial and other responsibilities for almost every case encountering distress is a very large, if not dangerous, order for governments,' he warned. True progress in developing social security should be 'based upon the insurance principle' and, because of the 'severe demands ... being made on the provincial economy,' now was not the right time for reform.[5]

But while a royal commission was ruled out, the prolonged length of the recession and the continued growth in assistance caseloads did push governments at the federal, provincial, and municipal levels to seek new approaches to welfare. One of the most popular remedies harkened back to the 1930s. Once the able-bodied unemployed became eligible for social assistance in Ontario after 1958, a number of communities began compelling them to 'work for their relief' on local make-work projects such as snow-shovelling in the winter or bush-clearing and road work in the summer. As unemployment began to rise, so too did the popularity of work for relief, especially among budget-conscious local councillors and welfare administrators in rural and northern Ontario and in some new suburbs. In Chippewa, five miles south of Niagara Falls, welfare recipients were told they 'must work in future for the money they receive unless they can produce a medical certificate that they are not able to work. This applies to both sexes. The women will be expected to wash windows and clean the town hall working 16 hours per month.' Scarborough divided the monthly welfare payments of its employables by an hourly rate of $1.55 and required them to work out its value through eight hour days 'clearing ... brush from undeveloped township land.' If a man refused to report for duty without legitimate medical reasons, his assistance was cut off and his 'wife [was] advised to seek a judgment of non-support.' Township officials claimed that their program was a great success. 'It keep[s] the recipients occupied and ... encourages [them] to seek and obtain employment elsewhere, thus reducing the welfare assistance payroll.'[6]

Similar support for making the jobless work for their assistance flooded into Queen's Park from other Ontario communities as the recession persisted. 'In many cases the breadwinners don't want to work,' Mayor Gordon Stronach of London told Premier John Robarts in endorsing the idea. Men on relief liked to work out their assistance. 'It took the stigma out of receipt of welfare and helped them to retain their self respect,' Sarnia's welfare administrator argued. 'Needless to say, it also outlined to us those who did not intend to work.' These views were echoed by both the Ontario Municipal Association and the Ontario Welfare Officers Association, which also supported work for relief at their 1962 annual conventions. 'The threat of work stimulate[s] people to find other support than welfare,' the province's municipal welfare administrators claimed.[7] Band, who had heartily endorsed and developed a variety of work-for-relief projects during his long tenure as a provincial relief inspector during the 1930s, saw nothing to criticize in these ideas. Making the jobless work for their support was a 'widespread practice throughout the history of the province,' he told his federal counterpart Joe Willard. 'There are many services that can be performed by recipients in return for the assistance granted which do not greatly affect the stream of economic life in the community ... Most of these projects are basically work tests ... of a temporary nature' such as cutting wood, 'incidental road work, brushing and other projects of this type.' They did not displace regular municipal workers, Band argued, and they kept 'needy employable persons ... usefully occupied while receiving financial assistance ... without prejudice to anyone.'[8]

Of greatest significance, however, was the growing support for work-for-relief projects emanating from some of Canada's provincial premiers, as both unemployment and welfare caseloads continued to rise. At a federal-provincial conference in the late summer of 1962, Quebec premier Jean Lesage voiced his concern about 'creating a class of people whose only occupation was receiving unemployment assistance,' views which were also echoed by Manitoba premier Duff Roblin and British Columbia's W.A.C. Bennett. 'There is a hard core of people who live on relief and who might be classed as professional relief recipients,' Roblin warned. Bennett said that in the past year his government had received 'probably five times as many complaints about people receiving assistance undeservedly than they had about people not receiving assistance when required.' 'There was very great interest in this matter by practically all of the Premiers,' federal finance department officials noted, 'and repeated expressions of the view that it was undesirable from the standpoint of the workers' morale to continue unemployment assistance payments over a long period of time without demanding some work in return.'[9]

But while the campaign for reinstituting work tests for the able-bodied reflected familiar responses to relief which had dominated public opinion and government policy throughout the 1930s, much had changed by the time prolonged unemployment returned once more in the late 1950s and early 1960s. Most important, perhaps, was the new strength of organized labour, particularly in the public sector. At a time of high unemployment, unions wanted extended unemployment insurance benefits and job creation projects with real wages. They did not want the restoration of punitive practices which, as the director of the National Union of Public Employees put it, 'create unemployment for regular municipal employees.' Despite a 'strong movement on the part of' ... municipalities' for work relief, Ontario welfare minister Louis Cecile warned Robarts that 'vocal groups, particularly labour unions ... are vigorously opposed to the restoration of this practice,' a point underscored by federal unemployment assistance director Dick Splane. 'I am inclined to believe that no municipality [in Ontario] will want to push its position on the matter too far,' Splane argued. 'And I do not think in view of Labor's position on the matter, that if it reached the floor of the House the opposition parties would want to espouse the municipalities favoring work relief.'[10]

Of almost equal importance was the repugnance, reflecting a changed public mood, towards policies that explicitly punished the unemployed along lines familiar from the 1930s. 'Older citizens ... will remember the "make-work" schemes of the depression, the devices by which relief recipients were required to "earn" the meagre aid received but which so often robbed this work of all dignity because it served no useful social purpose,' the *Belleville Intelligencer* commented on learning of Chippewa's work relief scheme. 'Lacking such a purpose, the enforced labor came very near to being a punishment for poverty.' According to the *Peterborough Examiner*, residents of that city 'were ashamed when a similar proposal was made by a local alderman.' Giving in to such demands would only allow 'penny-pinching municipalities ... to exploit those on welfare as a cheap source of labour for municipal projects.' It was a 'sure way to bring back the workhouse.' Other newspapers drew attention to the stark contrast between the tremendous affluence produced by the boom conditions of the past two decades and the pressing needs of the 'new poor' on relief. 'They are poor in the midst of plenty,' the *Globe and Mail* observed. 'They must count their pennies when people just like them are throwing around dollar bills.' Reinstituting work tests in the midst of so much prosperity also troubled the *Toronto Star*. 'Our wealthy society has the obligation to provide [the unemployed] with work at a living wage. Failing this, it has the obligation to support them and their families decently – not in exchange for forced labor, not as a matter of charity, but simply as a matter of right.'[11]

The decisive opposition to work for relief, however, came from Ottawa. Beginning in March 1961, federal officials presiding over the Unemployment Assistance Act told Queen's Park they would not provide any cost-shared funding to municipalities that made work for relief a condition of entitlement. The impetus for this decision, ironically, came not from within the Department of National Health and Welfare, which had administered the Unemployment Assistance Act since its inception in 1956, but from the Auditor-General's Office. Moreover, it soon became apparent that closing down local work relief schemes had more to do with the search for greater control over federal spending than with any moral repugnance towards punishing the poor.

The Unemployment Assistance Act was a highly unusual piece of legislation, unlike any other form of federal cost-sharing with the provinces. As part of the elaborate political compromise needed to bring

Ontario, Quebec, Alberta, and Nova Scotia under its terms after 1958, the Unemployment Assistance Act, unlike other shared-cost programs for hospital insurance, old age, blind, and disability pensions, contained no accompanying federal regulations and relied completely on provincial auditors' statements to confirm that Ottawa's money was being correctly spent.[12] Moreover, it contained only the loosest definition of the target population. As Health and Welfare administrators conceded, although the legislation required 'that persons included in the reimbursement claim to the Federal Government be unemployed and in need, IT DOES NOT DEFINE 'UNEMPLOYED' OR 'NEED.' An aim of the Act has been to fit into existing but diverse provincial general assistance programs in such a way as to share in their costs without imposing restrictive conditions.'[13] In other words, the language of the Unemployment Assistance Act was left deliberately vague. This, combined with the lack of accompanying regulations and the total reliance on provincial auditing, gave officials in the federal Department of Health and Welfare no independent capacity to scrutinize municipal welfare financial statements in order to ascertain how their money was being spent.

The federal auditor-general did possess this authority, however. As expenditures on unemployment assistance began to soar over $51 million by 1961, the legislation increasingly caught his eye as a classic example of one federal program out of control. Repeatedly in his annual reports after 1959, the auditor-general directed withering criticism at both the Unemployment Assistance Act and its administrators within the Department of Health and Welfare for presiding over poorly drafted legislation replete with open-ended funding, ambiguous terminology, no regulations, and seemingly no administrative checks on the appropriateness of provincial and local spending practices.[14] In order to demonstrate his point, the auditor-general sent his own staff, in 1961, to scrutinize spending under the act in selected local welfare departments. Within Scarborough, they uncovered the township's routine practice of requiring the able-bodied jobless to work for relief; when pushed for explanations, provincial welfare department officials freely admitted they had no objections to the use of unemployment assistance funds for these purposes which were 'customary long before the senior governments shared in the cost of assistance.'[15]

The auditor-general was unimpressed. Men and women working out their relief for local governments were in fact 'earning wages and reimbursing the municipality with the wages so earned for the relief received.' In other words, they were not unemployed under the meaning of the legislation. Municipalities using their labour were, in effect, diverting federal money intended for assisting the jobless to subsidizing their own work programs for community improvement. This was a totally unauthorized usage of unemployment assistance funds and should not be cost-shared by Ottawa, the auditor-general insisted.[16] It was in response to these criticisms that the health and welfare department explicitly told Ontario that work-for-relief schemes in the province would be ineligible for funding after March 1961.

It is clear that the explosion of controversy over work relief caught federal Health and Welfare officials administering the program completely by surprise. 'When the federal unemployment assistance legislation was drawn up this type of situation was not anticipated,' Willard told his provincial counterpart, Band, and so the act itself was silent on the question of work relief.[17] Although recognizing that the issue was highly controversial, the department's key policy-makers clearly had no desire to reintroduce work tests on the jobless. Most senior Health and Welfare administrators such as Willard, his predecessor George Davidson, or the director of unemployment assistance, Dick Splane, were either graduates of Schools of Social Work or had served key apprenticeships within the Canadian Welfare Council before moving into government. Unlike Band, whose views on welfare were shaped during his years as a provincial relief inspector in the 1930s, these federal administrators shared a professional social work consensus on welfare matters which viewed work relief programs as harsh, punitive, and degrading. When given a window of opportunity by the auditor-general, they were only too happy to eliminate federal cost-sharing for the practice. Work relief derived from 'old Poor Law concepts' that reflected a 'punitive approach to relief recipients,' Splane told Willard. 'Being requested to join a work gang may be physically and emotionally more damaging than being without employment,' and such projects were 'unlikely to help the individual to obtain new skills.' Willard agreed. Work relief risked the danger of disentitling those who 'might be unable for justifiable reasons, including that of health, to participate in such projects,' he told Band. It also reintroduced 'the problem of distinguishing between employables and unemployables for cost-sharing purposes,' which the open-endedness of the Unemployment Assistance Act had been designed to forestall.[18]

Federal officials also feared that if work relief caught on as a widespread municipal response to rising unemployment, Ottawa would slowly but surely be drawn ever more closely into a tangled web of subsidizing local public works budgets and perhaps displacing regularly paid municipal workers. 'How [can] the federal and provincial governments ... avoid becoming enmeshed in the normal public works and "housekeeping" programs of the municipalities if work for relief projects involving welfare funds were developed?' Willard asked his provincial counterparts. Keeping a semblance of fiscal control over the loosely drafted Unemployment Assistance Act was difficult enough when the funding was restricted only to providing relief. If it were expanded to include works projects, under legislation that lacked any independent federal audit or regulations, the administrative problems would become horrendous. Like the auditor-general, in other words, Health and Welfare officials viewed work relief as a policy which, if widely adopted, would immensely complicate, not alleviate, the problem of bringing ballooning welfare expenditures under control.[19]

Despite bitter protests from Ontario and its municipalities when funding for such programs was cut off, and growing demands from other provinces for making work relief eligible for cost-sharing under unemployment assistance, federal officials continued to resist the call to make the unemployed work for their assistance. If work-testing was such a good idea, Health and Welfare officials argued, let the provinces subsidize such schemes on their own and prove it. Within Ontario, neither Band nor his political superiors were prepared to pick up the challenge. A month after receiving the news that federal unemployment assistance funding would no longer be available for such projects, Band informed all municipal welfare administrators that the province was also cutting out its cost-sharing for them as well. By the end of 1961, Ontario welfare officials were willing to concede privately, although not publicly, that since such projects 'inevitably led to administrative complications,' work relief was an area 'the province was well advised to avoid.'[20]

Ironically, despite the flurry of publicity over work relief as a means of reducing unemployment assistance caseloads, both Ottawa and Queen's Park realized that most of the rapid expansion in the program's costs was caused by growing numbers of unemployables, not the able-bodied jobless. Even in the depth of the 1958–62 recession, employables within Ontario made up only 35 per cent of the General Welfare Assistance caseload, and only 30 per cent of those aided through the Unemployment Assistance Act across Canada as a whole (see appendix, table 6). The remainder was made up of those too ill, too old, or too handicapped to work, or mothers with dependent children who did not qualify for mothers' allowance benefits. As Health and Welfare officials in Ottawa conceded, the title of the legislation was really both a misnomer and a source of embarrassment, causing it to be 'misunderstood by the population at large and by many public officials.' Although it did not start out that way, in fact by 1962 the Unemployment Assistance Act had become a federal general welfare assistance scheme providing cost-sharing for those who could not qualify for or live on the benefits provided through existing categorical social programs.[21]

Why was an 'unemployment' assistance act providing two-thirds of its aid to those who were incapable of working? And why were their numbers growing rapidly after 1958? Unemployables became eligible for federal funding a result of Ontario premier Leslie Frost's insistence that this was the only basis on which Ontario would contemplate entering into the unemployment assistance program. Once Ottawa's elaborate statistical formula designed to exclude a province's normal unemployable relief burden from coverage was scrapped by the Diefenbaker government in 1958, all provinces, including Ontario, were handed an unprecedented opportunity to modernize and expand their general social assistance programs, which had previously been financed exclusively out of local and provincial revenues, and receive 50 per cent federal funding for every dollar they spent. The result, after 1958, was a major restructuring of social assistance across Canada on a scale unseen since the Great Depression. Herein lay the roots of most of the exponential growth in the caseload size and costs of unemployment assistance between 1958 and 1962.

In the Maritimes, poor laws were finally repealed and provincial governments began sharing the cost of local relief for the first time in order to take advantage of federal funding. Quebec, in the throes of the Quiet Revolution, took over complete administration of social welfare from local governments and charities. Manitoba, Nova Scotia, and New Brunswick abolished separate mothers' allowance schemes in favour of single general assistance programs, cost-shared through federal unemployment assistance. Within Ontario, through the General Welfare Assistance Act of 1958, the municipal share of relief was cut in half from 40 to only 20 per cent. The new availability of federal unemployment assistance funding made up all the difference.[22]

Moreover, under the revised terms of the unemployment assistance legislation after 1958, federal funding was now made available to institutionalized unemployables, chiefly the elderly and the disabled, in so-called homes for special care as well as to municipal governments willing to top up the inadequate $65 monthly benefits paid to those living on existing categorical allowances for old age, blindness, or disability. In fact, almost the only provincial and local welfare costs excluded from federal funding after 1958 were child welfare programs, care of the mentally ill, medical relief, aid to mothers with children administered through separate mothers' allowance programs, and the growing administrative costs of welfare itself. As a consequence, after 1958 provinces tried to 'case-shift' as many welfare clients as possible out of these programs, for which they were entirely responsible, and onto the federal unemployment assistance program. With the availability of federal money, provinces and local governments were also able to liberalize eligibility requirements and benefits levels modestly in their social assistance programs, a development that paid particular dividends to single people on welfare, widows under sixty-five, and to the elderly within nursing and old age homes.[23]

Unemployment, although important, was thus only a small part of the background reasons behind the enormous expansion in unemployment assistance costs between 1958 and 1962, a point underscored by the continued growth in unemployment assistance costs and caseloads long after economic recovery occurred in 1963. By 1965, spending on unemployment assistance would top $215 million annually, supporting a caseload of almost 800,000 people.[24] The remarkable growth of unemployment assistance during these years was really 'one indication of the unmet need that existed prior to the adoption of the program' in provinces such as Ontario which had failed to develop their own welfare programs until the arrival of open-ended federal funding after 1958. As Joe Willard observed, by the early 1960s unemployment assistance had become 'one of the most important developments in social welfare in Canada.'[25]

Despite the infusion of cost-shared federal dollars after 1958, life for those struggling to get by on general welfare assistance in Ontario did not markedly improve. Within the province's largest cities, such as Toronto, the widening gap between provincial and municipal welfare allowances and the real cost of living was critical, particularly with respect to shelter allowances. For a family of four, the shelter allowance had remained frozen at an effective ceiling of $40 a month since 1951, despite a 60 per cent increase in the cost of living over the same ten-year period (see appendix, table 7). During the 1950s food allowances had risen by only 30 per cent.[26] The end result for a mother with three children attempting to live on general welfare assistance in 1961 was a monthly welfare income of $105. Even including federal family allowance benefits, this sum approximated only 48 per cent of the minimum needed to reach a basic standard of adequacy, according to detailed calculations by the Toronto Social Planning Council. Single people under the age of sixty-five fared even worse, getting only $46 monthly or 29 per cent of the minimum budgetary standard (see appendix, table 8).[27]

The human costs of this structural gap received widespread publicity in the city's press throughout the early years of the 1960s through a well-orchestrated campaign for more adequate welfare allowances led by Toronto's Social Planning Council. 'We find people on relief are just half way through a month and out of food money,' a former director pointed out. 'They have used that food money to pay the rent.' Lillian Thomson, head of Toronto's largest social work agency, called on labour and other community groups to 'join in a war against poverty' early in 1961, and singled out housing as the key arena for action. 'Money for food, fuel, and clothing [is] being diverted to keep a roof of sorts over the family's head. The wolf is at the door alright, but he's looking for the rent.' To prove her point, Thomson cited the typical case of 'a young deserted mother who has to pay $60 a month for two rooms, yet her shelter allowance is only $27 a month ... Families spend food money for rent when threatened with eviction then seek help from the Red Cross, the churches, or others for food. This is typical of what's happening.' Rent allowances set at 'simply ridiculous' levels were condemning welfare families to lives of 'hunger, cold, and shame' in 'squalid, vermin-infested houses.' One fifty-three-year-old widow living alone on a welfare allowance of $57 a month spent $40 simply on rent for a 'small, chilly top floor room in Parkdale.' 'The biggest problem is food,' she told a reporter. 'I have 45 cents a day to spend for food, and find that I have to live mostly on bread, porridge, and soup ... I've been on relief for the past eight months. At first it wasn't so bad, but lately I seem to be hungry a lot of the time.'[28]

It was not long before Toronto's press began to give the problem of inadequate welfare incomes wide coverage. In a series of devastating columns, the *Toronto Star*'s Pierre Berton lambasted the province and the city for providing shelter allowances that drove welfare clients into abject misery. Drawing stories from case files provided by the city's private social agencies, Berton told of a fifty-one-year-old single woman 'who can't get a job because she's over age' living on a welfare allowance of $48.50 a month. 'As her tiny, furnished room costs $10 a week, she has $8 left for everything else. And she lives entirely on cream cheese, skim milk, stale bread, and packaged soup. She never goes out, for she has no street car fare, she has no entertainment. She buys no clothes or books or magazines. She is, in short, a vegetable, sustaining life and nothing more.' A mother with seven children, after paying shelter costs, had only $20 a week left over for food. 'How do you properly feed seven children and one adult on $20 a week? The answer is that you don't ... All Mrs. Lacer can do is to buy bulk food to stave off hunger pangs – gelatins, oatmeals, stale bread, beans, macaroni, and potatoes.'[29]

Berton then sent his research assistant out to find a five-room house at $40 a month, the city's maximum shelter allowance for a family of six. She could not come even close. After checking with ten real estate agencies and searching through 171 ads in the press, she came up with only two listing houses below $100 a month. One had no furnace and was infested with rats. The other was a 'ramshackle tenement' with broken windows, torn up linoleum floors, and holes in the walls. As for apartments, 'the rock bottom low was $60 a month for two rooms with a kitchen. There wasn't a flat available within $20 of the allowances.' Berton's conclusion was straightforward. 'Hundreds ... go hungry because they must use their food budget to pay the rent.'[30]

Other Toronto reporters confirmed the same results. One, who with his wife and three children tried to live on the city's general welfare assistance allowance for two weeks, discovered that 'the amounts allotted for shelter and heat are so unreal that food money must be diverted to these purposes.' Granted a maximum of $33.35 a month to pay for shelter, he discovered housing 'couldn't possibly be obtained for our family of five for less than $80 or $90 a month. Obviously rent money would have to come off the food bill. What would be left?' Two weeks later he found out. '[We] were an irritable, tired group, lacking energy, and lacking ambition. We were sick to death of cheese, of porridge and bread, or potatoes and thin stews, of stale loaves and the knowledge that we didn't even have a dime for a telephone call.'[31]

When the Scott Mission began to distribute free lunchtime sandwiches to children of families on welfare, even NBC news got into the act showing film of more than forty kids lining up for food at the mission on the Huntley and Brinkley evening news. The resulting publicity mortified the city's politicians. The Social Planning Council and the Labour Council both denounced the need for children of the poor to 'parade to a communal soup kitchen, feeling like second class citizens.' But civic leaders issued angry denials that welfare allowances were inadequate. News coverage of hungry Toronto children was 'irresponsible, unfounded, and slanderous,' Mayor Nathan Phillips claimed. 'No evidence of anyone starving ... because of inability to purchase food' had been reported to the city's Health Department. 'Irresponsible press and television reports which have been carried round the world have damaged the city's reputation.' Implicitly shifting the blame to relief families themselves, city welfare commissioner Robena Morris argued that no one need go hungry, 'if welfare money was spent wisely.'[32]

Privately, however, city officials acknowledged that the allowances they paid were inadequate and that these gross discrepancies caused problems for their workers. Given the department's large turnover in staff, it was essential to remind new personnel continually of the 'difference between the actual financial needs of the people for food, rent,

clothing, etc. and the allowance which can be granted under the regulations and departmental policy,' district supervisors were told. 'The private agencies tend to work on the basis of what they consider actual
needs of the family and expect us to assist on that basis.'[33]

On the issue of housing costs, however, even Morris conceded that
there was 'too much discrepancy between the actual rate of rental and
the shelter allowance' and that existing provincial ceilings on cost-
sharing for housing welfare recipients were 'not sufficient to meet minimum shelter requirements in most instances in a large city.'[34] In the
spring of 1961 Alderman Fred Beavis, chairman of the City of Toronto's Public Welfare Committee, led a delegation of civic officials to
welfare minister Louis Cecile's office demanding that something be
done to bring provincial shelter allowances into line with big city rents.
'Our welfare people [are] being driven crazy with cries of people being
hungry and starving to death,' he told Cecile. Two months later, in July
1961, the province responded by implementing, for the first time, differentials in shelter allowance ceilings it would cost-share for families,
but not single people, in cities with populations over 100,000. A 20 per
cent increase boosted maximum permissible shelter payments to $65 a
month for unheated premises. For welfare families living on shelter allowances frozen at levels set in 1951, this jump was long overdue. They
would not see another one until a further $10 a month hike was allowed
in 1965. However, even with this increase, the new shelter allowances
were 'still inadequate in terms of the actual rentals which must be paid
in a large city, particularly by families with children,' Toronto's mayor
told provincial officials. [35]

Minimal adequacy in relief allowances, however, was simply not a
priority issue for senior officials in the province's Department of Public
Welfare. Instead, the key energies of the department with respect to
welfare reform in these years were directed towards ensuring that every
effort possible was being made by local governments to control the
rapid expansion in welfare costs and caseloads. The first line of attack
was attempting to enforce more vigilant standards of home investigation into the lives of welfare recipients. The focus of their concern once
again remained Toronto, source of the fastest-rising growth in general
welfare assistance recipients and almost 27 per cent of all provincial
spending on direct relief.[36] Once the employable unemployed became
eligible for social assistance after 1958, the city's welfare department
gave up attempting to make home visits in order to check up on eligibility for relief. Because of 'insufficient staff for the volume of ...
work,' city welfare administrators simply handed applicants the appro-

priate forms 'to be completed by them in their homes and brought back to the district office for interview the next day.'[37]

Provincial welfare inspectors were appalled by these practices and, in most cases in which they reinvestigated and cancelled aid, the issue was the same: proving whether husbands really had deserted their families or whether men were living with welfare mothers common-law. 'Mrs. S. [a mother of five children] stated that husband deserted her,' one provincial investigator explained in a typical reinvestigation report of a Toronto welfare case file. '[I] called at 11:00 a.m. Two men and a woman in the kitchen – men left by back stairs ... House filthy, woman in shorts, children half dressed. During the conversation the woman admitted that she is living common-law with an ... unemployed [man] ... It was explained to her that ... if she intends to continue living common-law, her welfare assistance will be cancelled.' The common-law husband of another mother of five was discovered 'spend[ing] almost every day with her "because she needs a man in the house," but returns at night to his mother's home ... in order that the woman quali-fies for Welfare Assistance.' In other examples drawn to the deputy minister's attention, men reported to have deserted families granted city relief were found by provincial welfare investigators to be still living at home and working. In Toronto it was not uncommon for 'less than 10% of [general welfare] cases [to] have been visited in their own homes.' Without such investigations, 'we are going to have an ever-increasing number of persons receiving public assistance fraudulently.'[38]

James Band needed no reminding of the importance of home visits. As Ontario's roving relief inspector and chief trouble-shooter for the Department of Public Welfare during the 1930s, he had personally put in place systems of rigorous and systematic home investigation at the local level wherever he found relief costs running out of control. Con-sequently, Band lost no time in cracking the whip over the heads of Toronto's welfare department, the only 'major centre' in Ontario where routine home visits were not occurring. In March 1961 the province issued new regulations under the General Welfare Assistance Act re-quiring that every municipality conduct a home visit of welfare clients when they initially applied for aid or, in emergency cases only, not less than two weeks after relief was granted. When Toronto mayor Donald Summerville, along with a Board of Control delegation, protested to Leslie Frost that they could not possibly afford to hire the increased staff needed to comply with this new regulation, Band took his case directly to the premier. 'It has been demonstrated, time and again,' the deputy minister argued, 'that statements on the part of applicants inter-viewed in relief offices are incomplete, inadequate, and uncertain.' The true picture could 'only be brought to light when a visit is made to the home.' Nowhere was this more critical than in the 'numerous cases involving desertion, separation, and common-law unions.' With these women it was 'almost impossible' to know what was going on 'without a most careful screening through home investigations.' Band insisted that 'because of the reluctance of Toronto authorities to carry out ... home investigations I am restive as to whether there is actual need for the assistance that is being granted by the City to many individuals and families.' R.A. Farrell, the premier's executive assistant, agreed. 'Relief applications could run away like wild fire' without detailed home investigations, he advised Leslie Frost.

The deputy minister won his point. Frost agreed to give Toronto a three-month period of grace in which to hire the necessary additional staff systematic home visiting would require. Otherwise, welfare investigation in the city would have to be brought into line with practices occurring elsewhere in the province. Nor would Queen's Park provide any additional financial assistance to defray the city's increased expenditure on welfare staffing. 'We would be open for a very substantial cost if the practice of provincial sharing in administration costs were to be maintained throughout the Province,' Band argued in advising against such a move.[39]

Systematic home visiting was only one of a number of initiatives launched by Band's department in these years to bring welfare costs under control. A second was his campaign to place the maximum $65 monthly benefits paid to the elderly, the disabled, and the blind through categorical programs cost-shared with Ottawa on a 'budgetary needs' basis. As federal Health and Welfare officials in Ottawa conceded, despite a 'lack of data to determine [their] adequacy,' these categorical allowances had nonetheless 'helped to establish a national minimum level of aid ... [since] most recipients are granted the maximum benefit of $65.'[40] In principle, switching these *de facto* flat-rate benefits to individualized allowances calculated according to budgetary need could have enhanced benefits for some clients, since in 'some cases (particularly in large urban areas) [recipients] might qualify for ... amounts up to a maximum of $85 monthly,' Band noted. In practice, however, this was highly unlikely. Within Toronto, where living costs were highest and where general welfare assistance was already calculated on a budgetary needs basis, no single unemployables were getting $85 a month. Instead, the provincial regulations capped their monthly allowances at a maximum of $57, and city officials were already telling Queen's Park that it was 'questionable whether [this] amount ... can be considered of minimum adequacy ... in a large municipality where the majority of recipients are unemployable and there is no other income.'[41]

It is clear that Band really viewed the flat-rate allowances and the 'rigid' and 'inflexible' eligibility criteria Ottawa attached to categorical programs as inherently wasteful, not parsimonious. Federal regulations governing the exemption of liquid assets for means-testing 'in all three programs [allowed] recipients [to] have very substantial assets – in amounts not normally considered to be representative of needy circumstances – and still qualify for an allowance,' Band told his minister, Louis Cecile. By placing these programs, like general welfare assistance, on the basis of a 'budgetary allowance ... based on individual minimum needs,' Band was convinced 'there would ... be a great many individuals who would qualify for an amount less than the present flat-rate allowance of $65. In addition, other persons now receiving an allowance would not qualify for any assistance (under the budgetary approach) because of the substantial amount of liquid assets in their possession and which, from any reasonable point of view, would be regarded as more than sufficient to maintain [them] without resorting to the use of public funds, as is now permitted under the present federal regulations.'[42] Simply put, Band rejected out of hand any attempt to define or deliver national minimum standards of social assistance and chafed against federal programs which, even implicitly, compelled Queen's Park to match a level of need determined outside its jurisdiction. These views would be critical in negotiations leading to new federal-provincial cost-sharing arrangements governing social assistance in the years ahead.

In other moves to shift welfare costs, permanently unemployable men with families, who previously received benefits through the mothers' allowance program financed exclusively by Ontario, were transferred to the general welfare assistance caseload. Provincial officials 'admit[ted] quite frankly ... the primary reason ... [was] to obtain the additional financial assistance available under the Unemployment Assistance Agreement.' A new categorical program for widows and single women aged sixty and over was also created early in 1963 to take advantage of federal cost-sharing through unemployment assistance. Through this plan, former clients of mothers' allowances, cut off from the program when their last child turned eighteen, effectively gained eligibility for old age assistance five years before men. The numbers of such women living in poverty far exceeded the province's initial expectations. Within a year, almost 7000 women aged sixty and over were collecting the allowance and, two years later, their numbers were only marginally less than the mothers' allowance caseload itself. Almost 6000 senile, handicapped, and mentally ill patients within Ontario's mental hospitals were also shifted over the next five years to private 'homes for special care' in order to qualify for cost-shared federal funding as 'unemployables' under special provisions of the Unemployment Assistance Act. But while new sources of federal cost-sharing were exploited to the limit in order to subsidize the existing social welfare caseload, Ontario's welfare department refused to tell municipal governments about 'the possibility of federal sharing of amounts paid [through general welfare assistance] in excess of the provincial rates.' On this issue, Ontario officials were determined to maintain complete autonomy over their regulation of local welfare ceilings. 'The province would lose control if it passed on to the federal government claims from the municipalities based on assistance granted in excess of the provincial rates,' Dorothea Crittenden, one of Band's key executive officers, told Health and Welfare officials in agreeing to forgo this extra aid for Ontario communities that might wish to enrich their welfare benefits.[43]

Tracking down husbands who deserted their families was also pursued more systematically by the province. In 1961 Band's department created its own Deserted Wives Unit to help local governments trace the whereabouts of absconding fathers whose families were filling up welfare caseloads. Investigating about 500 cases a year, the unit claimed that its 40 per cent success rate was saving the province $100,000 annually. But some local officials questioned the effectiveness of this activity. 'Once they leave, very few of them come back and live as a happy family ... [I]f an order is made for $10.00, $50.00 or $100.00 a week, if it is not paid what good is [it]? ... Where is the solution? He will desert again.' The head of the unit, however, reminded municipal welfare officers that its activities were 'not entirely confined to husband hunting.' The work also included checking out 'desertions of convenience' in which fathers fled 'so the Welfare Department can meet the bills of the house. When they have reached a nice level he will return.' In a 'very large number of cases' there was also 'a lot of collusion between a man and his wife. If pressure is put on she can sometimes quite easily find him.' At other times early and late calls could be very productive in uncovering fraudulent claims of abandonment, or 'situations where there is alleged prostitution or other behaviour.' In other words, much of the unit's work involved monitoring the lives of the women left behind, rather than the men who fled. Since most husbands, in fact, could not be found, local resentment against the increased welfare costs produced by family fragmentation was directed against mothers seeking assistance. 'The big problem,' local officals complained, 'is the person who has been deserted, the unmarried mother and types of that kind.' For these women, community welfare administrators often had little sympathy. 'There must be some reason why men leave their families,' one pointed out. 'I hate to admit it, but there may be some women who are hard to live with. We let these men drift, we don't make too great an effort to bring them back.'[44]

Of all the remedies put forward for shrinking the assistance caseload in the early 1960s none proved more popular, at least in theory, than 'rehabilitation' of the long-term welfare client. The popularity of rehabilitating the poor flowed from a variety of sources: the predominance of psychiatric over community social work throughout the 1950s; success at rehabilitating veterans after the Second World War; the growing conviction that most unemployment was structural rather than cyclical in origin and was caused by the impact of rapid technological change on an insufficiently skilled workforce. Rehabilitation was also perceived as the most effective response to the growing moral panic that welfare families were reproducing themselves across two or even three generations, a fear soon captured in the richly evocative idea of a culture of poverty that swept through North American discussions of welfare in the early 1960s.[45]

Above all, the appeal of rehabilitation can be traced to its close fit with beliefs deeply entrenched since the nineteenth century concerning the character and motivation of the poor. This congruence was clearly visible in a series of studies of Long-term Assistance Families undertaken by Ontario's public welfare department in the early 1960s. Ostensibly, the idea behind these investigations, financed through welfare grants provided by Ottawa, was to show the benefits of intensive casework upon families mired in poverty. In Toronto, Hamilton, and Windsor, representative samples of one hundred families living on welfare for over a year were given to social workers whose normal caseloads were cut in half. Over a six-month period, these families were subjected to repeated visits, in some cases up to forty, to see if concentrated intervention by the caseworker could rehabilitate the family and get it off welfare. Control samples of one hundred similar families in two of the communities were also chosen to monitor the effect of routine levels of investigation.

All three studies produced the same result. There were significant differences in the proportion of cases closed after intensive and repeated visiting, compared with the control samples subjected to routine investigation. In Toronto, 42 per cent of study group cases were closed after the six-month trial period, and only 23 per cent of the control group. In Hamilton the respective figures were 56 per cent and 21 per cent. In Windsor, where no control group was selected, 32 per cent of the families subjected to intensive investigation had their cases closed.[46] These experiments, which represented some of the first research ever conducted by Ontario's public welfare department, were deemed a great success, proving conclusively, according to Band, that 'a high proportion of long-term assistance families will, with stimulation and guidance, become independent within a comparatively brief time.' The availability of welfare itself emerged from the research as a basic cause of long-term dependency. 'We should sometimes pause in the midst of planning what we can do *for* people to ask what we do *to* people in granting them public assistance.' Out of the three hundred cases examined intensively by these investigations, one client's comment most stood out in his mind. 'The worst thing the Department ever did was to give my husband his first welfare cheque.'[47]

On closer scrutiny, however, these results were far more ambiguous than the department claimed. In Toronto, only half the cases were closed because the family head found work. Of the remaining families, 43 per cent were simply transferred from the general assistance to the mothers' allowance caseload, and almost all the rest were cut off either through the discovery of undisclosed income or the existence of a 'man in the house.' Four 'voluntarily' withdrew their claims. Similarly, in Hamilton, one-third of the case closures were due either to case-shifting onto mothers' allowance or because the families were ruled ineligible for assistance.[48] In what sense these results constituted 'rehabilitation' as opposed to bureaucratic expediency was questionable. Since no follow-up of those who found employment was done after the studies ended, it is also impossible to say whether any lasting benefit was derived from this brief spell of intensive scrutiny. Many quite possibly took temporary work of any kind to escape from the unremitting gaze of twice-weekly home visits.

What does emerge clearly is the extent to which the project closely resembled nineteenth-century crusades for 'moral uplift' and character reformation among the poor. In none of the studies, for example, was the adequacy of welfare allowances or minimum wage employment, the quality of housing, the absence of vocational training, or lack of day care deemed worthy of mention as background causes of long-term dependency. Instead, virtually all the case commentary focused on the moral condition of families under surveillance, with inadequate housekeeping, hypochondria, and malingering the most common sources of caseworkers' complaints. Women deemed overweight were told to diet and to 'clean up their rooms.' Men were instructed to shave and use dentures. 'Decent housekeeping' was demanded as an imperative in all the studies. Children who were 'filthy and unwashed,' apartments with a 'strong smell' or with 'blinds and curtains falling down' and a 'veritable shamble of "things" piled all over' were recurring images used as evidence of the need for moral rehabilitation. Men who had decided that 'welfare assistance is an institution of which [they] can be justly proud' were given detailed lists to keep track of calls on employers, and their families were threatened with loss of assistance 'as a means of motivation.' Women suspected of living in common-law unions were visited intensively in order to detect hidden or phantom husbands. 'For most mothers, there is much guilt and conflict, so the welfare office is never informed,' the Toronto study observed. Once a 'sound trust [was] built up' through repeated visits, however, evidence of cohabitation could be discovered and their allowances cancelled. Many long-term assistance families had simply 'formed the habit of unemployment,' including deserted mothers with young children. Once their offspring were 'old enough to attend school and look after themselves' they too were expected to 'work toward full employment.' One father with a wife and ten children, getting $245 a month as well as free medical care through welfare, was told to 'lower his sights' when holding out for a job that paid at least $260 monthly for full-time work. Another man medically classified as only partially employable due to 'chronic neuritis, general disability, and chronic rheumatism' was diagnosed on the basis of 'a few visits' by a caseworker as 'immature and ... pushing the responsibility of supporting his family on to his wife.' He too was told to 'register for employment.'[49]

In all three studies, 'primary emphasis was placed on social rather than financial factors' as the key causes of long-term dependency. 'It was found that people withdrew from public assistance under frequent visiting' for reasons that could 'only be inferred,' although descriptions of clients who were 'generally resentful,' 'extreme[ly] hostile,' 'aggressive,' angry about 'hounding,' or suffering from a 'persecution complex' were endemic throughout the studies.[50] But the moral lesson of the research was quite plain. Hard-core poverty stemmed from the cultural and character deficiencies of the poor, or as the Toronto study put it, their 'general subjective inadequacies.' These defects could be remedied in many cases through intensive home visiting. Chronically dependent people 'display surprising resourcefulness and self-reliance when confronted by necessity,' the researchers concluded. 'The direct and firm approach of the welfare visitor gave structure and motivation to

some recipients who had let themselves adopt a rather passive acceptance of their life situation.' Uplift, in short, was still Ontario's principal
strategy for breaking the cycle of poverty.[51]

Within Ottawa the search for a new approach to financing and administering Canada's mushrooming welfare programs was underway by the
spring of 1962. A variety of internal bureaucratic factors converged to
drive the federal government and the provinces together in welfare
reform in the early 1960s. The most important was Ottawa's increasing
unhappiness with the Unemployment Assistance Act itself. As the auditor-general continually pointed out, the deliberate ambiguity of the legislation, its lack of regulations, and its failure to allow federal auditing
of provincial or local expenditures provided Ottawa with a poor vehicle
for controlling or even understanding rising welfare costs. When unemployment assistance expenditure almost doubled in a single year from
$51 million to more than $92 million between 1961 and 1962, this
absence of regulatory control within an open-ended cost-sharing program became a growing sore spot in relations between National Health
and Welfare and the Department of Finance. Early in 1962 a Treasury
Board Interdepartmental Committee on Unemployment Assistance was
established to sort out what could be done about improving 'the rather
limited controls ... the federal government is now able to exercise'
under the act.[52]

The committee was given two tasks: to draft a set of federal regulations for an amended Unemployment Assistance Act and to 'consider
the most appropriate approach for a new public assistance program,' an
alternative that officials in National Health and Welfare had been discussing tentatively for the past two years. After three meetings, its members quickly concluded that little was to be gained by attempting to
amend the act. Because the legislation was six years old, too much time
had elapsed to expect provinces to agree to a detailed set of federal
regulations that attempted to 'clarify ... [its] terms ... improve ... standards in provincial programs and strengthen ... federal control,' Ottawa's
three criteria for reform. A far better approach would be to abandon the
legislation altogether and replace it with a new general assistance scheme
that would include all the categorical assistance programs.[53]

When the provincial premiers raised the issue of work for relief as a
means of cutting back on rising unemployment assistance costs during
the summer, federal planning for a new public assistance act gained
extra momentum since, as deputy health and welfare minister Joe Willard
put it, Ottawa did not want 'to get entangled with this complicated
question' for reasons already discussed. Health and Welfare officials

instead hoped to divert discussions with the provinces over work relief into a more wide-ranging process of developing a new comprehensive public assistance act, through the proposed National Council of Welfare, an advisory body composed of federal and provincial deputy welfare ministers which Ottawa hoped to create in the upcoming session of Parliament. Officials within the department were soon at work drafting proposals for a new public assistance act that could be included in the 1963 Speech from the Throne.[54]

Although the Canada Assistance Plan, which would ultimately emerge from these discussions, would form the centrepiece of Ottawa's War on Poverty launched with great fanfare during the spring of 1965, the initial political attraction of a new national public assistance act for the federal government did not lie in any coordinated assault on poverty. Instead, the idea of merging unemployment assistance as well as the other three categorical programs into a single comprehensive public assistance act emerged out of more prosaic concerns. New legislation would allow Ottawa to develop standards of auditing, administrative efficiency, and clear definitions of eligibility which were at present missing from the most expensive of all the cost-shared programs – unemployment assistance. Such reforms might not reduce costs, but they would at least give federal officials a clearer sense of where and how they were occurring. The alternative of simply broadening coverage under unemployment assistance, as the provinces wished, to include the last anomalous assistance categories excluded from its terms, such as women and children in mothers' allowance programs, was far less satisfactory from Ottawa's viewpoint, given the absence of adequate administrative controls under the legislation. As well, federal officials argued that the word 'unemployment' was increasingly problematic as a title for the statute. Not only did it convey the erroneous impression that most recipients were capable of work, but it encouraged those who had exhausted their unemployment insurance benefits to believe they had an 'automatic entitlement' to assistance 'irrespective of whether they qualify on the basis of need.'[55]

Finally, it was increasingly clear to federal officials by the early 1960s that the alternative to reforming social assistance was simply greater reliance on far more expensive universal social programs such as family allowances or old age security as a means of responding to the problems of persistent hard-core poverty. 'Assistance programs offer the most economical way of meeting real need and thereby prevent irresistible demands building up for costly increases in other federal social programs,' Health and Welfare officials argued in lobbying cabinet for a new public assistance act. 'It may well be that for the next several years the best policy for Canada to pursue would be to improve its assistance programs while holding the line on its more costly transfer payment programs such as old age security and family allowances ... To do this adequately will require additional federal outlays but the magnitude of the cost is relatively small compared with other alternatives.'[56]

To make targeted social assistance more acceptable to the public as an alternative to universal income security, however, required basic reforms in how welfare was perceived and delivered by provincial and local governments. Because of the 'bad repute' surrounding means-tested local relief and provincial old age assistance, the image of needs-based programs required major rehabilitation. 'The pursuit of a policy that puts the emphasis back on social assistance,' Health and Welfare argued, 'would involve the encouragement of the provinces and muncipalities to improve their standards of assistance and its administration so that there is a general disposition on the part of Canadians to accept this approach.' This in turn would necessitate that assistance 'be granted to those in need in amounts that meet basic needs and in ways that recognize and preserve the rights and dignity of those who apply for aid.'[57] Such wholesale reform was simply not possible under the loosely worded terms of the Unemployment Assistance Act.

'Holding the line' on universal programs such as Old Age Security, however, was exactly what the Diefenbaker and Pearson administrations did not do between 1962 and 1963. During these years of intense political competition and instability, old age pensions were boosted twice, from $55 to $65 a month by Diefenbaker just prior to the 1962 federal election, and again to $75 a month by the incoming Pearson administration in the fall of 1963 as a first instalment on pledges for comprehensive pension reform during its initial 'Sixty Days of Decision' in office.[58] This 36 per cent hike in Old Age Security benefits between 1962 and 1963, undertaken without any provincial consultation, played havoc with the way in which provinces calculated social allowances through means-tested cost-shared programs for those under the age of seventy. Traditionally, benefits payable through provincially administered old age assistance, blindness, and disability allowances were kept identical to Ottawa's universal Old Age Security payments for those aged seventy and over. Put differently, through setting the level of Old Age Security, Ottawa effectively defined a national minimum for all those dependent on categorical assistance, although not general welfare, across Canada.[59]

In the Atlantic provinces this minimum was only rarely exceeded. In Quebec and the West, provincial governments topped up these benefits for thousands of needy recipients through supplemental payments they cost-shared through the Unemployment Assistance Act. Ontario remained 'the only province outside of the Atlantic region' not to comply, leaving the issue of supplementation entirely to local governments, which generally avoided it.[60] Ottawa's unilateral action in dramatically boosting Old Age Security effectively severed the linkage between benefits payable through this universal program and the cost-shared categorical programs. It also galvanized the provinces to press for a new comprehensive public assistance act. In Atlantic Canada, the cost of meeting even the $65 monthly standard set in 1962 for the other categorical assistance programs placed severe strains on provincial welfare budgets, officials claimed, and distorted their social policy priorities in other areas. A $75 monthly benefit was simply out of the question. At this level, old age assistance and blindness and disability allowances would be almost double the $40 monthly welfare entitlement for a single unemployable in Halifax cost-shared through unemployment assistance.[61]

Quebec and the western provinces faced a different dilemma. If they reduced their supplemental payments to recipients in these programs by the amount of Ottawa's increase, they would be accused of taking away from their poor with one hand what the federal government was granting with the other. If they kept their level of supplementation unchanged, however, they risked compromising their own definition of 'need.' Quebec, which viewed Ottawa's unilateral boost of allowance ceilings to $65 monthly in 1962 as an intrusion on its autonomy to set its own standards in social programs, decided to curtail its supplementation of categorical allowances. The western provinces, where pensioners were well organized, did not. In 'anticipation of public pressure,' and with considerable grumbling to Ottawa, they passed on the full benefits of the 1962 increase. But when Old Age Security leaped another $10 only a year later, the limits of provincial tolerance for allowance standards unilaterally set in Ottawa were reached. During the summer of 1963, when pensions were increased to $75, the provinces stepped up their demands for 'rationalizing ... the total area of public assistance ... and adopting new approaches which would allow them greater flexibility in developing assistance measures suited to their particular needs.'[62] At their first opportunity, during a September 1963 federal-provincial conference called to discuss the launching of Pearson's key campaign pledge – a contributory old age pension scheme – the premiers, led by Joey Smallwood of Newfoundland, insisted that the subject of a new public assistance act be placed on the agenda. Their demand was motivated not only by anger at the lack of consultation surrounding the recent dramatic hikes in Old Age Security, but also by deeper fears emanating from Ontario, Alberta, and Saskatchewan that 'relatively high benefit levels under the [proposed] Canada Pension Plan will set the standards of assistance granted under the various public assistance programs.'[63] Federal officials were also interested in developing a new approach to public assistance and, at a subsequent federal-provincial conference in November, Ottawa and the provinces agreed to establish a 'federal-provincial working group' to begin discussions of a new public assistance act to replace the entire basis of cost-sharing Canada's social welfare programs.[64]

The process that would culminate three years later in the Canada Assistance Plan had been launched. But at its heart lay a contradiction that would be critical for all subsequent attempts to fight poverty both in Ontario and across Canada throughout the remainder of the decade. For Ottawa, the quest for welfare reform was driven essentially by unhappiness with unemployment assistance and a desire for greater fiscal control over the standards and accountability of provincial and local welfare programs. Provinces, in contrast, wished to escape a federal regulatory presence in categorical programs that they already viewed as overly intrusive. As Ontario premier John Robarts put it, 'The conditions attached to the grants are too rigid ... Every effort should be made ... to modify these arrangements so that federal interference in affairs of provincial responsibility is kept to a minimum.'[65] In neither case, however, were governments principally concerned with putting more money into the hands of the poor to lift individuals or families out of dire poverty.

Indeed, the strategy of using federal authority to boost inadequate local and provincial welfare allowances had been explicitly ruled out by Ottawa long before detailed talks on a new general assistance scheme even began. Despite official statements that Ottawa's goal was to meet the poor's 'basic needs ... in ways that recognize and preserve [their] rights and dignity,'[66] Health and Welfare officials conceded in private that to define the budgetary components of what those basic needs might be in any new public assistance act, as the Canadian Welfare Council had advocated in 1961, was politically out of the question. Provinces that already objected to the indirect linkage between national Old Age Security benefits and their own categorical allowance programs were not likely to agree to new federal definitions of need in their general assistance programs. Indeed, it was precisely the flexibility they enjoyed to define benefit levels and eligibility requirements under unemployment assistance that they wished to see extended to all forms of welfare cost-shared with Ottawa.[67]

At bottom, what *was* the primary objective of the federal presence in social assistance, Health and Welfare officials asked? 'Is the purpose to ensure that all people in Canada who are in need will have their needs met adequately, or is it just ... to help the provinces meet their general assistance costs?' The question was no sooner asked than answered. 'It would appear that the legislation was primarily enacted to help the provinces to bear assistance costs as the provinces define and administer them.'[68] Consequently, in new legislation to replace unemployment assistance 'it would not be realistic to expect provincial acceptance of a quantitative definition of these components [of a public assistance budget] by the federal government.' Recommendations for public assistance reform emerging from Ottawa, Health and Welfare officials advised cabinet, should thus 'avoid any rigid definition of adequacy' if provincial agreement was to be secured.[69] Put differently, the definition of a national poverty line was ruled out even before substantial discussions on public assistance reform began in the early months of 1964. Recognition of this fact, however, was buried in public statements that Ottawa's goal was to allow provinces 'greater flexibility in setting assistance rates and determining conditions of eligibility so that programs can be designed to meet local requirements.'[70]

Before serious negotiations for a new public assistance framework could begin, however, one final hurdle needed to be cleared. In its 1962 campaign platform the opposition Liberal Party led by Lester Pearson, in response to the nationalist momentum of Quebec's Quiet Revolution, had promised if elected to implement a more 'co-operative federalism' that would allow provinces to 'opt out' of established shared-cost programs and receive appropriate fiscal compensation from Ottawa to run their own schemes.[71] Within the federal Department of Finance senior officials had never been enamoured of shared-cost programs, which they viewed as cumbersome, expensive, and difficult to monitor, arguments reinforced by the ballooning expenditures under unemployment assistance. Moreover, equalization payments developed since 1957 to smooth out disparities in provincial tax yields further undercut the need, in the eyes of Finance officials, for such a strong federal fiscal presence within areas of provincial jurisdiction. The growing nationalist insistence of Quebec Liberal premier Jean Lesage that Ottawa should get out of all conditional grant programs, combined with the victory of the Liberal Party in the 1963 federal election, soon placed the legitimacy of all shared-cost programs in question. During the summer of 1963 the Department of Finance developed new proposals that would allow provincial governments to 'contract out' of conditional grant schemes through a transfer of tax points equivalent to current levels of federal cost-sharing. With this additional tax revenue, provinces could run their own social programs free of all but minimal federal control.[72]

Within National Health and Welfare, officials were appalled by the contracting-out proposals, a move they viewed as devastating to the core of their department and one that would reverse the momentum for upgrading and standardizing welfare programs across Canada which had been ongoing since the early 1950s. 'I think we will see the time when Canadians as a whole will regret this action,' deputy minister Joe Willard warned Judy LaMarsh. More importantly, contracting out might well kill the prospect for developing a new comprehensive public assistance act. 'The ability and willingness of the provinces to establish assistance programs on an adequate basis, without federal support, has not been demonstrated,' Health and Welfare officials argued in a vigorous counterattack against the Finance initiative. 'Dramatic improvements in the provincial assistance programs' over the past decade were in large measure attributable 'to the federal support available through a specific grant program,' a point acknowledged by most provincial welfare administrators who 'almost without exception tend[ed] ... to support the use of conditional grants' and who 'were not unhappy with controls now exercised.' Given the increasing mobility of Canada's population, there was also a need for 'achieving national standards of certain services' in health and welfare. Left to their own devices, provinces 'could not be expected always to choose a course which would be in the national interests.' After all, 'if a province can be adequately compensated for withdrawing from a programme, why would it continue to meet federal conditions? Would the logical outcome of contracting out not be the end of the conditional grant programme to which it applies, and perhaps others as well?'[73]

Although these arguments carried some weight, in the end conditional grants programs survived because the alternative of widespread contracting out was fraught with too much financial uncertainty both for the provinces and for Ottawa. Only programs 'of a continuing nature which involved fairly regular annual expenditures' such as old age, blindness, and disability assistance, federal and provincial officials concluded, were logical candidates for contracting out, since their target populations were relatively stable and their costs could be easily predicted. However, they accounted for only a small fraction of shared-cost spending. The big drain was hospital insurance and unemployment assistance and, in these new areas, costs were still too volatile and unpredictable to be reduced to any neat taxation formula.[74] As even senior Finance Department officials eventually conceded, this fact sharply reduced the feasibility of any widespread implementation of contracting out:

The categorical welfare programs, which might otherwise be suitable for transfer have been ruled out because they cannot be divorced from unemployment assistance which presumably the provinces wish the federal government to remain in, because of its violent fluctuations ... Hospital insurance costs are so large and still so subject to fluctuations that it is considered unlikely that the federal offer to get out of hospital insurance with compensation will appeal to many (if any) of the provinces ... even ... Quebec.[75]

This proved to be the case. Although Ottawa offered the contracting-out option for all shared-cost programs to the provinces at both the November 1963 and April 1964 federal-provincial conferences, the federal proposals were vaguely worded and remained unaccompanied by any significant offer of additional tax room for cash-starved provincial coffers.[76] As a consequence, there were no takers outside Quebec. Ontario was the next most likely candidate. It had taken the lead in forcing Ottawa to liberalize conditions for sharing costs through unemployment assistance, grumbled continually about the 'rigidity' of most conditional grant programs, and disliked the extent to which they transferred income out of the province. As provincial welfare minister Louis Cecile told Robarts just prior to the November 1963 conference, Ontario's per capita recovery of revenues from Ottawa through conditional grant programs was the lowest in Canada, while its per capita contributions to the federal treasury were the highest. If Ottawa eliminated all shared-cost welfare programs and simply agreed to equalize transfer payments for welfare purposes on an average per capita cost basis across Canada, the province would receive almost two-thirds more than the $35 million it presently got through the shared-cost approach. 'In this manner, Ontario could readily design its own public welfare programs to suit the needs of its population,' Cecile argued, although he conceded this was a 'forlorn hope.'[77]

Robarts was sympathetic. 'Ontario ... was not a fat cat to be stripped,' he told Pearson and the premiers behind closed doors. However, the Ontario premier also recognized that his province had the largest stake in enhancing the free flow of capital and labour within a national economy. 'Canada-wide uniformity was desirable in many governmental services; conditional grants had achieved such uniformity in certain fields and Ontario was reluctant to see such uniformity as had been achieved imperilled.' Problems with conditional grants were 'not so serious as to dictate the wholesale abandonment of ... the system.' As he later explained within the Ontario legislature, 'we are Canadians first and foremost.' Robarts did serve notice, though, that he wanted to see the transfer of money within shared-cost programs become a lot more flexibile. Ontario's most pressing revenue needs were in education, not welfare, and his government had to 'allot priority to various programmes and to postpone those which lacked a high priority.' Why could specific conditional grants not be replaced by 'block or departmental grants which would retain the overall uniformity but allow the provinces greater freedom to employ methods based on their familiarity with and experience of local conditions'?[78]

Robarts's advice would become federal policy fourteen years later with the creation of Established Program Financing. For the moment, Ottawa simply tried to buy time by giving a vague commitment for a 'continuing review of fiscal arrangements and shared cost programs and the relation between them.' However, the provincial need for additional tax revenue was immediate, particularly within Quebec where the costs of modernizing the social infrastructure were ballooning rapidly. After a second inconclusive federal-provincial conference in April 1964 a furious Jean Lesage, by threatening to go it alone on contributory old age pensions, finally succeeded in winning major concessions from Ottawa for additional taxation revenue. With this breakthrough in revising overall fiscal arrangements between Ottawa and the provinces, specific discussions over the issue of contracting out of shared-cost programs faded into the background for the time being. After extensive consultations, federal officials reported that the provinces did 'not oppose in principle initiatives taken under the conditional grant programmes or wish them to cease.' They did wish to see 'greater consultation and cooperation and some need as well for the federal government to administer [them] with a less heavy hand' and to make them 'truly joint programmes from their inception or even before their inception.'[79] With this important caveat, the way was clear by the spring of 1964 to begin detailed negotiations on a comprehensive and completely new shared-cost approach to the field of public assistance, a development that received immense momentum from south of the border when America's new president, Lyndon Johnson, declared 'war on poverty.'

7

The War on Poverty in Ontario, 1964–6

While Ottawa and the provinces were moving slowly behind the scenes towards new administrative relationships for delivering programs to the poor, the entire issue of poverty across Canada and within Ontario exploded into public consciousness through dramatic initiatives launched by American president Lyndon Johnson early in 1964. Anxious to place his own stamp on the presidency in the wake of John F. Kennedy's tragic assassination and to solidify his credentials as a southern 'liberal' in the New Deal tradition, Johnson quickly transformed the tentative planning already begun by Kennedy's advisers for some modest initiatives aimed at the poor into an 'unconditional War on Poverty' that became the keynote of his January 1964 State of the Union address to Congress. It was a war that 'the richest nation on earth ... cannot afford to lose,' Johnson argued in pledging an all-out effort to 'help that one-fifth of all American families with incomes too small to even meet their basic needs.'[1]

Within Ontario and Ottawa Johnson's powerful metaphor, combined with the launching of his Office of Economic Opportunity later that August to extend a direct federal presence in the fight against poverty in cities across the United States, had dramatic spillover effects, particularly within Ontario where unemployment had dropped to only 3 per cent, yet welfare spending was up by 15 per cent. 'In Canada, we always do later what they have already started to do in the United States, but we cannot afford to be much later in launching our war on poverty,' the *Globe and Mail* observed two months after Johnson's address. 'No more than they, can we be a rich country while the poor are always with us.' As the London *Free Press* pointed out, Canada quickly got 'caught up in the spirit of President Johnson's ambitious crusade against poverty ... and declared a war of its own.'[2]

Within the Ontario legislature this heightened interest in poverty was soon apparent through the activities of a revitalized New Democratic Party and its newly elected MPPs Stephen Lewis and James Renwick, along with veteran social policy critic Ken Bryden. Demanding that the welfare department shed its 'mentality of the dole' and 'neanderthal social views ... [of] welfare recipients as unregenerate and undeserving,' as well as an approach to welfare in which 'we never hear talk of minimums, only maximums,' Lewis called on the government to heed the 'exciting new developments in the United States' and to launch 'an overall attack on the whole problem of poverty.' Americans such as Michael Harrington in *The Other America*, Bryden argued, had demonstrated that there was 'a whole subculture of poverty – of people and their families who are condemned to permanent poverty ... who live within the community but are not part of it and who have developed their own culture of poverty with its own conditions and its own customs.' To break out of the 'vicious circle of poverty,' these people and their children needed 'much more than financial assistance.' Apart from decent housing and health care, they required a 'new stress on personal services' such as 'individual counselling,' 'remedial training and retraining,' and 'rehabilitation services' all designed to 'assist them to reestablish themselves as independent, self-reliant citizens.' Lewis called on the government 'to throw the entire weight of the province behind a retraining and rehabilitation programme including that for disturbed children on the assumption that the welfare department exists primarily to encourage people to become self-sufficient, responsible and self-reliant.' Although there was 'no significant statistical study of the problem' in Canada, Bryden extrapolated from Harrington's statistics to conclude that, in 1964 '1.5 million of the men, women, and children of this province are living in poverty.' This was a 'startling fact' and Ontarians would hang their heads 'in shame when [the] 1967 [Centennial] comes, if we have not by that time adopted full-scale programmes which will eliminate poverty forever.'[3]

In the absence of any provincial war on poverty, the NDP instead launched a full-scale attack on the Department of Public Welfare and its hapless minister, Louis Cecile, during the presentation of the department's annual estimates that spring. The lawyer from Prescott made an inviting target. A cabinet holdover from the Frost era, Cecile clung to the Welfare portfolio not out of aptitude, but simply by virtue of representing francophone Ontario within the Conservative caucus. Against the informed and incisive social policy criticism of NDP members Lewis, Bryden, and Renwick, the deeply conservative and moralistic Cecile was simply out of his depth.[4]

Throughout a gruelling debate on his estimates, Cecile made a string of verbal gaffes and admissions that both delighted and appalled his opposition critics. The NDP's call for a war on poverty was merely the 'gospel of the socialist point of view.' Welfare allowances should not be 'too generous so as to permit [a man] to stay on welfare; because why should he work if he has so much?' Women deserted by their spouses could not be dealt with too liberally lest 'any of the deserting husbands ... take unfair advantage of welfare and be gone every now and then ... I have to draw the line some place.' Women who worked full time, according to Cecile, were neglecting their 'most important role of all, the role of wife and mother,' and were condemning 'several thousands of children in Ontario' to possible juvenile delinquency through 'this disregard ... for their offspring.' A few days later Cecile revealed that his department did not directly fund research, nor did he even know if it had anyone 'specially designated ... to [do] research.' Within children's institutions there were staff shortages, but 'to put a figure on it would be very difficult for me.' Asked why per capita welfare costs were 60 cents in North Bay and $3 in London, Cecile could only reply 'these things happen in ... local municipalities.' Nor did he 'know what I can do ... [about poor housing] except advise the municipalities.' Did he think the province's ceiling for general welfare assistance which paid 'a mother with six children ... $35.40 a week [or] 84 cents a day per child' was adequate? 'This I cannot answer,' Cecile lamely replied. 'I have to go along with the tables that are set forth by the experts ... It is not a very high living but it is a living of some sort until they can rehabilitate themselves.' Nor did he know if the province's ceilings on shelter allowances were sufficient. 'Surely ... the municipalities would ... have been on our back ... [and] ... they have not asked us for anything.' As for the wider issue of poverty itself, Cecile conceded 'to say that I have studied the topic really deeply, I must confess ... no.' For a minister who had held the Welfare portfolio since 1956, it was an appalling performance. 'Clearly, after years in the department, his detailed knowledge of what goes on ... is about as close to nil as is possible. One shudders to think of how little impact he must have in the Cabinet in fighting for welfare matters,' NDP leader Donald MacDonald aptly concluded. Even major newspapers such as the *Globe and Mail* soon picked up on the issue of Cecile's incompetence, noting that his 'continuing ignorance of the work of his department is a wondrous thing.'[5]

Despite lack of interest in poverty within the province's Department of Public Welfare, challenges soon came from other directions which forced the Roberts administration to react. The first was an important study of 'Poverty in Ontario' undertaken by the Ontario Federation of

Labour and adopted at its autumn 1964 convention. This analysis was the first of its kind to undertake a statistical estimate of the dimensions of poverty in the province using research methodologies and language borrowed from the American War on Poverty literature and an important new domestic research tool – the 'Population Sample' of the newly available 1961 census. Even Ontario welfare department officials conceded these data were 'a tremendous source of knowledge' for those wishing to undertake poverty research.[6] The federation booklet touched on all the key themes that would dominate the poverty debate for the remainder of the decade. The most important was its argument that the number of poor was 'constantly growing in an age of plenty.' This was the 'painful paradox' of the 1960s. 'Why are we so excited about poverty in what is one of the richest countries in the world and certainly the richest province in Canada?' the study asked. 'One of the reasons ... is that, for the first time in history, we have the means to eliminate mass poverty completely ... *[P]overty is no longer a dilemma but a problem that can be solved*. That is what is new.' Affluence, in short, made the continued existence of poverty intolerable.

Who were the poor? How many were there? How did they differ from their counterparts in the past? And what could be done to help them? The federation analysis was highly revealing in the answers it gave to these questions. Today's poor were different from those trapped within the 'general poverty ... [of] the hungry thirties.' Rather than living within an 'economy on the downgrade' in which 'unemployed engineers rubbed shoulders with impoverished factory workers,' the poor of the 1960s suffered from relative deprivation. Victims of the same automation, technological changes, and new methods of production that were delivering affluence to the general population, the new poor in effect were 'getting less and less of ... the expanding economy.' They were 'psychologically handicapped' because they had been 'denied the minimal levels of health, housing, food, and education that our present state of technological and scientific knowledge specifies for life as it is lived in this country.' An affluent society had created 'new needs and new concepts,' the most important of which was the 'right for a person to live decently, just because he is a human being and a fellow man.' The new poor, in other words, were the victims not simply of scarcity, but of a rising sense of expectations and entitlement.

They were also a marginalized and increasingly self-contained population: 'older workers and ... pensioners, the underemployed and the unemployed, the school drop outs and the undereducated, the widows and the fatherless families, the disabled and the sick, the retarded and the mentally ill, the small farmers and the migrant workers, the Indians and the new immigrants.' Their children were trapped within a self-perpetuating culture of poverty, 'most likely to be poor themselves because their parents are usually unable to give them the needed education, health, or in many cases, incentive to improve their lot.' Passive victims of progress, the poor could 'not pull themselves up by their own bootstraps simply because their environment has done little to prepare them to cope with the realities of today. So if and when the opportunity for improvement presents itself, they are not equipped to grasp it.' Nor could they organize on their own to improve their lot. They were the 'invisible poor, the unseen, the unheard.' They did 'not belong to any pressure groups or organizations that will champion their cause.' They constituted a 'massive problem, an enormous amount of human suffering that should stir us to action.'

How many were there? The federation's statistical calculations painted a 'picture of the poor that staggers the imagination.' Conceding that their report was plagued by 'lack of reliable information' and a general absence of research on the topic within Canada, the authors nonetheless argued that the federal government itself had drawn a *de facto* poverty line by allowing the average Canadian family of four $2700 in annual income before levying taxation. 'To avoid quibbling,' the study set its poverty line at $3000 for a family of four and $1500 for a single person,' the same definition of poverty used in the most widely cited American studies. On this basis, using income statistics derived from the 1961 census, the report concluded that among Ontario's non-farm population, 700,000 people, or 11 per cent, were living in destitution, 1 million or 19 per cent were living in poverty, and almost 2 million or 32 per cent were living in poverty, destitution, or deprivation. Within rural Ontario, 65 per cent of the farming population earned incomes below this level.

What could be done? Although optimistic that poverty could be abolished, the federation study was short on solutions. There was a 'great need for more low cost, low rental housing'; the province's $1 an hour minimum wage was far too low; automation was creating a 'growing number of hard core, chronic unemployed'; and maximum weekly benefits of $36 under unemployment insurance for families were 'woefully inadequate.' Although education was 'the key to long term economic expansion,' there did 'not seem to be an overall plan to train people for the kind of jobs available.'

But on the topic of welfare the report had a lot to say, singling out this area of provincial policy for its harshest criticism. Scales of assistance were set 'well below the cut off figure of $3000 and $1500 annual income which we are using as a definition of poverty.' Indeed, the province had made 'no proper survey ... regarding the needs of the people on welfare, or the amounts spent by the various ... private and public agencies in this field. We even lack such an elementary reference in this province as an up to date guide to family spending and cost of living budget.' Welfare allowances were 'decided arbitrarily at the whim of the department' and were 'designed to sustain life only ... There is no relationship between the constantly rising cost of living and the amount of welfare received by those needing it.' Pensioners on old age assistance had seen their incomes decline by 30 per cent in real terms since 1949, the report pointed out, a 'disgrace and an insult to our senior citizens.' All those dependent on relief had to endure 'rigid, economically unrealistic, and often humiliating means tests' most often administered by municipal governments whose staffs were usually 'not trained for this work.' Yet local governments, which contributed the least amount, had 'the final say on whether or not welfare assistance is given' and how much would be granted. The province's entire welfare system was a 'hodge-podge of public and private arrangements' that had 'grown up haphazardly ... depending on the political climate and pressures.' It was 'geared to subsistence levels' that were 'completely inadequate in today's affluent society.' The report concluded that 'nothing short of a thorough ... and complete overhaul of the present antiquated system will suffice.'

About the most impoverished section of Ontario society, the booklet had surprisingly little to say. Although acknowledging that 'the Indian is the most poverty-stricken of the poor' whose needs 'should have top priority,' the authors could only urge that on the eve of Canada's centennial 'our maturity as a nation can best be fostered by giving back to the Indian his dignity and the right to live as the true Canadian that he is.' This was an analysis of poverty in the province's urban, industrial south, not its isolated, rural north.[7]

The ferocity of the attack on Cecile during the spring estimates, the continuing popularity of the American War on Poverty, which even the welfare minister acknowledged had 'captured the imagination of the public,' and the 'Poverty in Ontario' report all combined to prod the Robarts administration into a reluctant response to the issue near the end of 1964. Because of the 'massive program ... commonly known as "The President's War on Poverty,"' Cecile wrote to Robarts soon after the release of the booklet, 'I am convinced that we will be under pressure to develop a provincial "War On Poverty."' Yet there were a number of reasons why Cecile thought this was a bad idea. Only Ottawa could 'inaugurate a plan that would be effective across the nation.' Because its economy was so much stronger than that of the rest of Canada, if

Ontario 'were to take separate measures of development we might expect an influx of persons from other provinces.' Finally, the 'major emphasis' of the American poverty war appeared to be directed towards 'work training, work study, and educational measures,' and Ontario already possessed 'as effective a training and education program as any to be found on the continent.' What then could be done to appease the growing public expectation for action? 'In view of the popularity of this topic,' Cecile recommended a trip to Washington in order to study the operation of America's Economic Opportunity Act first hand. In this way the province would be in a better position to exert pressure on Ottawa 'to institute similar studies.'[8]

That winter, deputy welfare minister James Band and his assistant journeyed to Washington and a selected group of American states to examine the American War on Poverty. Band was not impressed by what he saw. The programs were 'still very much in the planning stage,' were 'vaguely defined,' and involved 'almost total concentration upon employment or preparation for employment as the means of relieving poverty.' Some, such as the 'Work Experience' initiatives, seemed to 'bear a close resemblance to "work for relief" projects which have been so largely decried in Canada.' The community action programs which provided direct federal funding for newly formed citizens groups were amateurish and had fostered 'rivalry and criticism ... [of] experienced professional welfare people.' Band also was convinced that the single-minded American concentration on job training and employment was inappropriate for Ontario. Most of the province's welfare caseload was made up of 'people who because of poor health, or age, or family responsibilities are actually unable to work,' and the 40 per cent who were employable 'leave the rolls fairly quickly in a time like this of comparatively high employment.' Moreover, the deputy minister argued that Ontario was already doing more for its needy citizens than most states south of the border. Vocational education, hospital insurance, and medical welfare for the poor in Ontario was 'seldom available in any of the [American] states' and, taken together, would 'compare favourably with the Economic Opportunity Act.' Above all, and in marked contrast to the authors of the federation study, Band believed that the rhetoric and expectations surrounding America's War on Poverty were impossibly naïve:

Does anyone honestly see in the near future, a society where conspicuously lower standards are eliminated for the unemployable? ... American officials pointed out to us that the cost of raising every American family to $3000 level would be about 28 billion dollars a year ... an impossibly high sum. They were sure the American public are not ready and perhaps will never be ready for such massive taxation to redistribute wealth and income ... I think that anyone who talks about the 'elimination of poverty' should state clearly what he means ... [L]et us be honest with ourselves and ask 'can we utterly eliminate low standards of living, and if so, how will this be done?' ... The elimination of poverty may be accomplished in the remote future by evolutionary methods; if it is to be done in our day, the methods would have to be revolutionary.[9]

Robarts was impressed by this 'very interesting memo,' whose thinking closely matched his own views on poverty. Along with the authors of the federation study or NDP critics of his government, Robarts was quite willing to acknowledge the existence of a culture of poverty, but much like American conservative critics of the War on Poverty, the Ontario premier drew sharply different inferences from it.[10] 'Most social workers, sociologists, and psychologists would agree that the problem of poverty is often related to social attitudes and the motivation of people,' he replied to one of his constituents who asked whether he believed poverty could be 'substantially eliminated in this generation.' 'How far [should] society, through government ... go to aid people who are not prepared to help themselves? ... [E]ducation in a public school system cannot control or influence the home environment [which] ... is very important to the development of the individual personality ... As long as we are concerned with maintaining an open and free society, we must continue to rely on individual initiative as the main antidote to poverty.' Nor was Robarts convinced by the statistical arguments that families living on less than $3000 a year were necessarily 'poor.' 'The problem with this economic yardstick is that it applies to all families and individuals regardless of such factors as location, cost of living variations, ownership of home and other mitigating circumstances ... It is extremely difficult to establish any exact measure of poverty throughout the whole of Canada or even within a province.'[11]

Ironically, at the same moment that Ontario was decisively rejecting the American War on Poverty, Ottawa declared war on its own. At the beginning of 1965 Lester Pearson wrote to all his cabinet ministers asking for policy ideas that could be 'striking enough to help shift the focus of political attention away from opposition attempts to harry us on other matters ... thereby taking the spotlight off our difficulties and mistakes.' Pearson suggested that 'these problems ... might best be approached by developing a Canadian version of "the war on poverty" ... It is a heading under which one or two attractive and practical programs could be launched, possibly without much in the way of legislative requirements, and a shelf of further programs could be prepared for introduction as circumstances make them appropriate.'[12] The memo was drafted by Pearson's policy secretary and key adviser, Tom Kent, who hit upon the idea for a Canadian War on Poverty in late December 1964. The British-born and educated Kent was a man of diverse talents. A former industrial economist and ex-editor of the *Winnipeg Free Press*, Kent was a left-wing Liberal who, along with Walter Gordon and Maurice Lamontagne, had played a critical role in devising the creative policy agenda that helped to bring the Liberal Party under Lester Pearson back in from the political wilderness after its disastrous 1958 defeat.[13]

As Pearson's letter to cabinet suggests, in coming up with the idea of a War on Poverty, Kent was primarily guided by political considerations. Two years earlier, in preparing for the 1963 federal election, Pearson's policy secretary had given no prominence to the poverty issue whatsoever in drafting a list of social policy recommendations for the Liberal Party's platform. 'A few main policies for social progress – to improve educational opportunities, to make good health care financially available to all, to ensure that everyone has access to adequate contributory pensions' were initiatives Kent targeted squarely at the middle class, not the poor.[14]

The 'discovery' of poverty in 1965, however, occurred at an opportune moment for the Liberals. Although Pearson's minority government had accomplished much during its first two years in power, including the creation of the Canada Pension Plan, Kent later recalled that it 'felt and looked tired and worn by all the battering it had undergone' because of scandals, the embarrassment over Walter Gordon's first budget, and initial blundering in its dealings with Quebec on pensions and tax-sharing. 'If the death wish was to be overcome, if public confidence was to be restored, there had to be a sense of getting a second wind.' The government needed not 'more new measures than were already on the agenda,' but simply 'a way of giving them some new coherence as a program.' Pearson agreed, and Canada's short-lived War on Poverty was launched in the spring of 1965 through a throne speech, drafted by Kent, which promised 'a programme for the full utilization of our human resources and *the elimination of poverty among our people*.'[15]

Despite the grandiose rhetoric, Canada's War on Poverty contained a fair amount of 'window-dressing' and amounted to 'a good deal less than meets the eye,' as the press quickly pointed out after the April throne speech. Most of the fanfare represented an attempt to give 'political sex appeal' to several long-planned pieces of legislation 'which otherwise would seem to be only loosely related.'[16] As Kent knew full well from the difficult negotiations over contributory pensions, most of the terrain on which any poverty war would be fought lay within provincial areas of jurisdiction. Consequently, 'almost all of the relevant federal activities required consultation and co-operation with the provinces' at a time when federal-provincial relations, particularly with Quebec, were extremely volatile. Nor was he proposing that Canada 'copy the Americans by setting up a new agency to mount and administer programs.' There would be no Canadian equivalent to Washington's Office of Economic Opportunity, with its $2 billion budget and separate staff. Kent took great pains to reassure the provinces that 'the last thing that any Federal Government could possibly afford to think of doing would be to enlarge its own area of operation ... If what we tried to do became a replacement of provincial action, then the whole point would be lost.'[17]

Instead, Ottawa's poverty war would be a low-key campaign fought through programs for rural economic development, contributory pensions, vocational retraining, and the reform of public assistance, programs that were already in place or well on the way to fruition within existing government departments and through federal-provincial negotiations that had occurred long before the April throne speech. Its twin themes, reflecting Kent's own particular interests, would be enhancing labour market training and employability and regional economic development. Glaring by its absence was the omission of any reference to the plight of native people, who were living in the most acute poverty within Canada, or of women and immigrants. Indeed, neither the Departments of Indian Affairs nor Citizenship and Immigration were included in planning Ottawa's War on Poverty campaign. Essentially, the war would be fought through a new Special Planning Secretariat made up of a handful of officials seconded to the Prime Minister's Office from the Departments of National Health and Welfare, Labour, and Industry, and reporting to Kent himself. Their task was to act as a focal point somehow transforming disparate and ongoing bureaucratic activity, both within Ottawa and among the provinces, into a coordinated war on poverty. Apart from the creation of the Special Planning Secretariat itself and the Company of Young Canadians – an organization Kent hoped would 'channel ... the idealism and energy of ... young people ... in[to] community service' – there was little else that was new in Ottawa's program to eliminate poverty.[18]

The highwater mark of the War on Poverty was a major four-day conference in Ottawa on Poverty and Opportunity in Canada organized by the Special Planning Secretariat on 7–10 December 1965. Almost two hundred provincial and federal government officials, along with a few selected academics and representatives of senior private charitable organizations such as the Canadian Welfare Council, were in attendance. Significantly, no members or representatives of the poor were invited. Initially envisaged as the first of a series of such gatherings that would lead up to 'a great national conference on poverty and opportunity,' it became instead the first and only time federal and provincial representatives sat down specifically to discuss poverty for the remainder of the decade. 'By comparison with the hopes and the work that had gone into its preparation' the poverty conference 'was an anticlimax,' Kent later recalled, both because of the Liberals' demoralizing failure to win a majority government during the November 1965 election and the inability of the secretariat to articulate a clear framework for its work. 'The Federal role in this is ... to try to take an initiative toward the development of a sort of consensus out of which can grow more effective action,' Kent told provincial officials in attempting to explain the purpose of the gathering. It was all very vague and, as Kent later conceded, 'it came to nothing ... Good discussion could not conceal a sense of pointlessness.'[19]

Nonetheless, the very existence of a conference on poverty did force both federal and provincial government officials to engage in the rare exercise of articulating some of their ideas on the subject. Within both Ottawa and Queen's Park the task provoked considerable consternation and confusion within the bureaucracy. Officials in National Health and Welfare initially attempted to provide a frank overview of inadequacies and contradictions within federal social programs that contributed to poverty. Unemployment insurance, research director John Osborne pointed out in a lengthy background memo prepared for the conference, was available to only two-thirds of the total labour force, excluded the most vulnerable workers in agriculture and domestic service from protection, and demanded worker contributions that 'in relative terms are actually greater at low income levels than ... at higher income levels.' Above all, the benefits it paid out were woefully inadequate, providing a maximum of only $36 per week or $1870 a year, an income far below the secretariat's working poverty line for the conference of $3000 for average-size families. Family allowances, 'which formed a significant part of family income in 1948' and were Ottawa's principal tool for fighting child poverty, had been kept 'basically unchanged ... over a period of years during which wages and price levels have increased substantially.' As a consequence, the 1964 allowance was worth 'only $4.94 in 1948 terms ... compare[d] with an actual average payment in 1948 of $5.92.' It was the only federal social benefit whose value had declined in relation to personal income since the 1940s. Provincial social assistance programs also contributed to poverty. Many 'lack[ed] the administrative base necessary to provide adequate programs of assistance,' rates varied irrationally among provinces and among municipalities within provinces, and allowances based ostensibly on needs tests undermined the concept of adequacy 'if the allowance for any one item (for example, rent) is inadequate, if the total allowance granted is a fixed percentage of established need, or if a ceiling is placed on the total allowance which may be granted,' policies that were standard practice in all provinces including Ontario.[20]

Deputy finance minister Robert Bryce was appalled when he learned of these 'serious criticisms of the adequacy and scope of various Federal and shared-cost programs – criticisms which virtually amount to recommendations for major changes ... [which had received] ... no interdepartmental consideration within the Government.' Osborne's critique of federal programs was 'partial and tendentious' and his comments on the inadequacy of provincial social assistance would surely be 'resented by the provincial authorities.' Bryce demanded and received assurances from Health and Welfare deputy minister Joe Willard that the offending passages would be excised from the memo prior to the poverty conference. Ironically, even within a conference intended to promote 'an informal exchange of views' and restricted almost solely to government officials, honest internal assessments of government policy failures and anomalies could not be tolerated. In any event, the primary mission of the conference, Kent continually stressed, was to 'avoid emphasis on the alleviation of poverty and ... emphasize the opportunity side of the question.'[21]

Although highly sceptical of Ottawa's sudden conversion to a War On Poverty and concerned that 'a public conference would generate new pressures for programs that would strain [its] budget,' Ontario was determined not to be upstaged by the federal government at the December conference. The province prepared thoroughly for the gathering and sent an impressive thirty-two member delegation. All major departments were canvassed by Robarts's office for their views on poverty, and the province arrived at the meeting with a thick portfolio of background memoranda. In a revealing move, the task of strategizing and coordinating Ontario's presentation at the Poverty Conference was delegated by Robarts not to the Department of Public Welfare but to Ian Macdonald, the province's chief economist in the Department of Economics and Development. 'Although the "war on poverty" had been declared by Ottawa,' Macdonald pointed out, 'the battleground fell largely within provincial jursidiction' and, for this reason, it was critical that Ontario 'avoid the Ottawa imprint of poverty being placed upon us.' 'Policies should fit our profile rather than one set out by Ottawa,' he warned. 'Ontario should emphasize the dangers of rigid criteria at the national level ... We want the utmost flexibility. The final decision [on poverty] must be left to the provinces.'[22]

In preparing for the conference, Macdonald noted that there was 'at present no truly adequate definition and measurement of poverty in Canada.' Indeed, his staff suggested Ottawa should be 'ask[ed] ... for a paper on how to measure/recognize poverty.' If the rather arbitrary annual poverty line of $3000 for average-size families proposed by the Special Planning Secretariat was adopted, then almost 15 per cent of Ontario families were living in poverty, an index of need that varied dramatically from 45 per cent of all families in the County of Manitoulin or 26 per cent in Renfrew to less than 8 per cent in Halton. In other words, there was a geography of poverty in Ontario. 'Eastern Ontario from North to South has a lower average income and a higher welfare rate than the remainder of the province ... because the area lies within the Laurentian Shield whose rocky terrain and colder climate makes it less attractive to manufacturing and less profitable to agriculture,' Ontario officials pointed out. To focus too much on these regional variations, however, was deceptive. There were 'more people on welfare in the richer parts of the province than in the poorer,' and even a prosperous region such as York County had over 40,000 families earning less than $3000 annually, more than Ontario's twenty-six poorest counties combined.[23]

Another way of looking at poverty was in relation to the minimum wage recently set at $1 an hour. This was 'not ... a fair wage or [a] living wage, but [it] seems to provide for basic needs,' the labour department argued, and was 'designed to provide a basic living standard for employees without placing an undue burden on employers.' For someone working forty-eight hours a week it was 'more than adequate to meet the budget on which provincial welfare assistance is based,' even if it was only half 'the more generous health and decency standards outlined by other agencies' such as the Toronto Social Planning Council. From this perspective, 6.5 per cent of all wage and salary earners were in need, making less than the $1 an hour standard. Two-thirds of this group were women, most of them recent immigrants employed by 'submarginal firms that actually do depend on sub-standard wages and long hours of work to remain competitive.'[24]

A third view of poverty came from the Department of Public Welfare. If dependency on social assistance was the true measure of poverty, then only 2.8 per cent of Ontarians were in need, giving Ontario 'a low to average incidence of welfare' compared with 'other provinces and States.' Few of these people could work: 51 per cent were on social assistance because of poor health, mostly due to the 'feebleness of age';

28 per cent, mostly women, because they were the sole support of children; and only 21 per cent because they were unable to find employment. Within this category, many 'because of age, physical limitations or character defects, are unacceptable to employers.' For all these reasons, welfare officials estimated that the 'group who can, under present conditions, be restored to independence with a modicum of special attention represents probably less than 8% of the total welfare caseload.' These statistics left department officials sceptical about the emphasis placed on 'education, training, and various forms of rehabilitation all aimed at the one goal of commercial employment.' They were 'no panacea against dependency,' the department warned, although 'for the children of all welfare recipients [w]here our efforts are supplemented by medical and psychological treatment ... some inroads can be made in reducing the balance.'[25]

Given these conflicting images, 'perhaps the most difficult task is to establish our criterion of poverty. What yardstick are we to apply?' Macdonald asked the conference in his opening statement on behalf of Ontario's delegation. And what were the ultimate objectives of any war on poverty? Were governments 'seeking to relieve absolute poverty or to close the gap between the low income ... and higher income groups?' Did they wish to 'move [people] out of certain regions' or instead 'bring opportunity to the people? ... We may have to choose.' Above all, were poverty policies to be simply 'of the traditional welfare type to relieve misery and suffering' or should they be designed to 'lift ... the growing generation out of depressed conditions by policies of education, training, or mobility thereby not only improving their human condition but adding to economic productiveness as well'? From this 'dynamic' viewpoint, 'welfare policies become consistent with growth policies.'[26]

As an economist, Macdonald left no doubt where he stood. The key to 'alleviating poverty is economic growth. All programs and policies designed to alleviate poverty should be examined and evaluated in terms of whether they contribute to or detract from other policies and programs aimed at achieving high levels of economic growth and employment.' In specific terms this meant programs that 'provide[d] people with the help and opportunities to move out of poverty and become productive citizens, instead of relief payments that merely guarantee them minimum incomes. A remedial rather than a welfare approach is needed.'[27]

On this point Macdonald got no argument from Tom Kent. Also trained as an economist, Kent made no secret of his distaste for antipoverty strategies based on a welfare model and, like Macdonald, his preference was for policies aimed at using education, training, mobility grants, and regional economic development to break the cycle of poverty. One of his favourite metaphors was to liken society to 'a river where the good swimmers do beautifully but those who can't swim or are mired in the mud on the bank must somehow be carried (even if kicking and screaming) into the mainstream.' Indeed, much of Kent's campaign for a War on Poverty can be seen as preparing the ground for the new federal Department of Manpower and Immigration, of which he would soon become deputy minister, and which already was widely rumoured during the Poverty Conference itself. Pearson's policy secretary continually stressed that the primary theme of Ottawa's poverty war was creating opportunity, not relieving need, and that the Special Planning Secretariat was 'very suspicious of income measurements' and 'did not want to try to develop a rigid definition of poverty.'[28]

The main division that surfaced within the conference, in fact, was not between federal and provincial officials, but between economists and social welfare professionals working within both levels of government. While economists spoke the language of opportunity, mobility, training, and employment, delegates from the social sector instead talked of more accurate and adequate ways of measuring and responding to need. The panel on research pointed to the 'very large gap in our knowledge of the incidence and effect of poverty.' The panel on public assistance concluded that 'rates were generally too low' and 'there was no sense in the existing differentials' among various programs. 'Who can explain ... why an old person's need is assessed at $75 while that of a child ... at somewhere between $10 and $20, or a mother and four children at $74?' its members asked. New methods of 'income transfers' had to be found 'as an anti-poverty measure if we were going to be able to deal with poverty caused by family size,' including supplements for those living in poverty but working full-time at low wages. These were the poor for whom 'the government has made no provision,' and their numbers were substantial. Their plight stood in the way of providing 'adequate amounts of public assistance' to those on welfare, without provoking a backlash from 'their neighbours – those on low incomes.' The panel on welfare manpower noted that the 'available supply of competent personnel is totally inadequate' and that 'staff simply do not exist ... to implement the legislation we are putting on the books.' As a consequence, within existing welfare departments at all levels of government 'the underlying philosophy that people are poor through their own fault and ... that welfare personnel must be watchdogs of public funds ... still ... pervades the administrative ranks of public and private organizations.' Throughout all four days of the conference 'the concept of a minimum level of income as a universal right was discussed but not resolved.'[29]

In the end, the economists dominated within a conference that became, as Kent put it, the 'passing rite for [the war on poverty] as an organized, central activity of government.' Ontario officials reached the same conclusion. As one welfare department delegate summed up the proceedings for deputy minister James Band:

The discussions were very general ... No existing programs or plans for the future were considered in detail. Hence no conclusions were reached ... No announcements of any new plans or programs were made. My own impressions were that the Federal 'War on Poverty' will be a modest effort. No new administrative structures and no new programs will be created ... Great attention will be given to *training* with generous allowances for trainees. The emphasis is on giving help to those persons who are *employable* so that they can begin to earn money and giving help to *rural* impoverished areas rather than to *urban* areas. In summary: the 'War on Poverty' is *not* an attempt to raise the mass of poor people to any certain standard of living. Instead, a selected number of these people, and a selected number of geographical regions will get rehabilitative help that will reduce (but by no means eliminate) the poverty group.[30]

This was, in fact, a perceptive assessment of Ottawa's response to the poverty issue for the remainder of the decade.

After the December 1965 conference, Ottawa's War on Poverty rhetoric and the work of the Special Planning Secretariat fizzled to a halt. Tom Kent left the Prime Minister's Office and the Special Planning Secretariat early in 1966 to pursue his key interests in promoting labour market training and mobility as the first deputy minister of the newly formed Department of Manpower and Immigration. With his departure, what little coherence and bureaucratic support there was for the secretariat disappeared and it became, as one Health and Welfare official aptly put it, 'an organization with form but no content,' one that was increasingly perceived as an unnecessary administrative nuisance by most government departments both in Ottawa and the provinces. Although it would live on until the late 1960s, for all practical purposes both the Social Planning Secretariat and its vision of a coordinated national response to poverty were dead by the early months of 1966.[31]

Ironically, Canada's poorest citizens – native people – were left off the agenda, not only of the poverty conference but of most of the federal and provincial programs targeted at 'eliminating poverty' during the 1960s. Within Ontario, however, the devastating extent of their need, particularly in the North, was increasingly evident to provincial welfare officials throughout the decade as a result of a rapid population increase within aboriginal communities and, more importantly, the steady migration of native people off isolated northern reserves and into nearby communities such as Moosonee, Red Lake, Kenora, and Sault Ste Marie.

During the previous decade, Ontario had gradually expanded its responsibility for native welfare, extending the full range of categorical benefit programs such as old age assistance, disability, blindness, and mothers' allowances to native people in 1955 through the Indian Welfare Services Act. The province had also allowed band councils, for the first time, to act as local governments in administering relief to those in need through the General Welfare Assistance Act of 1958. This progressive extension of provincial welfare entitlement to aboriginal people was in keeping with an overall philosophy of assimilation through integration. As the province's 1953 Report on Civil Liberties and Rights of Indians optimistically put it, 'the time is not far off when the Indian will take his rightful place alongside his non-Indian neighbour with full equality – neither maintaining his present exceptional benefits *nor his now almost imaginary disadvantages.*'[32]

By the early 1960s as increasing numbers of poverty-stricken Indian families began to migrate off the reserves, where they were a federal responsibility, and into areas adjacent to northern Ontario single industry towns, this earlier complacency was shattered as the true extent of native deprivation in their own north was driven home to provincial officials. Living in 'shacks' and 'hovels' outside communities such as Red Lake, Moosonee, or Batchawana Bay, these non-treaty, off-reserve Indians, making up perhaps two-thirds of the province's northern native population, were a 'grossly deprived,' 'quite primitive,' and 'dissolute' people existing within 'conditions of squalor and disorder' and facing a 'total lack of hope for the future.' In these rural northern slums, Band told Robarts: 'Housing (if such it can be called) is of the most primitive, "shack-like" construction ... Sanitation is non-existent ... In consequence there is a marked degree of illness and disease. There is ample evidence of malnutrition; children are neglected, almost completely; the delinquency rate is high ... [and] the consumption of alchohol ... is ... highly excessive .... [M]ost of the older Indians hav[e] attained less than Grade 1, while in the younger age group schooling rarely goes beyond Grade 5.' Federal Indian Affairs officials had been 'almost studiedly indifferent to their plight,' Band continued, and he had 'nothing but repugnance and disdain for the manner in which [they] have dealt with Indians.'[33]

Although these conditions were appalling, they were not new. Indeed, they had existed within isolated northern reserve communities across the province and throughout Canada for decades. It was their export to the fringes of white settlements in northern Ontario which triggered such an outbreak of alarm within Queen's Park. Communities such as Moosonee were 'now saturated with Indians' who had 'no hope of making a livelihood.' Within Red Lake, the poverty of natives 'camping on the fringes' was so 'chronic and expanding ... that the local municipal authorities were unable to cope.' Problems of similar scale were developing on the outskirts of Kenora, Hornepayne, and even Sault Ste Marie. This growing migration of Indians off reserves was allowing Ottawa to walk away from its obligations to native people. 'Even if the federal government has legislative responsibility for these Indians – in practice, they are not meeting it,' Louis Cecile told Robarts, and Ottawa was 'more than anxious ... to rid themselves of the administrative responsibility for services' if the provinces were willing to step in.[34]

As a consequence, Ontario was increasingly drawn into developing a policy response to aboriginal poverty in the north. Communities demanded some help from Queen's Park in meeting the explosion of squalor outside their borders. Moreover, given the 'notable failure' of Ottawa's Indian Affairs policy, only concerted provincial action was likely to allow Indians to 'be more readily assimilated' through education, relocation, and retraining. Finally, a provincial response to the plight of off-reserve native families seemed the most likely means of winning a wider financial commitment from Ottawa for their care.[35]

Within Red Lake, provincial community development officers were sent in to help native men find jobs in the local mining industry, to locate better housing, to improve sanitation, and to get native children into the school system. They also helped to organize a recreational association, an adult education program, and an Indian Association within an off-reserve community made up of a 'number of tribal factions.'[36] The 'very encouraging results' of these efforts at Red Lake between 1963 and 1965 encouraged provincial officials early in 1966 to enter into a wider framework agreement with Ottawa for taking over the delivery of welfare services and community development for all native people, an endeavour some other provinces dismissed as a 'pig in a poke.' Under its terms, Ottawa, in recognition of the substantially higher than average incidence of poverty among native people, agreed to pay over 90 per cent of the cost of general welfare assistance and child welfare services delivered by Ontario to Indians both on and off the reserve. In addition, Ottawa also agreed to fund provincial community development efforts for native people off the reserve in education, training, job placement, housing, recreation, health, law enforcement, and economic development according to the 'ratio of Indians to the white population' in the surrounding area. For the federal government this 'pioneer' agreement represented the first step towards ending its special responsibility for native people, by placing the delivery of welfare services to them on the same basis as to the rest of the population. For Ontario, the 'financial benefit to the province' stemmed from finally winning special federal fiscal support for the growing burden of off-reserve Indians living in poverty. 'The way is now open to the province for an all-out action to eliminate conditions of poverty, squalor, and deprivation which exist with many Indian citizens,' Cecile declared when the agreement was announced.[37]

Within less than a year, however, these hopes lay in tatters as Ottawa and Queen's Park proved to have wildly divergent interpretations of what cost-sharing for community development implied. Soon after the negotiations were concluded the province created a new Indian Development Branch within the Department of Social and Family Services with a staff of seventeen, including ten field officers. Their goal was to 'make a concentrated effort to raise the standards of living wherever needed among Indian groups and open up new opportunities for integration into Canadian life.' It soon became apparent, however, that the promise of 90 per cent federal cost-sharing, including capital expenses, for social and economic development projects in Ontario's north was more illusory than real. 'When Indian development projects are proposed,' Cecile told Robarts only eight months after the agreement had been concluded, 'the interpretation is that if any other provincial program whatever provides a certain service to non-Indians, that service should be provided to the project under the provincial program, rather than come under the Agreement.' Education, training, housing, and roads were all examples Ottawa argued should be excluded from cost-sharing. As a result, federal money was available for 'little more than ... staff salaries [and] even here the contention is that such salaries are sharable only for certain areas at certain times.' Out of more than one million dollars initially authorized for five community development projects, the federal share under this interpretation would amount to only $31,500. This was a 'bit and pieces' approach, which 'yields so little value' that the agreement should be abandoned, Cecile advised.[38]

As a consequence, Robarts refused to authorize the expenditure of any significant funding of the $1.5 million allocated to the Indian Development Branch until Ottawa liberalized its definition of cost-sharing under the agreement. Ontario 'would not unilaterally fund such services to Indians who were constitutionally a federal responsibility,' Robarts told the legislature. Ottawa, for its part, was uninterested in yielding either the control of or credit for community development projects funded over 90 per cent by federal money to promote social and economic development within northern Ontario. In the meantime, by 1969, after over two years of stalemate, the patience of Indian Development Branch director Joseph Dufour reached an end. In an unprecedented move, early in the spring of 1969 he gave his minister, John Yaremko, an ultimatum. Either Ontario's $1.5 million already allocated for native community development projects would be released or he and his staff would resign en masse. Although understandable, this 'ultimatum from a civil servant to his political masters' was ineffective. Dufour received no reply and, true to his word, resigned along with seven of his ten field staff.[39]

To publicize his anger, Dufour also took the extraordinary move of holding a press conference and staging a two-hour demonstration, backed by more than one hundred supporters, outside the legislature, the first time any civil servant had 'staged a public protest against departmental action, or rather inaction.' Despite the unfavourable publicity, hours of debate, and an opposition motion of censure against his government, Robarts refused to budge. Without significantly expanded federal support, funding for native community development would take place 'only on a limited and discretionary basis.'[40]

By the decade's end provincial welfare personnel were openly disenchanted with the prospect of taking over further responsibility for social policy within native communities. 'The Welfare problems of Indians are too big and more than welfare is needed to improve Indian life,' Social Service officials concluded. For Ontario's poorest citizens, the War on Poverty thus fizzled to an end in 1969 without any real shots having been fired.[41]

The Canada Assistance Plan, Welfare Rights, and the Working Poor, 1966–70

Out of the War on Poverty emerged one long-standing objective of federal and provincial welfare officials and private social work agencies in Ontario and across Canada – a new national public assistance act known as the Canada Assistance Plan, which received parliamentary approval in July 1966. Although the Canada Assistance Plan was publicized as a key part of Ottawa's War on Poverty, its origins predated by almost two years Ottawa's sudden discovery of the poverty issue in 1965. Unlike the unilateral and somewhat derivative gestation of Ottawa's War on Poverty, the Canada Assistance Plan was the product of elaborate consultations and negotiations between the federal and provincial governments stretching back to the autumn of 1963, and internal Health and Welfare planning that dated from 1960. Of all the social measures introduced by the Pearson administration in the 1960s, it had the most 'direct bearing on the matter of poverty,' as health and welfare minister Judy LaMarsh noted at the time.[1] Yet despite its important accomplishments and the heady optimism that surrounded its passage, the Canada Assistance Plan ultimately failed to alter, in any fundamental way, longstanding approaches to the needs of the poor either in Ontario or in other provincial jurisdictions. The reasons why this was so reveal much about the limitations and contradictions of welfare policy during a decade of unprecedented affluence and economic growth.

Negotiations leading to the Canada Assistance Plan began in earnest with the formation of a federal-provincial working group on welfare programs after the November 1963 federal-provincial pension conference. Ottawa and the provinces had different reasons for seeking new arrangements in the field of shared-cost social assistance. For federal officials, unhappiness with the loose arrangements and soaring costs of unemployment assistance was the key triggering factor, a point federal deputy welfare minister Joe Willard made quickly at the first meeting of the working group in February 1964. 'We have now got into a program where we have over 700,000 recipients ... The federal outlay is more than $110 million [annually],' he told his provincial counterparts. 'When you add to that the provincial share it ... makes the programs that were provided during the 1930's seem rather small ... *[I]t is equal in one year to what was spent during the entire depression period.*' The explosive growth of unemployment assistance expenditure far beyond the $13 million level anticipated when the legislation was first implemented cried out for some form of rationalization and reform. 'The community generally is beginning to get restless in respect to welfare expenditures,' Willard observed. 'How is it, when we are in perhaps the most prosperous time in the history of the country, that welfare levels are at [their] greatest point?' Apart from gaining better control and understanding of soaring costs, federal officials also wished to see provinces and local governments spend welfare money more wisely in order to help break the cycle of poverty. Too many welfare departments were simply 'continu[ing] to pay money ad infinitum to certain problem families ... when we should have been thinking in terms of ... rehabilitation.' Unless welfare became more closely linked to 'vocational training and job placement, we may continue to spend very large sums of public money to no avail other than ... to keep ... particular people alive.'[2]

Ontario, in contrast, was not unhappy with the open-endedness and flexibility of the Unemployment Assistance Act, particularly in comparison with other shared-cost programs which, according to its officials, were too rigidly governed by federal regulations. From the province's perspective, the central objective in welfare reform was not to enhance Ottawa's authority, but simply to extend the flexible cost-sharing arrangements surrounding unemployment assistance to the other categorical benefit programs as well as to areas presently excluded from federal funding such as mothers' allowances, child welfare, and medical care for the poor.[3]

The Canada Pension Plan was an additional factor pushing both levels of governments towards new welfare legislation. As part of the complex negotiations leading to the plan, Ottawa agreed to phase eligibility for universal Old Age Security downwards to the age of sixty-five bringing to a gradual end the means-tested old age assistance program administered by the provinces. Inadequacies in Old Age Security benefits as well as in the low payments initially payable through the proposed Canada Pension Plan in its first ten years would require continued welfare supplementation for many of the elderly in need. In the absence of new legislation, these supplements could only take place through unemployment assistance, with all its inadequate fiscal and administrative controls.

Modernizing provincial public assistance was thus seen as essential for winning public acceptance of the new pension changes, particularly for groups inadequately protected by either the Canada Pension Plan or Old Age Security. Indeed, a new social assistance scheme could save the federal government 'some $300 million or $800 million' by allowing Ottawa to 'resist the pressure for increases in Old Age Security,' Joe Willard pointed out. Provinces had different concerns with pensions. As long as categorical benefits for the aged, the blind, and the disabled remained linked by tradition to Old Age Security, then provincial standards of welfare spending would be increasingly determined by decisions made in Ottawa. If all these welfare programs were merged into a single administrative framework, much like unemployment assistance, in which provinces and municipalities could set their own benefit ceilings and asset requirements, then provincial autonomy over the determination of 'need' could be restored.[4]

With a consensus on the need for close and ongoing federal-provincial consultations and the added momentum provided by the American War on Poverty, discussions on a new welfare act proceeded smoothly throughout the remainder of 1964. Health and Welfare officials worked intensively, with ongoing provincial consultation, in producing a comprehensive first draft of the scheme, and early in 1965 Judy LaMarsh proposed to Pearson that a new Canada Assistance Plan form the centrepiece of Canada's War on Poverty during the upcoming 1965 session of Parliament. The new legislation would replace unemployment assistance 'with a measure which would provide for sharing in all types of public assistance, including mothers' allowances, which are now excluded ... [and] the costs of administration of such programs, including ancillary social services.' Under the new plan, all existing categorical programs would 'eventually be eliminated ... [so] that people will be looked after *on the basis of their actual need* irrespective of cause, [and] free of arbitrary eligibility restrictions.' The Canada Assistance proposal was 'essential to supplement the age-reduced benefits under ... Old Age Security which begin on January 1 1966,' LaMarsh argued, and would also allow the government 'to indicate that the range of its programs dealing with poverty compare very favourably with the much-publicized "war on poverty" in the United States.' LaMarsh's reference to the War on Poverty was timely. The plan's fate as a new shared-cost venture would have been highly uncertain, given the tepid support from the Department of Finance for such measures, without the added political momentum provided by Pearson's decision to launch his own War on Poverty campaign. After receiving cabinet approval in April, the Canada Assistance Plan became a core component of Ottawa's pledge to eliminate poverty in the April 1965 Speech from the Throne.[5]

What remained unclear, even within National Health and Welfare, was how far Ottawa would go with the assistance plan to 'promote adequate levels of assistance so that Canadians will not, through poverty, be denied an adequate standard of food, clothing, shelter and other essentials for normal living and the preservation of family life,' a concern made all the more relevant by the legislation's stated intent to meet 'the fact, not the cause of need.' The first proposal sent to cabinet contained the proviso that Ottawa 'defin[e] ... the basic elements in the family budget.' Provinces would be required to 'set out in plans' their own 'rates to cover each of these items' as well their 'arrangements for setting assistance rates and assessing their adequacy from time to time.' Also included were a range of administrative procedures through which Ottawa and the provinces jointly could 'develop ... generally accepted indices of need.'[6]

Department of Finance officials quickly shot down these recommendations. '*Standards can only be decided upon locally* ... [I]t is impossible to get a fair standard for all of Canada and also unnecessary to attempt it,' deputy minister Robert Bryce tartly informed Willard. As a result, the interdepartmental committee recommending the Canada Assistance Plan to cabinet agreed that the legislation 'should provide only for *very general standards* in respect of the items of assistance that would be included.' It would be up to provinces to 'establish the more specific conditions and requirements governing the provision of assistance.' Simply put, the War on Poverty would be fought without any attempt by Ottawa to define the enemy.[7]

Unlike the Unemployment Assistance Act, the Canada Assistance Plan did have regulations that required the provinces to provide 'assistance rates that take into account the basic requirements of individuals and families for food, shelter, clothing, fuel and utilities, and household and personal needs.' However, the definition of basic requirements was left totally to the provinces. Welfare recipients would receive the difference between their 'budgetary requirements,' as determined by provincially or locally administered needs tests, and their 'available resources,' up to the level of whatever set maxima the provinces imposed. If in the case of shelter costs these maxima took no account of actual rents, there was no provision within the plan to ensure that the basic requirements or actual need of the individual or family would be met.[8]

Soon after the Canada Assistance Plan took effect, internal guidelines issued within Toronto's welfare department instructed case workers administering needs tests 'to ensure that ... [provincial] maximum allowances are adhered to. If a reduction is necessary to meet the maximum, the *adjustment deduction* should be taken off the shelter allowance.' Such adjustment deductions, although never publicized, became routine bureaucratic procedures to ensure that the basic requirements of all those applying for aid never exceeded 'the allowable maximum for the family size.' In other words, despite all the rhetoric of meeting actual need and eliminating poverty, welfare administration under the Canada Assistance Plan was simply business as usual. The idea of needs testing remained a fiction when the actual financial requirements of families, particularly for shelter, were bureaucratically manipulated to fit within preset provincial maximums.[9]

The main significance of the plan lay not in defining national standards, which in the political context of the mid-1960s was unlikely in any case,[10] but in markedly expanding the scope of federal financing for social assistance costs across the country. Here the provinces, including Ontario, played a leading role in pushing Ottawa far beyond its initial willingness simply to include mothers' allowance cases within a new general assistance scheme. Two critical new frontiers for federal cost-sharing were in social administration and child welfare. Ontario had little interest in the former, which James Band viewed simply as an unwelcome opportunity for federal meddling in his own bureaucracy.[11] Cost-sharing for the hiring of new welfare personnel was included within the assistance plan, despite such grumbling, because it was desperately needed to modernize welfare departments in the Atlantic provinces and because it fit so well into the rehabilitative thrust of Ottawa's War on Poverty, with its commitment to breaking the cycle of hard-core dependency. 'We must ... get ... better welfare staffs out into the homes,' Joe Willard argued in selling the proposal to cabinet. 'Otherwise our efforts on rehabilitation and efforts to cut down on malingering will be greatly reduced. If we want to keep the federal incentives in the right place ... we must share in these costs.' War on poverty czar Tom Kent agreed, arguing it was 'the only sensible approach to the problem.' Within Ontario, Band was mollified by Willard's promise that Ottawa would simply provide a straight 50 per cent subsidy but would attach no conditions to 'what kind of people you hire.'[12]

But Ontario did play a decisive role in drawing Ottawa into cost-sharing the field of child welfare. Band made this a key provincial objective throughout the entire Canada Assistance Plan negotiations, with strong assistance from his premier, John Robarts. Although federal finance department officials put up fierce opposition, two arguments ultimately worked in Ontario's favour. The first, and perhaps most important, flowed logically from including mothers' allowances within the plan. Within this caseload were numerous children, who although not wards of the crown, were cared for as 'assistance cases' by foster parents. Although their needs would now be eligible for federal cost-sharing as part of the plan, those of children under the legal protection of Children's Aid Societies would not. Why should the fact of 'guardianship' deprive needy children of the added resources federal funding could provide? This distinction was as artificial as the one that previously excluded women and children on mothers' allowances from unemployment assistance funding, provincial officials argued.[13]

Despite complaining that 'at each step we are solving one problem but ... are creating additional anomalies,' federal officials conceded the logic of such arguments. On the one hand, they feared provinces might prove reluctant to take children into guardianship if this made them ineligible for CAP funding. On the other hand, they also acknowledged that a War on Poverty could hardly be won if children were left out. 'Child welfare services ... are increasingly under stress across Canada,' LaMarsh argued in a final plea to cabinet noting Ontario's concerns. '[They] represent one of the most vital of preventive services, and measures to strengthen them deserve priority in any concerted war on poverty.' If the Canada Assistance Plan did 'not deal comprehensively with child welfare,' it would 'fall short of its goal' of developing an integrated and adequate public welfare system.[14]

At the last minute, and with the decisive intervention of Quebec welfare minister René Lévesque, these arguments prevailed. 'If we neglect this field,' Lévesque told Ottawa, 'then we will only breed more cases which are going to cost more than the rest of the Canada Assistance Plan ... We are going to fabricate more customers for whom you are going to pay, one way or the other, much more.' Lévesque's 'emphatic ... emphasis [of] the needs of youth,' combined with the 'strong and unanimous demand for including child and youth welfare in the Plan' among the other provinces, clearly tipped the balance. Shortly after the final January 1966 federal-provincial conference on the plan, Ottawa announced it would include full funding for all provincial child welfare costs within the legislation, at an additional cost estimated at $16 million a year.[15]

The arrival of open-ended Canada Assistance Plan funding came at a propitious moment for Ontarians in need. Unemployment in the province during the mid-1960s averaged only 2.5 per cent, a low-point it would never reach again. Ontario was in the midst of a phenomenal economic boom that would see real personal income in constant dollars grow by more than 40 per cent over the next five years.[16] In response to internal administrative reforms launched by the Robarts government, the province also had developed a provincial civil service capable, for the first time, of rivalling Ottawa's in its planning, research, and administrative capability, including the establishment of a separate research and policy planning unit within the newly renamed Department of Social and Family Services. 'In the early post-war years ... [t]he provinces simply did not have the necessary revenues, the personnel, nor the planning skills that were necessary to bring [social] programs into being,' Robarts's chief executive officer Keith Reynolds conceded to federal officials near the end of the decade. 'The situation is different today.' Because of a phenomenal growth in its activities over the past two decades, the province had now developed its own cadre of 'competent and expert advisors and administrators' and it would 'no longer accept the right of the federal government alone to define the national interest as it relates to areas of provincial jurisdiction ... over social security.'[17] In the midst of unprecedented affluence, how would Ontario use this newly found administrative and economic strength to realize the plan's stated intentions of seeking 'the prevention and removal of the causes of poverty,' particularly in the face of a public debate on the issue that sought, if only briefly, to eliminate poverty altogether?

The first answers appeared in the summer and fall of 1967, Canada's centennial year, as Ontario's new minister of social and family services, John Yaremko, introduced legislation incorporating the changes necessitated by the Canada Assistance Plan into a new framework for social assistance within the province. A new Family Benefits Act consolidated the existing categorical programs for the old, the blind, the disabled, for elderly widows and unmarried women, and for women with dependent children into one single long-term assistance program administered by the province. With this change, mothers' allowances as a separate and distinct program within the province disappeared after forty-seven years of existence. A revised General Welfare Assistance Act, however, continued to hold municipalities responsible for administering and financing 20 per cent of the cost of supposedly short-term welfare clients, for the most part single men, employable men and their families, and all those who fell within the three-month waiting period normally needed to qualify for long-term family benefits.

The province's new welfare allowances under the assistance plan 'would be generous' and would 'ensure acceptable living standards' for all those dependent upon social assistance, retiring welfare minister Louis Cecile assured Robarts. 'As has been made abundantly clear, the intent of the federal legislation is that additional funds are to be used to improve existing allowances and services to needy persons. It is not to be expected that there will be much saving to the province because of the increased federal aid.'[18] On an across-the-board basis, welfare benefits in Ontario jumped 15 to 20 per cent through the new legislation introduced in 1967, the first increase in over two years. Municipalities also received a 50 per cent subsidy of their new welfare administration costs as an incentive to modernize their staffs. For those on family benefits, a new 'needs test' replaced 'means-testing,' although the extent to which this alleviated individual need was more fictional than real. 'In theory [we] will ... provide the difference' between needs and available resources, department officials observed of the new setup under the Family Benefits Act. 'In practice, we have introduced maximums into our regulations.' Although individual circumstances varied, the range of aid under family benefits in 1967 extended from $85 to $115 a month for single people, from $130 to $180 for couples, and from $226 to a ceiling of $300 a month for a family of four. In effect, these ceilings now became the provincial definition of 'an adequate and decent social minimum.'[19]

Opposition critics and Ontario's social policy community disagreed fiercely. The ceilings proposed through family benefits came to only 60 per cent of the Toronto Social Planning Council definition of a minimum cost-of-living budget for a family of four in that city, NDP welfare critic Stephen Lewis charged. Given the 'great hopes' aroused by the Canada Assistance Plan, the legislation was a 'bitter, bitter, disappointment ... [and] a betrayal of the people it is designed to serve.' In an entirely new departure that borrowed heavily from recent American debates on poverty, Lewis called instead for a 'radical overhaul' of Ontario's welfare state through the development of a guaranteed annual income of at least $4000 to $5000 a year for a family of four, an amount that would provide both those on welfare as well as the 'working poor' with a decent minimum. Lewis's reference to the working poor and his call for a guaranteed annual income were new ideas that 'really [put] some meat on the platter,' Cecile conceded, but such a system was in operation nowhere else and, within Canada, could only be implemented at the national level. 'There is only so much money available ... The question of standards is always a difficult one and open to controversy for here we are trying to answer the question of how much is enough, or how much is too much.'[20]

Within the legislature, the strongest criticism of the province's new welfare legislation was directed against the government's decision to retain municipal responsibility for the administration of general welfare assistance. Why 'arbitrarily and unjustly ... discriminate between different kinds of recipients?' both Liberal and NDP members asked. Why, for example, did families on family benefits (FBA) need $12 a month for utilities while those on general welfare (GWA) needed only $8? This retention of arbitrary categorical distinctions 'violates every single social principle [of] the Canada Assistance Plan.' Was the only reason because the province wanted to 'charge some of the cost back to the municipalities?'[21]

This accusation was only partially correct. Widows, the elderly, the disabled, and the blind liked distinctions that kept them separated from a general program of 'direct relief,' provincial officials argued. More important, however, were 'problems in defining needs in relation to community standards,' particularly for those who could work. If the province took over administration of general welfare assistance, it would 'face serious problems of interregional economic disparities.' Put differently, municipal governments were best able to keep welfare rates in line with local wages. Although a cliché, there was a strong element of truth to the old poor law argument that the government closest to home was best suited to administer welfare, the province's brief to the Senate Committee on Poverty noted. 'Welfare services must start and finish with a personal confrontation between the applicant and a representative of the appropriate welfare service in the community.'[22]

'Personal confrontation' aptly described the tone of local welfare administration in many Ontario communities throughout the remainder of the decade. By the late 1960s almost five hundred of the province's nine hundred municipalities still ran their own welfare systems. The remainder had delegated the responsibility to nineteen county and district welfare units. All these local agencies continued to enjoy considerable discretion in how they interpreted eligibility and benefit entitlement under general welfare assistance, including how many liquid assets applicants were allowed to possess before applying, how much of their earnings from part-time work would be deducted from their allowances, whether items of special assistance such as eye glasses, prescription drugs, or dental care would be provided, and whether they were looking hard enough for work in order to retain their benefits. Municipalities had also developed 'investigatory procedures ... tailored to local standards ... [and] designed to detect fraud'; provincial welfare officials conceded that these procedures aroused 'criticisms of infringement of privacy and individual rights.' Above all, local welfare departments, like the province through the Family Benefits Act, never revealed the basis on which they calculated the specific amount of a recipient's entitlement, even for basic necessities such as food, clothing, and household necessities. For reasons of administrative efficiency, the estimated cost of all such items was blended into one 'pre-added budget' and provincial officials argued that it was 'not possible for recipients to know how this part of their basic allowance is made up ... Needs tested income maintenance programs are complex and not easily explained. Some recipients are disadvantaged in their ability to comprehend.'[23]

Although too dull to grasp the cost of their needs, welfare clients were nonetheless expected to spend their money wisely. If not, they could be easily blamed if their pre-added budget failed to meet their actual requirements. 'We do not allocate any specific sums for any amount,' Yaremko replied to opposition critics demanding to know how much the province and local governments provided for food. 'The schedules work out to a total figure. The social assistance recipient gets that cheque and he or she has to figure out his own way and he has complete discretion as to the expenditures.' Some of them might 'like to sleep with the windows wide open and get a lot of cold fresh air and spend the money on something else. It may be vice versa.' For mothers who could not manage there was always family counselling or department nutritional advice 'to guide and assist them in budgeting in order to make the dollars provided for them go as far as possible.'[24]

Because of Ontario's decision to keep local governments in charge of general welfare assistance, there were dramatic variations across the province in the average local monthly expenditures for recipients, ranging from $25.79 in Nipissing District to $71.38 in Ottawa-Carleton. In contrast, the range of difference under the provincially administered family benefits program was modest – $62.59 in Sudbury compared with $76.05 in Toronto.[25] As local welfare costs crept steadily upwards by the end of the 1960s, soaring in communities like Kingston from 3.4 per cent to 11.7 per cent of the city's total expenditures between 1961 and 1971 in response to a growing burden of youth unemployment, tax-conscious local councils increasingly pressed their welfare administrators to use their discretionary authority to keep costs under control.[26]

As a result, reports of abusive treatment of welfare applicants at the hands of local departments mushroomed within the legislature. Peterborough's welfare department denied the deaf child of a family on General Welfare the cost of batteries for her hearing-aid, and some local councillors threatened employable men with jail if they failed to report for work activity projects. Brantford's welfare administrator was accused of telling women applying for aid to 'get some guy to live with,' 'go back and live with your husband for the money,' or 'get the money [you need] in the best way you know how.' Kingston's welfare department, in response to a 'constant stream of complaints from irate taxpayers,' refused welfare to those who quit their jobs or were fired unless the department decided that the employer was unfair. In rural townships, applicants seldom received money for household necessities or items of special assistance and often did not even get the province's pre-added budget schedule for food and clothing. Those applying for assistance in Scarborough were required to sign forms authorizing that 'anyone may enter the home on behalf of the department.' As a provincial Task Force on Community and Social Services later concluded, in many municipalities across Ontario 'attitudes to welfare are reflected in an administration that is mean, arbitrary, combative, grudging, and destructive of dignity.'[27]

Even within Toronto, where welfare administration had traditionally been more liberal than elsewhere, a crackdown on the general welfare caseload was increasingly evident as the decade wore on. Alarmed by the rapid rise in single employables on relief and the growth of what they termed 'welfaritis,' senior welfare administrators instructed their staff to be 'as stringent as possible in the processing of all applications,' including withholding aid until after home visits, putting all allowances on a weekly rather than a fortnightly basis, allowing 'no physically and emotionally healthy single[s] ... to stay on welfare for several months,' and pressuring single parent mothers 'to force daughters out of the home as a measure of work motivation.' Case workers were also advised to use 'bluffs ... where appropriate' in convincing any applicants not from Ontario that they would be 'forcibly repatriated' back to their own communities in violation of CAP's primary guarantee of a right to relief anywhere in Canada. Special assistance for glasses, dentures, and drugs, previously issued automatically with hospital approval, would now be subjected to 'considerable discretion ... by the district administrators to ... reduc[e] costs.' Above all, welfare visitors were told to abandon their 'negative approach ... of assuming that all clients cannot exist another day without emergency [aid].' Instead, 'indirect motivating methods' were needed, including telling applicants to 'do as much for themselves as they are able to do.'[28]

As the Senate's report on *Poverty in Canada* remarked in 1970, it was 'difficult if not impossible for one person or one department to be a dispenser of casework services and a financial investigator at the same time. Saving money and saving people are often goals in conflict.' By the end of the 1960s as the proportion of employables on general welfare assistance rose from 42 per cent to 64 per cent of an increasingly youthful caseload, and the numbers on family benefits and general welfare combined almost doubled from 80,000 to more than 150,000 between 1961 and 1971, the province's welfare system, according to John Yaremko, was 'under the greatest strain since the depression.'[29]

By far the largest share of this rising assistance caseload was composed of single mothers. Between 1966 and 1969 the number of families led by women on family benefits more than doubled from 10,056 to 20,428, boosting the cost of the program by over 200 per cent. Three years later more than 33,000 mothers would be collecting family benefits. Mother-led families on family benefits and general welfare combined jumped by 302 per cent in Ontario between 1961 and 1973, representing exactly a third of the province's entire welfare caseload by 1973 and over half the total increase in the numbers collecting social assistance. These soaring caseload numbers were fuelled by liberalized eligibility requirements and a rising rate of family fragmentation. In 1964 the period of desertion by a husband was dropped to three months as a requirement for eligibility under the program. Two years later wives not technically deserted, but merely separated from husbands whose whereabouts were known, also became eligible for benefits. The addition of these two new categories to family benefits 'accounted for most of the 10,372 additional cases that more than doubled the caseload in that brief period.'[30]

This 'feminization of poverty' remained one of the most neglected features of the entire debate on need within Ontario during the 1960s. As Diana Pearce has pointed out in analysing similar developments south of the border, 'much of women's poverty is due to two causes that are basically unique to females. Women often must provide all or most of the support for their children, and they are disadvantaged in the labor market.' Moreover, when relationships fractured, most often 'the man becomes single while the woman becomes a single parent.' Within Ontario these unique aspects of female poverty were mostly overlooked by government policy-makers concerned with the War on Poverty. As in the United States, most of the language and program activity flowing out of Ottawa's anti-poverty initiatives in labour market training and regional development 'assumed that the overwhelming majority of those who needed jobs, and therefore needed the skills to obtain jobs, were men,' even though single mothers were the fastest-growing component of the welfare caseload. As a consequence, the particular structural obstacles 'lock[ing] them into a life of poverty' were ignored.[31]

Nowhere was this clearer than around the issue of day care. From the end of the Second World War onwards, Ontario rapidly lost interest in providing support for publicly funded child care for working mothers.

By 1964 the province was actually spending less money on day care than it had twenty years earlier. Compared with twenty-eight municipal day nurseries in Ontario in 1946, there were only twenty-nine by 1962, providing publicly funded full day care for between 1000 to 2000 children. Over the next six years, and with the stimulus of federal funding through CAP, the number of municipal spaces subsidized according to the mother's ability to pay jumped to over 5000, but as the province's former director of general welfare assistance pointed out, 'this.was like hoisting a small umbrella to shelter a stadium full of people in a downpour ... In any month, the children of recipients of Mothers' Allowances and General Assistance exceeded 100,000.' Across the province, more than 95,000 single mothers not on social assistance were also working full time.[32]

Given the absence of subsidized day-care spaces, women with small children heading single parent families often had little alternative but complete reliance on inadequate social assistance benefits as a means of economic survival, and little ability to compete effectively in the labour market. Across Ontario by 1967 only 15 per cent of mothers on family benefits reported any part-time earnings whatsoever, and women's average duration on social assistance was over twice the length of men's.[33] Yet Ontario officials adamantly refused to see the provision of adequate subsidized day care as an urgent need for women who wished to escape from poverty. For Cecile, the very desire of mothers to combine 'employment and homemaking has contributed to many of the social problems which have to be faced and treated.' Their 'primary responsibility [is] for family life,' he insisted. Nor was Cecile convinced that his department had any pressing obligation to provide child care. 'There might be a lot of these women who have children – one ... or two, or three – and have next-door parents who will take care of them, or some other neighbour. They do not all need help.' These 'condescending ... 19th century ... male-dominated' attitudes towards day care infuriated NDP critics in the legislature. Throughout the 1960s the party kept up a fiery barrage of criticism against the government's tortuously slow pace in creating more subsidized public spaces for the care of young children, but by the decade's end affordable child care for welfare mothers remained only marginally more available. Significant progress on this issue would not begin in earnest until the 1970s.[34]

Despite the emphasis on training and rehabilitation in the War on Poverty, Ontario's burgeoning army of welfare mothers also found themselves left beyond the battlefield during the 1960s. Women caring for their children and therefore out of the labour force for over three years were deemed ineligible for financial support for retraining provided by

Ottawa's flourishing Canada Manpower programs after 1966. For the minority of mothers who found part-time employment, high clawbacks on their earned income, combined with the absence of financial support for child care, provided few incentives for seeking work. Apart from a $24 monthly exemption for the mother and $12 for each child, 75 per cent of any additional income a women earned was simply deducted from her monthly allowance, 'a pretty large bite into what anybody is earning over and above assistance,' critics in the legislature pointed out, and far higher than the 50 per cent clawback rate proposed by even the most stringent conservative proponents of a guaranteed annual income.[35]

Finally, women on family benefits, like their predecessors on mothers' allowances, simply did not get enough to provide even minimal standards of food, clothing, and shelter for themselves and their children despite the program's stated intentions of 'meeting actual need' and the infusion of 50 per cent federal funding through the Canada Assistance Plan. Once again the roadblock remained arbitrary maximum ceilings on the standards of assistance provided. As deputy welfare minister Burne Heise had pointed out in the 1940s, attempts to combine needs-testing with maximum ceilings of support produced a 'bastard system.' In the 1960s NDP critic Stephen Lewis picked up on this same 'contradiction ... in the [Family Benefits] Act which completely nullifies its intent ... The Act says that the allowance will mean an allowance provided on the basis of need ... Then under the regulation it prescribes maximum amounts of benefits ... It is absolutely impossible, it defies all the rules of logic, to say on the one hand that you will base an income on need and then on the next hand that you will prescribe the maximum needs allowable. It cannot be done.' Mothers getting only '60 per cent of the absolute minimum subsistence level' as calculated by Toronto's Social Planning Council were not benefiting from 'a needs test programme. That is a crude and arbitrary fixing of people at a poverty level, nothing more, nothing less.'[36]

Arbitrary formulas were simply a fact of life, Cecile replied. 'How are we going to judge a person? We have to have a basic formula some place ... We have to arrive at some rule, some norm, and then go from there.' His successor, John Yaremko, answered similar criticisms by arguing that mothers in the program, paying no taxes and enjoying in-kind medical and dental benefits, were often better off than households with a full-time wage earner. 'If families on social assistance are having problems, they are having problems which many people in our society with these kind of earnings are facing.'[37]

Women dependent on the program had a different frame of reference. Why did the government 'pay foster mothers more money to look after youngsters than it gives to the natural mothers of these children?' the manifesto of Women Trapped in Poverty asked at the decade's end. 'The government obviously recognizes the expense of foster mothers in looking after children and pays them for the work they do, but it gives no recognition of the work done by a natural mother and it makes her task more difficult by making her do it for less money ... There is no recognition of our contribution to society.' In arguments harkening back to the original premise of mothers' allowances as a 'reward for service to the state,' these women demanded that natural mothers under family benefits assistance 'deserve pay for work equal to the foster mother's at least,' as well as 'adequate shelter for our family' and 'greater opportunities and support to gradually upgrade our education and eventually phase out of government assistance.'[38]

Instead, despite or perhaps because of the program's greatly expanded caseload and much wider framework of eligibility, the level of benefits under family benefits assistance by 1971 as a proportion either of the average Ontario family income or the Toronto Social Planning Council's *Guide for Family Budgeting*, remained virtually unchanged over the course of the decade, regardless of major increases in government spending on the program. As Lorna Hurl concludes, 'over time the programme ... changed to ensure more equitable treatment of one group of sole-support ... mothers in relation to another, but not to provide greater adequacy or equality of recipients in relation to the population as a whole.'[39] For women on family benefits, the War on Poverty swelled their ranks but did not substantially alter their prospects for a better life.

In response to soaring welfare caseloads during a time of affluence, attitudes and policies towards those on relief, particularly at the local level, began to harden. Within this context, the right of appeal for those denied benefits by local governments assumed increasing political importance. The creation of some appeal mechanism was one of the few new conditions Ottawa had succeeded in attaching to the cost-sharing of social assistance through the Canada Assistance Plan in order to raise, albeit indirectly, local welfare standards. The ability to appeal the denial of aid was critical to establishing the concept that welfare was indeed a legal right, and not merely charity. 'The power to create legal relationships is a form of political power,' a Kingston anti-poverty study pointed out. 'If the welfare recipient is able to effectively challenge and criticize official behaviour, he is, in effect, enfranchised and representative in the decision-making process.' This was all the more critical given the plan's language, which promised 'the provision of

adequate assistance to and in respect of persons in need and the prevention and removal of the causes of poverty.' How were these phrases to
be interpreted and what legal force did they have? How could the right
to adequate assistance be guaranteed if recipients were never told how
their budgetary needs had been assessed or if the province continually
refused to publish the basis on which it calculated its pre-added welfare
budgets? Welfare appeal boards could have a critical impact in breaking down this veil of administrative discretion and secrecy that traditionally enveloped relief administration by developing a welfare case
law and uniform standards of interpreting the rights of those in need
throughout the province, NDP critics pointed out. Through participating in this process, the poor could also 'develop a sense of community'
around which they could 'organiz[e] ... to increase their social and
political power.'[40]

This prospect had little attraction for Ontario's welfare administrators. Early in the negotiations for the Canada Assistance Plan, James
Band made no secret of his dislike of Ottawa's intentions to insist on
some form of appeal mechanism being incorporated into the legislation.
The process would only clutter up the courts and might be a very
expensive operation, he told federal officials. The absence of an appeal
process in Ontario had 'not given [us] too many worries,' nor had his
department devoted any particular thought to how such a structure might
develop. Canada was 'at the stage where this kind of thing is important
to many people,' his federal counterpart Joe Willard insisted. However,
in the face of continued provincial opposition to any detailed regulations, he agreed finally that 'a provision for right of appeal will be
made and we can let it go at that.'[41]

Even this minimal requirement within the Canada Assistance Plan,
however, became a source of irritation to Ontario, and the province put
off creating an appeal structure for as long as possible. When a new
General Welfare Assistance Act was introduced in 1967, no provision
was contained for appeals. 'If the [welfare] administrator, in ... fixing
the eligibility and the amount of assistance is wrong, I am sure that the
members of the [municipal] council will hear about it,' Ontario attorney-general Arthur Wishart reassured the legislature, 'so ... I do not
think you need to have another ... appellant authority to deal with the
matter.'[42] Two years later, welfare recipients in Ontario still lacked any
mechanism for appealing unfavourable decisions. After continued agitation by local welfare rights organizations, including frequent complaints to Ottawa that Ontario was not living up to the terms of the plan,
the province finally established a board of review in 1969 consisting of
Robena Morris, Toronto's recently retired welfare commissioner, news-

paper columnist Frank Drea, and a retired Carleton County reeve, Earl Armstrong. Ironically, before the year's end, the board would be chaired by none other than James Band, who also retired from his extensive government service that year. Six months later the board still had not met, no regulations governed its operations, and no forms existed within local welfare offices to inform recipients how to launch an appeal. Under intense questioning in the legislature, Yaremko conceded that out of 108,000 general welfare recipients, only seven had so far requested an appeal, all from Peterborough through the efforts of the United Citizens, Ontario's oldest welfare rights organization. Only a seventeen-hour filibuster of his department's estimates by the NDP extracted a commitment from Yaremko that welfare recipients would be informed of the board's existence as well as how to apply to it. These efforts, combined with effective publicity by the United Citizens and continued pressure from Ottawa, finally resulted in the Board of Review's first hearings in Peterborough later that year. Nonetheless, opposition critics rightly questioned how any appeal board, composed of retired senior welfare administrators and with no representation from the poor themselves, could possibly provide an objective review of the very decisions they 'might have had something to do with.' The board was nothing more than a 'green pasture for retired bureaucrats ... the very people who made unfair and degrading policies that must be challenged and changed,' the Just Society, a Toronto welfare rights group, complained to the legislature.[43]

The proliferation of groups like the United Citizens and the Just Society, by the late 1960s, drove home to provincial welfare officials that 'the poor, including welfare recipients [were] organizing' and 'for the first time [were] shed[ding] their sense of shame or inferiority.' In scattered communities across the province such as Peterborough, Kingston, Ottawa, Brantford, and Toronto, a diverse range of welfare rights groups such as the United Citizens, Association for Tenants' Action Kingston (ATAK), Action 70, the Just Society, and Women Trapped in Poverty had formed to press governments, most often at the local level, to provide more adequate housing and welfare allowances. The roots of this fledgling poor people's movement were diverse. Some organizations, such as Peterborough's United Citizens, were the product of a local left-wing labour and community activist tradition dating back to the 1940s. More typically, though, welfare rights groups flowered briefly between 1967 and 1970 through a combination of 1960s New Left activism, the devastating impact of urban redevelopment on poor people's neighborhoods, and direct government sponsorship of community organization efforts through agencies such as the Company of Young Canadians or welfare grants channelled through the Department of National Health and Welfare.[44]

What they all shared in common was a sense of anger and frustration at the widening gap between government rhetoric on the poverty issue and the actual operation of welfare and housing programs. The language of the War on Poverty fostered high expectations that combatting need was a key government priority. It also created a growing sense of entitlement to a decent minimum standard of living, an expectation strengthened by Prime Minister Pierre Trudeau's 1968 election campaign for a Just Society and his Throne Speech promise to 'define, with as much clarity as possible, the essential components of a minimum standard of satisfactory living – not a subsistence standard, but one which allows for dignity and decency.' As a consequence, 'in a short time clients rights groups and poor people's organizations were approaching government aggressively at every level.'[45]

As the decade drew to a close, moreover, government organizations themselves raised the stakes in the poverty debate. In its fifth annual review in 1968, the Economic Council of Canada made the most systematic attempt yet undertaken to measure the depth of poverty in Canada. Defining it as the expenditure of 70 per cent or more of annual income on the basic necessities of food, clothing, and shelter, the council argued that (in 1961 dollars) the poverty line for individuals was $1500 and for the average family of four, $3500 a year, a figure subsequently revised upwards to $4200 by 1969. According to this standard, one out of four Canadians was living in need. Moreover, two-thirds of poor families worked at least part of the year but were unable to get help from social assistance. 'Serious poverty should be eliminated in Canada ... [T]his should be designated as a major national goal,' the council concluded.[46] In late autumn 1968, in response to these recommendations, the Senate of Canada appointed its own Special Committee on Poverty, chaired by Senator David Croll, former welfare minister in Ontario during the Hepburn years and most recently chairman of a highly influential Senate Committee on Aging. Two years later, after conducting numerous hearings across Canada, listening to 810 witnessess, and receiving 109 briefs, the committee concluded that despite the unprecedented affluence of the past decade, 'in absolute terms poverty in Canada had increased at the same time and at a similar rate.' Like the Economic Council, the Senate poverty report agreed that one out of four Canadians in 1970 were still living below the poverty line, over a million of them or about one-quarter of the total in Ontario – about 13 per cent of the province's population. The idea that economic growth 'could in time "solve" poverty' was simply 'fallacious.' 'The welfare system is a hopeless failure. The matter is not even contro-versial,' the senators argued. Reforming it necessitated, among other things, giving 'the poor themselves ... a right to participate, to be heard, and indeed, to share in the organization and administration of programs created for them.' Federal officials agreed. 'Given the present stage of eco-nomic development in Canada, the extent to which poverty continues to exist is nothing less than obscene,' the research director for National Health and Welfare argued. 'Some doubt legitimately that any real rehab-ilitation can come until the poor constitute such a social force that it would be political suicide to deny their demands any longer,' his minis-ter, John Munro, told a conference of Vancouver social workers.[47]

The very existence of this research and widespread public debate over the extent and causes of poverty gave legitimacy and voice to welfare rights and anti-poverty organizations across Ontario. Given a chance to organize and reasonable expectations that their voices would be heard, the poor were not, as it turned out, the passive, helpless victims so frequently depicted in the 'culture of poverty' literature of the mid-1960s. Because of their circumstances, the poor shared a dis-tinctive 'life style' but not a 'culture,' one Hamilton study of over two hundred randomly sampled families living below the poverty line pointed out. There was 'no clear evidence ... for major value differences be-tween the poor and others.' Three-quarters of those interviewed sup-ported the idea that 'organizing ... low income people to ... get changes made in ... government policies' was a 'good idea.'[48]

By the end of the decade, organizations of the poor had greater confidence and more frequent opportunities to confront government officials directly with the consequences and contradictions of provin-cial and municipal welfare policies. 'People on welfare cannot live like human beings, because your welfare rates allow survival; not life ... [S]helter allowances [do] not even cover the rents of slum houses,' members of the Just Society told the Ontario legislature during debates on the 1970 estimates for the Department of Social and Family Serv-ices. Basic necessities such as prescription drugs, dental care, and eye-glasses were 'left up to the discretion of ... the local welfare administra-tor' and it was 'not surprising that most municipalities exercise this "discretion" by refusing [them].' The government 'persistently refused to let people know what their rights and entitlements are' and kept thousands of working poor families living below the poverty line by failing to provide a realistic minimum wage or supplementing their income 'as you could do under the Canada Assistance Plan.'[49]

An Ottawa conference – Action 70 – sponsored by local poor peo-ple's organizations gave over four hundred welfare recipients the rare chance to have a 'lively confrontation' with Social and Family Services Minister John Yaremko over the absurdities and injustices of provincial welfare policies. 'It's very hard ... We've been waiting three years [for an increase in welfare allowances],' delegates told Yaremko. 'We had one in 1967 ... We've waited three years, but since then everything went up and all the scales went up except us, us poor people. We're almost starving. But now we want it ... not in three years from now. Now ... Everybody else has got raises, you've got your raise in pay, but we haven't got one. But we want to live too.' Why could welfare scales not simply be 'brought in line with the cost of living 'and readjusted each year?' Why should families paying over $160 a month in rent receive only $105 in shelter costs and so be forced to 'take the [money] out of their food and clothing to make up for it. Either the people have a need and it should be provided for or they don't have a need. And there's little use in giving them halfway measures.' Why was there no welfare appeal board in Ottawa? Assistance was 'a right, as such, and not charity, so I don't think [a woman] should have to go to any member of Parliament as if it were some favour that she's being done.' Poor people at the conference wanted 'written information outlining their rights and describing how their allowances are calculated' as well as 'representatives on boards, commissions or departments' dealing with social assistance. Their key demand, however, was income supplements for the working poor. 'At the moment, persons with dependents and working for the minimum wage receive less than they would on Welfare,' conference delegates pointed out. 'There is no incentive for ... welfare recipients to return to work.' Poor families needed a 'supplementation of income in order to attain a minimum and decent standard of living.'[50]

This demand for income supplements cut to the heart of the dilemma of the War on Poverty and its aftermath within Ontario. By the decade's end a growing volume of research into poverty by governments, social planning councils, and individual researchers revealed two disturbing and intractable facts. On the one hand, even within Ontario, the nation's richest province, maximum welfare benefits for individuals and families of all sizes never came close to reaching existing federal government or social planning council definitions of a poverty line. Four years after the arrival of the Canada Assistance Plan and its promise to seek the 'prevention and removal of the causes of poverty,' individuals and families on welfare in Ontario were getting sufficient income to meet only 40 to 60 per cent, respectively, of their basic budgetary needs as measured by the most reliable existing guides to family spending.

This was a higher percentage than they had received at the beginning of the decade. Living standards on social assistance had improved, but not enough to approximate an income sufficient to lift people out of poverty as it was currently defined. Yet 60 per cent of the poor lived in families where the household head was working and, in most cases, these individuals and their dependants were worse off economically than if they were living on welfare. In other words, although minimum welfare standards throughout the 1960s had not improved sufficiently to lift families out of poverty, they had become good enough to be markedly superior (including in-kind benefits) to those of many families whose heads were earning the minimum wage and paying income tax, unemployment insurance, and Canada Pension Plan premiums.[51]

The fact that most of the poor were working and were worse off, in strictly economic terms, than families on welfare was the most powerful finding revealed by the report of the Special Senate Committee on Poverty in Canada. It was also the most striking evidence that Canada's welfare state at the decade's end was perverse. Welfare was a 'trap,' *Poverty in Canada* concluded, from which it was difficult to escape into full-time employment given the existing disincentives provided through the work/welfare tradeoff, particularly as family size increased. In order to resolve this conundrum the Senate Committee endorsed the concept of a guaranteed annual income, or negative income tax, which would provide all Canadians, working or otherwise, with a basic allowance sufficient to raise them to at least 70 per cent of the poverty line – defined as the point at which an individual or family was spending 70 per cent of income on basic requirements for food, clothing, and shelter. People would be allowed to retain a proportion of this basic allowance, while working, until their earned income reached the existing poverty line threshold for their family size. For the average family of four in 1970 this would mean a basic allowance of $3500 annually and the retention of some fraction of it, on a sliding scale, until earned income reached $5000. In other words, a combination of work and welfare would allow everyone to enjoy at least a minimum standard of adequacy.[52]

Although the anomalous position of the working poor received its greatest exposure through the Senate's *Poverty in Canada* report, it had long been known to government officials. As early as 1964, during negotiations on the Canada Assistance Plan, the dilemma of what to do about low-wage earners with large families living in poverty had been a disturbing conundrum for federal and provincial welfare administrators. 'Should the provinces and municipalities provide enough to raise the family's income to the level that they have an adequate standard of aid, and if so what does this do to the economy?' federal director of unemployment assistance Dick Splane asked provincial welfare officials at that time:

Do we, if we follow that line in our public assistance programs, run the risk of the kind of [Speenhamland] system they had in England in the early 19th century? ... So there are two choices: families going without their needs being adequately met, on the one hand, or assistance being granted to low income families with an employed family head on the other. If that problem is dealt with through granting assistance to such families do we then face the problem of subsidizing the fully employed low income?[53]

The specific focus of this Speenhamland dilemma, named after the famous eighteenth-century British poor law parish that first used relief to subsidize the low wages of farm labourers, became whether to allow partially or fully employed citizens in need to qualify for welfare cost-shared through the Canada Assistance Plan. Such income supplementation of the working poor might 'lead to the subsidization of unproductive employment or to the encouragement of low wages,' federal officials acknowledged. Nonetheless, in the final text of the Canada Assistance Plan full cost-sharing for this group was permitted over the specific objections of Ontario. The intention, however, was deliberately modest. The target group for income supplements was not the large numbers of poor already working, but those on welfare and capable of seasonal or short-term employment 'who feared to go off assistance ... because aid would not be granted during the transitional period.' For these people, temporary income supplements could be used 'as a part of a rehabilitation program' to ease them back into the labour force.[54]

Ontario refused to participate in any form of income supplements for the working poor even though federal officials, in response to growing pressure from anti-poverty groups in the late 1960s, continually reminded the province that nothing in the plan prohibited federal cost-sharing for 'assistance ... to persons employed full time who are also persons in need.'[55] The work/welfare tradeoff was growing increasingly unfavourable to low-income earners within the province as the decade drew to a close, Yaremko acknowledged. Since the 'general scale of maintenance allowances in the province of Ontario has gone up considerably,' he told a conference of welfare ministers in 1968, 'you reach the point where people on welfare ... are almost better off than the comparable man who is working. [T]hat ... is where a considerable difficulty may arise.' There was always 'that level of person who is just above, who earns just a little more than an allowance ... The wages a man earns are geared to the job he does, the benefits we pay are geared to the type of family ... This is one of the great problems that have to be solved.'[56]

In their appearance before the Senate Committee on Poverty, provincial officials provided a rare glimpse of just how critical this less eligibility dilemma was to their calculations of welfare entitlement. In response to intense questioning, deputy minister Merian Borczak conceded that 'when you move to a large urban centre there is a bigger gap between the actual shelter costs and the amounts provided for' through the province's maximum shelter allowances. How, then, could Ontario claim it was operating a needs test if it was 'not meeting basic costs of shelter,' Senator David Croll asked. 'The problem here [is] in terms of how high the level of allowances may be,' Borczak replied: 'The higher they are the greater becomes the differential between the person who is working full time on low wages and the persons on public assistance ... That is to say that we find that the person on public assistance begins to be in a position of marked advantage over the person working full time at low wages. If our allowances were higher than they are at the present time by removing the maximum, this spread would become even greater than it is at present.'

Welfare rates in the province, Ontario officials assured the Senate Committee, although 'still somewhat below poverty lines,' were nonetheless 'extremely generous.' To prove their point they simply compared the annual income of a family of four living at the maximum provided through family benefits with that of the same family of a full-time wage-earner making $2.30 an hour, one dollar more than the provincial minimum wage. The province's conclusion was that there was little to be gained by working. Although in terms of gross income the working-poor family was ahead by $1200 a year, after income taxes, unemployment insurance, Canada Pension Plan, and health insurance premiums, along with dental costs and work-related expenses, the difference shrunk to only $205 a year or a paltry $18 a month. This was a 'new differential' that favoured those on welfare over full-time low-wage workers, Ontario argued. It had arisen as an 'unintentional side effect' of government policies that historically had responded to the area of greatest need – 'those persons who were either unable to work or could not obtain work and consequently had almost no sources of income.' 'Our big job now,' Yaremko argued, 'is to solve the problem of how to bring up the income of a family whose head is working full time and who we call, for want of a better term, the working poor.'[57]

But this was a challenge Ontario was unwilling to undertake on its own. While the dilemma of less eligibility could always be employed as an argument against enhancing welfare entitlement for the poor, it did not incline the Robarts administration towards supplementing the incomes of those in need working at or near the minimum wage. Although such payments could be cost-shared through the Canada Assistance Plan, Yaremko told Robarts, the financial and social risks were simply too great:

Our Research and Planning Branch has made a rough estimate, based on available income figures, that there could be 1,450,000 persons in Ontario receiving incomes below the levels of Family Benefit Allowances and therefore potentially eligible. This figure was arrived at by taking the estimate of the Department of Treasury and Economics of those below the poverty line (1,100,000) and adding our own estimate of those above the poverty line but below the family benefits levels (350,000). This total figure would represent between 400,000 and 500,000 cases ... [W]e have not yet reached a position where we can establish a useful cost approximation. Would such a program tend to maintain wages in low paying industries at a depressed level? In the agricultural economy, would income supplements encourage marginal farmers to remain on small and uneconomical holdings? Would those in low paying and unrewarding jobs find increasing dependence on public assistance more attractive than continued employment?[58]

Ontario officials added a host of additional reasons why large-scale income supplementation to lift families of the working poor out of poverty was simply out of the question at the present time. Census 'information concerning the working poor is almost completely lacking,' Borczak pointed out. 'It is possible to determine the number of greenhouses in the province, the monthly production of soft drinks, [or] ... purchases and sales of scrap aluminum ... Accurate and highly current data is available concerning the Consumer Price Index, wages and salaries, and the labor force. Yet, there is virtually no data available concerning the working poor ... The problem is simply that the information system has not been developed to produce the type of data which is required for an attack on poverty.' Nor was enough known about the sociological and psychological effects of income supplements on the work ethic of those potentially eligible.[59]

Finally, such a program, if developed on a large scale, would be an administrative nightmare, Borczak maintained. Unlike income supplements for senior citizens who were outside the labour force and whose annual income and needs were relatively stable, supplements to the working poor would be targeted at a group whose income and needs might fluctuate dramatically from month to month. Consequently, it would be extremely difficult to tie monthly supplements to real needs without encountering constant problems of over- and underpayments. His department's experience with the administrative problems of monitoring part-time earnings of mothers on family benefits was enough of a warning of what might follow from a full-blown income supplements program for all the working poor, including those working full time. It was also 'not difficult to imagine some of the possible results which this might produce in the area of collective bargaining and employer-employee relations.'[60]

In effect, supplementing the incomes of the working poor through the Canada Assistance Plan would be an attempt to 'start ... a guaranteed annual income program ... through the back door.' For one province to do this on its own would 'incorporate most of the major administrative problems of the negative income tax system without the advantages offered by integration with the income tax structure,' Ontario officials argued. Moreover, without a strict residence requirement, which did not appear feasible, there was also the 'chance that needy families from other provinces might take advantage of the scheme.' Despite being 'one of the great national challenges of today,' supplementing the income of the working poor was simply too big a policy shift to do under the Canada Assistance Plan and too big for Ontario to do alone. Instead, it was axiomatic that any large-scale program targeted to the needs of the working poor had to involve the 'effective coordination of the taxation and income maintenance structure,' something that could only occur at the national level. This was 'essentially ... the question of a guaranteed annual income.'[61]

A national guaranteed annual income was the favoured final solution to the War on Poverty for reformers across the political spectrum in the late 1960s, including the Senate Committee on Poverty, the New Democratic Party, and, for a brief time, the federal Progressive Conservative party led by Robert Stanfield. It would also form the core element of Ottawa's sweeping but unsuccessful Social Security Review between 1973 and 1976. For Ontario officials, the concept held few attractions and many potential risks. Although frequently viewed as 'a complete panacea to all our welfare problems,' the guaranteed annual income was 'unlikely to bring us into the promised land in welfare or ... in any other area,' veteran deputy minister James Band warned cabinet in the late 1960s. A guaranteed income would be 'an extremely costly venture ... [A]t the present time we are in no position and I doubt that any jurisdiction in the industrialized world is in a position to implement such a plan,' he argued. 'One of the major unanswered problems ... is that of the relationship between ... incentive on the one hand and ...

adequacy on the other.' A guaranteed income that met basic adequacy would provide few incentives to work. One that contained strong work incentives could hardly meet basic needs. 'There is no simple solution to this dilemma and whichever of these advantages one wished to seize ... the plan would be weakened in another way.'[62]

Other advisers to Robarts made similar arguments against the guaranteed income concept. 'Do we need more social security programs or less ... Can we afford to keep on redistributing our wealth before we have actually created that wealth?' Keith Reynolds, the premier's chief executive officer, asked prior to a 1970 federal-provincial conference on income security. 'We have reached the point where the basic objectives of social security measures have now been largely attained ... [T]he task is not to introduce further large scale government programs, which ... are both unnecessary and undesirable, but to consolidate and rationalize the existing web of programs.' The idea of a guaranteed annual income begged the question of whether 'governments have the financial capacity to introduce programs of this magnitude.'[63]

From within the provincial Conservative Party came warnings that the idea could be 'politically suicidal.' It would be 'sheer folly for us not to learn from the experience our Party nationally has already lived through,' the executive assistant to Attorney-General Arthur Wishart told Yaremko and Robarts. When Stanfield endorsed the idea during the 1968 federal election campaign, 'opposition ... within the Party was swift and strong.' Stanfield's own 'wishes were shrugged off' and the idea was 'shelved until after the election.' Much of the criticism came 'from a sizeable number of Ontario delegates. These are Progressive Conservatives. The problem, therefore, is not one of having the party unanimously adopt a program which it subsequently finds difficult to sell to the people: the problem is that of opening up a serious division within the Party in the process of adopting the idea in the first place.' For Conservatives, Wishart's assistant observed, the semantics of the phrase 'guaranteed annual income' was like 'opening a can of worms.' After all, 'can the State really "guarantee" anything to citizens, at least in the economic realm?'[64]

Within the Ontario legislature, Robarts quickly distanced himself from Stanfield's support of the concept, and in private voiced fears that such a scheme might well 'encourage ... "professional" welfare families. The problem of what to do with people like this is a great one ... How far does one go in making sure they do not reproduce themselves?' the Ontario premier asked. 'I do not know whether our people generally realize what a constant battle we must wage against the demands for increased public spending.' Throughout the next decade, negotiations over a guaranteed annual income to meet the plight of the working poor would dominate federal-provincial discussions on social policy. Although the reasons behind the collapse of these efforts have been well analysed elsewhere and are beyond the scope of this study, the seeds of failure can be easily discerned by 1970. Within Queen's Park there was simply little support for a program whose ultimate costs and potential impact on the welfare caseload, the provincial labour market, and the provincial budget were so uncertain. Nor did provincial officials trust Ottawa's intentions, in light of the existing open-ended spending available through the Canada Assistance Plan. 'The Social Security Review wasn't going to get us any more money. They were going to get a better control on our expenditures. They were going to rationalize the amount spent ... It was financial control that Ottawa wanted,' one former official recalled. Even a scaled-down guaranteed income proposal, Ontario officials argued in the mid-1970s, would cost three times more than Ottawa's $1 billion estimate. It would also draw tens of thousands of new working-poor clients into the welfare system. 'We don't think that the taxpayers in Canada can afford a massive program at the present time,' provincial treasurer Darcy McKeough maintained within the context of an inflationary 1970s economy. Ultimately these concerns would seal the fate of any comprehensive attempt to lift Ontario's working poor out of poverty.[65]

The 1960s was a pivotal decade for welfare policy both in Ontario and throughout Canada. In most respects, the range of programs and entitlements still available to the poor today took their final form in this turbulent era. Although never exceeding 5 per cent of the total population, not since the Great Depression had Ontario witnessed such a rapid rise in the numbers on social assistance or such a far-reaching debate over the fundamental causes and consequences of poverty. Indeed, for one brief moment between 1965 and 1970, government promises of a War on Poverty held out the hope that the condition itself could be eliminated or abolished and all citizens raised, as Pierre Elliott Trudeau put it, to at least the 'minimum standard of satisfactory living which allows for dignity and decency.'[66]

Although the rhetoric was uplifting, the programs that followed were not. Material circumstances for Ontario's poor did improve over the course of the decade, particularly for the aged. Partly as a result of enriched federal funding provided through the Canada Assistance Plan after 1966, social assistance allowances for a typical welfare family of four in Ontario rose by almost 100 per cent over the course of the decade, or from 48 per cent to 60 per cent of basic adequacy, according to later estimates by Toronto's Social Planning Council. Combined with the inauguration of universal health insurance and a significant expansion in rent-geared-to-income public housing, the gap between needs and resources for Ontario's poorest citizens narrowed modestly over the course of the decade. At the same time, the range of services available to them in areas such as child care, homemaking, and family counselling expanded. So too did Ontario's total welfare spending, which also jumped 335 per cent during the 1960s.[67]

Although impressive, these statistics must be placed in context. Government spending was fuelled not simply by enhanced allowances but, more importantly, by a ballooning welfare caseload that grew by 122 per cent over the course of the decade, and it was financed by an increasingly dynamic Ontario economy. During the affluent 1960s average family income more than doubled in the province. As a consequence, although families on social assistance within Ontario were better off in absolute terms by the decade's end, relative to the rest of the population their position had not changed at all and, despite the lofty promises surrounding the Canada Assistance Plan and the War on Poverty, they were not even close to 1960s definitions of a poverty line. Ironically, rather than standing on the threshold of an end to poverty or 'The World We Leave Behind,' as a chapter in the Senate's *Poverty in Canada* report was optimistically titled, Ontario's poor by the end of the 1960s had instead reached the limits of affluence. Almost all the core entitlements or relative income shares they would ever receive within Canada's wealthiest province had been attained by 1970. More importantly, in terms of finding and holding on to work or locating affordable shelter, their position would deteriorate badly over the next two decades.[68]

The 1960s War on Poverty was driven by political developments south of the border as well as by the galling paradox of increasing welfare dependency in the midst of affluence. Why were the numbers of the poor continuing to grow within an economy operating at almost maximum performance? Who were they and how should they be counted? What could be done to lift them out of dependency? Were those in need prisoners of their own 'culture of poverty' or simply victims of material circumstances? Within a 1960s context, what constituted an adequate and decent minimum standard of living? How much would it cost and how could it be guaranteed to those existing below it? The decade spawned a host of core questions about poverty, but in the end provided little consensus on the answers. By 1970 Ontario officials could only observe that there might be 'one million men, women, and children [in Ontario] living ... in poverty or this may be an overestimate ... no one knows.' Nor could they even provide a working definition of what an adequate and decent social minimum might be. Canada required 'commonly accepted, objective, quantified standards' to measure need, standards that were 'scientifically sound,' department officials told the Senate Committee on Poverty, but after four decades of regulating the province's welfare allowances they still could not say what these standards should be. Apart from food allowances devised several years before, Ontario's other criteria for setting welfare entitlements, the department conceded, were less precise. The province did not like existing definitions of adequacy, but could offer none of its own beyond comparing the income available through welfare to that earned by the province's lowest-income earners.[69]

In the end this was the only standard that mattered. Although welfare increases in Ontario throughout the 1960s were periodic and haphazard, it is incorrect to conclude that they 'follow[ed] no discoverable logic' or that policy formation in this area was 'ambiguous at best, and apparently without objectives.'[70] Throughout this pivotal decade a continual tension existed between the search at the national, provincial, and local levels for an acceptable definition of what constituted a decent social minimum, as well as for the political and economic impact of such a definition on the province's labour market and economy. Simply put, although the rhetoric of the War on Poverty was about defining such a standard, poverty policy within Ontario was about avoiding it. Existing national standards implemented by Ottawa through categorical allowance programs were explicitly jettisoned during negotiations on the Canada Assistance Plan at the insistence of provinces such as Ontario which demanded more flexibility in determining their own definitions of need. Indeed, the arrival of the Canada Assistance Plan itself – the most lasting and tangible achievement of the 1960s War on Poverty – had little to do with its stated intention of bringing about the 'prevention and removal of the causes of poverty.' Instead, the plan's origins can be traced to far more prosaic concerns: Ottawa's own search for better administrative control over welfare spending already mushrooming through the loosely drafted Unemployment Assistance Act; the unintended consequences for other categorical programs of enhancing benefits to the elderly through Old Age Security; and provincial unhappiness with the arbitrary exclusions, rigidities, and accounting complexities of existing cost-shared programs.

Throughout all the plan negotiations, Ontario deputy welfare minister James Band explicitly rejected any attempts by National Health and Welfare officials to draw his province into mutually agreed upon definitions of adequacy and basic needs. During the remainder of the 1960s provincial welfare officials consistently refused to reveal their own criteria for formulating pre-added welfare budgets and were singularly uninterested in any welfare appeal process that might legally challenge these powers of administrative discretion. By the decade's end, shelter allowances were still as far removed from the existing cost of housing as they had been at the beginning, meeting in medium to large cities only 58 per cent on average of actual rents paid by welfare recipients and consuming about 62 per cent of their total allowances.[71] No cost-of-living formulas governed the calculation of welfare benefits, nor at any point during the decade was the province interested in taking over the administration of general assistance from local governments in order to promote more uniform and adequate standards of social assistance. Instead, welfare entitlement for those still active within the province's labour market was deliberately kept at the local level in order, as Ontario officials put it, to keep the definition of need in line with community standards and interregional economic disparities.[72]

What did emerge out of the 1960s poverty debate was the discovery, or more accurately rediscovery of the working poor, a group forgotten since the 1930s. As standards of and eligibility for social assistance were liberalized, however modestly, during the 1960s, the plight of poor families working outside the welfare system was thrown into ever sharper relief, particularly as new data available from the 1961 census made their sizeable numbers more apparent. For government officials, as well as poverty investigators, welfare programs that made it more economically advantageous not to work were clearly irrational. Barring major rollbacks or disentitlements within the welfare system, the greater attractiveness of work itself could only be brought back into balance through the delivery of some form of income supplementation to the poor within the labour force. Although possible through the Canada Assistance Plan, this option was rejected by Ontario. Its ten-year search for greater flexibility in the determination and alleviation of need did not, as it turned out, extend to acting on its own to meet the plight of low-wage earners and their families who constituted 60 per cent of the province's poor. On this issue Ontario wanted federal leadership, although not, as it turned out, on the terms and conditions sought by Ottawa.

During the 1960s, within an economy delivering unprecedented prosperity to most of its citizens, Ontarians contemplated momentarily the paradox of poverty in the midst of plenty as well as the cost and means of bringing an adequate and decent standard of living to everyone. The vision, however blurred, was glimpsed but soon forgotten during the more difficult economic times ahead.

Conclusion

'Welfare,' Michael Katz argues, 'never will be satisfactory. It cannot escape the contradictions between its goals – deterrence, compassion, discipline and control ... or resolve the tension between entitlements and the market.'[1] This enduring paradox of welfare is the central theme of this book. It is our most complex, least understood, and most unpopular social program, and, at a cost of more than $6 billion annually within Ontario, it is also one of our most expensive areas of social policy. While everyone accepts its necessity, few people, least of all its clients, believe it is an effective or adequate response to poverty. As *Transitions*, the final report of Ontario's three-year inquiry into social assistance put it, welfare is a 'system that has a history, but no overall rationale.'[2]

This book has attempted to unravel this history and make sense of the often convoluted process through which welfare evolved within Ontario, from an uncoordinated structure of private charity, houses of refuge, and local poor relief into one of our most complex and controversial bureaucratic structures. What insights does it offer towards a wider understanding of the making of the welfare state? To answer this question it is worth returning to the six theoretical approaches towards social policy outlined in the introduction.

At perhaps the broadest level of generalization, the history of Ontario's welfare policy does confirm the functionalist perspectives put forward by Wilensky and others which view welfare programs as a necessary response to industrialization, urbanization, and increased family fragmentation and economic vulnerability attendant upon the expansion of a wage-earning labour force. Increasing poverty among widows, single mothers, the elderly, and the unemployed was a consequence of Ontario's urbanization and industrialization in the twentieth century and the growing inability of family structures to cope with widening dimensions of need. In this sense economic necessity was a goad to more adequate social provision within Ontario, as it was in other modernizing industrial economies in this century – a point driven home by the aging of its population, the depth and duration of the dependency crisis provoked by the Great Depression, and Ontario's creation of a public welfare bureaucracy to dispense relief to the elderly and the jobless during that decade. Rapid economic expansion and the widening of affluence after 1945 also provided the material basis for financing the incremental liberalization of welfare eligibility and benefits, in modest fashion during the 1950s, and with increasing force under the impetus of the 1960s War on Poverty. However, simply interpreting welfare as an inevitable response to the 'logic of industrialism' is not very helpful in explaining why the bureaucratic welfare state emerged when it did, why it incorporated some of the poor but not others, and why it failed to provide its clients with minimally adequate standards for meeting their basic human needs.

To what extent can the answers to these questions be found by looking at the core values and beliefs imbedded within Ontario's political culture? Did a conservative 'Red Tory' province produce a particularly distinctive response to the problems of human need thrown up by an industrializing economy? Here the answer is a qualified no. Certainly, there is no evidence that conservative traditions led to more activist state leadership within the welfare field in Ontario, relative to other provinces or adjacent American states. If anything, tendencies within the province's political culture led in the opposite direction. The strength of local government in Ontario and its large role in financing and administering social welfare throughout the entire half century under review acted as a restraining influence on demands for more adequate welfare assistance. One-party dominance by the Conservatives for most of this century also contributed to caution, stability, and resistance to change, at least on most welfare matters, within Ontario's Department of Public Welfare, particularly during the twenty-year reign of deputy minister James Band. Compared to more ideologically charged provinces in western Canada, particularly British Columbia, movements by old age pensioners or the unemployed for better social provision were also relatively weak.

In the pension field, differences in political culture contributed to Ontario's comparative stinginess relative to other less affluent western provinces. Although political culture is thus of some help in interpreting aspects of Ontario's response to poverty, it does not take us very far. Little within the design or implementation of mothers' allowance, old age pension, or general welfare assistance programs suggests a distinctively Ontario-based approach to problems of meeting human need. In all these programs the legislative models as well as much of the financing and leadership came from other jurisdictions.

If the 'strength of labour in civil society' is seen as a key determinant for understanding the comparative development of most western welfare states, to what extent is it a relevant factor within Ontario? Here the evidence is ambiguous at best. Although organized labour did not originate the campaign for mothers' allowances – Ontario's first income security program in 1920 – it did lend critical support to the measure at a time when union membership and militancy, under the influence of wartime conditions, was rapidly rising. The legislation was also introduced and implemented by Walter Rollo, labour party cabinet minister within the UFO-ILP coalition of 1919. However, despite labour's support, the leadership of the movement for mothers' allowances clearly lay within the hands of a middle-class and mostly female child-saving coalition, within which labour was a junior partner. Moreover, the legislation was originally prepared by the previous Conservative government of William Hearst and would have been implemented regardless of who won the 1919 provincial election. Its provisions were also far more restrictive than those put forward by union leaders. As Theda Skocpol argues, mothers' pensions provide weak evidence for the centrality of labour to the building of the welfare state.

What about old age pensions? Here, too, the evidence is inconclusive. There is no doubt, given the scant support for the idea within Ontario's Conservative party, that old age pensions would never have come to Ontario in 1929 had it not been for the crucial leadership provided by the federal government. Here the critical role of labour MPs J.S. Woodsworth and A.A. Heaps is well known. Within Toronto's Old Age Pension Board, moreover, labour's influence and leadership was clearly a major factor in pushing that city to pioneer the most generous interpretation possible for determining old age pension entitlement before a municipal role in pension administration was terminated in 1933.

During the early 1940s, another era of peak union militancy, labour councils also flooded Queen's Park with resolutions demanding a long overdue cost-of-living increase for pensioners. On old age pensions, in other words, labour's voice could not be ignored. It would be a mistake, however, to conclude that it was decisive. Once Ontario's pension scheme was established, questions of fiscal control and regulation fuelled by the crisis of Depression, not labour or left-wing pressure, governed its administration as a form of state charity rather than earned entitlement. On most pension issues, bureaucratic leadership, particularly within the federal-provincial arena, not pressure from the left, is more important for understanding, in Hugh Heclo's terms, 'political learning' as a determinant of policy evolution within Ontario.[3]

Nor did organized labour or socialist parties such as the CCF exercise any discernible influence over the shaping of unemployment relief policy during the Great Depression, a decade in which both unions and the province's fledgling socialist party were politically weak and fighting for their own survival. During the following decade, particularly between 1943 and 1945, labour militancy, union growth, and electoral support for the CCF reached unprecedented heights within the province, establishing a political climate conducive to comprehensive social planning and welfare reform. Despite small victories on issues such as food allowances in Toronto, however, it is surprising how little the upsurge in social democratic strength in the 1940s actually accomplished in the fight against poverty in Ontario. Able-bodied men were cut off welfare, shelter allowances remained grossly deficient, municipalities were left in charge of most welfare administration, and comprehensive plans for reorganizing the province into a system of welfare units were scrapped. Wide-ranging plans for constructing a more comprehensive welfare state fell victim to the collapse of the Reconstruction Conference of 1945–6, in which a Conservative Ontario government, led by George Drew and Leslie Frost, played a critical role.

Had the CCF rather than the Conservatives won the 1943 provincial election, the subsequent relationship between social democracy and the building of Ontario's and even Canada's welfare state doubtless would have been stronger. Clearly, the 1945 election, along with the coming of the Cold War, were watershed events in altering the course of welfare reform within Ontario, as was the revival of economic prosperity in the late 1940s.[4] But within Ontario politics, after the Second World War, there is little discernible linkage between the burgeoning strength of organized labour and a more coherent or aggressive assault on poverty – in large part, perhaps, because of the critical collapse of the CCF in the 1950s.[5] Throughout the postwar era, labour concentrated on expanding the entitlements of 'industrial citizenship' for its members through collective bargaining and on lobbying Queen's Park and Ottawa for more universal social programs in health, housing, pensions, and education. Its interest in welfare reform, or the needs of Ontario's poorest citizens, during an era of high employment and job security remained ephemeral at best. The key advocates of the poor came from other sectors of society, most notably professional social work.

The Ontario Federation of Labour's 1964 report on *Poverty in Ontario*, along with biting and incisive criticism from a small but effective NDP caucus, did help to focus political debate within the province around poverty during the 1960s. Clearly these contributions were of secondary importance, however, compared with the spillover effects of America's War on Poverty, or the ongoing impact of Ottawa's bureaucratic initiatives in shaping the reform of Ontario's welfare system throughout the decade.

Are Marxian theories more helpful in understanding welfare policy within Ontario? In many respects the answer must be yes. Marxist analysis captures well the paradoxical nature of the state's role in attempting to reconcile social justice with market incentives. Welfare is, ideally, the fulfilment of basic human needs for food, clothing, shelter, and comfort, in a manner that is neither stigmatizing nor degrading, as a basic social right of citizenship in order that individuals can participate fully and freely within a democratic society.[6] Within Ontario, as within most if not all market societies, social assistance for either single mothers, the elderly, or families of the unemployed has never come close to meeting such objectives. Consistently, attempts to move welfare standards towards minimal levels of adequacy have foundered against the argument that such improvements would undermine the work ethic, most typically by making the lives of those on social assistance preferable to the standard of living obtainable by the working poor. In this sense, the continued inability of welfare to approximate minimal definitions of a poverty line as it has evolved through time is unequivocal evidence of the power of social control in shaping welfare policy.

Does this mean that welfare policy is only about social control or that business ultimately dictates what form it will take? This is a too simplistic and monocausal reading of state social policy which leaves no scope for the influence of other social actors such as women, professional social work, competing levels of government, or the poor themselves. As Frances Fox Piven and Richard Cloward argue in their studies of American welfare policy, insurgent poor people's movements can act to liberalize welfare entitlement. Within Ontario, this was most apparent during the early 1930s in bankrupt communities, when organizations of the unemployed, through exerting pressure on local governments and relief officers, pushed standards of assistance above the Campbell Report ceilings set by the province. However, the political agency of the poor was short-lived at best. By 1936, through a combination of more elaborate bureaucratic regulation and fiscal control over local governments and those on relief, the provincial government had reasserted its power over the level of welfare entitlements in order to control costs and to reinforce work incentives.

Nor, despite the revival of a welfare rights movement in the late

1960s, can the clients of social assistance be said to have exerted any major influence on welfare policy outside their own private battles with individual caseworkers or welfare agencies to maintain or enhance their own levels of entitlement.[7] In this regard, Ontario's welfare history fails to confirm the Piven and Cloward thesis concerning the cyclical nature of welfare expansion and contraction. Reforms, although usually modest, have been incremental rather than explosive. Apart from the denial of relief to employables in 1941 (a group subsequently reinstated in 1958), entitlements have not subsequently contracted, and they have rarely emerged in response to the demands of the poor themselves. Quite simply, there is no equivalent within Ontario's welfare history to the impact of America's National Welfare Rights Organization in pushing for radically expanded welfare eligibility, particularly for single mothers, during the 1960s.[8] The dynamics of race, a burgeoning civil rights movement, and welfare reform that fuelled much of America's War on Poverty are simply absent within the Ontario context, and yet the province's welfare caseload, much like America's, grew rapidly throughout the decade. To this extent, the emphasis Piven and Cloward place upon social unrest and social control as a factor in cycles of welfare expansion must be questioned, although, as has been shown, events, policy shifts, and a changing climate of opinion towards poverty south of the border had important spillover effects within Ontario and Canada.

Demographic changes, increasing family fragmentation, the confidence bred by the seeming success of Keynesian full employment policies, along with a rapid growth in living standards during the 1960s, must be assigned more interpretative weight in explaining simultaneous increases in welfare spending during this decade, particularly in understanding that decade's brief flirtation with ideas of abolishing poverty. But if the process of welfare expansion in Ontario does not confirm the Piven and Cloward thesis, their central argument concerning the enduring power of 'less eligibility' as a constraint on the limits of welfare reform is amply reaffirmed.

How much autonomy did the state within Ontario enjoy in framing its response to poverty? A major theme of this book has been the building of an 'admininistrative state' in the area of welfare policy.[9] Before 1920 Ontario had virtually no administrative knowledge of poverty or the bureaucatic capacity for dealing with it, beyond sporadic institutional provisions such as houses of refuge by local governments. By 1970 a massive welfare bureaucracy had been put it place, spending over $250 million annually, employing thousands of officials, and regulating the most intimate details of the lives of the poor. Clearly any

attempt to understand poverty or welfare policy must take, as its starting point, the influence of bureaucracy.

Several themes are worth re-emphasizing here. First, in contrast to
much 'state-centred' writing on social policy, there is no evidence that
bureaucratic leadership in and of itself was a major force for expanding
the entitlements of the poor. Within the field of mothers' allowances,
the critical leadership for establishing the program came from a private
child-saving coalition outside government itself. Bureaucratic development within the program during its first decade in the 1920s, particularly once the initial reform leadership of Peter Bryce and Elizabeth
Shortt departed from the commission, actually contracted the overall
level of monthly entitlement while modestly expanding the scope of
program eligibility. Most importantly, despite the lofty rhetoric surrounding its origins, mothers' allowances within Ontario failed to attain
the non-stigmatizing status of a pension or reward to mothers in return
for their service to the state. Grossly inadequate monthly benefits, and
ongoing and intrusive moral supervision of women's lives, rendered the
program only marginally better than local relief and far below standards of assistance or supervision provided to the families of injured
men through workmen's compensation. As the program matured during
the 1930s, 1940s, and 1950s, the tendency within Ontario's public welfare department was increasingly to converge the terms and conditions
of aid provided with general welfare assistance. In other words, bureaucratic regulation standardized benefits and conditions of eligibility for
women in need, without enhancing their status within the welfare state
or lifting them or their children out of poverty. As Skocpol has concluded in her study of similar programs south of the border: 'The starvation of early mothers' aid programs for public funds ensured that
the gaps between worthy and unworthy, and between givers and receiv-
ers, would become ever more entrenched in the practices of mothers'
pensions ... turning them into the forerunners of demeaning "welfare"
rather than the honorable salaries for mothers that their original supporters had envisaged.'[10]

Similar tendencies can be seen at work in the early development of
old age pensions and unemployment relief within Ontario. Although
initially justified as an 'earned right' in return for contributions in building up the nation, old age pensions quickly degenerated into little more
than a separately administered and degrading scheme of relief for the
indigent elderly, or in the words of one government official, little more
than 'charity from a benevolent state.' Increased bureaucratization eroded
rather than enhanced the status and dignity of the aged served by the
program between 1929 and the late 1940s. Only within local pension

boards, such as Toronto's, where labour and social activist groups enjoyed influence flowing from their previous agitation for pensions, were the elderly treated as rights-bearing citizens, a divergence lasting until local pension boards were terminated in 1933. Since the principal motivation for growing bureaucratic regulation was to contain the program's rapidly rising costs rather than to entrench new social rights for the aged, its overall failure to raise the aged out of degrading poverty is not altogether surprising.

On the other hand, widespread dissatisfaction with the costs and difficulties of administering means-tested, non-contributory pensions over the two decades between 1929 and 1949 did provoke a search, within both levels of government, for administratively simpler and less stigmatising forms of aiding the elderly, a movement that would lead to the adoption of universal old age security in 1951. To this extent, a process of 'political learning' and 'policy feedback,' as described by Heclo within Sweden and Great Britain, also influenced the development of pension policy within Canada as well.[11]

Mass provision of unemployment relief was a product of the Depression. Here, too, the early unsystematic local framework of relief-giving could produce tight-fisted frugality or, where the jobless were organized and militant, comparatively generous standards of provision. Bureaucratization of welfare at the provincial level, particularly between 1933 and 1936, eliminated or severely constrained the local scope for moving the poor towards adequacy, while at the same time leaving counties and municipalities free to pay the jobless as little as they chose. During the 1940s, as relief loads contracted, pressure for moving food allowances towards minimal nutritional standards came from agencies outside government, not from within the state. Even within the context of a poverty caseload below 1 per cent of the population, the modest bureuacratic leadership exercised by a progressive deputy minister such as Burne Heise was not adequate to effect any significant changes in welfare standards or administration.

Once James Band replaced Heise at the top of Ontario's welfare structure, the scope for bureaucratic leadership increased, if only through Band's close identification with the reigning Conservative Party and his unprecedented twenty-year tenure as deputy minister. Given the circumstances of Heise's departure, however, Band's influence was contingent on the sagacity of his political judgment and the confidence he enjoyed from Leslie Frost and John Robarts not to undertake far-reaching reforms within welfare policy which might alienate public opinion, local politicians, or Conservative Party members. Cautious and conservative by training and inclination, and harbouring a thinly veiled contempt for professional social work, Band was not a likely source for exercising state-centred leadership in social policy reform.

To the extent that a 'polity-centred framework' for understanding social policy does apply, it pertains particularly to the role of federalism.[12] Consistently in Ottawa and Ontario as well as at the local level, governments modified, abandoned, or launched programs aimed at the poor in response to the availability or curtailment of cost-sharing, in relation to changes within analogous programs aimed at other categories of need, or in the light of negotiations surrounding the division of taxation revenue. The importance of this theme has been so pervasive within this book that it need only be briefly summarized here. Policy deliberations surrounding means-tested old age pensions between 1927 and 1951, unemployment relief in the 1930s and 1950s, the Reconstruction Conference of 1945–6, the Canada Assistance Plan of 1966, and the unsuccessful attempt to develop a guaranteed annual income in the early 1970s were all intimately bound up with the dialectics of fiscal federalism. This is not to argue that, over the entire half century under review, federalism in itself was a force for either expanding or constraining welfare policy.[13] It was, however, a critical field within which policy-makers developed their response to poverty, and it did influence the initial timing and shape of the programs that were developed, particularly in the areas of unemployment and social assistance.

Bureaucratic leadership did exist in the field of welfare. Given the stigma that traditionally surrounds dependency and relief, the enduring moral power of the work ethic, ideas about proper mothering, and the remarkable longevity of distinctions between the deserving and undeserving poor, it would be foolhardy to suggest that state officials in Queen's Park or Ottawa somehow lagged behind public opinion in their ideas about welfare entitlement.[14] Clearly this was not so. Given the widespread ambivalence that surrounds public attitudes towards the poor, both then and now, few programs are less likely to win public approval than comprehensive welfare reform, particularly reforms designed to make assistance more attractive.[15]

Given these constraints, policy-makers faced a range of choice between bowing to or challenging prevailing attitudes towards the poor. For the most part federal officials within the Department of National Health and Welfare attempted to move public opinion forward. Ontario welfare officials more often reflected traditional stereotypes. This distinction is particularly apparent from 1958 onwards in debates over the efficacy of work relief, income supplements for the working poor, and the different responses of Ontario and Ottawa towards the American War on Poverty. In part these differences reflect a more intense level of political competition in federal politics during an era of electoral instability. Most of the Liberal Party's progressive ideas on social policy were developed while the party was out of office between 1957 and 1962. Ontario's ruling Conservatives, in contrast, remained comfortably in power through the entire post–Second World War era.

The difference also reflects the different training and background of federal as opposed to Ontario welfare officials. Within National Health and Welfare, George Davidson, Joe Willard, Richard Splane, and others came out of a professional social work community and had served apprenticeships within the Canadian Welfare Council. Ontario officials, until the late 1960s, typically rose up through the ranks of the province's welfare bureaucracy and lacked any social work training or socialization.[16] Accounting or bookkeeping experience, not knowledge of social work, represented the fastest route to promotion within the provincial welfare state.[17] The Canada Assistance Plan, the single most important piece of legislation affecting the poor to emerge out of the 1960s, owed its origins to provincial as well as federal bureaucratic imperatives (particularly the unintended consequences of earlier unemployment assistance legislation), an unexpectedly deep recession, and the impact of increases in old age security on other forms of categorical social assistance. Its scope and shape were also influenced by the social work training of National Health and Welfare's bureaucratic elite and their commitment to widening the coverage as well as modernizing the administration of Canada's public assistance system. To this extent, state-centred leadership emanating from Ottawa must be given some weight in accounting for policy change in the fight against poverty.[18]

Gender represents the last theme running throughout this book. Women reformers built Ontario's first income security program – mothers' allowances – on the basis of a woman-centred commitment to protecting and dignifying the role of mothering as an essential contribution to the nation's welfare. Mothers' pensions, Skocpol argues in her analysis of similar developments in the United States, represent the most tangible vision of a 'maternalist welfare state' through which middle- and upper-class female reformers, in tandem with other 'child-savers,' sought to 'embrace as sisters, as fellow mothers, the impoverished widows who would be helped by mothers' pensions ... [They] intended to include needy mothers in the same moral universe as themselves, providing them with regular and nondemeaning material assistance to make it possible for them to realize a vision of the same basic ideals of homemaking and motherhood to which the ladies themselves aspired.'[19]

Women's groups, such as the Visiting Homemakers and the Women's Electors, along with women leaders within public health agencies, schools of nutrition, and private charity or social work, also played key roles between 1935 and 1945 in the successful campaign to develop adequate nutritional standards for families on relief and in developing Canada's most sophisticated measurements of a poverty line for families in need. Women constituted the overwhelming proportion of Ontario's professionally trained social workers and, from the 1950s onwards as heads of families, they also dominated the province's social assistance caseload. To what extent, then, were women primary agents in the construction of Ontario's welfare state? How important is gender for understanding the successes and failures of the province's response to poverty?

There can be no doubt of the centrality of an ethic of mothering, or of cross-class gender identification with the skills and needs of poor women and their children, to the development of political campaigns aimed at expanding welfare entitlement. To this extent, the evidence in this book confirms the insights of Linda Gordon and Theda Skocpol that gender plays a more complex role in the welfare state than simply reinforcing the patriarchal domination of women by men within a 'family ethic.'[20] Women in Ontario, as elsewhere, fought for increased state provision for mothers either as 'worthy widows' in the 1910s, or as the lynchpin of relief families during the Great Depression. At times when class identities were politically silenced, as in the 1920s or later 1930s, gender loyalties often provided the only crucial bridgehead for developing interest in or campaigns around the plight of families living in poverty – an insight easily applicable to our current welfare crisis.[21]

However, it is important not to exaggerate the extent to which shared loyalties based on gender overcame class identities or market criteria in shaping the overall provision of state welfare. On the one hand, the key decision-making authority within Ontario's Mothers' Allowance Commission, its Department of Public Welfare, or the various relief-giving agencies of local governments always lay in the hands of men who actually ran Ontario's social welfare state. Although women could and did lobby on behalf of their 'poorer sisters,' and most frequently staffed the lower echelons of Ontario's welfare organizations, men decided how much assistance families living in poverty would receive as well as who would be eligible to receive it. On the other hand, it is not at all clear that women possessed starkly different assumptions about the moral character of the poor, by virture of their gender, strong enough to construct a 'maternalist' and more caring welfare state. Mothers' allowances both in Ontario and the United States never lived up to the lofty ideals of decent, adequate, and non-stigmatizing social assistance put forward by the movement's mostly female leadership – even when confined to the most deserving of the poor, worthy widows with two or more children – during the program's first decade. Ironically and unintentionally, mothers' pensions, although designed to keep mothers within the home, ended up 'pushing poor women into marginal wage-labor markets' in order to make ends meet.[22] Why? What logic, as Gordon asks, drove women to design 'inferior programs for other women?'[23] According to Skocpol, once the broad coalitions of middle- and upper-class female reformers had put such programs into place, they lacked the 'political clout to achieve adequate levels of funding' for the locally varied programs and 'gradually lost interest' in them. Skocpol also argues that once implemented, mothers' pensions fell under the control of 'bureaucrats and social workers, most of whom did not see their clients as part of the same moral universe as themselves.'[24]

Within Ontario, the evidence for such arguments is inconclusive. Through their experience with the Patriotic Fund in aiding soldiers' wives, women advocates of mothers' pensions had a good idea of the minimum monthly amounts needed to keep a family of three or more living in adequacy, yet Ontario's mothers' allowance scheme paid only half this amount. Although responsibility for this decision must lie with government, not women's organizations, there is no evidence that the program's low level of benefits became a major source of complaint on their part. Instead, their most intense concern was centred not on the fiscal adequacy of the scheme, but on the moral adequacy of its recipients. Male trade unionists, not women's groups, provided the strongest arguments for a liberal plan extended to all single mothers whether widowed, deserted, unwed, or divorced. Women reformers, in contrast, expressed the greatest fear that the program not pauperize indigent families through providing automatic entitlement without ongoing and rigorous moral supervision, or encourage men to abandon their domestic responsibilities. Throughout the 1920s women who helped to create the scheme remained adamant that it not be extended to deserted, divorced, or unwed mothers, who constituted the overwhelming proportion of their sex living in poverty. Through a kind of moral parallel to 'less eligibility' and its relationship to the male work ethic, women advocates of mothers' allowances insisted that social assistance provided by the state should in no way subvert the natural economic dependency of women on men wherever possible, lest the sanctity of marriage and the family be undermined.[25] Women leaders also insisted that a mother's entitlement to state support was not a right, but a discretionary 'allowance' contingent on her continuing moral fitness as a good housekeeper and mother. Within this framework, inability to manage on funding that was made available, demoralization, sloppy housekeeping, or failure to seek part-time work were used frequently as arguments, by women investigators, to disentitle other women from assistance.

In short, the moralizing and maternalist assumptions underpinning the reformers' arguments for mothers' allowance harboured the seeds of continued stigmatization and regulation of women within the scheme. These assumptions provided needy women with a poor defence for demanding more adequate levels of assistance or more individual freedom based on their human rights as citizens, rather than on their duties as mothers. Arguments for liberalization on a more nonjudgmental basis during the 1930s and 1940s emerged instead among professional social workers and state officials who, according to Skocpol, did not share their clients' 'same moral universe.'

In assessing the overall importance of gender to the shaping of welfare policy in Ontario, one must also ask, as do Piven and Cloward, how important mothers' pensions were to the overall welfare caseload.[26] They were not important, until eligibility within the program was liberalized in the late 1950s as a result of bureaucratic and professional initiatives rather than lobbying from women's groups. The overall assessment of need, the determination of benefits, and the intrusive style of home investigation within mothers' allowances did not differ significantly from practices in grossly inadequate and degrading general relief programs, nor did the program lack an ongoing and vigilant concern with enforcing the work ethic and women's participation in the labour market.[27] In short, although the rhetoric surrounding mothers' allowances upheld a distinctive maternalist ethic that celebrated the claims of motherhood, the actual administration and benefit levels provided by the program were only marginally different from the general framework of the province's wider provision for the poor. An examination of the plight of women living on social assistance within Ontario confirms that 'market concerns and market actors were overwhelmingly determining in the politics of ... welfare state programs.'[28] Mothering provided Ontario women living in poverty with a weak basis for entitlement compared with other insurance-based forms of social provision aimed principally at men.

To what extent were social work and its professional needs-based discourse a factor in pushing government and society forward in the fight against poverty? Over the entire half-century reviewed here, social work must be credited with some significant victories, in particular the creation of nutritionally adequate food allowances in 1944 and the passage of the Unemployment Assistance Act of 1956, even if it clearly lost the overall War on Poverty.

Three caveats are important here. First, it is difficult to generalize about the profession as a whole in discussing attitudes towards poverty. As in other professions, political orientations within social work spanned the ideological spectrum from arch conservatives such as Charlotte Whitton or Robena Morris to radicals such as Margaret Gould or Bessie Touzel. Most working with the profession fell somewhere in the middle. Second, since social work was a profession created and dominated by women, it is not always easy to separate gender from professional ideology in analysing the social work response to poverty. As Gordon argues in a provocative analysis of the gendering of state welfare, the 'needs-based' discourse of social casework itself was constructed on feminine skills 'involving attentiveness, empathy, [and] asking the right questions.' Within this framework, 'the needs tradition called up a female experiential and discursive realm of nurturance and of authority through the power to give.'[29] Finally, social workers were not disinterested bystanders in arguments surrounding social policy. Building welfare state programs also meant creating employment for social work and expanding the profession's potential power through enhancing the claims of its specialized knowledge and expertise.

Having said this, it is apparent that social work influence on welfare in Ontario had both conservative and liberalizing tendencies. Casework emphasis on the therapeutic 'rehabilitation' and 'adjustment' of clients living in poverty, which reached an apogee in the late 1950s and early 1960s, clearly carried on, in professional guise, earlier individualizing assumptions about character reformation as the most effective strategy for preventing conditions of dependency.[30] At the same time, casework put social workers directly into the homes of many of those living in poverty. During the 1930s it exposed ill health, gross nutritional inadequacies in food allowances, and lack of decent shelter and household necessities among families on welfare. Casework also led in 1939 to Canadian social work's most influential attempt to quantify a minimum standard of health and decency, the publication of *The Cost of Living*. Thereafter, in spite of concerted opposition from business and studied indifference from government, organizations such as the Toronto and the Canadian Welfare Council have carried on a systematic attempt to define minimum basic needs and to measure the extent to which state welfare provision falls below them. Although, within Ontario, provincial and local governments often ignored or disputed social work's quantification of minimum needs, they never put in place alternative definitions other than the maximum ceilings on social assistance. Ironically, on the most critical question affecting the lives of Ontario's poorest citizens, the department entrusted with their care did almost no discernible research and left private welfare organizations to define the meaning of poverty.

Perhaps the most enduring weakness within the professional social work vision was the assumption, typified most clearly in the work of Harry Cassidy, that solving poverty was a technical question best left within the aegis of social work expertise. Much of Cassidy's emphasis upon bureaucratic reform, rationalization, and professionalization of the province's welfare system rested on the assumption that placing social workers (like himself) in charge of welfare administration would resolve the inadequacy, stigmatization, and demoralization that surrounded social assistance within the province. His widely shared professional vision was typical of a generation of welfare 'consolidators,' to use Heclo's term, who acted in the faith that among competing values of liberty, equality, and security, 'no final choice was necessary.'[31] Efficient public administration of social policy by informed professionals could resolve the inherent contradiction between expanding citizenship rights and enduring market-based inequalities – a conflict that lies at the heart of the welfare state.

Cassidy, along with most social work leaders before 1970, was wrong. Deteriorating economies, ballooning budget deficits, and a growing backlash against the expanding army of dependent poor after 1970 would demonstrate just how quickly the fragile consensus around welfare entitlement could unravel. In losing sight of the extent to which welfare policy is about moral choices and competing values, not simply professional expertise and bureaucratic efficiency, many within social work as well as the wider social policy community forgot that the political will to fight poverty must be created and sustained within every generation.[32] It cannot be entrusted only to experts and advisers within or outside government. To this extent, social workers, along with all those interested in combatting poverty, have much to learn from the complex political origins of Ontario's welfare state.

Appendix

TABLE 1
Schedule of Weekly Food Costs

Summer schedule as follows	
For one adult per week	$1.50
For the second adult in a family, per week an additional	.95
For the third member of the family, per week an additional	.90
For the fourth member of the family, per week an additional	.85
For the fifth member of the family, per week an additional	.80
For the sixth member of the family, per week an additional	.75
For the seventh member of the family, per week an additional	.70
For the eight member of the family, per week an additional	.65
For the ninth member of the family, per week an additional	.60
For the tenth member of the family, per week an additional	.55
This will work out to a standard wherein the full food supply needs of families can be made as follows	
Family of one per week	$1.50
Family of two per week	2.45
Family of three per week	3.35
Family of four per week	4.20
Family of five per week	5.00
Family of six per week	5.75
Family of seven per week	6.45
Family of eight per week	7.10
Family of nine per week	7.70
Family of ten per week	8.25

SOURCE: Ontario, *Report on Provincial Policy on Administrative Methods in the Matter of Direct Relief in Ontario* (Toronto 1932), 17.

TABLE 2
Public Assistance in Ontario: Direct Relief Expenditures, 1930–43

Assessed population 1942	Municipality	Gross expenditures ($)	Governmental share ($)	Municipal share ($)	Percentages	
					Gov't	Municipal
669,130	Toronto	67,671,913	46,658,229	21,013,684	68.9	31.1
109,948	Windsor	20,371,270	17,372,474	2,998,796	85.3	14.7
167,505	Hamilton	16,542,121	11,383,772	5,158,349	68.8	31.2
158,581	Ottawa	14,524,717	9,833,507	4,691,210	67.7	32.3
79,485	York	14,022,505	12,399,601	1,622,904	88.4	11.6
41,477	York East	7,075,251	6,338,978	736,273	89.6	10.4
77,438	London	5,415,381	3,742,212	1,673,169	69.1	30.9
32,778	Brantford	4,294,765	3,078,003	1,216,762	71.7	28.3
23,847	Scarborough	3,810,931	3,409,468	401,463	89.5	10.5
20,118	Niagara Falls	3,469,067	2,823,443	645,624	81.4	18.6
32,559	St Catharines	2,899,637	2,000,484	899,153	70.0	30.0
26,843	Oshawa	2,785,607	2,194,616	590,991	78.7	21.3
35,745	Kitchener	2,134,546	1,489,605	644,941	69.8	30.2
34,184	Sudbury	1,916,595	1,574,658	341,937	82.2	17.8
22,953	York North	1,696,395	1,371,348	325,047	80.8	19.2
29,061	Fort William	1,645,689	1,130,342	515,347	68.7	31.3
9,997	Stamford	1,626,421	1,143,783	482,638	70.3	29.7
6,579	Midland	1,612,472	1,242,915	369,557	77.1	22.9
24,424	Port Arthur	1,603,776	1,116,569	487,207	69.6	30.4
26,224	Sault Ste Marie	1,588,888	1,178,869	410,019	74.2	25.8
4,213	Sturgeon Falls	1,576,286	1,363,868	212,418	86.5	13.5
30,569	Kingston	1,568,239	1,075,979	492,260	68.6	31.4
23,195	Guelph	1,501,406	1,023,735	477,671	68.2	31.8
18,477	Etobicoke Twp	1,479,442	1,254,151	225,291	84.8	15.2

Municipality						
North Bay	15,933	1,387,546	1,101,530	286,016	79.4	20.6
Peterborough	27,776	1,313,621	906,882	406,739	69.0	31.0
Hawkesbury	6,177	1,262,904	968,953	293,951	76.7	23.3
Stratford	16,993	1,184,702	823,507	361,195	69.5	30.5
Mimico	8,075	974,139	815,095	159,044	83.7	16.3
Eastview	7,972	951,826	887,498	64,328	93.2	6.8
St Thomas	17,773	902,484	621,265	281,219	68.8	31.2
Timmins	25,790	846,957	568,212	278,745	67.1	32.9
Sarnia	17,840	700,872	482,902	217,970	68.9	31.1
Orillia	9,503	686,935	473,780	213,155	69.0	31.0
Chatham	17,241	584,730	400,761	183,969	68.5	31.5
Teck Twp	17,831	557,413	382,493	174,915	68.6	31.4
Kenora	7,809	491,309	349,560	141,749	71.1	28.9
Alexandria	1,975	347,117	286,580	60,537	82.6	17.4
Fort Frances	5,410	331,889	243,799	88,090	73.5	26.5
Cornwall Twp	13,809	316,381	227,023	89,358	71.8	28.2
Total province	3,660,632	238,008,876	180,606,569	57,402,307	75.9	24.1
40 municipalities	1,923,237	195,674,145	145,740,454	49,933,691	74.5	25.5

SOURCE: AO, RG 29, Deputy Minister, box 125. The forty municipalities in the province accounted for 82.2 per cent of gross expenditures, 80.7 per cent of governmental expenditures, 87.0 per cent of municipal expenditures, and 52.5 per cent of estimated provincial population.

TABLE 3
Monthly Budget for Family of Five

Item		Cost	Per cent
Rent		$30.00	19¹/₂
Food			
Man	$13.00		
Woman	11.60		
Boy 6	7.60		
Girl 10	10.55		
Boy 12	10.55		
Total	$53.30	53.50	34¹/₂
Clothing			
Man	6.40		
Woman	6.00		
Boy 6	3.05		
Girl 10	4.15		
Boy 12	4.50		
Total	$24.10	24.10	15¹/₂
Operation			
Coal	7.75		
Gas	2.70		
Light	1.08		
Water	.90		
Ice	1.00		
Cleaning supplies	1.50		
Replacements	2.50		
Carfare	3.50		
Total	$20.93	20.93	13¹/₂
Advancement and Recreation			
Newspaper	.75		
Allowances	1.00		
Radio license	.20		
Vacations and parties	4.25		
Church	1.40		
Shows, sports, etc.	1.60		
Postage, reading	1.00		
Carfare	1.30		
Total	$11.50	11.50	7¹/₂
Medical and Dental care: $1.80 per person		9.00	6
Savings		4.50 }	3¹/₂
Insurance (life policy for man)		0.84	
Total per month		$154.17	100
Total per week		$35.85	

SOURCE: Toronto Welfare Council, *The Cost of Living* (Toronto 1944), 31.

TABLE 4
Monthly Relief Maximum Total Allowance, 1950–61

Date	Single person, unattached		Four-person family		Seven-person family	
	Allowance ($)[a]	Percentage increase from 1950	Allowance ($)	Percentage increase from 1950	Allowance ($)	Percentage increase from 1950
14 Sept. 1950	35.65	–	135.00	–	175.00	–
30 Oct. 1951	38.57	8.2	135.00	–	175.00	–
16 July 1952	40.07	12.4	135.00	–	175.00	–
12 April 1956	45.07	26.4	135.00	–	175.00	–
24 May 1957	48.36	35.7	150.00	11.1	180.00	2.9
31 Oct. 1960	48.50	36.0	150.00	11.1	180.00	2.9
16 Feb. 1961	57.10	60.2	150.00	11.1	180.00	2.9
3 July 1961	57.10	60.2	150.00	11.1	180.00	2.9
			(225.00)[b]	(66.6)[b]	(255.00)[b]	(45.7)[b]

NOTES: Regulations under the Unemployment Relief Act and the General Welfare Assistance Act.

[a] There is no stipulated maximum total allowance for a single person, unattached. Hence, these amounts are the sum of the monthly maximum regular component allowances (food, heated shelter, household sundries, clothing, and electricity for cooking) for a single person, unattached.

[b] Applies to municipalities with population over 100,000 and area municipalities in Metropolitan Toronto. This amount is calculated by adding the maximum regular heated shelter allowance for three municipalities to the maximum total allowance as allowed in Ontario Regulation 172/61.

SOURCE: J.D. Wismer, 'Public Assistance in Ontario, 1950–61' (Master of Social Work, University of Toronto 1964), table 17, 86.

TABLE 5
Maximum Shareable Relief Shelter Allowance, 1950–60

Date	Maximum shareable
1 Jan. 1950	24.00 (30.00)[a]
14 Sept. 1950	30.00
16 July 1952	40.00
12 April 1956	50.00
24 May 1957	50.00
7 Jan. 1958	45.00
31 Oct. 1960	Revoked

NOTES: Regulations under the Unemployment Relief Act and the General Welfare
Assistance Act.
[a] Applies only to municipalities with population over 500,000.

SOURCE: Wismer (see table 3), table 13, 80.

TABLE 6
Ontario Social Assistance Caseload by Reason for Dependency, 1961–73

March of year	Unemployment GWA[a] only	Blindness, disability, major health problem			Mother-led single-parent family			Other reasons: old age, women age 60–5, etc.		
		GWA	FBA[b]	Both	GWA	FBA	Both	GWA	FBA	Both
1961	13,884	11,862	17,791	29,653	4,806	7,510	12,316	1,539	22,736[c]	24,275
1962	14,690	13,227	18,315	31,542	5,567	7,652	13,219	1,675	22,868[c]	24,543
1963	15,324	12,198	19,492	31,690	7,471	7,446	14,917	3,126	23,925[c]	27,051
1964	12,500	11,803	20,792	32,595	7,451	7,747	15,198	3,064	31,995[d]	35,059
1965	10,645	12,374	22,380	34,754	7,933	8,821	16,754	2,949	34,915[d]	37,864
1966	9,178	12,248	23,791	36,039	7,824	10,056	17,880	3,764	29,738[d]	33,502
1967	10,036	12,486	25,205	37,691	7,892	11,775	19,667	3,606	23,544[d]	27,150
1968	18,885	13,268	26,507	39,775	8,181	17,179	25,360	3,892	18,208	22,100
1969	15,583	12,965	28,528	41,493	9,672	20,428	30,100	4,010	13,427	17,437
1970	20,564	18,783	29,225	48,008	10,795	24,247	35,042	3,832	10,232	14,064
1971	40,529	25,038	31,433	56,471	13,901	27,895	41,796	4,270	12,273	16,543
1972	34,847	26,321	34,706	61,027	14,485	35,040	49,525	7,119	10,362	17,481
1973	20,230	23,980	36,131	60,111	12,733	36,749	49,482	7,691	11,157	18,848

NOTES
[a] General Welfare Allowance.
[b] Family Benefit Allowance.
[c] Figure represents Old Age Assistance cases only.
[d] Figure represents Old Age Assistance and widows and unmarried women cases only.

SOURCE: Social Planning Council of Metropolitan Toronto, *Social Allowances in Ontario: An Historical Analysis of General Welfare Assistance and Family Benefits (with special focus on adequacy of allowances), 1961–1976* (Toronto 1977), 89.

TABLE 7
Monthly Relief Maximum Total Allowance as Percentage of Ontario Monthly Average
Wages[a] by Years, 1950–61

Year	Four-person family (%) (per cent)	Seven-person family (%) (per cent)	Wages ($)
1950	66.9	86.7	201.69
1951	60.3	78.1	223.82
1952	55.3	71.7	224.04
1953	52.2	67.7	258.33
1954	50.8	65.8	265.69
1955	49.0	63.5	275.17
1956	46.6	60.4	289.50
1957	49.0	58.9	305.52
1958	47.3	56.7	316.96
1959	45.3	54.4	330.77
1960	44.0	52.8	340.81
1961	42.6	51.2	351.34
	(64.0)[b]	(72.6)[b]	

NOTES: Regulations under the Unemployment Relief Act and the General Welfare
Assistance Act; and Canada, Dominion Bureau of Statistics, *Employment and Payrolls*
(Ottawa: Queen's Printer, monthly, 1950–61).
[a] Average weekly wages multiplied by 4.3.
[b] Applies to municipalities with population over 100,000 and area municipalities in
Metropolitan Toronto.

SOURCE: Wismer (see table 3), table 19, 89.

TABLE 8
Budget Ratios[a] of Four Families Receiving Ontario Social Assistance Allowances, 1961–76

	Single person under age 65	Mother, child age 4		Mother, children ages 3, 6, 8		Father, mother, children ages 10, 13	
	GWA[b]	GWA + FA[c]	FBA + FA	GWA + FA	FBA + FA	GWA + FA	FBA + FA
				Per cent			
1961	29	40	57	48	60	41	49
1962	31	44	57	52	59	45	48
1963	30	43	67	51	69	44	59
1964	33	53	66	57	68	49	58
1965	37	58	69	62	71	54	61
1966	35	58	68	57	64	50	57
1967	43	62	65	64	66	59	60
1968	42	61	61	63	63	57	57
1969	38	56	60	58	58	53	53
1970	38	58	58	59	59	53	53
1971	38	58	58	59	59	53	53
1972	35	54	54	55	55	49	49
1973	36	55	61	55	59	48	53
1974	40	61	63	62	64	52	55
1976	43	61	63	62	64	53	55

NOTES:

[a] Ratio of allowance income (assistance, plus family allowances) to guides, family budgets. Indicates adequacy of income on an annual basis, where 100 per cent indicates complete adequacy of income to satisfy budgetary needs.

[b] General Welfare Allowances.

[c] Family Benefit Allowance.

SOURCE: Social Planning Council of Metropolitan Toronto (see table 6), 56.

Notes

INTRODUCTION

1 Ian M. Drummond, *Progress without Planning: The Economic History of Ontario from Confederation to the Second World War* (Toronto 1987); K.J. Rea, *The Prosperous Years: The Economic History of Ontario, 1939–75* (Toronto 1985); Desmond Morton, 'Sic Permanet: Ontario People and Their Politics,' 7, S.F. Wise, 'The Ontario Political Culture: A Study in Complexities,' 52–3, and Richard Simeon, 'Ontario in Confederation,' 171, in Graham White, ed., *The Government and Politics of Ontario*, 4th edition (Toronto 1990); Christopher Armstrong, 'The "Mowat Heritage" in Federal-Provincial Relations,' in Donald Swainson, ed., *Oliver Mowat's Ontario* (Toronto 1972), 117.
2 Senate of Canada, Report of the Special Senate Committee on *Poverty in Canada* (Ottawa 1971), xiii–xviii; Rea, *The Prosperous Years*, 248.
3 The primary monographs on the evolution of the Canadian welfare state are Kenneth Bryden, *Old Age Pensions and Policy-Making in Canada* (Montreal 1974); Malcolm Taylor, *Health Insurance and Canadian Public Policy* (Montreal, 1979); C.D. Naylor, *Private Practice/Public Payment: Canadian Medicine and the Politics of Health Insurance, 1911–1966* (Montreal 1986); *James Struthers, No Fault of Their Own: Unemployment and the Canadian Welfare State, 1914–1941* (Toronto 1983); Leslie Pal, *State, Class and Bureaucracy: Canadian Unemployment Insurance and Public Policy* (Montreal 1988); Dennis Guest, *The Emergence of Social Security in Canada* (Vancouver 1980). On the critical connection between the evolution of 'social rights' and national citizenship in the making of the welfare state, T.H. Marshall's seminal 1949 essay 'Citizenship and Social Class,' reprinted in his *Class, Citizenship, and Social Development* (Chicago 1977), has yet to be surpassed.
4 For the most convincing arguments concerning the gendered and two-tiered structure of the welfare state as it developed within the United States see Linda Gordon, 'What Does Welfare Regulate?' *Social Research* 55, 4 (winter 1988), 609–30 and 'Social Insurance and Public Assistance: The Influence of Gender in

Welfare Thought in the United States, 1890–1935,' *American Historical Review* 97, 1 (February 1992), 19–54. For a spirited if not entirely convincing rebuttal to Gordon see Frances Fox Piven and Richard A. Cloward, 'Welfare Doesn't Shore Up Traditional Family Roles: A Reply to Linda Gordon,' *Social Research* 55, 4 (winter 1988), 631–47. Other important contributions to this literature include Barbara Nelson, 'The Origins of the Two-Channel Welfare State in the U.S.: Mothers' Aid and Workmen's Compensation,' and Nancy Fraser, 'Struggle over Needs: Outline of a Socialist-Feminist Critical Theory of Late-Capitalist Political Culture,' in Linda Gordon, ed., *Women, the State, and Welfare* (Madison 1990).

5 Ontario, *First Annual Report of the Mothers' Allowance Commission of Ontario, 1920–21*, 15; Rea, *The Prosperous Years*, 131; Lorna Hurl, 'The Nature of Policy Dynamics: Patterns of Change and Stability in a Social Assistance Programme,' paper prepared for the 4th National Conference on Social Welfare Policy, Toronto, 24–27 October 1989, table 1; Vernon Lang, *The Service State Emerges in Ontario: 1945–1973* (Toronto 1975), 53; Ontario, *Time for Action: Towards a New Social Assistance System for Ontario* (Toronto 1992), 3–4; Toronto *Globe and Mail*, 30 January 1993. For two classic statements on the 'withering away' of means-tested welfare within an increasingly univeralistic welfare state see T.H. Marshall, 'Citizenship and Social Class,' and Richard Titmuss, 'Universal and Selective Social Services,' in his *Commitment to Welfare* (London 1968), 113–123.

6 Although the literature on the welfare state since the 1970s is too vast to list here, some of the more notable contributions include James O'Connor, *The Fiscal Crisis of the State* (New York 1973), Ian Gough, *The Political Economy of the Welfare State* (London 1979), Claus Offe, *Contradictions of the Welfare State* (Cambridge 1985), Hugh Heclo, *Modern Social Politics in Britain and Sweden: From Relief to Income Maintenance* (New Haven 1974), Gosta Esping-Andersen, *Politics against Markets: The Social Democratic Road to Power* (Princeton 1985), Peter Evans, Dietrich Rueschemeyer, and Theda Skocpol, eds., *Bringing the State Back In* (Cambridge 1985), Margaret Weir, Ann Shola Orloff, and Theda Skocpol, eds., *The Politics of Social Policy in the United States* (Princeton 1988), and Peter Flora and Arnold Heidenheimer, eds., *The Development of Welfare States in Europe and America* (London 1981). Within a Canadian context, two notable collections of essays are Leo Panitch, ed., *The Canadian State: Political Economy and Political Power* (Toronto 1977), and Allan Moscovitch and Glenn Drover, eds., *Inequality: Essays on the Political Economy of Social Welfare* (Toronto 1981).

7 The key exceptions to this generalization remain the seminal revisionist historical studies by Frances Fox Piven and Richard Cloward, *Regulating the Poor: The Functions of Public Welfare* (New York 1971) and *Poor People's Movements: Why They Succeed, How They Fail* (New York 1979), as well as books by Michael Katz, *Poverty and Policy in American History* (New York 1983), *In the Shadow of the Poorhouse: A Social History of Welfare in America* (New York

1986), and *The Undeserving Poor: From the War on Poverty to the War on Welfare* (New York 1989).

8 Clarke A. Chambers, '"Uphill All the Way": Reflections on the Course and Study of Welfare History,' *Social Service Review* (December 1992), 493–5, 501, and 'Toward a Redefinition of Welfare History,' *Journal of American History* 73, 2 (September 1986), 415. As Michael Katz has also argued, 'The history of welfare looks very different when the historian perches on the shoulder of a poor person and looks outward than it does when the story is told from the perspective of governments, agencies, or reformers.' See his *In the Shadow of the Poorhouse*, 293. For a recent Canadian reflection on this theme see the review essay by Cynthia Commacchio, 'Another Brick in the Wall: Toward a History of the Welfare State in Canada,' *Left History* 1, 1 (spring 1993), 103–8.

9 Harold L. Wilensky and Charles N. Lebeaux, *Industrial Society and Social Welfare* (New York 1958), and Wilensky, *The Welfare State and Equality: Structural and Ideological Roots of Public Expenditures* (Berkeley 1975). As Wilensky summed up this perspective in his later book, 'economic growth and its demographic and bureaucratic outcomes are the root causes of the general emergence of the welfare state,' xiii. The phrase 'logic of industrialism' school is taken from Jill Quadagno, *The Transformation of Old Age Security: Class and Politics in the American Welfare State* (Chicago 1988), 3.

10 Wilensky and Lebeaux, *Industrial Society and Social Welfare*, 140. Their conceptual distinction between 'institutional' and 'residual' approaches to welfare has since been repeated in almost all professional social work writing on the welfare state. See, for example, Kathleen Woodroofe, *From Charity to Social Work in England and the United States* (Toronto 1962), 219, and for an influential Canadian view see Dennis Guest, *The Emergence of Social Security in Canada* (Vancouver 1980).

11 For a useful summary of these criticisms see Flora and Heidenheimer, eds., *The Development of Welfare States in Europe and America*; Quadagno, *The Transformation of Old Age Security*, 3–4; and most recently Theda Skocpol, *Protecting Soldiers and Mothers: The Political Origins of Social Policy in the United States* (Cambridge 1992), 12–14.

12 See for example Seymour Martin Lipset, *First New Nation: The United States in Historical and Comparative Perspective* (New York 1963); Louis Hartz, *The Liberal Tradition in America* (New York 1955) and *The Founding of New Societies* (New York 1964); Gaston Rimlinger, *Welfare Policy and Industrialization in Europe, America, and Russia* (New York 1971). For a specific application of the 'national values' approach to U.S. social policy see Roy Lubove, *The Struggle for Social Security* (Pittsburgh 1968). The 'national values' characterization is taken from Skocpol, *Protecting Soldiers and Mothers*, 15.

13 Gad Horowitz, *Canadian Labour in Politics*, chapter 1 (Toronto 1968), 3–57.

14 John Wilson, 'The Ontario Political Culture,' in Donald MacDonald, ed., *Government and Politics of Ontario*, 1st edition (Toronto 1975), 211–33; Wise, 'The

Ontario Political Culture,' 44–62; H.V. Nelles, *The Politics of Development: Forests, Mines, & Hydro-Electric Power in Ontario, 1849–1941* (Toronto 1974); S.J.R. Noel, *Patrons, Clients, and Brokers: Ontario Society and Politics, 1791– 1896* (Toronto 1990), especially chapters 1 and 2.

15 This paragraph relies heavily on the critique in Skocpol, *Protecting Soldiers and Mothers*, 15–23.

16 Nancy Fraser, 'Women, Welfare, and the Politics of Need Interpretation,' in her *Unruly Practices: Power, Discourse, and Gender in Contemporary Social Theory* (Minneapolis 1989), 145.

17 Francis G. Castles, *The Working Class and Welfare: Reflections on the Political Development of the Welfare State in Australia and New Zealand, 1880–1908* (London 1985) and also his *The Social Democratic Image of Society* (London 1978); Walter Korpi, *The Democratic Class Struggle* (Boston 1983); Esping-Andersen, *Politics against Markets* and more recently *The Three Worlds of Welfare Capitalism* (Princeton 1990). In a broader sense, one might also fit T.H. Marshall's classic 1949 three-stage interpretation of the welfare state, 'Citizenship and Social Class,' into this perspective, given his insight that within the twentieth century 'citizenship and the capitalist class system have been at war ... [and] it is quite clear that the former has imposed modifications on the latter' (121), although Marshall was not precise on the process through which these new 'social rights' of citizenship were put into place. The quotation in the text is from Skocpol, *Protecting Soldiers and Mothers*, 24.

18 Elements of such an interpretation may be found in Bryden, *Old Age Pensions and Policy-Making in Canada*, 61–80; Struthers, *No Fault of Their Own*, chapter 6, 175–207; Laurel Sefton MacDowell, 'The Formation of the Canadian Industrial Relations System during World War Two,' *Labour/le travailleur* 3 (1978), 175– 96; Taylor, *Health Insurance and Canadian Public Policy*, 69–104, 239–330.

19 Quadagno, *The Transformation of Old Age Security*, 4. Esping-Andersen's recent work explicitly acknowledges the critical importance of cross-class coalitions, particularly with agrarian interests, for interpreting variations in the scope and timing of welfare state developments across nations. See his 'The Three Political Economies of the Welfare State,' *Canadian Review of Sociology and Anthropology* 26, 1 (1989), 10–36.

20 For an analysis of comparative social policy development which is highly sensitive to the explanatory importance of federalism as a variable, see Christopher Leman, 'Patterns of Policy Development: Social Security in the United States and Canada,' *Public Policy* 25, 2 (spring 1977), 261–91.

21 Skocpol, *Protecting Soldiers and Mothers*, 24–6.

22 Quadagno, *The Transformation of Old Age Security*, 7.

23 Ian Gough, *The Political Economy of the Welfare State* (London 1979), 12.

24 Quadagno, *The Transformation of Old Age Security*, 5. For two influential

collections of essays articulating a similar perspective on the Canadian welfare state see Panitch, ed., *The Canadian State*, and Moscovitch and Drover, eds., *Inequality*.

25 Piven and Cloward, *Regulating the Poor* and *Poor People's Movements*. See also their *The Politics of Turmoil: Essays on Poverty, Race, and the Urban Crisis* (New York 1974) and *The New Class War* (New York 1982). Although more than two decades have passed since *Regulating the Poor* first appeared, the debate surrounding its arguments remains ongoing. For two informative discussions see Walter I. Trattner, ed., *Social Welfare or Social Control? Some Historical Reflections on Regulating the Poor* (Knoxville 1983), and Linda Gordon, 'What Does Welfare Regulate?' *Social Research* 55, 4 (winter 1988), 609–30, as well as Piven and Cloward's spirited and incisive replies to their critics in each volume.

26 Piven and Cloward, *Regulating the Poor*, xiii.

27 Francis Fox Piven and Richard Cloward, 'Humanitarianism in History: A Reply to the Critics,' in Trattner, ed., *Social Welfare or Social Control?* 144.

28 For two excellent interpretations of American welfare state development which assign primacy of place to the role of business see Quadagno, *The Transformation of Old Age Security*, and Kim McQuaid and Edward Berkowitz, *Creating the Welfare State: The Political Economy of 20th Century Reform* (Lawrence 1992). A less convincing Canadian example may be found in Alvin Finkel's *Business and Social Reform in the Thirties* (Toronto 1979). On coercion and control within state welfare bureaucracies, the best single interpretation remains Frances Fox Piven and Richard Cloward, 'The Professional Bureaucracies: Benefit Systems as Influence Systems,' in their *The Politics of Turmoil*, 7–27.

29 On the tendency of many Marxists theorists to deny the 'agency' of the working class or the poor in the creation of social policy see Quadagno, *The Transformation of Old Age Security*, 5. The agency of the working class and the poor is the core argument of Piven and Cloward's *Poor People's Movements*.

30 Quadagno, *The Transformation of Old Age Security*, 5. See also James Leiby, 'Social Control and Historical Explanation: Historians View the Piven and Cloward Thesis,' in Trattner, ed., *Social Welfare or Social Control?* as well as the introduction to this volume by Trattner, who argues that 'there are serious historical problems in attempting to explain American social welfare history as ... Piven and Cloward do, in some single, unchanging, almost mechanical fashion,' 10.

31 Skocpol, *Protecting Soldiers and Mothers*, 28.

32 See for example Struthers, *No Fault of Their Own*, and Pal, *State, Class, and Bureaucracy*.

33 Skocpol, *Protecting Soldiers and Mothers*, 29.

34 Ibid., 42. The growth of 'state-centred' explanations of social policy has been rapid over the past decade. One of the earliest and most influential examples is Hugh Heclo's *Modern Social Politics in Britain and Sweden: From Relief to*

Income Maintenance (New Haven 1974). More recently the prolific output of
Theda Skocpol and her collaborators has dominated the field. See for example the
collection of essays in Evans, Rueschemeyer, and Skocpol, eds., *Bringing the
State Back In*; Weir, Orloff, and Skocpol, eds., *The Politics of Social Policy in the
United States*; Ann Shola Orloff, *The Politics of Pensions: A Comparative
Analysis of Britain, Canada, and the United States, 1880–1940* (Madison 1993);
as well as Skocpol's recently published *Protecting Soldiers and Mothers*. Within
Canada, Pal's *State, Class and Bureaucracy*, and more recently his *Interests of
State: The Politics of Language, Multiculturalism, and Feminism in Canada*
(Montreal 1993), represent important interpretations of social policy from this
perspective. See also Rodney Haddow, 'The Poverty Policy Community in
Canada's Liberal Welfare State,' in William Coleman and Grace Skogstad, eds.,
Policy Communities and Public Policy in Canada: A Structural Approach
(Mississauga 1990), 212–37, as well as his *Poverty Reform in Canada, 1958–
1978: State and Class Influences on Policy-Making* (Montreal 1993).

35 All these points are elaborated cogently in Skocpol, *Protecting Soldiers and
Mothers*, 41–60.

36 The most extensive treatment of this theme remains Keith G. Banting, *The
Welfare State and Canadian Federalism* (Montreal 1982). See also Richard
Simeon and Ian Robinson, *State, Society, and the Development of Canadian
Federalism* (Toronto 1990).

37 Chambers, 'Uphill All the Way,' 502.

38 Pal, in *State, Class and Bureaucracy*, 134–5, argues that an 'actuarial ideology'
derived from the private sector insurance industry dominated policy deliberations
within Canada's Unemployment Insurance Commission. For Pal this constitutes
compelling evidence that 'policy may be determined largely within the state
itself, in relatively autonomous bureaucratic organizations.' Why perspectives on
the boundaries of entitlement of the unemployed, derived from a private sector
insurance metaphor and inserted into state policy, should be seen as compelling
evidence for the 'autonomy' and 'independence' of the state vis-à-vis business is
not clear.

39 Alan Wolfe, 'The Mothers of Invention,' review of Theda Skocpol's *Protecting
Soldiers and Mothers*, in *The New Republic*, 4 and 11 January 1993.

40 Skocpol, *Protecting Soldiers and Mothers*, 31. This massive monograph represents a major analytical shift on Skocpol's part away from her celebrated state-
centred explanations of the origins of U.S. social policy and towards more
society-centred explanations, in this case through asserting the influence of a
social feminist mass movement of American women upon the forging of a
distinctive 'maternalist' welfare state protecting women and children. As Alan
Wolfe points out in a recent review of the book, this marriage of state-centred and
society-centred explanations is not always successful. 'Skocpol ... tries to
preserve her 'state-centred' theorizing even while furnishing the evidence that

contradicts it ... What we really have in the new Skocpol is a criticism of the old Skocpol ... [She] is arguing here that American women made a difference ... In her new picture, real people move across the stage, people who know that their actions and their emotions matter.' *The New Republic*, 4 and 11 January 1993.

41 Gordon, 'What Does Welfare Regulate?' 611–14; the term 'family ethic' comes from Mimi Abramovitz, *Regulating the Lives of Women: Social Welfare Policy from Colonial Times to the Present* (Boston 1989); Carole Pateman, 'The Patriarchal Welfare State,' in Amy Gutmann, ed., *Democracy and the Welfare State*, 238–42.

42 Linda Gordon, 'What Does Welfare Regulate?' 612; Nelson, 'The Origins of the Two-Channel Welfare State,' in Gordon, ed., *Women, the State, and Welfare*, 123–51. See also Linda Gordon's introduction to this volume, 'The New Feminist Scholarship on the Welfare State,' 9–35. As Gordon puts it, 'Needs language was often brought into political debate by women ... The rights legacy has been male traditionally.' See her 'Social Insurance and Public Assistance,' 34–5.

43 Gordon, 'The New Feminist Scholarship on the Welfare State'; Mary Jo Bane, 'Politics and Policies of the Feminization of Poverty,' in Weir, Orloff, and Skocpol, eds., *The Politics of Social Policy in the United States*, 381–97; Pateman, 'The Patriarchal Welfare State,' 247.

44 Abramovitz, *Regulating the Lives of Women*, 39. For a Canadian variant of this theme see Jane Ursel, 'The State and the Maintenance of Patriarchy: A Case Study of Family, Labour, and Welfare Legislation in Canada,' in J. Dickinson and B. Russell, eds., *Family, Economy, and State: The Social Reproduction Process under Capitalism* (Toronto 1986), 150–91.

45 Skocpol, *Protecting Soldiers and Mothers*, 37. See also Seth Koven and Sonya Michel, 'Gender and the Origins of the Welfare State,' *Radical History Review* 43 (1989), 112–19.

46 Gordon, 'What Does Welfare Regulate?' 630.

47 Skocpol, *Protecting Soldiers and Mothers*, 33. From theorists of the 'patriarchal' welfare state, Skocpol argues, 'we do not learn of the celebration of the universal civic value of mothering – by mothers of all classes and races – that was so central to women's movements for mothers' pensions.' Eli Zaretsky has also stressed the extent to which women themselves were leading advocates of a 'family wage' in order to provide relief to working-class mothers from the double burden of wage-earning work. See his 'The Place of the Family in the Origins of the Welfare State,' in Bonnie Thorne and Marilyn Yalom, eds., *Rethinking the Family: Some Feminist Questions* (New York 1982). For a recent interpretation of child welfare policy in Canada which assigns primary place to such cross-class gender solidarities see Carol Thora Baines, 'From Women's Benevolence to Professional Social Work: The Case of the Wimodausis Club and the Earlscourt Children's Home, 1902–1971' (PhD dissertation, University of Toronto 1990).

48 Gordon, 'Social Insurance and Public Assistance,' 21. On the importance of race

see her 'Black and White Visions of Welfare: Women's Welfare Activism, 1890–1945,' *Journal of American History* 78, 2 (September 1991), 559–90.

49 Linda Gordon, as cited in Alan Wolfe, 'The Mothers of Invention,' *The New Republic*, 4 and 11 January 1993, 34.

50 Piven and Cloward, 'Welfare Doesn't Shore Up Traditional Family Roles,' 644–5.

51 Wolfe, 'The Mothers of Invention,' 32. Similar points are made by Zaretsky, 'The Place of the Family in the Origins of the Welfare State,' 211–12, 216, and Koven and Michel, 'Gender and the Origins of the Welfare State,' 117.

CHAPTER 1 *'In the Interests of the Children'*

1 On the mothers' pension movement in the United States see Gwendolyn Mink, 'The Lady and the Tramp: Gender, Race, and the Origins of the American Welfare State,' and Barbara J. Nelson, 'The Origins of the Two-Channel Welfare State: Workmen's Compensation and Mothers' Aid,' in Linda Gordon, ed., *Women, the State, and Welfare* (Madison 1990), 93–151; Joanne Goodwin, 'An American Experiment in Paid Motherhood: The Implementation of Mothers' Pensions in Early Twentieth-Century Chicago,' *Gender and History* 4, 3 (autumn 1992), 323–42; and most recently, Theda Skocpol, *Protecting Soldiers and Mothers: The Political Origins of Social Policy in the United States* (Cambridge 1992), 424–79. For an analysis of the same movement in Canada see Veronica Strong-Boag, ' "Wages for Housework": Mothers' Allowances and the Beginnings of Social Security in Canada,' *Journal of Canadian Studies* 14, 1, (spring 1979), 24–34, and more recently, Margaret Hillyard Little, 'A Fit and Proper Person': The Moral Regulation of Single Mothers in Ontario, 1920–1940,' paper presented to the Canadian Women's Studies Association, Kingston, 30 May 1991, and Suzanne Morton, 'Women on Their Own: Single Mothers in Working-Class Halifax in the 1920s,' *Acadiensis* 21, 2 (spring 1992), 90–107.

2 Linda Gordon, 'The New Feminist Scholarship on the Welfare State,' in her *Women, the State, and Welfare*, 9.

3 Skocpol, *Protecting Soldiers and Mothers*, 424–79.

4 Mink, 'The Lady and the Tramp,' 101.

5 Archives of Ontario (AO), RG 7, series II-1, box 2, 'Memo on Mothers' Pensions Prepared by the Superintendent of Trades and Labour,' 1917, 2.

6 On Kelso and the origins of the Children's Aid Societies of Ontario see Andrew Jones and Leonard Rutman, *In the Children's Aid: J.J. Kelso and Child Welfare in Ontario* (Toronto 1981), and John Bullen, 'J.J. Kelso and the "New" Child-Savers: The Genesis of the Children's Aid Movement in Ontario,' *Ontario History* 82, 2 (June 1990), 107–28.

7 As cited in Margaret Hillyard Little, ' "No Car, No Radio, No Liquor Permit": The Moral Regulation of Single Mothers in Ontario, 1920–1993' (PhD dissertation, York University 1994), 53. I am indebted to Little for drawing the centrality

of Kelso's early role in Ontario's mothers' allowance movement to my attention.

8 The list of organizations involved in Toronto's Committee on Mothers' Allow-
ances included, besides Peter Bryce as convener, representatives from the
Juvenile Court, the Social Service Council of Ontario, the Trades and Labour
Council, the Social Service Commission of Toronto, the Superintendent of
Catholic Charities, the Bureau of Municipal Research, the Local Council of
Women, the Department of Public Health, the Superintendent of Neglected and
Dependent Children, the Neighborhood Workers' Association, the Women's
Institutes, the Machinists' Union, the Inspector of the Feeble-Minded, and the
Head of Separate Schools. Ontario, Department of Labour, *Mothers' Allowances:
An Investigation* (Toronto 1920), 15.

9 Biographical material on the Reverend Peter Bryce is taken from Carol Thora
Baines, 'From Women's Benevolence to Professional Social Work: The Case of
the Wimodausis Club and the Earlscourt Children's Home, 1902–1971' (PhD
dissertation, University of Toronto 1990), 48–50; the quotation is originally cited
in Doug Owram, *The Government Generation: Canadian Intellectuals and the
State, 1900–1945* (Toronto 1986), 124.

10 Mink, 'The Lady and the Tramp,' 93, 97–8, 107. See also Mimi Abramovitz,
*Regulating the Lives of Women: Social Welfare Policy from Colonial Times to the
Present* (Boston 1988), and Jane Lewis, *The Politics of Motherhood: Child and
Maternal Welfare in England, 1900–1939* (London 1980). Skocpol, in *Protecting
Soldiers and Mothers*, 442–8, provides the most important new interpretation of
the mothers' pension movement in the United States, arguing that its origins can
be traced to the power of a middle- and upper-class women's reform movement,
led by organizations such as the National Congress of Mothers and the General
Federation of Women's Clubs, which had branches in cities and towns across the
nation. 'These upper and middle-class women were trying to embrace as sisters,
as fellow mothers, the impoverished widows who would be helped by mothers'
pensions' (479).

11 On the symbiotic relationship between exposure to the needs of working-class
women and the achievement of social power by women charity workers see
Baines, 'From Women's Benevolence to Professional Social Work,' 60–93.

12 AO, RG 7, 'Memo on Mothers' Pensions,' 1917.

13 Ibid.

14 Mariana Valverde, *The Age of Light, Soap, and Water: Moral Reform in English
Canada, 1885–1925* (Toronto 1991), 160; AO, RG 7, 'Memo on Mothers'
Pensions,' 1917.

15 On the primary role of orphanages in providing care for the children of indigent
parents see Bettina Bradbury, 'The Fragmented Family: Family Strategies in the
Face of Death, Illness, and Poverty, Montreal, 1860–1885,' in Joy Parr, ed., *Childhood and Family in Canadian History* (Toronto 1982), 109–28. As Ann
Vandepol writes, 'These asylums quickly developed into the major social

mechanism for sustaining children of low-income parents faced with unemployment, financial collapse, or death of a male breadwinner. At many asylums, half-
orphans (children with one parent alive) outnumbered full orphans by a wide
margin. In California by 1900 there were 5399 half-orphans and only 959 full
orphans housed in institutions throughout the state,' cited in Nelson, 'The Origins
of the Two-Channel Welfare State,' 137–8; Baines, 'From Women's Benevolence to Professional Social Work,' 104–6; Ontario, *Mothers' Allowances*, 22–3.

16 Ontario, *Mothers' Allowances*, 24–6, 28–9. The risk to children in institutional
care of death from infection was quite real in this era. Within the Earlscourt
Home, fourteen children died between 1913 and 1929 owing to contagious
disease. Baines, 'From Women's Benevolence to Professional Social Work,' 110.
Even official institutional death rates among children were often understated. As
one doctor testifying before Ontario's 1919 Inquiry into Mothers' Allowances
pointed out, 'the main advantage of this Pension scheme is that it will take these
children out of Infant Homes, no matter how well they may be managed. In some
of these places, in order to keep their mortality down, they ship the sick child into
hospitals, and then the death does not appear in the books.' AO, RG 7, series II,
box 2, file 'Mothers' Allowance, 1919,' verbatim testimony, 'Mothers' Pension
Allowance: Hamilton Enquiry, 20 February 1919,' testimony of Dr Mullin.

17 Ontario, *Mothers' Allowances, an Investigation*, 1920, 26–7; AO, RG 7, series
II-1, box 2, 'Mother's Pension Allowance: Hamilton Enquiry, 20 February 1919,'
testimony of Mrs Evans; RG 7, 'Memo on Mothers' Pensions, 1917,' citation
from Report by Dr Bruce Smith, April 1913. Chronic overcrowding and high
death rates among institutionalized children were also critical factors in the
success of campaigns for mothers' pensions in American states. As Mimi
Abramovitz notes, 'In 1910, one year before the enactment of the first Mothers'
Pension program, the number of children housed in institutions peaked at more
than 126,000, representing more than three per 1000 of the child population ...
High infant mortality rates, outbreaks of contagious diseases, the exploitation
of child labor, and the overall poor care provided to the children who survived
discredited the original child-saving methods as a way to socialize children and
conserve them as an important national resource.' *Regulating the Lives of Women*,
196.

18 *Toronto Star*, 15 January 1920, cited in Ontario, *Mothers' Allowances*, 19; ibid.,
12, 15; AO, RG 7, series II-1, box 2, 'Mother's Pension Allowance: Hamilton
Enquiry, 20 February 1919,' testimony of Walter Rollo. On similar arguments
for mothers' pensions by organized labour in American states see Nelson, 'The
Origins of the Two-Channel Welfare State, 139, and Goodwin, 'An American
Experiment in Paid Motherhood' (327). Nelson observes that although union
leaders lent their support to the mothers' pensions movement, unlike workmen's
compensation legislation it was 'never a priority for organized labor.' This was

probably the case in Ontario as well. It is also important to note the critical distinction Nelson makes between the conceptualization and operation of these two early state initiatives into income security. 'Workmen's Compensation was a program developed for the white northern men employed in heavy industry ... [and] it set the tone for the first channel of the welfare state, which was male, judicial, public, and routinized in origin. In comparison, Mothers' Aid was origi- nally designed for white impoverished widows of men like those eligible for Workmen's Compensation. It set the tone for the second channel of the welfare state, which was female, administrative, private, and nonroutinized in origin' (133).

19 Strong-Boag, 'Wages for Housework,' 25.

20 Ontario, *Mothers' Allowances*, 17.

21 AO, RG 7, 'Memo on Mothers' Pensions, 1917'; Ontario, *Mothers' Allowances*, 84; RG 7, series II-1, box 2, 'Mothers' Pension Allowance: Hamilton Enquiry, 20 February 1919,' testimony of W.H. Lovering.

22 Ontario, *Mothers' Allowances*, 75.

23 Ibid., 17; RG 7, series II-1, box 2, 'Mothers' Pension Allowance: Hamilton Enquiry, 20 February 1919,' testimony of W.H. Lovering.

24 'Mothers' Pension Allowance: Hamilton Enquiry, 20 February 1919,' testimony of W.H. Lovering.

25 Ibid. This was an amount adjusted for postwar price increases. During the war itself, the Patriotic Fund paid up to a ceiling of $45 per month for the mother and a progressively smaller amount for each child, depending upon the circumstances of each family. Local committees in each community were given discretionary authority to set their own scales up to the level of this maximum. See Philip Morris, ed., *The Canadian Patriotic Fund: A Record of Its Activities from 1914 to 1919* (np, nd), 30. See also Margaret McCallum, 'Assistance to Veterans and Their Dependants: Steps on the Way to the Administrative State, 1914–1929,' in W. Wesley Pue and Barry Wright, eds., *Canadian Perspectives on Law and Society: Issues in Legal History* (Ottawa 1988), 157–77.

26 Ontario, *Mothers' Allowances*, 9–10; AO, RG 7, series II-1, box 2, 'Mothers Allowance, 1919,' W.H. Hearst to W.A. Riddell, 16 January 1919.

27 Ontario, *Mothers' Allowances*, 10.

28 Ibid., 30.

29 Ibid., 30–1. By the end of 1921–2 mothers' allowances in Ontario would have a caseload of 3559 widows and 10,922 children at a total cost of $1,382,138, compared with $774,667 spent on 2660 mothers in its first year. Ontario, *First Annual Report of the Mothers' Allowance Commission of Ontario 1920–21* (hereafter *First Annual Report, 1920–21*), 15; *Second Annual Report, 1921–22*, 9. On the gross inaccuracy and lack of administrative preparation surrounding Ontario's first foray into old age pensions see James Struthers, 'Regulating the

Elderly: Old Age Pensions and the Formation of a Pension Bureaucracy in Ontario, 1920–1945,' *Journal of the Canadian Historical Association*, new series, 3 (1992), 235–55.

30 Ontario, *Mothers' Allowances*, 16.

31 Ibid., 21–2.

32 Ibid., 23–5, 49–50.

33 Ibid., 35, 50–3, 68.

34 Ibid., 54–8; RG 7, series II-1, 'Mothers' Pension Allowance: Hamilton Enquiry, 20 February 1919,' testimony of Mrs Hawkings, Walter Riddell, and Mr Axford. For further support by labour for the rights of unwed mothers, see the testimony of Walter Rollo.

35 AO, RG 7, series II-1, box 2, 'Mothers' Pension Allowance: Hamilton Enquiry, 20 February 1919'; Mothers' Allowances, 31, 53, 68, 86, 88.

36 *Mothers' Allowances*, 59–65, 88 (original emphasis); AO, RG 7, 'Mothers' Pension Allowance: Hamilton Enquiry, 20 February 1919,' testimony of W.H. Lovering.

37 AO, RG 7, series II-1, box 2, 'Mothers' Pension Allowance: Hamilton Enquiry, 20 February 1919,' testimony of Mrs P.D. Crerar; *Mothers' Allowances*, 82–4.

38 Nelson, 'The Origins of the Two-Channel Welfare State,' 124, 133, 136, 140–1. As Nelson points out, 'a key difference in the administration of the two programs is that Mothers' Aid was given in return for an ongoing service rather than in response to a realized risk ... [T]he administrators of Workmen's Compensation cared if alcohol contributed to accidents ... but they did not care, or, more important, they could not control the beneficiary who spent all of his or her benefits on drink. The behaviour of Mothers' Aid beneficiaries, on the other hand, was closely monitored. Thus, it was the *capacity to care* that was supported in Mothers' Aid' (original emphasis).

39 *Mothers' Allowances*, 60.

40 Ibid., 80; *First Annual Report, 1920–21*, 10. Patronage in the appointment of Mothers' Allowance investigators was a frequent complaint from the ranks of Canadian social work in the 1920s. See James Struthers, 'A Profession in Crisis: Charlotte Whitton and Canadian Social Work in the 1930s,' *The Canadian Historical Review* 62, 2 (1981), 169–85, and Margaret Kirkpatrick Strong, *Public Welfare Administration in Canada* (Chicago 1930), 135.

41 *First Annual Report, 1920–21*, 16–17.

42 Ibid., 10–11; *Tenth Annual Report, 1929–30*, 13. On Elizabeth Shortt's resignation see Clifford J. Williams, *Decades of Service: A History of the Ontario Ministry of Community and Social Services, 1930–1980* (Toronto 1984), 38.

43 *First Annual Report, 1920–21*, 12, 23, 27. On the prevalence of 'fit and proper person' clauses in most mothers' pensions schemes see Abramovitz, *Regulating the Lives of Women*, 200–3; Mink, 'The Lady and the Tramp,' 93, 110.

44 *First Annual Report, 1920–21*, 20, 23–4; *Second Annual Report, 1921–22*, 24, 26–9.

45 *First Annual Report, 1920–21*, 27–8; Valverde, *The Age of Light, Soap, and Water*, 28.

46 *Fifth Annual Report, 1924–25*, 12–13; *Second Annual Report, 1921–22*, 27.

47 *Second Annual Report, 1921–22*, 30.

48 *Third Annual Report, 1922–23*, 18–19; *Fourth Annual Report, 1923–24*, 15.

49 *Fourth Annual Report, 1923–24*, 16.

50 Ibid., 16.

51 AO, MG 26 1739/31, vol. 1, Lanark County Mothers' Allowance Board, Minutes, 8 January 1921; *First Annual Report, 1920–21*, 65.

52 *First Annual Report, 1920–21*, 28, 65.

53 Ibid., 15; *Tenth Annual Report, 1929–30*, 5. The length of time required for the desertion of husbands whose whereabouts were unknown, as a requirement for eligibility, was dropped from seven years to five in 1921. Physical incapacitation of husbands, as a criterion for eligibility, jumped from 7.6 per cent to 22 per cent of the total caseload between 1921 and 1930.

54 *First Annual Report, 1920–21*, 21; *Second Annual Report, 1921–22*, 21.

55 *First Annual Report, 1920–21*, 10–11.

56 *Third Annual Report, 1922–23*, 17.

57 *Fourth Annual Report, 1923–24*, 16; *Third Annual Report, 1922–23*, 20, 22.

58 *Second Annual Report, 1921–22*, 27-28; *Third Annual Report, 1922–23*, 18, 22.

59 AO, Lincoln County Records F 1741, 'Minutes of the Lincoln County Mothers' Allowance Board,' meeting of 18 May 1927.

60 Ibid., meeting of 20 October 1927; *First Annual Report, 1920–21*, 18, 27; *Second Annual Report, 1921–22*, 30–1; *Third Annual Report, 1922–23*, 18; AO, F 1741, Lincoln County Mothers' Allowance/Pension Commission, Case Records for Mothers' Allowances, 1920–1949, box 3, Jean Davidson to H. Bentley, 31 1938; case of E.H., 10 May 1939; letter from Mrs E. Nolan to the *Toronto Star*, 3 February 1926, originally cited in Margaret Hillyard Little, '"A Fit and Proper Person": The Moral Regulation of Single Mothers in Ontario, 1920-1940,' paper presented to the Canadian Women's Studies Association, Kingston, 30 May 1991, 10.

61 AO, MG 26 1739/31, vol. 1, Lanark County, Minutes, Mothers' Allowance Board, 1920–38, meeting, 12 March 1921, 19 December 1925; AO, F 1551/14/1, Brant, County of: Mothers' Allowance Board Minutes, 1920–1937, 15 December 1920, 22 January 1921; F 1741, box 3, Lincoln County Mothers' Allowance/Pension Commision, Case Records for Mothers' Allowances, 1920–49, case of E.J., 16 February 1928; case of M.J., 4 December 1938 (original emphasis).

62 AO, F 1741, box 3, H. Bentley to Jean Davidson, 15 December 1938.

63 AO, MG 26 1739/31, vol. 1, Lanark County, Minutes, Mothers' Allowance Board, 1920–38, 16 March 1922.

64 *First Annual Report, 1920–21*, 28.

65 AO, F 1551/14/1, Brant, County of: Mothers' Allowance Board Minutes, 1920–37, 16 May 1925; AO, MG 26 1739/31, vol. 1, Lanark County, Minutes,

Mothers' Allowance Board, 1920–38, 18 March 1927; AO, F 1741, Lincoln
County Pension/Mothers' Allowance Commission, 1937–49, Minutes, 25 May
1934, 5 January 1937, 27 July 1937; Little, 'No Car, No Radio, No Liquor
Permit,' 14–15. As Little points out, Mothers' Allowance Commission investigators also took the same strict approach to enforcing sexual propriety. 'They
interrogated the mother, her parents, her friends and neighbours, public officials
– asking them to comment on the number and type of visitors to the home, the
number of times the mother socialized outside the home and with whom, and
the type of clothing the mother bought and wore' (15). See also her 'The Policing
of Ontario's Single Mothers during the Dirty Thirties,' paper presented to the
Canadian Historical Association Annual Meeting, Charlottetown, May 1992.

66 University of Western Ontario (UWO), Regional History Collection, London,
Minutes of Seventh Meeting of Mothers' Allowance Board, 27 September 1929,
case no. 609; AO, F 1741, Lincoln County Mothers' Allowance/Pension Commission, Case Records, box 3, Jean Davidson to Central Board, 19 November
1938; case of I.H., 22 April 1940; case of L.C., 21 October 1936; case of J.B., 3
January 1939. In this instance the central commission overruled the recommendation of the local board on the grounds that the mother was using up the balance
of her husband's estate correctly to improve the home conditions of her children.
H. Bentley to Jean Davidson, 3 January 1939.

67 UWO, Regional History Collection, Minutes of Seventh Meeting, Mothers'
Allowance Board, 27 September 1929, case no. 613.

68 AO, F 1551/14/1, Brant, County of, Mothers' Allowance Board Minutes, 1920–
37, 16 July 1932; F 1741, box 3, Lincoln County Mothers' Allowance/Pension
Case Files, 1920–49, case of M.D., 10 June 1935; AO, MG 26 1739/31, vol. 1,
Lanark County, Minutes, Mothers' Allowance Board, 1920–38, 18 February
1935, 14 September 1936; Brant, County of, Mothers' Allowance Board Minutes,
1920–37, 28 December 1925. On old age pensions see Struthers, 'Regulating the
Elderly.'

69 AO, F 1741, Lincoln County Pensions/Mothers' Allowance Commission, 1937–
49, box 1, Minutes of the Lincoln County Mothers' Allowance Board, meeting of
18 May 1927.

70 *Eighth Annual Report, 1927–28*, 14; AO, MG 26 1739/31, vol. 1, Lanark County,
Minutes, Mothers' Allowance Board, 1920–38, meetings of 31 July and 14
November 1929 (names changed from original).

71 *Seventh Annual Report, 1926–27*, 21.

72 *Eighth Annual Report, 1927–28*, 14–15. For a stimulating application of the ideas
of Michel Foucault to the state's 'moral gaze' over family life, through a web of
interconnected social agencies, see Jacques Donzelot, *The Policing of Families*
(New York 1979), especially chapter 4.

73 *Tenth Annual Report, 1929–30*, 14; Warren E. Kalbach, 'Growth and Distribution of Canada's Ethnic Populations, 1871–1981,' in Leo Driedger, ed., *Ethnic
Canada* (Toronto 1985), table 8.

74 Little, 'A Fit and Proper Person,' 26–8; AO, F 1741, Lincoln County Mothers'
Allowance/Pension Commission, Case Records, 1920–49, box 3, case of M.S.,
21 September 1938; case of K.O., 12 June 1940; case of H.P., 12 March 1941;
case of C.M., 17 December 1940. Little also notes, from her research, that black
and aboriginal women 'suffered most. Almost every Black mother who applied
had experienced neighbours attempting to besmudge her reputation.' Aboriginal
mothers often had their claims dismissed because of inadequate documentation
by Ottawa of Indian births.

75 *Second Annual Report, 1921–22*, 31–33.

76 AO, F 1741, Lincoln County Mothers' Allowance/Pension Commission, Case
Records, 1920–49, box 3, case of R.H., 20 December 1934; case of M.D., 16
January 1929; case of S.C., 26 September 1935; case of M.D., 17 November 1927.

77 AO, RG 3, Ferguson Papers, box 100, file 'Mothers' Allowance Commission,'
Mrs Ethel Bagley to Howard Ferguson, 30 October 1928; Howard Ferguson to
Mrs Ethel Bagley, 5 November 1928; Howard Ferguson to F.W. Stapleford, 14
January 1927. See also the quite typical case of B.F. with five children under the
age of sixteen whose husband died of a brain tumour in 1928. She applied for and
received a mothers' allowance at the age of thirty-four in February 1928. After
sixteen years of support, her allowance of $30 a month was cut off automatically
in June 1944 'as the last child turned 16.' She thus faced the labour market at the
age of fifty, without any income or savings, and with a twenty-year wait for
eligibility for a means-tested Old Age Pension. AO, F 1741, Lincoln County
Mothers' Allowance/Pension Commission, Case Records, 1920–49, box 3, case
of B.F., 21 February 1928.

78 In her recent study of mothers' pensions in the United States, Theda Skocpol
argues that inadequate benefits, averaging $21 monthly across the United States,
reflected the inability of women's reform organizations, which pioneered the
legislation, to exercise continuing influence over its administration once such
programs passed into the hands of 'bureaucrats and social workers.' Within
Ontario, however, there is no evidence that women's organizations campaigned
vociferously for higher benefits levels than the ones provided. See Skocpol,
Protecting Soldiers and Mothers, 476–9. Suzanne Morton notes that in Nova
Scotia, mothers' allowances initially paid $35 a month, while workmen's
compensation paid benefits to a maximum of $60 a month. Morton, 'Single
Mothers in Halifax,' 100, n55.

CHAPTER 2   *Regulating the Elderly*

1 National Archives of Canada (NA), RG 29, Department of National Health and
Welfare Records, vol. 127, file 208-1-18, letter from anonymous writer to James
Murdock, minister of labour, 30 March 1925.

2 Veronica Strong-Boag, *The New Day Recalled: Lives of Girls and Women in
English Canada, 1919–1939* (Toronto 1988), 179.

3 For a convincing refutation of the myth of a 'golden age' for the elderly see
   Carole Haber, *Beyond Sixty-Five: The Dilemma of Old Age in America's Past*
   (New York 1983), chapters 1, 2. See also David Hackett Fischer, *Growing Old in
   America* (New York 1978), chapters 1, 2, and W. Andrew Achenbaum, *Old Age
   in the New Land: The American Experience since 1790* (Baltimore 1978), part 1,
   2. The statistics on mortality are from Fischer, *Growing Old in America*, 106.

4 Michael Katz, *In the Shadow of the Poorhouse: A Social History of Welfare in
   America* (New York, 1986), 85–6; Stormie Elizabeth Stewart, 'The Elderly Poor
   in Rural Ontario: Inmates of the Wellington County House of Industry, 1877–
   1907,' *Journal of the Canadian Historical Association*, new series, 3 (1992),
   217–33.

5 Wilson A. Hunsberger, 'A History of the Ontario County Home' (MSW thesis,
   University of Toronto School of Social Work, 1951), 14, 22, 26.

6 John C. Bacher and J. David Hulchanski, 'Keeping Warm and Dry: The Policy
   Response to the Struggle for Shelter among Canada's Homeless, 1900–1960,'
   Urban History Review 16, 2 (October 1987), 148; Michael J. Piva, *The Condition
   of the Working Class in Toronto 1900–1921* (Ottawa 1979), 111.

7 Haber, *Beyond Sixty-Five*, 71, 80–1.

8 Ibid., 120; Fischer, *Growing Old in America*, 139.

9 Haber, *Beyond Sixty-Five*, 126; Achenbaum, *Old Age in the New Land*, 39–54.
   Fischer calls the formation of this perspective on old age 'gerontophobia.' See
   his *Growing Old in America*, 154. For a revisionist viewpoint, however, which
   argues that the situation of the elderly improved with industrialization see Brian
   Gratton and Carole Haber, 'Rethinking Industrialization: Old Age and the Family
   Economy,' in Thomas Cole et al., eds., *Voices and Visions of Aging: Towards a
   Critical Gerontology* (New York 1993), 134–59.

10 Daniel Scott Smith, 'Accounting for Change in the Families of the Elderly in the
   United States, 1900–Present,' in David Van Tassel and Peter N. Stearns, eds.,
   Old Age in a Bureaucratic Society (Westport 1986); Ann Shola Orloff, *The
   Politics of Pensions: A Comparative Analysis of Britain, Canada, and the United
   States, 1880–1940* (Madison 1993), 104–5; Lisa Y. Dillon, 'Your Place or Mine?
   Household Arrangements of Widows and Widowers in Nineteenth Century
   Ottawa: A Study of Three Wards,' paper presented to the Canadian Historical
   Association, Annual Meeting, Charlottetown, 1992. As Orloff notes, 'Much of the
   co-residence of the past occurred in the context of conjugal family households;
   the elderly were simply living with their own unmarried children. This form of
   co-residence has declined as life expectancy has increased and as people have had
   fewer children, closer together and earlier in life, leading to a longer period of the
   empty nest.' The key change affecting living arrangements of the elderly in the
   first half of this century, as Orloff points out, 'was not values and willingness
   to live with one's elderly kin. Rather, the proportion of elderly people in the
   population relative to younger people increased; there were fewer adult children

to go around, so more were called upon to help in the support of those elderly people who needed it.' *The Politics of Pensions*, 105, 109.

11 James G. Snell, 'Maintenance Agreements for the Elderly: Canada, 1900–1951,' *Journal of the Canadian Historical Association*, new series, 3 (1992), 197–216; David Gagan, *Hopeful Travellers: Families, Land and Social Change in Mid-Victorian Peel County, Canada West* (Toronto 1981), 50–7; W.H. Graham, *Greenbank: Country Matters in 19th Century Ontario* (Peterborough 1988), 195, 294; Jane Synge, 'Work and Family Support Patterns of the Aged in the Early Twentieth Century,' in Victor Marshall, ed., *Aging in Canada: Social Perspectives* (Don Mills 1980), 138–9.

12 Kenneth Bryden, *Old Age Pensions and Policy-making in Canada* (Montreal 1974), 30; Metropolitan Toronto Records and Archives (MTRA), RG 5.1, Commissioner of Public Welfare Records, file 48, graph 'Distribution of Population by Age: Ontario 1901–1961.'

13 MTRA, Commissioner of Public Welfare Records, RG 5.1, file 48.1, 'Old Age Assistance, 1921–1944,' Charles Hastings to Mayor Hilz, 26 June 1924. For alternative viewpoints, however, see Gratton and Haber, 'Rethinking Industrialization.'

14 Sharon Anne Cook, '"A Quiet Place ... to Die": Ottawa's First Protestant Old Age Homes for Women and Men,' *Ontario History* 81, 1 (1989), 1, 38.

15 On the role of women in such charity reform and institution building see Cook, 'A Quiet Place ... to Die'; Christina Simmons, 'Helping the Poorer Sisters: The Women of the Jost Mission, Halifax, 1905–1945,' *Acadiensis* 14, 1, (autumn 1984), 3–27; Patricia T. Rooke and R.L. Schnell, 'The Rise and Decline of British North American Protestant Orphans' Homes as Woman's Domain, 1850–1930,' *Atlantis* 7, 2 (spring 1982), 21–35; R.L. Schnell, 'Female Separatism and Institution-Building: Continuities and Discontinuities in Canadian Child Welfare, 1913–1935,' *International Review of History and Political Science* 25 (May 1988), 14–41; John T. Cumbler, 'The Politics of Charity: Gender and Class in Late Nineteenth-Century Charity Policy,' *Journal of Social History* 14, 1 (fall 1980), 99–110, and, more recently, Theda Skocpol, *Protecting Soldiers and Mothers: The Political Origins of Social Policy in the United States* (Cambridge 1992), 321–72. On the institution as surrogate for the family see David Rothman, *The Discovery of the Asylum: Social Order and Disorder in the New Republic* (Boston 1972). As Haber points out, 'the medical conception [of old age] emphasized numerous weaknesses and diseases that were present in the last stage of life ... [O]ld age was a time when separation from society was both necessary and desirable.' *Beyond Sixty-Five*, 80–1.

16 Archives of Ontario (AO), RG 8, series II-10-F, box 1, file 14, chart on 'Charitable Institutions,' May 1928. See also Provincial Secretary's Department, *Annual Report of the Inspector for Hospitals, Charities, and Asylums*, 1926, 21–3.

17 Cook, 'A Quiet Place ... to Die,' 30, 36–7, 39.

18 MTRA, RG 5.1, file 48, reports by G. Horne, 28 October 1943.

19 AO, Department of Public Welfare, *Annual Report*, 1934–5; RG 3, Mitchell Hepburn Papers, box 191, file 'Public Welfare Dept re Pensions, 1935,' 52nd *Annual Report* of the Aged Women's Home, October 1935; 32nd *Annual Report* of the Aged Men's Home, October 1935; Cook, 'A Quiet Place ... to Die,' 38.

20 Ontario, Department of Public Welfare, *Annual Report*, 1939–40, 'Report of Refuges, Statistical Summary January 1–December 31 1939.' By 1939 city refuges spent $1.12 each day per patient compared with 69 cents in the county homes. For an excellent case study of one such county refuge see Stewart, 'The Elderly Poor in Rural Ontario.'

21 See clippings in AO, RG 21, County of Lanark, House of Industry Management Committee Minutes, 1903–52; Stewart, 'The Elderly Poor in Rural Ontario,' and Hunsberger, 'A History of the Ontario County Home,' 15–29. Until 1937 the Revised Statutes of Ontario required that 'every inmate of a house of refuge, if able to work, shall be kept diligently employed at labour.' Hunsberger, 28. On the late nineteenth-century Ontario response to 'tramping' and vagrancy see James Pitsula, 'The Treatment of Tramps in Late Nineteenth Century Toronto,' Canadian Historical Association, *Historical Papers*, 1980, 116–32, and Richard Splane, *Social Welfare in Ontario, 1791–1893* (Toronto 1963), 99–116. For an overview of Ontario's Houses of Refuge see Norma Rudy, *For Such a Time as This: L. Earl Ludlow and a History of Homes for the Aged in Ontario, 1837–1961* (Toronto 1987), chapters 2–3, 15–66. As Rudy notes, Ontario's permissive legislation regarding the construction of County Houses of Refuge between 1867 and 1903 was largely ineffective 'for in over twenty-two years only nine counties built houses of refuge and many municipalities housed their elderly in gaols under the pretext that they were vagrants.' Only after 1903, when construction of such county houses was made mandatory, did their numbers increase significantly, reaching thirty-one in total by 1912. Rudy, *For Such a Time as This*, 22–7.

22 Ontario, Department of Public Welfare, *Annual Report*, 'Report of Refuges, Statistical Summary, January 1–December 31 1939.' Stewart, 'The Elderly Poor in Rural Ontario,' 224. Males made up 69 per cent of the inmates in the Wellington County House of Industry between 1877 and 1907. Among aged inmates, 82 per cent were males, Stewart has discovered. This gender discrepancy, she argues convincingly, most likely reflects the larger male composition of a migratory rural labour force, reduced to poverty in old age, as well as the more explicit 'work test' inherent in the nature of these rural poorfarms. The predominance of women in city refuges can be accounted for by the higher incidence and association between widowhood and poverty for elderly women in cities, as opposed to men, as well as their dramatically lower rate of labour-force participation after the age of sixty. For both reasons elderly women in cities bore a higher risk of pauperism than did men.

23 Katz, *In the Shadow of the Poorhouse*, 24–5. The 'deterrent' nature of Ontario's county houses of refuge is aptly captured in the description provided by Cy Atkinson, a former provincial inspector of these institutions:

> Upon entering ... the first impression was an over-powering odour composed of a mixture of human excrement, body odours, boiled cabbages, and strong disinfectant ... [T]here were one or two large dormitories on each side filled with white iron beds, as many as 20 lined in a row ... In the basement ... were wooden benches on which the male inmates sat to smoke ... Superintendents had received no training for their jobs and ... some ... were suspected of being almost sadists ... In ... several cases ... the cells in the basement were ... obviously in use ... It was ... clearly evident that the stigma of the old-time 'poorhouse' ... still existed.

Cited in Norma Rudy, *For Such a Time as This*, 34–5.

24 Hunsberger, 'A History of the Ontario County Home,' 14, 37–8; AO, RG 21, United Counties of Stormont, Dundas & Glengarry, House of Refuge, Minutes of Board of Management, 1928–48, 13 June 1929, 15 April 1931, 13 February and 1 April 1936, 5 February and 19 April 1937, 8 June 1948; Stewart, 'The Elderly Poor in Rural Ontario,' 232.

25 Hunsberger, 'A History of the Ontario County Home,' 60; Stormont, Dundas & Glengarry House of Refuge Minutes, 27 April 1937 (my emphasis).

26 Stormont, Dundas & Glengarry House of Refuge Minutes, 19 April 1937, 16 May 1945, 20 March 1931, 18 February 1932, 13 May 1936, 12 April 1934, 19 September 1938; University of Western Ontario (UWO), Weldon Library Regional History Collection, London Department of Welfare Collection, box B411, 'Correspondence – re Admissions to Hospitals and Nursing Homes, 1912–1929,' E.B. to relief inspector, 23 January, 1927, Relief Inspector to E.B., 26 January 1927 (my emphasis). Seven months later the Glengarry farmer finally succeeded in getting his wife out of the poorfarm after signing 'a satisfactory paper with the Township ... that both he and [his wife] will never ask for relief from said township.' Stormont, Dundas & Glengarry House of Refuge Minutes, 27 April 1939.

27 Cited in Hunsberger, 'A History of the Ontario County Home,' 62–3.

28 Stormont, Dundas & Glengary House of Refuge Minutes, 10 October 1944; circular from G.S. Tattle, Department of Public Welfare, cited in minutes, 29 February 1940; the attempted marriage incident and its aftermath appears in the minutes for 27 and 29 July 1938.

29 Hunsberger, 'A History of the Ontario County Home,' 91.

30 Stormont, Dundas & Glengarry House of Refuge Minutes, 24 February 1930, 18 August 1938, 29 August and 2 November 1940, 13 May and 18 November 1936, 5 October 1934, 11 February and 3 June 1938, 23 May 1944, 5 August 1940.

31 See Hunsberger, 'A History of the Ontario County Home,' 88, 61–2, 52. Stormont, Dundas & Glengarry House of Refuge Minutes, 27 July 1938. As the Board of Management noted, 'The field day was well attended and a good success. Dr. Barton, department of agriculture, together with other notable speakers addressed the meeting. A class of aged cows were judged together with a class of calves. Many favourable comments were heard from the visitors in regards to the buildings and crops and cattle.' No reference is made to the inmates or to their care. On the preoccupation of County Refuge management with agriculture see also the County of Lanark, House of Industry Management Committee Minutes, 1903–52. According to Norma Rudy, Earl Ludlow, provincial inspector of county houses of refuge, shared this perception. 'Ludlow recalls that many board members took pride in the farm and on many occasions visited the barns to view the cattle. They rarely, and in some instances never, visited the house of refuge where the inmates lived. Frequently the barns were cleaner and more cheerful than the houses.' *For Such a Time as This*, 38.

32 Hunsberger, 'A History of the Ontario County Home,' 80, 88, 107, 74; MTRA, RG 5.1, file 48.1, 'Old Age Assistance, 1921–1944,' Dr Charles Hastings to Mayor Hilz, 26 June 1924.

33 AO, RG 8, series II-10-F, box 1, file 14, Charts on Charitable Institutions and Houses of Refuge, May 1928; Ontario, Department of Public Welfare, *Annual Report*, 1939–40, 'Statistical Chart – Houses of Refuge,' *Annual Report*, 1931–2, 'Houses of Refuge'; Census of Canada, 1931, vol. 9, pt 3, *Institutions*, tables 6, 9, 10, cited in Bryden, *Old Age Pensions and Policy-making in Canada*, 36. Those over sixty also made up about 20 per cent of the population of Ontario's mental health institutions in 1937. About 700 senile elderly were housed in these chronically overcrowded institutions. See Harvey G. Simmons, *Unbalanced: Mental Health Policy in Ontario, 1930–1989* (Toronto 1990), 4, 38.

34 See for example MTRA, RG 5.1, file 481, Charles Hastings to Mayor Hilz, 26 June 1924.

35 J.R. Podoluk, 'Income Characteristics of the Older Population,' testimony to the Special Senate Committee on Aging, 22 October 1964, appendix U-1, 1252. UWO, London Welfare Department Collection, box B411 'Correspondence – Re Admissions to Hospitals and Nursing Homes, 1912–1919, A–Z; 1929–1944, A–L,' S.C. to city council, 3 October 1913; M.A. to Relief Inspector Saunders, 25 October 1930; Inspector McCallum to city council re M.C., 23 March 1920; A.C. to mayor, 4 February 1924.

36 AO, RG 21, Lincoln County Pensions/Mothers' Allowance Commission, 1937–47, Case Records, Old Age Pensions. Calculations and conclusions are taken from a detailed examination of this commission's 195 surviving case files, which include all old age pension applicants in Lincoln County who had last names beginning with the letters G–O between the years 1937 and 1947. For similar arguments concerning co-residence as an urban strategy for pooling scarce

housing resources between the elderly and their children see Orloff, *The Politics of Pensions*, 116–17.

37 Cited in Hunsberger, 'A History of the Ontario County Home,' 108.

38 UWO, London Welfare Department Collection, box B411, J.C. to city clerk, 7 November 1913; B.M. to city clerk, 12 December 1923; J.L. to city council, 19 June 1921; J.W. McCallum, relief inspector, to city council, 21 November 1912; J.W. McCallum to city council re K.B., 30 July 1914.

39 Ibid., A.B. to Relief Inspector J.W. McCallum, 25 November 1915; M.B. to Frank McKay, 26 November 1936; J.W. McCallum to Welfare Committee, 10 September 1923; A.C. to Mayor G.A. Wenige, 4 February 1924; J.W. McCallum to Mayor G.A. Wenige, 13 February 1924.

40 James G. Snell, 'Filial Responsibility Laws in Canada: An Historical Study,' *Canadian Journal on Aging* 9, 3 (1990), 270.

41 Achenbaum, *Old Age in the New Land*, 76. As Achenbaum notes, by 1860 'eighteen of the nation's thirty-three states had enacted laws designed to cope with dependency among family members of all ages; thirty-two states had passed such measures before 1914.' Only in the early twentieth century, however, did these laws begin to single out aged *parents* as a special category of obligation.

42 Charles M. Johnston, *E.C. Drury: Agrarian Idealist* (Toronto 1986), 154.

43 James G. Snell, 'Maintenance Agreements for the Elderly: Canada, 1900–1951,' *Journal of the Canadian Historical Association*, new series, 3 (1992), 198.

44 Smith, 'Accounting for Change,' 87–109; Scott argues that 'the high proportion, more than 60 percent, of persons aged sixty-five and older in 1900 who lived with children may be explained by the fact that Americans simply were too poor to afford independent residence of adult generations within the family,' 95–6; Orloff, *The Politics of Pensions*, 114–18, provides an able summary of the conflicting historical findings concerning patterns of co-residence of the elderly with their kin in the first four decades of this century. Despite variations among urban, rural, and small town settings, extended family co-residence was on the rise during this period, Orloff concludes. 'Differences in critical material conditions – the availability and cost of housing, the need for child care services, and the availability of sources of income to permit independent living by the nonworking ... can explain the different levels of co-residence. It certainly appears that independent living was the preferred alternative, of which people availed themselves when either social provision or private resources allowed.' Whether the elderly in need would be taken in by children living in poverty was also 'contingent on the aged relatives being able to offer something in return for their care. Whether or not the elderly would have that something to offer depended in turn on the character of state social provision.' For these reasons, Orloff argues, arguments for old age pensions gained increasing popularity (120).

45 See for example Piva, *The Condition of the Working-Class in Toronto, 1900–1921*, 56–8, 171. The UnMarried Parenthood Act, a statute similar in intent to the

Parents' Maintenance Act, passed the UFO administration during the same time period, but proved to be ineffective in extracting financial care for illegitimate children from putative fathers.

46 Snell, 'Filial Responsibility Laws in Canada.' Snell's thorough combing through the records of Carleton and Ontario counties between 1922 and 1963 uncovered only forty-seven cases in which the Parents' Maintenance Act was invoked. As Snell concludes, 'Despite the widespread adoption and long-term maintenance of filial responsibility laws in all Canadian jurisdictions, these laws have played a strikingly minor role in the lives of the dependent elderly' (272, 275).

47 On the coming of Canada's first old age pension scheme see Bryden, *Old Age Pensions and Policy-making in Canada*, and Orloff, *The Politics of Pensions*, 240–68.

48 Bryden, *Old Age Pensions and Policy-making in Canada*, 30, 36; MTRA, RG 5.1, file 48, graph, 'Distribution of Population by Age: Ontario 1901–1961'; AO, RG 8, Provincial Secretary, series II-10-F, box 1, file 14, Charts on Charitable Institutions and Houses of Refuge, May 1928; AO, Department of Public Welfare, *Annual Report*, 1939–40, 'Statistical Chart – Houses of Refuge'; AO, RG 3, Ferguson Papers, box 91, file 'Old Age Pension, 1926,' R.J. Browne, police magistrate, Toronto, to Howard Ferguson, 5 October 1926.

49 The $20 monthly benefit ceiling appears to have been derived from the $19 a month pension benefit paid in the 1920s by the Australian scheme, which formed the principal basis for cost estimates of the Canadian legislation. See Canada, House of Commons, *Second and Final Report of the Special Committee on Old Age Pensions*, 1 July 1924, 63–6. Pat Thane's argument concerning the rationale behind low levels of benefits in the British non-contributory old age pension scheme launched by Herbert Asquith's Liberal government in 1908 applies equally well to the thinking behind Canada's 1927 legislation. 'He [Asquith] believed that the central problem was that of helping the existing aged poor who had suffered from bad industrial conditions of the past, and that the younger generations should be induced to save. He believed that they had greater capacity to do that than previous generations and hence would be less in need to support from the state when they reached old age – there was therefore no need to establish complex insurance machinery.' *The Foundations of the Welfare State: Social Policy in Modern Britain* (London 1982), 82.

50 AO, RG 6, Records of the Ministry of Treasury and Economics, Series I-2, box 23, file 'Old Age Pensions, 1925–30,' letter to Provincial Treasurer J.D. Monteith from A.C., 9 January 1930. Although most letters in this series express gratitude, some were more critical, labelling the pension 'a mere pittance to keep any old couple from ... the poorhouse' and demanding a pension that would 'give old people over seventy a chance to live a little above the starvation line.' See J.R. to Monteith, 11 February 1929.

51 AO, RG 6, series I-2, box 23, file 'Pensions – Old Age, 1925–30,' George
    Crummer to J.D. Monteith, 27 April 1927; RG 3, Ferguson Papers, box 69, file
    'Old Age Pensions – 1925,' Jack Truman to Ferguson, 26 August 1925; box 91,
    file 'Old Age Pensions – 1926,' E.A. Giles to Ferguson, nd, but circa January
    1927; Ferguson to R.J. Browne, 8 October 1926. See also report of speech by
    Ferguson on old age pensions in *Hamilton Spectator*, 24 March 1926.
52 Peter Oliver, *G. Howard Ferguson: Ontario Tory* (Toronto 1977), 313–14.
53 Ferguson's administration began to collect data on how many Ontarians might
    be eligible for an old age pension under the terms of the 1924 Parliamentary
    Committee report only in 1928, three years after it had promised Ottawa it would
    begin the process. The procedure Ontario used to determine this information pro-
    vides a revealing glimpse into the incompetence and disorganization of adminis-
    tration at the provincial level. Refuge directors across the province were asked
    how many of their inmates were aged seventy or over and would be eligible if
    a pension of $20 a month was enacted. At the same time, municipal and town
    clerks were sent a mail survey by the Bureau of Municipal Affairs during the
    spring and summer of 1928 asking them to estimate, from their assessment rolls,
    the numbers of elderly in their communities with annual incomes under $365, the
    cutoff point for pension eligibility under the federal scheme. When replies were
    not forthcoming, two officials from the bureau were sent by car and train across
    the province to ferret out the information. The bureau's final tally revealed, late
    in 1928, that 14,607 Ontarians would be eligible for a pension should Ontario
    implement the federal legislation, a figure later revised upwards in March 1929 to
    20,665 when higher estimates from Toronto and the refuges were factored in.
    Even this latter figure was grossly wide of the mark, underestimating by almost
    100 per cent Ontario's actual pension caseload of 39,925 during the scheme's
    first full year of operation in 1930. Since local officials were given no money to
    conduct their survey and were told by Queen's Park officials to ignore property
    owners and to assume 'that not more than 30% of the balance [of those over
    seventy] would be eligible,' this range of inaccuracy is hardly surprising. AO,
    RG 8, series II-10-F, Bureau of Municipal Affairs: Old Age Pension Commission,
    box 1, file 5, circular from Bureau of Municipal Affairs, 10 May 1928; file 14,
    'Re Old Age Pensions No. Returns Received,' November 1928; AO, MU 1034,
    Howard Ferguson Papers (Private), box 18, file 4, 'Old Age Pensions in Ontario,'
    J.A. Ellis to Ferguson, 22 March 1929; AO, COMSOC, Minister's Correspond-
    ence, 1939–47, reel no. 3, undated memo, circa 1937; Ontario, Department of
    Public Welfare, *Annual Report*, 1947–8, chart 1, 'Old Age Pensions,' 9; AO, RG
    8, series II-10-F, box 3, file 23, 'Windsor,' J.A. Ellis to M.A. Dickinson, 28 May
    1928, 'Re Old Age Pensions.'
54 AO, MU 1034, Ferguson Papers (Private), box 18, file 4, 'Old Age Pensions in
    Ontario,' speech of Premier Ferguson in the Legislative Assembly, 21 March

1929 (my emphasis). The idea of non-contributory pensions as an 'earned' right of citizenship in reward for years of building up a nation became a prominent feature of the New Liberalism justifying Britain's old age pension scheme launched in 1908. See Orloff, *The Politics of Pensions* 167–81.

55 AO, RG 3, Ferguson Papers, box 107, file 'Old Age Pensions, 1930,' memo on 'Old Age Pensions – Qualifications.'

56 AO, MU 1034, box 18, file 4, 'Old Age Pensions in Ontario,' 21 March 1929.

57 NA, RG 29, vol. 137, file 208-5-5, 'First Annual Report of the Toronto Old Age Pensions Board,' 31 December 1929; 'Second Annual Report of the Toronto Old Age Pensions Board,' 31 December 1930. By the end of 1930 there were 6897 old age pensioners in Toronto, 4226 were women and 2671 were men. The chairman of Toronto's Pension Board was John O'Connor, secretary of the Masonic Temple. Other members included Mrs W.L. McFarland, past president of the Local Council of Women; John Dillon, a member of the Toronto Separate School Board; and C.M. Carrie, a member of the Toronto School Board. Its secretary and guiding spirit was Bert Merson. According to *Toronto Star* editorial writer and political radical, Margaret Gould, Merson's 'connection with old age pensions dates back many years when as a member of the Trades and Labour Council he, together with Tom Moore and others, strove to secure this valuable piece of legislation.' Gould also noted that when Toronto's pension board was first established, a conscious decision was made not to entrust its administration to the city relief officer. 'It was placed instead in the health department which then had a family welfare division. The board has since functioned so as not to attach any relief stigma to the pensioner.' *Toronto Star*, 19 October, 4 November 1937.

58 AO, RG 6, series I-2, box 23, file 'Old Age Pensions, 1935–30,' Dr D. Jamieson to E.T. Dunlop, 13 December 1932; AO, RG 3, Henry Papers, box 143, file 'Old Age Pensions, 1931,' 'Indignant Taxpayer' to Henry re Mrs B.B., 6 July 1931; W.P. Martin to Henry, 5 October 1931; Pension Commission to Mrs B.B., 7 October 1931, noting that her pension had been cancelled owing to her 'mode of living.' 'There are certain requisites for the granting of old age pensions and in your case these are not being met,' the commission told her. There was no reference in either federal or provincial pension legislation to 'mode of living' as a criterion for entitlement; same box and file, Dr D. Jamieson to Henry, 13 November 1931; NA, RG 29, vol. 137, file 208-5-5, E.A. Thomas to Peter Heenan, 4 April 1930; AO, RG 21, Lanark County Old Age Pension Board Minutes, 1929–48, minutes of meetings 15 October 1929 and 26 November 1929, 29 January 1930, 13 May 1931. Typical comments from these minutes were 'having granted a full pension to your wife, the Board feel that you are able to earn sufficient to maintain yourself;' 'having granted a pension to your wife ... your family should be able to support one of their parents'; 'pension granted husband should be sufficient to live on'; 'her position as housekeeper should ensure her maintenance'; and 'she is earning her living as housekeeper for her son.'

59 AO, RG 21, Lincoln County Pensions/Mothers' Allowance Commission, 1937–47, Case Records, Old Age Pensions. Commission members denied a pension to one seventy-year-old, for example, on the grounds that he was a 'young man for his age, well preserved and well able to work.' Another man of seventy-three with no savings or income was granted only a half-pension of $10 a month 'as long as he is able to give assistance in return for his board.' Similarly, a seventy-one-year-old woman, also with no wages or savings, was refused a pension because she was 'receiving [her] keep for services as a housekeeper.' See cases no. 1069 (8 June 1938); no. 1254 (12 February 1941); no. 1188 (8 May 1940), no. 1301 (9 April 1941); UWO, London Welfare Department Records, box B419, 'Old Age Pension Applications – Correspondence A–Z.'

60 Snell, 'Filial Responsibility Laws in Canada,' 268–77.

61 NA, RG 29, vol. 137, file 208-5-5, '3rd Annual Report of the Toronto Old Age Pension Board,' 31 December 1931 (which for the first time lists ineligibility 'due to parent's maintenance'); AO, RG 21, Lanark County Old Age Pension Board Minutes, 1929–48, 15 October 1929, 13 May and 23 June 1931; RG 3, Henry Papers, box 154, file 'Old Age Pensions, 1932,' Dr D. Jamieson to R.H., 5 February 1932; NA, RG 29, vol. 137, file 208-5-5, memo 'Re Old Age Pensions –Province of Ontario,' 4 March 1930; AO, RG 21, Lincoln County Pensions/ Mothers' Allowance Commission, 1937–47, Case Records, Old Age Pensions. Quotation is from case no. 1301, 9 April 1941.

62 Ontario, Department of Public Welfare, *Annual Report*, 1930–1, 4-4, 11–12. By December 1932 the average monthly pension was $18.29; NA, RG 29, vol. 137, file 208-5-5, memo on 'Old Age Pensions: Province of Ontario,' nd but circa 1933.

63 Bryden, in *Old Age Pensions and Policy-making in Canada*, 83, refers to a petition on pensions from a Toronto-based Old Age Pension Association in 1924, but no lasting record or evidence of this organization exists beyond this single reference. Ontario's first provincial organization of the elderly, the United Senior Citizens of Ontario, was not launched until 1956, twenty-four years later than the formation of British Columbia's Old Age Pensioners' Organization. AO, RG 18, Records of Commissions and Committees, series D-1-70, box C121, Select Committee on Aging, Minutes of Hearings, 21 June 1965, submission of the United Senior Citizens of Ontario. Unlike their counterparts in western Canada, the elderly as a pressure group in Ontario appear to have played little role in the launching of the province's pension scheme in 1929. On the strong grassroots support for pensions in the west see Bryden, *Old Age Pensions and Policy-making in Canada*, 71–2, 81–3. On the significance of the aged as a political force in pension implementation and administration see James G. Snell, *From 'Old Folks' to 'Senior Citizens': the Elderly in Canada, 1900–1951*, chapters 4 and 8. Interprovincial comparisons in pension benefits and takeup rates are from Snell, chapter 4, tables 44 and 45. I am indebted to James Snell for allowing me to read his forthcoming monograph.

64 NA, RG 29, vol. 137, file 208-5-5, memo to the deputy minister 'Re Old Age Pensions – Ontario', 19 March 1930; E.A. Thomas to H.H. Ward, 23 March 1930; E.A. Thomas to Peter Heenan, 4 April 1930.

65 AO, Department of Public Welfare, *Annual Report*, 1934–5, 3; *Annual Report*, 1939–40, 15. As the *Annual Report* for 1933–4 noted, 'many pensioners have families of sons and daughters who, under normal circumstances, would be able and willing to maintain or assist in the support of their aged parents, but on account of unemployment ... are unable to do so. Our experience in endeavouring to enforce the Parents' Maintenance Act has not been at all satisfactory. We have found that in more than 90 per cent of the cases brought before magistrates, no order was made against the children' (14–15).

66 Clifford Williams, *Decades of Service: A History of the Ontario Ministry of Community and Social Services, 1930–1980* (Toronto 1984), 4–6.

67 Biographical information on Dr David Jamieson is from G.D. Roberts and A.L. Tunnell, eds., *The Canadian Who's Who*, vol. 2: *1936–37*, (Toronto 1936), 554. On his political career under Howard Ferguson see Oliver, *G. Howard Ferguson*, 274–5, 360. On Jamieson's tenure as chairman of the Mothers' Allowance Commission see Williams, *Decades of Service*, 38.

68 *Windsor Star*, 20 February 1932; AO, Department of Public Welfare, *Annual Report*, 1930–1, noting that 'owing to the large number of applicants for pension it was impossible for either the Local Boards or the Commission to investigate fully the status of every applicant' (4–5).

69 MTRA, RG 51, file 481, 'Fourth Annual Report of the Toronto Old Age Pension Board,' 31 December 1932; NA, RG 29, vol. 137, file 208-5-5, vol. 1, 'Old Age Pensions – Ontario,' 'Second Annual Report of the Toronto Old Age Pension Board, 31 December 1930'; Report of Old Age Pension Commission, 'Third Annual Report 1932.'

70 AO, RG 3, Hepburn Papers, box 320, file 'Public Welfare Dept re: Old Age Pensions 1934,' David Croll to Hepburn, 29 October 1934; Toronto *Mail and Empire*, 26 October 1934; Department of Public Welfare, *Annual Report*, 1933–4, 3–4, 14–15.

71 NA, RG 29, vol. 29, file 208-1-1 pt 1, memo from J.W. MacFarlane to W.C. Clark, 'Problems Arising from the Joint Administration of Old Age Pensions,' 23 December 1938. As this memo pointed out, 'these initial [pension] schemes were not adequate or satisfactory presumably because no one in Canada at that time had had experience in the administration of Old Age Pensions ... The approval of a number of incomplete and inadequate schemes not only resulted in bad administration and loss of money, but also gave the provincial officials the impression that they were not in any real way subject to supervision by the Dominion.' AO, COMSOC, MS 728, Minister's Correspondence 1937–47, reel no. 3, Microdex no. 1, 'Mothers' Allowance and Old Age Pensions – Miscellaneous,' Jack Leith, secretary, Hamilton Old Age Department, to George Tattle, 15 June 1937; NA, RG 29, vol. 147, file 208-6-5 pt 1, J.W. MacFarlane to the

minister, 'Re Regulations Made Pursuant to the Ontario Old Age Pensions Act, 1929,' nd but circa June 1937; vol. 147, file 208-6-5 pt 1, J.L. Ilsley to M.F. Hepburn, 8 July 1937.

72 NA, RG 29, vol. 147, file 208-6-5 pt 1, J.W. MacFarlane, 'Re: Regulations Made Pursuant to the Ontario Old Age Pensions Act, 1929,' nd but circa June 1937; J.L. Ilsley to Mitch Hepburn, 6 July 1937; AO, Department of Public Welfare, *Annual Report*, 1937–8, 5–6, 9, 17.

73 AO, Department of Public Welfare, *Annual Report*, 1938–9, 16. A 'farm report' was also adopted at this time 'giving in detail particulars of the operation of the farm which aids in arriving at the net revenue derived therefrom.' Copies of these tables can be found in NA, RG 29, vol. 137, file 208-5-5 pt 3, memo dated 2 June 1941, and in AO, COMSOC, MS 728, Minister's Correspondence 1937–47, reel no. 3, microdex no. 5, 'Old Age Pensions – General, B.W. Heise, 1941.'

74 NA, RG 29, vol. 137, file 208-5-5 pt 3, memorandum by E.R. Sweettenham for J.W. MacFarlane, 18 December 1941; AO, Department of Public Welfare, *Annual Report*, 1949–50, 10.

75 NA, RG 29, vol. 29, file 208-1-1 pt 2, 'Report on the Administration of Old Age Pensions and Pensions for the Blind in Canada,' 30 April 1944; AO, Department of Public Welfare, *Annual Report*, 1942–3, 20, 23. As the *Annual Report* for 1940–1 noted, 'A reduction has also been made in the Old Age Pension rolls and it is felt *once again* that the earnings of children have placed them in a position to contribute to the support of their parents' (my emphasis). After 1939 many children of pensioners enlisted in the armed forces and, as the Department of Public Welfare pointed out, 'insofar as dependency can be proven, their parents have become eligible for Federal assistance, thus relieving our Province from further responsibility as regards the Old Age Pension.' *Annual Report*, 1939–40, 15. In Ontario, finance department officials noted in 1943, 'pension is stopped when the pension authority is notified by the pensioner that he is working. It remains suspended until such time as employment ceases ... One difficulty is that the pensioners do not always inform the pension authority that they have obtained employment.' NA, RG 29, file 208-1-1 pt 2, W.C. Clark to C.F. Needham, 1 September 1943. Statistical information is from NA, RG 29, vol. 137, file 208-5-5 pt 2, 'Old Age Pensions: Analysis of the Pay-List of the Province of Ontario for the Month of January 1939,' 17 March 1939; AO, Department of Public Welfare, *Annual Report*, 1932–3, 3–4; Toronto, City of Toronto Archives, CTA, SC 40, Records of the Metropolitan Toronto Social Planning Council, box 91, file 5, memorandum by Bessie Touzel for the Advisory Committee on Reconstruction, 'Old Age and Retirement,' January 1943.

76 NA, RG 29, vol. 29, file 208-1-1 pt 1, W.C. Clark to Stuart Edwards, 25 January 1937; J.W. MacFarlane to W.C. Clark, nd but circa 1938; J.W. MacFarlane, 'Memorandum to the Deputy Minister, Old Age Pensions, Payment of Reduced Pensions to Spouses and Pensioners Living Together,' 1 March 1939.

77 AO, RG 3, Gordon Conant Papers, box 414, file 'Public Welfare – General

Correspondence, 1942,' anonymous letter from a pensioner, London, Ontario, to Conant, 3 December 1942; Hepburn Papers, box 333, file 'Welfare, Dept of (Old Age Pensions) 1943,' F. Goodin to Hepburn, 11 November 1942. These letters are typical of dozens from individual pensioners which can be found in the Hepburn and Conant Papers and in COMSOC, MS 728, Minister's Correspondence, 1937–47 reel no. 3, for this time period.

78 MTRA, RG 5.1, file 48, A.W. Laver to L.H. Saunders, chairman, Committee on Public Welfare, 5 March 1943; file 48.1A, copy of resolution from City of Stratford, 6 March 1944; AO, COMSOC, MS 728, Minister's Correspondence, reel no. 3, microdex no. 5, C.B. Voaden, welfare administrator, St Thomas, to Old Age Pension Commission, 17 December 1943. As Voaden noted, 'the old age pension is not sufficient to keep them, and the City has to supplement the pension in order to arrange a home for them.'

79 AO, RG 3, Hepburn Papers, box 317, file 'Public Welfare: Old Age Pensions, 1941,' Fred Conboy, mayor of Toronto, to Hepburn, 10 November 1941, urging a 15 per cent boost in pension rates 'to cover the increase in the cost of living'; see also Hepburn Papers, box 333, file 'Welfare, Dept of – (Old Age Pensions) 1943,' resolutions to Hepburn from city councils of Stratford, London, Niagara Falls, Fort William, Chatham, North Bay, and Windsor, requesting a cost-of-living increase in old age pensions, February 1943. Ironically, although the Old Age Pension Commission did adjust its sliding-scale table of earnings for children to the cost of living in order to enforce parental maintenance during the war more effectively, it was not willing to push for a cost-of-living adjustment in pensions themselves. See AO, COMSOC, MS 728, Minister's Correspondence, reel no. 3, microdex no. 5, George Tattle to R.P. Vivian, 16 November 1943. Bessie Touzel, executive director of the Toronto Welfare Council and a hired consultant for the Advisory Committee on Reconstruction, noted that, compared with Britain where 80 per cent of those age seventy or over received a pension, in Canada less than 50 per cent did. The difference, she argued, was due not to the 'greater comfort of the aged in Canada' or their ability to provide from themselves, but rather to the pension scheme's 'rigid system of eligibility requirements ... which makes it difficult for many aged persons, genuinely in need ... to qualify for allowances.' In particular, Touzel pointed to the onerous residence requirements in the Canadian pension plan, the 'scaling down of allowances below the amount permitted by the Statute,' and the 'zealous adherence' to the principle of parental maintenance by children as the most critical shortcomings. CTA, SC 40, box 91 file 5, Touzel, 'Old Age and Retirement,' January 1943.

80 NA, RG 29, vol. 125, file 208-1-1 pt 1, memorandum from R.B. Bryce to J.W. MacFarlane, 'Re: Letter and Memorandum on Old Age Pensions,' 28 August 1941; W.C. Clark to J.W. MacFarlane, 11 September 1941.

81 NA, RG 29, vol. 125, 208-1-1 pt 2, 'Memorandum on Old Age Pensions,' 22 July 1943, noting that 'the additional burden should be thrown on provincial govern-

ments rather than added to the colossal burdens now being borne by the Dominion as a result of the war'; 'Memorandum Regarding Wartime Policy and Action of the Government in Respect of Old Age Pensions and Civil Service Salaries,' 1943. Although provincial governments paid only one-quarter of all pension expenditures, federal finance department officials complained, they continually attempted 'to block any encroachments by the Dominion on what they considered to be their own field of jurisdiction.' Provincial pension administrators were often appointed 'for some political reason' and quite frequently 'use[d] the Old Age Pension scheme for political propaganda,' blaming Ottawa for its inadequacies but at the same time 'jealously guard[ing] any attempt by the Dominion to influence [their] decisions.' Finance department officials also worried about the potentially 'staggering' costs of continuing an unfunded, non-contributory pension scheme as the population aged. Transforming the entire pension scheme 'as far as practicable onto a contributory basis' would provide 'relief to the Treasury,' Ottawa's chief actuary, A.D. Watson, and Deputy Finance Minister W.C. Clark agreed. See NA, RG 29, vol. 29, file 208-1-1 pt 1, J.W. MacFarlane, 'Problems Arising from the Joint Administration of Old Age Pensions,' 23 December 1938; A.D. Watson to W.C. Clark, 2 February 1937; W.C. Clark to A.D. Watson, 8 February 1937; vol. 126, file 208-1-8, memo on 'Old Age Pensions,' January 1939.

82 AO, RG 3, Conant Papers, box 422, file 'Public Welfare Dept. – Re Old Age Pensions 1943,' telegram from Gordon Conant to all premiers, 12 January 1943; Conant to W.J. Patterson, 16 January 1943. Because of Ottawa's incursions on provincial tax revenue, Ontario could 'not make any commitments involving the expenditure of substantial amounts,' Conant told the Saskatchewan premier; Reverend John Frank, Trinity Church Social Action Committee, to Conant, 17 March 1943; AO, COMSOC, MS 728, Minister's Correspondence 1937–47, reel no. 3, microdex no. 5, George Tattle to Farquhar Oliver, 27 May 1943, noting that the cabinet initially planned on a 20 per cent pension bonus, which was reduced to only 15 per cent one month later. The incoming administration of Conservative premier George Drew did not rescind the decision to pay the bonus only after a case-by-case review.

83 NA, RG 29, vol. 126, file 208-1-8, anonymous memo on 'Old Age Pensions,' January 1939.

CHAPTER 3   *How Much Is Enough?*

1 Ontario, *Report of the Ontario Commission on Public Welfare* (Toronto 1930).
2 Harry Cassidy, *Unemployment and Relief in Ontario, 1929–1932* (Toronto 1932), 79.
3 For a good description of the Toronto structure see Elizabeth King, 'The Experience of Some Canadian Cities from the Angle of the Private Agency,' Canadian

Conference on Social Work, *Proceedings*, 2nd Biennial Meeting, 1930; and James Pitsula, 'The Emergence of Social Work in Toronto,' *Journal of Canadian Studies* 14, 1 (spring 1979), 35–42. The best description of the municipal relief structure in Ontario circa 1930–2 is in Cassidy, *Unemployment and Relief in Ontario*, 121–2.

4 Indeed, in the early years of the Depression most Ontario municipalities did not provide any direct relief at all. Out of 901 municipalities in the province, only 206 participated in provincial relief works and direct relief in 1930–1; 341 provided direct relief in 1931–2, and 550 in 1932–3, the worst year of the Depression. Archives of Ontario (AO), RG 29, 74.3, box 1, file 1.3, J.A. Ellis, 'Memo Re Unemployment Relief,' July 1933.

5 For example, during the winter of 1930–1, the first full year of provincial unemployment relief, the federal, provincial, and municipal governments spent $18,500,000 on all forms of aid to the jobless. Of this amount, only $2,500,000 was spent on direct relief. The remainder was spend on relief works. AO, RG 3, George Henry Papers, box 148, file 'Unemployment Relief May 1931–July 1931, memo from J.A. Ellis to Dr J.D. Monteith, 13 May 1931.

6 Cassidy, *Unemployment and Relief in Ontario*, 87, 96; AO, RG 29, 74.3, box 1, file 1.1, memorandum, 'Ontario Unemployment Relief, October 1931'; RG 3, Henry Papers, box 148, file 'Unemployment Relief – December 1930 – April 1931,' memorandum from J.A. Ellis to George Henry, 9 February 1931.

7 Metropolitan Toronto Records and Archives (MTRA), RG 5.1, Commissioner of Public Welfare Records, box 9, file 9, 'Civic Unemployment Relief Committee Report,' May 1931.

8 MTRA, RG 5.1, box 9, file 9, 'Unemployment Relief Committee Report,' May 1931; A. Ethel Parker, 'Strengthening Bulwarks in Toronto,' *Social Welfare*, March 1931; RG 5.1, box 9, file 9, A.W. Laver, 'City of Toronto Department of Public Welfare: Special Commentary Report on Departmental Activities,' paper 2: 'Unemployment Relief Problems, 30 January 1933.'

9 Laver, 'Special Commentary Report on Departmental Activities, 30 January 1933.'

10 'Civic Unemployment Relief Committee Report,' May 1931.

11 A. Ethel Parker, 'Family Casework Goes Through the Deep Waters of Unemployment,' *Social Welfare*, September 1930.

12 Laver, 'Special Commentary Report on Departmental Activities, 30 January 1933.'

13 Ibid.; AO, RG 3, Hepburn Papers, box 182, file 'City of Toronto 1935,' 9th Annual Report of the House of Industry, 1932–3.

14 MTRA, RG 5.1, box 33, file 45.4, 'Nutrition,' memo on 'Calculations for Present House of Industry Food Supplies for 1 Week for Family of 5 as Compiled by Miss A.L. Laird, Department of Household Science, University of Toronto,' nd but circa 1931.

15 MTRA, RG 5.1, box 52, file 56, 'Food,' memo on 'Standard Supplies for the House of Industry,' Department of Public Health, City of Toronto, 21 October 1931.

16 Cassidy, *Unemployment and Relief in Ontario*, 183–5; AO, RG 29-01, box 42, file 1704, Ontario Medical Association, 'Relief Diets,' December 1933.

17 Don Spanner, '"The Straight Furrow": George S. Henry and the Politics of Depression, 1930–1934,' paper presented to the Annual Meeting of the Canadian Historical Association, Charlottetown, June 1992. See also Spanner, '"The Straight Furrow": The Life and Times of George S. Henry, Ontario's Unknown Premier' (PhD dissertation, University of Western Ontario 1993).

18 Ellis, 'Memo Re Unemployment Relief,' July 1933.

19 On this switch in policy from public works to direct relief see James Struthers, *No Fault of Their Own: Unemployment and the Canadian Welfare State, 1914–1941* (Toronto 1983), 59–66.

20 AO, RG 3, Henry Papers, box 169, file 'Unemployment Relief,' 'Report of the Relief Situation and How It Is Being Handled, Hamilton, 1932.'

21 Henry Papers, James Malcolm, 'Report of the Unemployment Situation and How It Is Being Handled, East Windsor, 1932.'

22 Henry Papers, James Malcolm, 'Report on the Unemployment Situation and How It Is Being Handled, North York Township, April 1932.'

23 AO, RG 29, 74.1, box 1, file 1.3, *Report on Provincial Policy on Administrative Methods in the Matter of Direct Relief in Ontario* (Campbell Report), Toronto 1932.

24 Campbell Report, 4, 6–7.

25 Ibid., 4, 17; AO, MU 1352, George Henry Papers, 1933, file '1 October–16 October,' George Henry to Allan Ross, 4 October 1933; Ross to Henry, 7 October 1933; H.L. McNally to Ross, 13 October 1933.

26 Campbell Report, 20–1, 13, 15–16, 10, 5–6.

27 AO, RG 18, series B-81, 'Inquiry as to the Handling of Unemployment and Direct Relief at Sturgeon Falls Ontario, 1933,' report of Judge James McNairn Hall, February 1933.

28 AO, RG 18, series B-84, 'Commission of Inquiry into the Handling of Direct Relief in the Township of York, 1933,' report of Judge James McNairn Hall, September 1933.

29 AO, RG 29, 74-1, box 1, file 1.6, memo to David Croll, 'Re: Relief Administration and Auditing of Relief Expenditures in Supervised Municipalities,' 17 September 1935; see also Patricia V. Schulz, *The East York Workers' Association: A Response to the Great Depression* (Toronto 1975), 8; Roger E. Riendeau, 'A Clash of Interests: Dependency and the Municipal Problem in the Great Depression,' *Journal of Canadian Studies* 14, 1 (spring 1979), 50–8.

30 AO, RG 29, 744, box 1, file 1.7, 'Weekly Grocery Orders for the Guidance of Local Welfare Boards,' December 1932.

31 AO, RG 29-01, box 42, file 1704, Ontario Medical Association, *Relief Diets*, reprinted from the *Bulletin* of the Ontario Medical Association, December 1933.

32 Margaret Gould, 'Actions Speak Louder Than Words,' *Toronto Star*, 13 May 1938.

33 Civic Unemployment Relief Committee Report, May 1931.

34 Things would get worse. In February 1934 Toronto's relief caseload peaked at almost 31,500 families or 120,000 individuals, including single men. Over 85,000 separate families and 53,000 single claimants would go on and off Toronto's relief rolls between 1930 and 1932. MTRA, RG 5.1, box 9, file 9, A.W. Laver to Mayor Fred Conboy, 26 January 1942.

35 AO, RG 3, Hepburn Papers, box 182, file 'City of Toronto 1935,' 96th Annual Report of the House of Industry, 1932–3. In 1933 total relief spending in Toronto topped $6.7 million, of which the city's share was $2.4 million. As Roger Riendeau points out, 'Already facing accumulated budgetary deficits of $2.8 million over the past three years, civic authorities had to resort to borrowing in order to finance the unbearable burden of direct relief. Accordingly the entire amount of the direct relief expenditure was funded by a five year serial instalment debenture issued at an interest rate of 4.5%.' The city continued this policy of postponing the real costs of relief by borrowing almost its entire expenditure throughout the Depression. It was 'not until 1945 that current expenditures for direct relief finally fell below $1 million per annum.' Riendeau, 'A Clash of Interests,' 52. Toronto, of course, was fortunate in its ability to borrow. Its surrounding suburbs simply went bankrupt owing to the unbearable costs of relief expenditure on inadequate local taxation bases.

36 MTRA, RG 5.1 box 39, file 46.21, A.W. Laver, 'Memorandum for the Ontario Unemployment Relief Department,' 22 April 1933.

37 Laver, 'Memorandum for the Ontario Unemployment Relief Department,' 22 April 1933; 'Memorandum for the Ontario Relief Department,' 13 September 1933. For an excellent study of the creation of Toronto's Department of Public Welfare see Allan Bass, '"A Properly Socialized Service": Unemployment Relief and the Formation of Toronto's Civic Department of Welfare' (research paper, York University 1989). I am indebted to Professor Christopher Armstrong for this source.

38 A.P. Kappele, 'The Administrative Set-Up for Local Welfare Services,' Canadian Conference on Social Work, *Proceedings*, 6th Conference, 1938; also see London *Free Press*, 7 November 1934.

39 John T. Saywell, *'Just Call Me Mitch': The Life of Mitchell F. Hepburn* (Toronto 1991), 92–3.

40 R. Warren James, *The People's Senator: The Life and Times of David A. Croll* (Vancouver 1990), 19–31; interview with Bessie Touzel, 26 October 1989; *Saturday Night*, 10 November 1934; *Border Cities Star*, 11 August 1934. For a

brief time Croll would also hold three portfolios, when he took over the Department of Labour.

41 See *Border Cities Star*, 5 April 1935, and *Windsor Star*, 18 March 1936, for the text of Croll's speeches on relief policy in the Ontario legislature, 4 April 1935 and 17 March 1936.

42 *Border Cities Star*, 8 and 29 December 1934; *Toronto Star*, 18 October 1934; AO, RG 29, 743, box 2, file 1.5 – 1933, 'Memorandum as to "Work and Cash" Plan of Direct Relief,' 26 April 1935. The plan, which allowed jobless heads of families to earn one-third above their relief allowance through municipal work relief schemes, was initiated on 11 August 1934. It also functioned as a work test. Men who refused to participate could be cut off the dole.

43 As Croll told one audience, 'Hamilton's system of handling relief was so satisfactory to the Ontario authorities that it had been adopted by the government where for financial reasons the province had been compelled to take over administration.' *Border Cities Star*, 7 November 1934. Croll hired Nell Wark, a University of Toronto School of Social Service graduate, away from Hamilton's relief department specifically to implement that city's relief reforms elsewhere in the province. Ibid., 29 December 1934. As Croll told the legislature, home investigation of the unemployed 'allows the visitor a chance to discover what the family has perhaps been concealing, possibly an undisclosed income from an old age pension paid an aged parent who lives with the relief applicant. Perhaps it is an income from a child. It also makes it possible to learn what the husband is doing and what his earning capacity may be. It may be that he is working and the family continuing to draw relief ... [I]n the past there was no way of learning this except through a tip-off from some neighbor.' Ibid., 5 April 1935.

44 Ibid., 18 August 1934, 5 April 1935, 15 August 1934; Warren James, *The People's Senator*, 42.

45 Toronto *Globe*, 3 November 1934. The background of the first twenty graduates of this 'relief inspectors' school is instructive. All were men. Seventeen had bookkeeping, accounting, engineering, or clerical experience. Two were former schoolteachers, and only one was a graduate from a school of social work. AO, RG 29, 74.1, box 2, file 1.5, memo from D.H.B. Harkness to J.A. Ellis, 'Suggestions re Staff Adjustments as of end of November,' 3 December 1934. The salary range recommended was $80 to $100 a month.

46 Toronto *Telegram*, 27 September 1934; *Border Cities Star*, 5 April 1935; Toronto *Mail and Empire*, 22 January 1935. Reregistration of those on relief proved 'beyond a shadow of a doubt,' Croll argued, 'that there was a lamentable lack of investigation; that many, a great many, far too many people were improperly receiving relief ... [I]n many municipalities no record was kept of those on relief, nor why they were on relief, nor what income was coming into the house.' *Border Cities Star*, 5 April 1935; Croll was 'amazed to learn that Sarnia had no

relief investigators.' London *Free Press*, 22 January 1935. Brantford, in contrast, 'saved $4500 in the first month of the home visiting system in addition to cutting 365 families off relief.' Toronto *Mail and Empire*, 7 May 1935. 'Queen's Park is stressing ... the advantage of home relief ... claim[ing] that this does away with chisellers.' Toronto *Globe*, 20 February 1935.

47 *Windsor Star*, 18 March 1936, text of Croll's speech on relief policy to the legislature; Toronto *Mail and Empire*, 7 November 1934.

48 Riendeau, 'A Clash of Interests,' 52; John Taylor, 'Sources of Political Conflict in the Thirties: Welfare Policy and a Geography of Need,' in Allan Moscovitch and Jim Albert, eds., *The Benevolent State: The Growth of Welfare in Canada* (Toronto 1987), 149.

49 Peter Hunter, *Which Side Are You On Boys ... Canadian Life on the Left* (Toronto 1988), 25.

50 The detailed history of the unemployed movement in Ontario during the 1930s awaits its historian. The best single local study remains Schulz, *The East York Workers' Association*. See also Lorne A. Brown, 'Some Responses to the Canadian Unemployed as a Political and Organizational Constituency, 1930–1935,' paper presented to the Annual Meeting of the Canadian Historical Association, Quebec City, June 1989. For an evocative memoir by one former organizer of the unemployed in Ontario during the 1930s see Hunter, *Which Side Are You On Boys*. Here is how Croll described to the legislature the process at work in one of these communities: 'New Toronto was hopelessly in default ... In spite of that on November 1, 1934, just as municipal elections were drawing near, members of the council increased the scale of relief another 14 per cent, raising the schedule to 39 per cent above the Campbell report. This was nothing less than an outrageous bribe of the municipal electors, with the province called on to pay the major portion of it ... We then [took over the administration of] relief in accordance with the maximum for the province. But once we had taken over the administration, the council immediately passed a resolution asking that we increase the allowance to its previous scale; took sides with the unemployed and had the audacity to pass a resolution asking me to come to New Toronto for the purpose of meeting the imported agitators who had intimidated the council ... [V]ote-greedy councillors ... are playing ball with the agitators ... Wherever stirs agitation and trouble we invariably find a politically-hostile council falling in with the views and the game of the local trouble-makers.' *Border Cities Star*, 5 April 1935.

51 Hunter, *Which Side Are You On Boys*, 21.

52 Ibid., 26.

53 See, for example, the 1933 Ontario Medical Association publication *Relief Diets*. Relief scales in Calgary were the highest in Canada throughout the Depression. Struthers, *No Fault of Their Own*, appendix 4. On a provincial 'average' basis, Ontario's relief scales were higher than in other provinces, but with its urbanized

population relative to the rest of the country this is not surprising, nor is it evidence of basic nutritional adequacy.

54 AO, RG 29, 74.1, box 2, file 1.6, memo from A. Ethel Parker and Frieda Held to D.B. Harkness, 8 April 1935. Parker and Held added, 'How can we hope to keep people on farms under such conditions when they can come to the city and get relief under our present conditions?' The department, they argued, should 'avoid changes or increases until we can get a good administration working, especially in these areas around Toronto. In their present spirit each increase granted seems to encourage them to work for another.' This conservative social work perspective on relief, not uncommon among social workers trained in a casework tradition during the First World War or the 1920s, contrasts with the more radical orientation of welfare professionals who came to maturity and positions of leadership in the 1930s, such as Harry Cassidy, Margaret Gould, and Bessie Touzel. Needless to say, such divisions within the profession over social reform versus 'individual adjustment' through casework continue to persist. For an example of the most prominent spokesperson of the conservative position in social work during the 1930s see Struthers, 'A Profession in Crisis: Charlotte Whitton and Canadian Social Work in the 1930s,' *Canadian Historical Review* 62, 2 (June 1981), 169–85.

55 Schulz, *The East York Workers' Association*, 28–9.

56 For accounts of these relief disturbances see AO, RG 3, Hepburn Papers, box 408, clippings from Toronto *Telegram*, 14 November 1934, 9 January and 16 April 1935; Toronto *Globe*, 10 January 1935; *Windsor Star*, 9 and 22 July, 19 August 1935; AO, RG 3, Hepburn Papers, box 185, file 'Hunger March, 1935,' 'One Year of Hepburn Liberalism,' June 1935.

57 *Border Cities Star*, 5 April 1935.

58 *Toronto Star*, 25 July 1935; Toronto *Telegram*, 26 July 1935; London *Free Press*, 31 July 1935. For a good description of the Windsor woodyard strike see *Windsor Star*, 22 July 1935.

59 *Toronto Star*, 25 and 31 July 1935; *Windsor Star*, 26 and 29 July 1935; London *Free Press*, 31 July 1935; Toronto *Globe*, 25 July 1935; AO, RG 3, Hepburn Papers, box 250, file 'Unemployment Relief 1935,' Hepburn to Andrew Dodds, 23 July 1935. For a good contemporary analysis of the effect of the 1935 summer of unrest in provoking Hepburn's abrupt reversal of policy see *Windsor Star*, 19 August 1935. According to the *Star*, the combination of the Crowland and Windsor relief strikes, the On-to-Ottawa Trek, and a chorus of rural complaints about the shortage of harvest help crystallized a 'change in public opinion' from 'sympathy for the unemployed ... to a feeling of resentment.' Taxpayer anger at relief costs is well captured by the Star's editorial comment: 'The actual fact is that a substantial percentage of the taxpayers have suffered far more during the last seven years than have those on welfare ... Often the small taxpayer has had to deprive himself and his family of what relief recipients consider necessities in

order that the tax bill may be met, and the citizen kept off welfare.' *Windsor Star*, 18 May 1938.

60 *Windsor Star*, 2 August 1935; Toronto *Globe*, 2 August 1935; Struthers, *No Fault of Their Own*, 141.

61 See *Windsor Star*, 18 March, 31 December 1936, for the text of Croll's speeches to the legislature on relief policy. The system of 'double controls' was worked out by H.L. Cummings, deputy minister of municipal affairs. See AO, RG 3, Hepburn Papers, box 250, file 'Unemployment Relief – 1935,' memo from Cummings to Hepburn, 'Re: Unemployment Relief,' 6 August 1935. For a good assessment of the impact of these mill-rate increases in breaking the back of the unemployment movement in East York and York Township see Schulz, *The East York Workers' Association*, 38–9; for Croll's battle over the mill-rate levy with Mayor Louis Auger of Hawkesbury see Toronto *Globe*, 27 October 1936; Toronto *Telegram*, 27, 29, 30 October 1936.

62 Croll's department, in a memo sent to all municipal clerks, defined 'chisellers' as 'those who prefer relief to labour ... those who conceal assets ... [and] those who conceal income.' Cities were also told to detect 'children ... earning good wages' within relief families as well as 'full-time workers who receive a wage so low that supplementary relief must be given if the family is to have the necessities of life. You must be aware that many employers are paying starvation wages and candidly informing their workers that "you can get partial relief."' AO, RG 29, 742, box 1, file 2, 'Memo to G.V. Waters,' 5 February 1936.

63 Toronto *Mail and Empire*, 4 February 1936; *Windsor Star*, 18 March 1936. The fiscal effects of these ceilings on municipal relief budgets were severe. Although the province ostensibly raised its percentage contribution for relief from 66 2/3 per cent to 75 per cent of local relief spending, the latter applied only to municipal expenditure up to the ceiling of the block grant. In Windsor, for example, actual provincial transfer payments for relief dropped by 41.2 per cent averaged over the last nine months of 1936, compared with the January–March period. In Toronto, by 1938, the city's share of total relief spending had risen from 28.8 per cent to over 40 per cent because of federal and provincial cutbacks in funding. As welfare commissioner A.W. Laver told Mayor Ralph Day, his department had made 'every effort ... by thorough investigation to purge the rolls of those who ... might not now require assistance ... [and] several thousand families were stricken from the rolls.' MTRA, RG 5.1, box 34, file 46.1, A.W. Laver to Ralph Day, 8 September 1938.

64 Ottawa *Citizen*, 18 August, 12 September 1936; *Social Worker*, November 1936. For coverage of this incident in greater detail see Struthers, *No Fault of Their Own*, 149–50. Hiring detectives to root out welfare 'fraud' has recently made a comeback in response to soaring welfare costs and caseloads during the 1990s recession. In November 1993 London's city council voted to hire fifteen employees to create a new 'welfare fraud squad.' According to the London *Free Press*,

at least four of the new employees were 'to be trained and experienced criminal investigators – perhaps former police officers.' As the *Free Press* editorialized, 'There are two good reasons for council's move – to save money lost to fraud and, by so doing, to enhance the credibility of legitimate welfare expenditures in the eyes of disgruntled taxpayers paying the bills. Supporters of the initiative say it will produce millions of dollars in savings to taxpayers. If that's true, it will have been worthwhile.' London *Free Press*, 16, 17 November 1993.

65 For Simpson's verbal battles with Hepburn over the premier's attempt to cut single men off relief see Toronto *Globe*, 30 July, 1 August 1935. Commenting on his election victory in 1935, the *Globe* prophetically remarked: 'Mr. Simpson will endeavour to don the spending cloak inseparable from socialistic ambitions, but in which he is likely to be checkmated by more conservative colleagues ... [He] will be surrounded by a Board of Control and a Council which will be in no temper for adventure at a time requiring steadiness.' *Globe*, 2 January 1935. Relief scales in Toronto remained 3 per cent below the provincial ceiling of the Campbell Report plus 25 per cent. On Arthur Williams see Schulz, *The East York Workers' Association*, 38–9. On the East York and York Township tax strikes see Toronto *Telegram*, 5 August 1936; Toronto *Mail and Empire*, 12 August 1936; Toronto *Globe*, 22 August 1936.

66 University of Western Ontario (UWO), Regional History Collection, London Department of Welfare Records, box B450, Frank McKay, memorandum re interview with Mr Croll, 23 April 1936.

67 As the Toronto Welfare Council (TWC) told the Rowell Commission, children fed at the province's maximum food relief schedule faced the prospect of 'faulty bone formation, bad teeth, lower resistance to disease, and general lack of well-being. For girls there is also the danger of a high death rate when they reach the child bearing age because of faulty formation of the pelvic bones. The situation is even more menacing in the case of a woman bearing or nursing a child.' Toronto *Star*, 13 May 1938.

68 *Windsor Star*, 18 June 1936.

69 Lorne Brown also agrees that 'communist-led unemployed organizations in the cities appear to have been on the decline' by the end of 1934. 'Some Responses to the Canadian Unemployed as a Political and Organizational Constituency,' 37.

70 Apart from protecting the government against 'extravagances, frauds, and abuses' and enforcing its own maxima, it was 'expedient to leave [municipalities] free to establish their own [relief] policies,' H.L. Cummings, Croll's deputy minister of municipal affairs, argued in 1935. Queen's Park should particularly avoid 'impos[ing] exacting conditions as to persons to whom, and the scales upon which relief is to be afforded.' AO, RG 3, Hepburn Papers, box 250, file 'Unemployment Relief – 1935,' memo from Cummings to Hepburn 'Re: Unemployment Relief,' 6 August 1935. As a result of such advice, a 1937 survey of 107 Ontario municipalities by the Canadian Association of Social Workers could find

only four cities paying above the provincial maximum relief scale of the Campbell Report plus 25 per cent. Twenty-nine gave only the Campbell Report scales, and another twenty-six paid even less than this amount. City of Toronto Archives (CTA), SC 40, box 89, file 13, Lois Fraser to A.W. Laver, 15 May 1938.

71 Ontario, Department of Public Welfare, *Annual Report, 1935–36.*

72 AO, Ontario, Department of Public Welfare, *Annual Report, 1934–35*; RG 3, Henry Papers, box 160, file 'Legislation – Mothers' Allowances, 1933,' copies of resolutions sent to Henry from various Ontario municipalities, circa January 1933.

73 AO, RG 3, Hepburn Papers, box 190, file 'Public Welfare Department re Mothers' Allowances, 1935,' Mrs W.J.M. to Hepburn, 30 January 1935; Mrs R.H. to Hepburn, 21 February 1935.

74 Ontario, Department of Public Welfare, *Annual Report 1933–34*; *Annual Report 1935–36*; AO, RG 3, Hepburn Papers, box 203, file 'Public Welfare Department re Mothers' Allowances, 1936,' secretary of Prime Minister's Office to Mrs S. Nicholson, 6 September 1935; H.J. Choates, treasury department, to Chester Walters, controller of finances, 19 December 1936, 'Re Mothers' Allowances.'

75 Department of Public Welfare, *Annual Report 1935–36*; Margaret Hillyard Little, 'The Policing of Ontario's Single Mothers during the Dirty Thirties,' paper presented to the Canadian Historical Association Annual Meeting, Charlottetown, May 1992, 34; Lorna F. Hurl, 'The Nature of Policy Dynamics: Patterns of Change and Stability in a Social Assistance Programme,' paper presented to the 4th National Conference on Social Welfare Policy, Toronto, October 1989, table 2.

76 Ontario, Department of Public Welfare, *Annual Report 1936–37*; Williams, *Decades of Service*, 38.

77 Ontario, Department of Public Welfare, *Annual Report 1935–36*; *Annual Report, 1936–37*; AO, RG 3, Henry Papers, box 162, file 'Mothers' Allowance Commission,' Dr David Jamieson, chairman, OMA Commission, to Henry, 20 October 1933, noting in the case of one widowed mother with four children, two of whom were older teenagers: 'It is the policy of the Commission not to consider a woman eligible simply because she is a widow with dependent children, but rather to take into consideration all the circumstances, and if by any means the family can be self-sustaining without being chargeable to the state, we think they should continue to do so.' *Annual Report 1934–35*, noting that 'in the majority of cases the applicants were ineligible because the whereabouts of the husband had been known within the period of three years required by the Act.' OMA Commission chairman cited in Little, 'The Policing of Ontario's Single Mothers,' 35.

78 Ontario, Department of Public Welfare, *Annual Report 1938–39.*

79 Ibid.

80 Margaret McCready, 'Relief Diets,' Canadian Conference on Social Work, *Proceedings* of the 4th Biennial Meeting, 1934.

81 CTA, SC 40, box 115, file 2, Federation for Community Services (FCS) Social Policy Committee, Minutes, 11 and 26 November 1936.

82 Ibid., Social Policy Committee, Minutes, 4 January 1937.

83 Interview with Bessie Touzel, 26 October 1989.

84 CTA, SC 40, box 89, file 10, Lois Fraser to Joseph Flavelle, 31 March 1937.

85 CTA, SC 40, box 115, file 1, 'Synopsis of Paper Presented to a Joint Meeting of the Executive Committee and the Social Policy Committee,' 12 April 1937, presented by Mary Jennison.

86 CTA, SC 40, box 115, file 1, FCS Social Policy Committee, Minutes, 23 April 1937; 'Statement Presented to the Executive Committee of the Federation for Community Service in Connection with the Matter of Welfare Policies,' 16 June 1937; FCS Social Policy Committee, Minutes, 22 September 1937. For an excellent analysis of the origins, impact, and gender implications of the campaign by the TWC for adequate nutritional standards in relief see Jacqueline Gayle Wills, 'Efficiency, Feminism, and Cooperative Democracy: Origins of the Toronto Social Planning Council, 1918–1957' (PhD thesis, University of Toronto 1989), 185–243.

87 CTA, SC 40, box 89, file 10, TWC, Public-Private Relations Committee, Minutes, 20 January 1938; Lois Fraser to Majorie Bell, 27 January 1938, enclosing an outline for 'A Study of the Food Habits of Poor Families,' box 87, file 9, TWC Minutes, 28 January 1938.

88 CTA, SC 40, box 89, file 10, TWC, 'Report from a Conference of the Members of the Public-Private Relations Committee Held in Mr. A.W. Laver's Office,' 6 May 1938; excerpt from 'Report on the Relations of the Scale of Relief to Growth, Health, and the Prevention of Illness,' submission by TWC to Eric Cross, minister of public welfare, 12 July 1938.

89 AO, RG 3, Hepburn Papers, box 280, file 'Public Welfare Department – 1937,' E.A. Horton to Hepburn, 14 January 1938; CTA, SC 40, box 87, file 9, TWC Minutes, 13 July 1938.

90 CTA, SC 40, box 89, file 10, Majorie Bell to E.J. Urwick, 27 July 1938; box 87, file 9, TWC Minutes, 13 July 1938.

91 E.W. McHenry, 'Toronto Poor Families Get Too Little Food,' *Health*, April 1939; 'Nutrition in Toronto,' lecture given at a meeting of the Royal Canadian Institute, 17 December 1938.

92 Ibid.

93 Toronto *Globe and Mail*, 2 June 1939; *Toronto Star*, 24 April 1939.

94 CTA, SC 40, box 88, file 1, TWC Minutes, 6 April 1939; Toronto Welfare Council, *The Cost of Living* (Toronto 1939), 1.

95 E.W. McHenry, 'Nutrition in Canada,' *Canadian Public Health Journal*, September 1939; 'Toronto Families Get Too Little Food.'

96 Toronto *Telegram*, 25 April 1939.

97 CTA, SC 40, box 88, file 1, TWC, Minutes, 20 April 1939; AO, MS 728, COMSOC, Minister's Correspondence, reel 1 1937–49, microdex no. 1, resolu-

tion to Eric Cross from Oshawa Branch, Ontario Federation on Unemployment, 4 May 1939 (more than two dozen identical copies of this resolution can be found in this file from local trades and labour councils and unions across Ontario); *Toronto Star*, 25 April 1939.

98 Toronto *Telegram*, 25 April 1939.

99 AO, RG 29, 74.1, box 1, file 1.11, memorandum to Eric Cross from E.A. Horton, 'Re: City of Toronto Relief Administration,' 11 April 1940. Relief fraud, however, was in the eye of the beholder. Unreported income from boarders, part-time work, or the earnings of children was precisely the way families survived on nutritionally inadequate relief diets during the 1930s.

100 AO, RG 29, 74.3, box 1, file 1.10, memorandum from James Band, Unemployment Relief Branch, to district relief inspectors, 19 July 1940.

101 AO, RG 29, 74.2, box 2, file 7, memo by James Band, 'Direct Relief Costs of Principal Cities of Ontario,' 1941; 74.1, box 1, file 1.15, memo to B.W. Heise, 'Re: Relief Allowances,' 29 February 1944; RG 29-01, box 61, file 2422, memo 'Re Unemployent Relief,' 1944.

102 CTA, SC 40, box 89, file 12, 'Points in Council – Considerations re Tisdall-Willard-Bell Report on Nutrition,' 20 March 1942.

103 CTA, SC 40, box 91, file 1, Bessie Touzel, 'Memorandum Based on Questions Posed for the Committee by Mr. J.L. Cohen in His Letter to the Chairman of May 19, 1942,' 22 May 1942; box 89, file 12, 'Points in Council – Considerations re Tisdall-Willard-Bell Report on Nutrition,' 20 March 1942.

104 CTA, SC 40, box 9, file 1, TWC Committee on Relief Problems, Minutes, 30 October 1940; box 168, file 1, Minutes of the Board of Directors, 21 November 1940.

105 CTA, SC 40, box 91, file 1, Bessie Touzel to Florence Christie, 19 December 1941; box 168, file 1, TWC, Minutes of the Board of Directors, 18 September 1941. In Touzel's opinion the agitation by the Women Electors Association had made the critical difference.

106 CTA, SC 40, box 89, file 12, Adelaide Plumptre to Lois Fraser, 7 July 1941. One of the most prominent women activists of her generation in Toronto, Plumptre ran unsuccessfully for the Board of Control in 1941, after five years on city council, stressing the need to bring 'woman's point of view' into city politics, particularly in the areas of health, welfare, and postwar reconstruction. See Toronto *Globe and Mail*, 24 and 27 December 1940.

107 CTA, SC 40, box 89, file 12, Bessie Touzel to John Innes, 7 July 1941; box 90, file 6, 'Extracts from Minutes of the Meeting of the Committee on Public Welfare, Monday 14 July 1941.'

108 CTA, SC 40, box 91, file 1, Bessie Touzel to Florence Christie, 19 December 1941; box 89, file 12, A.W. Laver to Alderman D.C. MacGregor, 18 February 1942.

109 CTA, SC 40, box 89, file 11, Bessie Touzel, 'Memorandum on History of Relief Standards Discussions,' 23 June 1942.

110 Ibid.; box 89, file 12, A.W. Laver to D.C. MacGregor, 18 February 1942.
111 CTA, SC 40, box 89, file 12, A.W. Laver to D.C. MacGregor, 18 February 1942;
    RG 29, 74-2, box 2, file 7, 'Direct Relief Costs of Principal Cities of Ontario.'
112 CTA, SC 40, box 89, file 12, 'Special and Final Meeting of the 1942 City Coun-
    cil,' 19 December 1942; box 168, file 1, TWC Board of Directors Minutes,
    19 March 1942.
113 AO, RG 29-01, box 4, file 131, memo by Farquhar Oliver, 1942; Touzel, 'Mem-
    orandum on History of Relief Standards Discussions.' For labour's use of and
    employer reaction against *The Cost of Living* see Wills, 'Efficiency, Feminism,
    and Cooperative Democracy,' chapter 5.
114 CTA, SC 40, box 168, file 1, TWC Board of Directors Minutes, 19 March 1942.
115 CTA, SC 40, box 89, file 12, 'Special and Final Meeting of the 1942 City Coun-
    cil,' Saturday, 19 December 1942. A motion to move Toronto relief allowances
    to 99 per cent of the Tisdall-Willard-Bell schedule was defeated 12 to 8 at this
    meeting. However, two months later council reversed its position and relief
    schedules were raised to the levels recommended by the Tisdall-Willard-Bell
    Report. In accordance with the report's recommendations, the city welfare
    department also hired its first trained nutritionist. See MTRA, RG 5.1, box 29,
    file 37.2A, memo from A.W. Laver to all relief recipients, May 1943; Board of
    Control Report no. 3, adopted 7 February 1944. Welfare Committee Report no. 2.
    Until 15 September 1947 Toronto maintained its relief allowance schedule on the
    basis of the Tisdall-Willard-Bell standard and independent of provincial ceilings
    for shared-cost funding. After this point, the city once again adopted provincial
    relief allowance ceilings as the basis for its relief schedule. See MTRA, 5.1, box
    29, file 37.2A, G.A. Lascelles, acting welfare commissioner, to Mayor Robert
    Saunders, 19 August 1947.
116 CTA, SC 40, box 89, file 12, clipping from *Toronto Star*, 23 January 1943.
117 E.W. McHenry, *Report on Food Allowances for Relief Recipients in the Province
    of Ontario* (Toronto 1944), 17; Toronto Welfare Council, *The Cost of Living*, 2nd
    ed. (Toronto 1944), 31.
118 McHenry, *Report on Food Allowances for Relief Recipients*, 2, 13, 15, 23.
119 AO, RG 29, 74.1, box 1, file 1.15, 'Some Questions and Answers Relating to
    Direct Relief,' 27 June 1944; McHenry, *Report on Food Allowances for Relief
    Recipients*, 17. Only 3.2 per cent of the provincial relief load was composed of
    families of five. Only 21 per cent was composed of families of more than two
    people.
120 Toronto *Globe and Mail*, 22 September 1944; AO, RG 29, box 123, 'Unemploy-
    ment Relief Act 1943.'
121 Wills, 'Efficiency, Feminism, and Cooperative Democracy,' 220–3, makes this
    point especially well, but she also notes women's loss of control over the
    nutrition debate through the bureaucratization of welfare nutritional standards at
    the provincial level after 1944. The key importance of women's voluntary groups,
    such as the Visiting Homemakers' Association (VHA) and the Women Electors,

in the campaign for adequate food allowances within Toronto parallels Theda
Skocpol's argument concerning the forging of a 'maternalist' vision of the welfare state by women reformers in the United States in the years before the First
World War. As Skocpol argues: 'America came close to forging a maternalist
welfare state, with female-dominated public agencies implementing regulations
and benefits for the good of women and their children ... [N]ation-spanning
federations of local women's clubs were the chief proponents of such maternalist
policies ... Women aimed to extend the domestic morality of the nineteenth
century's "separate sphere" for women into the nation's public life. For a while,
this vision was a remarkable source of moral energy and political leverage for the
female instigators of the first U.S. programs of public social provision.' *Protecting Soldiers and Mothers: The Political Origins of Social Policy in the United
States* (Cambridge 1992), 2–3.

122 AO, RG 29, Deputy Minister, box 123, 'Unemployment Relief Act 1943'
(my emphasis).

123 Ibid.

124 On this point see Struthers, *No Fault of Their Own*, 212.

CHAPTER 4 *Reconstructing Welfare*

1 As the Toronto Welfare Council told the Royal Commission on Dominion-
Provincial Relations in 1938, 'the whole matter [of relief] is regarded as a burden
upon the taxpayers which, almost at all costs, must be kept down to the smallest
possible amount.' Cited in Harry M. Cassidy, *Public Health and Welfare Reorganization in Canada* (Toronto 1945), 348.

2 Leonard Marsh, *Report on Social Security for Canada* (1943; new ed., Toronto
1975), 273–4.

3 Among these studies the most notable, apart from the Marsh Report itself, were
Harry Cassidy's *Social Security and Reconstruction in Canada* (Toronto 1943)
and *Public Health and Welfare Reorganization in Canada*, as well as Charlotte
Whitton's *The Dawn of an Ampler Life* (Toronto 1945). Also noteworthy, given
his subsequent appointment as Canada's first deputy minister of national health
and welfare, was George Davidson's 'The Future Development of Social Security
in Canada,' *Canadian Welfare*, January 1943, 1–17.

4 Hugh Heclo, 'Toward a New Welfare State?' in P. Flora and A. Heidenheimer,
eds., *The Development of Welfare States in Europe and North America* (London
1981), 391.

5 Roger Graham, *Old Man Ontario: Leslie M. Frost* (Toronto 1990), 79–80.

6 Heclo, 'Toward a New Welfare State?' 395.

7 Ontario, Department of Public Welfare, *Annual Reports*, 1938–9, 1943–4,
1947–8.

8 Ibid., 1940–1, 1942–3.

9 City of Toronto Archives (CTA), SC 40, box 91, file 5, Bessie Touzel, memo on 'Mothers' Allowances, Survivors' Insurance, etc.' prepared for Marsh's *Report on Social Security for Canada*, January 1943; National Archives of Canada (NA), RG 29, vol. 1882, file R170/100-1/1, Committee on Reconstruction, Interim Report on 'The Residual Social Services,' memo by George Davidson, Canadian Welfare Council, nd but circa January 1943; Ontario, Department of Public Welfare, *Annual Report*, 1952–3, 'Changes in the Curve of the Mothers' Allowance Average Index Rate Compared to Changes in the Curve of the Cost of Living Index from 1921 to 1953'; Archives of Ontario (AO), RG 3, Hepburn Papers, box 317, file 'Public Welfare: Old Age Pensions, 1941,' Fred Conboy to Hepburn, 25 October 1941.

10 Metropolitan Toronto Records and Archives (MTRA), RG 5.1, box 43, file 47, 'Mothers' Allowances and Dependent Fathers, 1931–1961'; letter from the chairman of the Toronto Welfare Council to Harold Kirby, 31 March 1943; J.W. Somers, city clerk, to A.W. Laver, commissioner of public welfare, 8 April 1943, citing comments by TWC executive director Bessie Touzel.

11 AO, MS 728, COMSOC, Minister's Correspondence 1937–49, reel 1, microdex no. 3, brief submitted to R.P. Vivian, minister of health and public welfare, by Fred Conboy, mayor of Toronto, 29 September 1943.

12 Ibid.

13 AO, RG 29-01, box 62, file 2435, Mothers' Allowance Commission, 'Budget for a mother and three children over 13 years of age,' 22 January 1943. The breakdown of the commission's minimum budget for such a family each month was as follows:

Rent	$24.00
Fuel average	9.75
Light	1.10
Food & clothing	16.68
(each child)	16.68
	16.68
	16.68
Replacements	6.00
Sundries	10.00
Total	$117.57

14 AO, COMSOC, MS 728, Minister's Correspondence 1937–49, reel 1, microdex no. 2, memo from B.W. Heise, 'Re: Mothers' Allowances,' nd but circa 1944.

15 AO, MS 728 COMSOC, Minister's Correspondence 1937–49, reel 1, microdex no. 2, B.W. Heise, 'Re: Mothers' Allowances,' nd but circa 1944; RG 29-01, box 40, file 1621, 'Departmental Memo Incorporating Understanding of Principles

and Procedures re Adjustments of Existing Mothers' Allowances Payments on Basis of Budgetary Requirements,' 23 November 1943; H. Bentley to B.W. Heise, 28 February 1944.

16 AO, MS 728 COMSOC, Minister's Correspondence 1937–49, memo from B.W. Heise 'Re: Mothers' Allowances,' nd but circa February 1944; memo by B.W. Heise, 'Proposed Basic Philosophy Governing Provincial Assistance (with specific application to Mothers' Allowances),' nd but circa 1944. In this detailed memo Heise argued that 'consideration should be given to the following as a plan which would cover all forms of Social Assistance, including Old Age Pensions, Children's Aid, Mothers' Allowances, etc.'

17 Ontario, Department of Public Welfare, *Annual Reports*, 1943–4; 1944–5; AO, RG 29-01, box 40, file 1621, press release from R.P. Vivian announcing commencement of $10 monthly supplemental benefits based on need, 24 November 1943. Bessie Touzel, executive director of the Toronto Welfare Council, went so far as to argue in her background work for Marsh's *Report on Social Security for Canada* that family allowances would 'largely take care of the needs of children ... The sole remaining problem will be to provide an income on the basis of security maintenance to enable the widow to maintain herself while looking after her family.' This prediction proved to be unduly optimistic. CTA, SC 40, box 91, file 5, Bessie Touzel, 'Mothers' Allowances, Surivors' Insurance etc.,' January 1943. On the genesis and impact of family allowances see Brigitte Kitchen, 'The Origins of Family Allowances in Canada,' in Jim Albert and Allan Moscovitch, eds., *The Benevolent State: The Growth of Welfare in Canada* (Toronto 1986). Other changes in Ontario's mothers' allowance program during the 1940s did provide some significant additional benefits. In 1942 families under the program became eligible for free medical care within the province's Medical Relief Plan, originally developed for families on unemployment relief during the 1930s. In 1946 the period of desertion as a criterion for becoming eligible for mothers' allowances was reduced from three years to only one year. In 1947 the differential in basic assistance rates between large- and medium-size cities and rural areas was abolished as all rates were brought up to the large city level. And in 1948 the basic rate of assistance for a mother with one child was increased to $50.00 from $42.00, and the rate for each child was raised from $6.00 to $10.00, bringing the maximum benefit for a mother with three children to $70.00. These changes, however, failed to keep pace with changes in the overall cost of living during these years. AO, RG 29, 748, file, 'History of the Department of Public Welfare, 1959,' chapter on 'Mothers' and Dependent Children's Allowances'; Lorna Hurl, 'The Nature of Policy Dynamics: Patterns of Change and Stability in a Social Assistance Program,' paper presented to the fourth National Conference on Social Welfare Policy, Toronto, 24–27 October 1989, table 4.

18 See, for example, AO, RG 3, Frost Papers, accession 9635, box 3, letters of protest from George Drew to Mackenzie King, 6 January and, 14 March 1944.

Ottawa's announcement of a national health program within the exclusive jurisdiction of the provinces and prior to a dominion-provincial conference on reconstruction 'makes co-operation next to impossible,' Drew complained.

19 AO, RG 3, Frost Papers, accession 9635, box 3, Chester Walters to Leslie Frost, 'Re: Bill No. 161: An Act to Provide for Family Allowances,' 31 July 1944. Walters went on to argue that with the same $100 million of Ontario taxpayers' money used for federal family allowances, the province could provide its own family allowances scheme on a more generous basis, provide 8 mills in property tax relief to municipal governments, take over $10 million in educational costs from local governments, expand its hospital and road construction program, and still have $12 million left over to retire provincial debt. Whether the Drew administration would have embarked on a family allowance scheme, in the absence of the federal initiative, is highly debatable, since the idea did not form part of Drew's twenty-two point election platform in 1943 and the Ontario premier vigorously attacked the federal program once it was implemented. On the family allowance issue, Ontario's anger seems clearly rooted in taxation revenue diverted to Ottawa rather than in a lost opportunity to embark on its own sweeping social policy agenda. See also box 4, file 'Dominion-Provincial General Files I, 1942–1946,' memo on 'The Dominion-Provincial Conference,' 2 August 1945, which notes 'another spur for an immediate conference is that the Family Allowances Act ... is in a measure contrary to the spirit of the Agreement between the Dominion of Canada and the Province for the suspension of certain taxing acts of the Province during the war.'

20 Graham, *Old Man Ontario*, 104; AO, RG 29-01, box 4, file 131, 'Cabinet Legislative Material, 1942–53,' speech by George Drew in the Ontario legislature, 22 February 1945.

21 AO, RG 3, Frost Papers, accession 9635, box 4, file 'Dominion-Provincial General Files I, 1942–46,' memo 'The Dominion-Provincial Tax Conference: Ontario's Role,' 31 July 1945; 'Dominion-Provincial General Files II, Private and Confidential: Memorandum of Conversations between the Honourable Maurice Duplessis, Premier of Quebec and the Honourable L.M. Frost, July 4 1945.'

22 AO, RG 3, Frost Papers, accession 9635, box 4, file 'Dominion-Correspondence, Drew-Frost 1946,' Drew to Frost, 9 July 1946. Another Treasury Department memo summed up the connection between Ottawa's *Green Book* taxation and social policy proposals and the perceived threat to Ontario's economic autonomy. According to its author the 'chief disadvantages' of Ottawa's proposals were: '1) Full provincial autonomy is only preserved so long as each provincial government has power to impose its own rate of tax and to raise such sums of money as it deems necessary for the efficient carrying out of the province's business and the development of its resources ... 5) ... the net transfer of tax money from Ontario residents to residents of other provinces will probably be greater than under conditions where provincial tax powers are retained. The tax money raised

by the Government of Ontario is spent for the benefit of the inhabitants of Ontario; a considerable fraction of the money raised by the federal government from Ontario's taxpayers will be spent elsewhere.' AO, RG 6, series II-6, box 19, 'Dominion-Provincial Conference on Reconstruction,' 3 October 1945.

23 This is also Marc Gotlieb's conclusion. Gotlieb notes that Ontario's Treasury Department estimates for postwar expenditures 'amounted to nearly double what the province had spent before the war. The increases involved primarily resource development and traditional provincial social responsibilities. Indeed, despite Queen's Park's insistence that it was responsible for social security, there were no plans for any significant new measures in this field.' See his 'George Drew and the Dominion-Provincial Conference on Reconstruction of 1945–6,' *Canadian Historical Review* 66, 1 (March 1985), 31.

24 AO, RG 3, Frost Papers, accession 9635, box 3, file 'Dominion-Provincial Conference I, 1945,' 'Notes made by Mr. D.R. Michener at Sub-Conference on Finance, August 9 1945'; same box and file, memo on 'Health Insurance,' nd but circa August 1945.

25 Ibid., box 4, file 'Dominion-Provincial General Files I, 1942–46,' 'Suggested Alternative to Proposals of Government of Canada,' 12 September 1945. The idea for complete provincial administration of all social welfare expenditure in the province, including family allowances, old age pensions, mothers' allowances, and unemployment assistance, regardless of the percentage of federal financing, came from Harry M. Cassidy of the University of Toronto and was contained in his 'Public Welfare Plan for Ontario,' 20 July 1945, commissioned by provincial welfare minister R.P. Vivian and presented to him on the eve of the 1945 Reconstruction Conference. Cassidy, of course, had no influence in shaping Ontario's fierce resistance to the surrender of its taxing authority to Ottawa. This opposition made his proposals for provincial administration of programs completely financed by Ottawa, such as family allowances or unemployment assistance, politically outrageous. AO, RG 29, series 74.9, box 1, file 14, 44.

26 AO, RG 3, Frost Papers, accession 9635, box 4, file 'Dominion-Provincial Memos, 1945–46,' minutes of Economic Committee Meeting, 15 January 1946; box 3, Chester Walters, 'Memorandum re Forthcoming Dominion-Provincial Conference,' 30 March 1944.

27 Gotlieb, 'George Drew and the Dominion-Provincial Conference on Reconstruction,' 47.

28 AO, RG 29, series 74.1, file 2.2, memo from B.W. Heise to Gordon Hogarth, Office of the Prime Minister, 4 March 1946.

29 AO, RG 29, series 74.9, box 1, file 1.2, Charlotte Whitton, 'The Administration of Welfare Services in the Province of Ontario, 1944,' summary of Major Findings and Recommendations, 1944. Over half the remaining relief caseload was over the age of sixty, and almost three-quarters were over fifty years old. More than half were single, and for 'the first time in Provincial statistics' there were more women than men collecting relief (3–4).

30 See for example, AO, RG 29, series 74.9, box 1, file 1.2, Charlotte Whitton, 'The Administration of Welfare Services in Ontario, 1943,' February 1944. In this 200-page report, commissioned by Ontario welfare minister R.P. Vivian, Whitton noted that 'the present surcease in Assistance needs, due to economic conditions, should be utilized for careful assessment of the problems ... and for the organization and mobilization of resources, the better to meet them ... whatever the future may have in store ... [for] the people of Ontario.' In commissioning Whitton's report, Vivian called for a 'comprehensive review of the entire Ontario set-up, and especially of the relations of the Province and its municipalities, and of the local public authority to the voluntary agencies.'

31 Harry M. Cassidy, *Unemployment and Relief in Ontario* (Toronto 1932). For more details on Cassidy's life and work and his seminal influence on Canadian social policy development see Allan Irving's excellent doctoral dissertation, 'A Canadian Fabian: The Life and Work of Harry M. Cassidy' (PhD dissertation, University of Toronto 1983). In addition to *Social Security and Reconstruction in Canada* and *Public Health and Welfare Reorganization in Canada*, Cassidy also was a contributing author on social policy for the League for Social Reconstruction's classic text, *Social Planning for Canada* (1935; new ed., Toronto 1975).

32 AO, RG 29, series 74.9, box 1, file 1.4, Harry Cassidy, 'A Public Welfare Plan for Ontario,' 22 July 1945.

33 Cassidy, *Public Health and Welfare Reorganization in Canada*, 350–1.

34 Ibid., 361–3.

35 Cassidy, 'A Public Welfare Plan for Ontario.'

36 On Whitton's career and influence in Canadian social welfare see Patricia Rooke and R.L. Schnell, *Charlotte Whitton: Feminist on the Right* (Vancouver 1988), as well as James Struthers, 'A Profession in Crisis: Charlotte Whitton and Canadian Social Work in the 1930s,' *Canadian Historical Review* 62, 2 (June 1981), 169–85. Besides serving as welfare adviser to the Drew administration in Ontario in 1943–4, Whitton wrote a commissioned analysis of Canadian social policy in the 1940s for national Conservative leader John Bracken; it was subsequently published as *The Dawn of an Ampler Life*.

37 Whitton, 'The Administration of Welfare Services in Ontario, 1944,' Feburary 1944, 54.

38 Whitton, 'The Administration of Welfare Services in the Province of Ontario, 1944,' 45–7, 54, 134–6; NA, MG 28, I 10, Canadian Council on Social Development Records, vol. 154, Canadian Association of Social Workers, 'Brief on Social Security and Public Welfare Services in Ontario,' to the Committee on Social Security and Reconstruction of the Legislature of Ontario, January 1944. Like Cassidy and Whitton, the CASW also endorsed the 'county welfare unit' model that had 'so successfully proved [itself] in the United States.'

39 Clifford J. Williams, *Decades of Service: A History of the Ontario Ministry of Community and Social Services, 1930–1980* (Toronto 1984), 11, 41–2.

40 AO, RG 29, series 74.1, box 2, file 2.1 – 1945, memo B.W. Heise to Drew,

'Summary for the Prime Minister,' 28 December 1945, setting the Department of Public Welfare's policy agenda. Heise notes under 'Problems to be Dealt With: ... the continuance of present reorganization plans, both internal and external, that would accompany the development of county welfare units in accordance with an outline appearing in "A Proposed Public Welfare Plan for Ontario."' In 1946 George Davidson hired Cassidy to undertake a similar sweeping survey of national health and welfare needs for his department. See Cassidy's 'A Canadian Programme of Social Security' completed for National Health and Welfare in 1947. See also AO, MS 728, COMSOC, Minister's Correspondence 1937–49, memo by B.W. Heise, 'Proposed Basic Philosophy Governing Provincial Assistance,' nd but circa 1944.

41 AO, RG 29, series 74.1, box 1, file 1.15 – 1944, memo by B.W. Heise, 'Some Questions and Answers Relating to Direct Relief,' 27 June 1944; NA, Charlotte Whitton Papers, MG 30, E256, vol. 37, file 1946, B.W. Heise, 'Trends in Public Welfare Administration,' Toronto, 27 August 1946. In selected Ontario cities in 1943, relief costs per capita of population varied from seventy-five cents in Toronto to only twenty cents in Brantford. In counties, the variation ranged from six cents in Victoria County to twenty-one cents in nearby Haliburton County; AO, MS 728, COMSOC, Minister's Correspondence 1937–49, reel 1, microdex no. 2, 'Municipal Expenditures for Direct Relief: Per Capita of Population Costs Based on Relief Expenditures 1939, 1943, and 1947 for 11 Selected Municipalities.'

42 Heise, 'Trends in Public Welfare Administration,' AO, MS 728, COMSOC, Minister's Correspondence, 1937–49, reel 1, microdex no. 2, memo from B.W. Heise to W.A. Goodfellow, re 'Establishment of Welfare Areas,' 17 January 1948.

43 AO, MS 728, COMSOC, Minister's Correspondence 1937–49, reel 1, microdex no. 2, undated memo re 'Welfare Units'; memo from B.W. Heise to W.A. Goodfellow, 'Re Establishment of Welfare Areas,' 27 January 1948.

44 As cited in Graham, *Old Man Ontario*, 80 (my emphasis).

45 AO, RG 29, series 74.1, box 1 – 1944, file 115, B.W. Heise, 'Some Questions and Answers Relating to Direct Relief,' 27 June 1944.

46 AO, MS 728, COMSOC, Minister's Correpondence 1937–49, reel 1, microdex no. 2, letter to George Drew from H.E.M. Payne, clerk and treasurer of the Town of Orillia, 5 October 1945.

47 NA, Canadian Council on Social Development Records, MG 28, I 10, accession 83, box 105, Harry M. Cassidy, 'Partnership in Social Welfare – The Provincial Contribution,' address to the Ontario Conference on Social Welfare, 14 June 1947.

48 AO, RG 29, series 741, box 2, file 2.3, address by K. Grant Crawford on 'The Municipalities and Social Welfare,' to the Ontario Conference on Social Welfare, Toronto, June 1947 (my emphasis).

49 *Fort William Daily Times-Journal*, 10 May 1950; Port Arthur *News Chronicle*, 10 May 1950.

50 *Stratford Beacon-Herald*, 6 June 1951.

51 NA, MG 30, E 256, Charlotte Whitton Papers, vol. 36, file: 1925–49, copy of 'The Welfare Units Act, 1948'; AO, MS 728, COMSOC, Minister's Correspondence 1937–49, reel 1, microdex no. 2, B.W. Heise to W.A. Goodfellow, 30 December 1949, 'The Welfare Units Act.'

52 AO, MS 728, reel 1, Heise to Goodfellow, 30 December 1949, 'The Welfare Units Act.'

53 AO, RG 3, Frost Papers, series E-16-A, box 158, file 228G, W.A. Goodfellow to Frost, 1 February 1950 (Frost's comment is handwritten on this copy); Goodfellow to Frost, 8 August 1950.

54 AO, MS 728, COMSOC, Heise to Goodfellow, 30 December 1949, 'The Welfare Units Act'; Heise to Goodfellow, 28 November 1950, 'Payments for Welfare Units – Hamilton, Windsor and Toronto'; RG 3, Frost Papers, box 158, file 228G, Goodfellow to Frost, 8 August 1950.

55 Williams, *Decades of Service*, 69–70.

56 NA, MG 28, I 10, accession 83, vol. 61, Harry Cassidy to R.E.G. Davis, 25 June 1951; Harry Cassidy, 'Administrative Reorganization in the Ontario Department of Public Welfare,' 5 January 1951.

57 Interview with Albert Rose, 3 August 1989; interview with Bessie Touzel, 26 October and 2 November 1989.

58 Interview with Dorothea Crittenden, 23 July 1990; interview with Bessie Touzel, 2 November 1989.

59 Williams, *Decades of Service*, 70; interview with Albert Rose, 3 August 1989.

60 Jacquelyn Gale Wills, 'Efficiency, Feminism, and Cooperative Democracy: Origins of the Toronto Social Planning Council, 1918–1957' (PhD thesis, University of Toronto 1989), 228.

61 CTA, Social Planning Council of Metropolitan Toronto Records, SC 40, box 168, file 1, 'Minutes of Board of Directors,' 18 November 1943.

62 Ibid., file 2, 'Minutes of Board of Directors,' 30 October 1947.

63 Ibid., 3 June 1948.

64 Ibid., 23 September 1948.

65 Ibid., 21 October 1948.

66 Wills, 'Efficiency, Feminism, and Cooperative Democracy,' 231.

67 CTA, SC 40, box 168, file 2, 'Minutes of the Board of Directors,' 29 September 1949.

68 Heclo, 'Toward a New Welfare State?' 396. On the rapid waning of support for the Ontario CCF during the later 1940s see Dan Azoulay, '"A Desperate Holding Action": The Survival of the Ontario CCF/NDP, 1948–1964,' *Ontario History* 85, 1 (March 1993), 17–42.

69 Azoulay, 'A Desperate Holding Action,' 19.

CHAPTER 5   *Poverty in Progress*

1 K.J. Rea, *The Prosperous Years: The Economic History of Ontario, 1939–75* (Toronto 1985), 27, 34, 84.
2 Robert M. Campbell, *Grand Illusions: The Politics of the Keynesian Experience in Canada, 1945–1975* (Peterborough 1987), 70, 85.
3 Metropolitan Toronto Records and Archives (MTRA), RG 5.1, box 29, file 37.2A, memo from Robena Morris to H.S. Rupert, 'Effects of Increased Cost of Living on Food Allowances,' 15 March 1948.
4 Archives of Ontario (AO), RG 29-01, box 62, file 2437, memo to W.A. Goodfellow from Hamilton delegation, nd but circa February 1947; A.P. Kappele to Board of Control, 16 December 1946.
5 AO, RG 29-01, box 42, file 1704, E.W. McHenry to James Band, 25 September 1946; James Band to B.W. Heise, 21 May 1947; *Toronto Star*, 4 July 1947; E.W. McHenry to James Band, 19 January 1948; James Band to B.W. Heise, 20 January 1948; MTRA, RG 5.1, box 29, file 37.2A, Robena Morris to H.S. Rupert, memo on 'Effect of Present Cost of Living – Relief Recipients,' 3 September 1948; J.D. Wismer, 'Public Assistance in Ontario, 1950–61' (MSW thesis, University of Toronto 1964), 46–63. In the 1950s Dr E.W. McHenry, Ontario's chief adviser on relief food allowances, remained unimpressed by stories of welfare hardship and hunger. 'Too many people go to the corner grocer at the last minute to buy what is available without consideration of price and as a result might find their allowance for food to be inadequate,' he told Toronto's assistant commissioner of welfare, Robena Morris, in 1951. MTRA, RG 5.1, box 33, file 45.4, 'Nutrition,' Robena Morris to H.S. Rupert, 9 March 1951.
6 AO, RG 29-01, box 62, file 2435, James Band to B.W. Heise, 'Re: Shelter Costs for Recipients of Relief – Toronto,' 4 March 1944; MTRA, RG 5.1, box 47, file 49A, 'Shelter: 1941–1965,' A.W. Laver to B.W. Heise, 17 November 1945; A.W. Laver to D.C. MacGregor, Committee on Public Welfare, 23 January 1942.
7 AO, RG 29, series 74.1, box 2, file 22, memo to B.W. Heise 'Re: Proposed Adjustment in Relief Allowances,' 20 August 1946.
8 Ibid.; interview with Dorothea Crittenden, 23 July 1990. The connection between relief shelter allowances and old age pensions was also made explicitly by Toronto's welfare department. In 1951 department officials argued that 'as far as possible and in keeping with other forms of public assistance including Old Age Pensions ... and Mothers Allowances, the allowance for a single person, including rent, should not exceed $40 per month and monthly rental allowances on behalf of a family should not exceed $40.00.' MTRA, RG 5.1, box 47, file 49A, 'Shelter, 1941–1965,' 'Minutes of the Shelter Allowance Committee,' 9 February 1951. J.D. Wismer has also noted the direct linkage between setting Ontario shelter allowances and the benefit rates payable under federal old age pensions in this era. See his 'Public Assistance in Ontario, 1950–61,' 99–100.

9 MTRA, RG 5.1, box 47, file 49A, H.S. Rupert to W.A. Goodfellow, 17 November 1949; D.C. Parker to H.S. Rupert, 19 February 1952.

10 MTRA, RG 5.1, box 47, file 49A, D.C. Parker to H.S. Rupert, 5 November 1952; H.S. Rupert to W.A. Goodfellow, 28 October 1954; D.C. Parker to H.S. Rupert, 17 November 1952; A.W. Laver to Robena Morris, 11 March 1942; AO, RG 29-01, box 63, file 2470, D.G. Gardner to J.S. Band, 'Progress Report: Survey of Unemployment Relief Cases in Toronto,' 10 February 1958 (my emphasis).

11 AO, RG 29 Deputy Minister, box 123, file 'Relief Allowances, 1947,' 'Standard Relief Allowances, 1947'; J.D. Wismer, 'Public Assistance in Ontario, 1950–61,' 44; MTRA, RG 5.1, box 47, file 49A, W.A. Goodfellow to Hazel McCallum, 27 March 1951; D.C. Parker to H.S. Rupert, 17 November 1952; file 46.1.73, 'Minutes of a Meeting of Senior Staff,' 22 May 1958.

12 *Financial Post*, 30 June 1962; MTRA, RG 5.1, box 47, file 49A 'Shelter, 1941–1965,' 'Minutes of meeting of district welfare officers, City of Toronto,' 11 August 1960; file 46.17, 'GWA – District Work, June/52 – May/54,' box 96, file 4, memo from H.S. Rupert to all staff, 27 October 1955; box 47, file 49A 'Shelter, 1941–1965,' letter from H.S. Rupert to W.A. Goodfellow, 17 November 1949. By 1960 Toronto was paying slightly over $10,000 a month in supplemental rental allowance costs, compared with more than $14,500 a month in 1949.

13 Wismer, 'Public Assistance in Ontario, 1950–61,' 80–4; MTRA, RG 5.1, file 46.17.4, Social Planning Council of Metropolitan Toronto, 'Toronto Department of Public Welfare Cases Who Received Supplementation from Voluntary Agencies,' November 1959.

14 'Toronto Department of Public Welfare Cases Who Received Supplementation from Voluntary Agencies,' November 1959 (my emphasis); Wismer, 'Public Assistance in Ontario, 1950–61,' 108.

15 Wismer, 'Public Assistance in Ontario, 1950–61,' 88–9. According to Wismer, the province's maximum welfare allowance ceilings for a family of four fell from 67 per cent to less than 43 per cent of the average Ontario monthly wage throughout the 1950s.

16 MTRA, RG 5.1, box 28, file 37, memo from Harold Lawson, Toronto Social Planning Council, 'Regulations under the General Welfare Assistance Act – 1960' (my emphasis).

17 AO, RG 29-01, box 51, file 2075, 'Re: Report by Social Planning Council of Metropolitan Toronto on Supplementation of Department of Public Welfare Cases from Voluntary Agencies,' November 1959; 'Notes on the Report of the Social Planning Council of Metropolitan Toronto on the Supplementation of Public Welfare Cases from Voluntary Agencies,' November 1959.

18 AO, RG 3, Frost Papers, box 21, file 44-2G, *Social Security for Canada*, a policy statement adopted at the Annual Meeting of the Canadian Welfare Council, 2 June 1958.

19 AO, MS 728, COMSOC, 'Minister's Correspondence 1937–1949,' reel no. 2, microdex no. 1, 'Report of George Gathercole on the Second Meeting of the Preparatory Committee of the Federal-Provincial Conference, May 26, 27, and 30, 1955,' 6 June 1955; RG 29, series 74.1, box 2, file 2.9, memo on 'Rural Municipalities Association,' 1953.

20 MTRA, RG 5.1, box 33, file 45.4, 'Nutrition,' memo by Robena Morris for the 'Conference Regarding Nutrition Services,' 8 May 1957. Morris, who would go on to become Toronto's first female commissioner of welfare, had been making this same 'less eligibility' argument regarding welfare allowances since the Great Depression. As she told a Canadian Conference on Social Work audience in 1940, 'there is a prevalent belief that public assistance comes very much as "manna from heaven" and that there is no limit to the amount of money that can or should be spent by the State on behalf of its dependants. To me, there is no question that individual need should be met. That it should always be met by the State from public funds is quite another matter. We believe that the State should not treat its dependants better than it treats its citizens, and should not insist upon the average taxpayers maintaining a higher standard of living for dependent families than they themselves can maintain for their own families. There is a limit to what can be collected from home-owners by taxation for the purposes of public assistance, unless we are to discourage the individual ownership of their own homes by families of moderate means, and the stability of family life that goes with it in every large Municipality.' Morris, 'Uses of Relief in the Case Work Programme of a Public Agency,' Canadian Conference on Social Work, *Proceedings*, 7th Conference, 1940.

21 AO, RG 29-01, box 63, file 2464, F.A. Nobile to A.T. Bosanquet, 'Re: City of Toronto Home Investigations of General Welfare Assistance Recipients,' 8 September 1959.

22 MTRA, box 34, file 46 'GWA,' H.S. Rupert to Allan Lamport, 13 August 1952; file 46.17, 'GWA – District Work June/52–May/54,' box 96, file 4, H.S. Rupert to W.F. Clifton, 24 January 1956.

23 MTRA, RG 5.1, file 46.17.1, memo from V. Morrow, welfare visitor, to Eleanore Songhurst, 'Caseload of District Number Five,' 22 June 1953; AO, RG 29-01, box 63, file 2467, memo by Robena Morris on 'Social Work' in the 'Final Report of Howard S. Rupert to Committtee to Study Proposed Amalgamation of the Department of Public Health and the Department of Public Welfare,' 2 September 1947; MTRA, RG 5.1, file 45, Eleanore Songhurst, 'Public Assistance – Its Philosophy and Practice,' 12 April 1956.

24 AO, RG 29-01, box 63, file 2467, 'Final Report of Howard S. Rupert to Committee to Study Proposed Amalgamation of the Department of Public Health and the Department of Public Welfare,' 2 September 1947; MTRA, RG 5.1, file 46.17 'GWA – District Work June/52–May/54,' memo from Eleanore Songhurst to

Robena Morris, 'Welfare Visitors – Volume of Work,' 30 July 1954; memo from H.S. Rupert complaining of the 'inadequate number of competent personnel' in his department, August 1956.

25 'Final Report of Howard S. Rupert to Committee to Study Proposed Amalgamation of the Department of Public Health and the Department of Public Welfare,' 2 September 1947.

26 MTRA, RG 5.1, file 46.17 'GWA – District Work – June/52–May 54,' H.S. Rupert to Alderman Clifton, chairman, Committee on Public Welfare, 4 October 1956, noting that 'Since the maximum salary for [welfare visitors] in the civil service is so much below that paid by other comparable organizations in the city the department is unable to secure a sufficient number of qualified applicants to fill vacancies.'

27 MTRA, RG 5.1, file 46.17, 'GWA – District Work – June/52–May 54,' H.S. Rupert to A.C. King, director of personnel, 24 February 1956; H.S. Rupert to Alderman Clifton, 4 October 1956, noting that during 1955 and 1956 his department had experienced twenty-one resignations of welfare visitors grade 1 out of a total complement of twenty-nine. 'At least nine of them resigned to accept other welfare positions at increased salary ranges, lower work loads, and or improved status on the staff.'

28 MTRA, RG 5.1, file 46.17, see, for example, case report by Alice Watson on K. family, 5 November 1947; file 46.17.3, 'General Welfare Assistance – District Work – Minutes of Meetings, Nov 49–May 53,' minutes of first meeting of superintendents and supervisors, 23 November 1949.

29 MTRA, RG 5.1, file 46.17, 'GWA – District Work – June/52–May/54,' H.S. Rupert to A.F. Clifton, 24 January 1956; 'GWA – District Work – Jan/39–Aug/49,' memo from Robena Morris to H.S. Rupert, 'Families and Individuals on Relief,' 29 June 1949.

30 MTRA, RG 5.1, file 46.17.3, 'General Welfare Assistance – District Work – Minutes of Meetings, Nov 49–May 53,' file 3, minutes of first meeting of superintendents and supervisors, 23 November 1949; file 46.17.1, Miss H. Robb, 'Report re Memorandum for Welfare Visitor,' 26 November 1952; V. Morrow to E. Songhurst, 'Caseload of District Number Five,' 22 June 1953; AO, RG 29-01, box 63, file 2464, D.G. Gardner to James Band, 'RE: Survey of Unemployment Relief Cases in Toronto,' 10 March 1958; MTRA, RG 5.1, file 46.17, 'GWA – District Work – June/52–May/54,' Eleanore Songhurst to Robena Morris, 'Welfare Visitors – Volume of Work,' 30 July 1954.

31 AO, RG 29, series 74.1, box 3 – 1956, file 3.2, 'Address of the Honourable Louis P. Cecile, Minister of Public Welfare, on Presentation of the Estimates, March 22, 1956'; RG 3, Frost Papers, series E-16-A, box 133, file 287G, Louis Cecile to Frost, 13 May 1958.

32 MTRA, RG 5.1, file 46.17, Report of R.G. Humphrey, acting assistant director of

personnel, 'Investigation of Duties of Welfare Visitors,' 20 September 1954; Robena Morris to H.S. Rupert, 'Centralized Intake in District Offices,' 20 December 1950.

33 For a pioneering application of moral regulation theory to an analysis of social and moral reform in English Canada between 1885 and 1925 see Mariana Valverde, *The Age of Light, Soap, and Water: Moral Reform in English Canada, 1885–1925* (Toronto 1991). As Valverde argues: 'Neither liberal nor Marxist accounts [of the welfare state] ... consider the possibility that moral regulation might be an important social process, which is intertwined with but is not an effect of either the economic or the political. Moral regulation is very closely linked to state formation ... but ... the state has no monopoly on moral regulation, and private organizations – notably, the medical and legal professions and philanthropic groups – have exercised crucial leadership in the regulatory field ... Moral regulation is an important aspect of ruling, helping to constitute class, gender, sexual and race relations by interpreting both social action and individual identity as fundamentally ethical' (165–7).

34 MTRA, RG 5.1, box 98, file 46.17.3, 'General Welfare Assistance – District Work – Minutes of Meetings, Nov 49 – May 53,' file 3, 6 August 1952; AO, RG 29-01, box 63, file 2469, H.S. Rupert to G. Arthur Walsh, commissioner of LCBO, 19 August 1952; MTRA, RG 5.1, file 46.17, 'GWA – District Work – Oct/49 – Apr/52,' memo from R.J. Smith to H.S. Rupert, 20 October 1950; 'Instructions to Tenants in Receipt of Welfare Assistance,' nd circa 1953.

35 MTRA, RG 5.1, file 46.17, 'Analysis of Case Load Carried by Students of the School of Social Work in this Department,' 8 July 1949; file 46.17.1, Paul Ayles to H.S. Rupert, 'Report on Make-Up of Caseload,' 22 January 1953.

36 MTRA, RG 5.1, file 46.17, 'GWA – District Work – Oct/49–Apr/52,' memo from H.S. Rupert to Robena Morris, 10 April 1951; box 34, file 46 'GWA,' memo from H.S. Rupert to All Division, Section, and Unit Heads, 13 October 1955.

37 MTRA, R.G 5.1, file 46.17 'GWA – District Work – Oct/49–Apr/52,' box 96, file 3, memo from Robena Morris to H.S. Rupert, 15 November 1950; 'GWA – District Work – June/52 – May/54,' box 96, file 4, memo by E. Songhurst, 'Statement of Income Forms,' 30 June 1952; file 46.17.3, 'General Welfare Assistance – District Work – Minutes of Meetings, Nov 49–May 53, file 3, meeting 4 April 1951 on 'Importance of Intake'; file 46.17, 'GWA – District Work – June/5 – May/54,' memo from Robena Morris to H.S. Rupert, on 'Emergency Assistance,' 14 April 1953; 'GWA – District Work – Nov/53–Dec/57,' Box 98, file 4, meeting on 'Approving for Regular Relief,' 8 November 1954. It is worth noting that once public hospital insurance came into effect in Ontario after 1957, the department completely reversed its policy on emergency assistance. Supervisors were told of 'the importance of putting cases on regular assistance as quickly as possible and not keeping them on emergency assistance month after month. This is increas-

ingly important now, as if they are kept on emergency assistance they will not
get registered under the Hospital Plan.' In this case, of course, the city would be
liable for paying the complete cost of their hospital medical bills if ill. File
46.17.3 'GWA – District Work, Minutes of Meetings, Jan/58–Nov/65,' box 98,
file 5, minutes of meeting, 20 November 1958.

38 MTRA, RG 5.1, file 46.17.1, Paul Ayles to H.S. Rupert, 'Report on Make-Up of
Caseload,' 22 January 1953; M. Planzer to E. Songhurst, 'Caseload of District
Number 4,' 12 June 1953; file 46.17.3, box 98, file 3, 'General Welfare Assist-
ance – District Work – Minutes of Meetings Nov 49–May 53,' meeting on
'Support from Putative Fathers,' 11 May 1950; file 46.17, D.E. Atkinson to H.S.
Rupert, 'Analysis of Case Load Carried by Students of the School of Social Work
in this Department,' 8 July 1949.

39 MTRA, file 46.17, D.E. Atkinson to H.S. Rupert, 'Analysis of Case Load Carried
by Students of the School of Social Work in this Department,' 8 July 1949 (my
emphasis); similar advice in other abusive situations is found in case summaries
of Toronto's welfare department throughout this era. See, for example, file
46.17.1, Paul Ayles to H.S. Rupert, 'Report on Make-Up of Caseload,' 22
January 1953, the case of Mrs H, whose husband 'abused her and the children
and separation was arranged ... In subsequent visits, the worker discussed the plan
[of reconciliation] carefully with the woman *whose object in considering
reconciliation was to provide more adequately for the children.* He explained that
there was little hope for success *unless both partners were willing to forgive* ... [A
reconciliation was effected and] as a result, Mrs H and her family were able to
dispense with public assistance and the worker feels ... the advice that he was able
to give increased the chances for a lasting and beneficial reunion' (my emphasis).
In all these cases women were advised that reconciliation with an abusive
husband was a preferable alternative to separation and support through public
assistance, and that the burden of 'adjustment' was theirs.

40 MTRA, RG 5.1, file 82, 'Remarks presented by Mr. James Band, Deputy
Minister of Public Welfare at the Welfare Officers' Association, Ninth Annual
Convention – 1959.'

41 MTRA, RG 5.1, file 46.1.73, 'GWA – District Work, Minutes of Meetings, Jan/
58–Nov/65,' box 98, file 5, minutes of meeting on 'Common Law Unions,' 9
April 1959.

42 Ibid.

43 AO, RG 29-01, box 63, file 2464, Clifford Williams to James Band, 8 December
1958.

44 MTRA, RG 5.1, file 46.1.73, 'GWA – District Work, Minutes of Meetings, Jan/
58–Nov/65,' box 98, file 5, meeting on 'Common Law Unions,' 9 April 1959.

45 MTRA, RG 5.1, file 46.17.1, M. Planzer to E. Songhurst, 'Caseload of District
Number 4,' 12 June 1953 (my emphasis).

46 MTRA, RG 5.1, file 46.1.71, M. Planzer to E. Songhurst, 'Caseload of District

Number 4,' 12 June 1953; file 46.17, D.E. Atkinson to H.S. Rupert, 'Analysis of Case Load carried by Students of the School of Social Work in this Department,' 8 July 1949.

47 MTRA, RG 5.1, file 45, Eleanore Songhurst, 'Public Assistance – Its Philosophy and Practice,' 12 April 1956; CTA, SC 40, box 29, file 7, Hugh Lawson, president, United Welfare Chest, to Mayor Robert Saunders, 'Subject – Appointment of a Welfare Commissioner' 21 January 1947.

48 AO, MS 728, COMSOC, Minister's Correspondence 1937–49, reel 1, microdex no. 3, brief submitted to R.P. Vivian, minister of health and public welfare, by Fred Conboy, mayor of Toronto, 29 September 1943.

49 City of Toronto Archives (CTA), SC 40, box 168, file 4, 'Interim Report' of the Special Committee of the Child and Family Welfare Division set up to study *Survey Recommendations on Services to Unmarried Parents*, May 1952.

50 Charlotte Whitton, 'Some Social Factors in the Treatment of Illegitimacy,' *Child and Family Welfare* 9, 5 (1934). In an earlier 1920 article, Whitton described illegitimacy as 'an offence that has ranked only with murder in the public disgust of history,' one that flourished 'where subnormality is a strong predisposing factor.' Whitton, 'Unmarried Parenthood and the Social Order,' *Social Welfare*, April 1920. By the 1930s Whitton had dropped her eugenicist arguments associating illegitimacy with feeble-mindedness, but her essentially moralizing approach to unwed parenthood remained intact.

51 A.F. Carver, 'Discussion of Miss Morlock's Paper on "Some Aspects of Illegitimacy,"' Canadian Conference on Social Work, *Proceedings* 10 (1946); Winona Armitage, 'The Unmarried Mother and Adoption,' Canadian Conference on Social Work, *Proceedings* 9 (1944).

52 A.F. Carver, 'Casework Service to the Unmarried Mother in Time of War,' Canadian Conference on Social Work, *Proceedings* (1944); Mary Speers, 'Case Work and Adoption,' *The Social Worker* 16, 3 (February 1948); Betty Isserman, 'The Casework Relationship in Work with Unmarried Mothers,' *The Social Worker* 17, 1 (October 1948); 'Mothers Not All Unhappy,' Toronto *Telegram*, 22 November 1956.

53 Carver, 'Case Work Service to the Unmarried Mother in Time of War.'

54 Speers, 'Case Work and Adoption.' Given these governing assumptions and the absence of financial support for unwed mothers wishing to keep their children, it is hardly surprising that a 1955 Toronto CAS study of 546 unwed mothers coming into contact with the agency revealed that less than 30 per cent kept their children. 'The rest were made permanent wards of the Children's Aid and either are adopted, or will be adopted, or were adopted through the agency without being made permanent wards.' 'Unhappy Homes Behind Many Unwed Mothers,' Toronto *Telegram*, 19 November 1956.

55 Svanhuit Josie, 'The American Caricature of the Unmarried Mother,' *Canadian Welfare* 31, 5 (December 1955).

56 Ibid. Josie's article prompted a harsh rebuttal from the supervisor of the Unmar-

ried Parents Department of the Toronto CAS. Most of the women who kept their children, in the experience of her agency, 'were emotionally sick people and only the future will tell what becomes of the children involved ... [W]hat she would like for herself is at war with what seems best for her child, in light of the social situation confronting both. It is with this group that the caseworker tries to be of assistance in helping her assess the realities of her situation,' this social worker argued. See Kathleen Sutherton, 'Another View,' *Canadian Welfare* 31, 5 (December 1955).

57 Canadian Welfare Council citation is from 'Interim Report' of the Special Committee of the Child and Family Welfare Division set up to study *Survey Recommendations on Services to Unmarried Parents*, May 1952.

58 Ontario, Department of Public Welfare, *Annual Report*, 1955–6, 45. Ontario's illegitimacy rate reached a peak of 5.2 per cent of all live births in 1945, before beginning a steady decline to only 3.1 per cent of live births ten years later. Ontario officials attributed the rise in illegitimacy at the war's end to 'disturbed and broken homes with fathers away and mothers working.' The postwar decline was explained by prosperity. 'Rising incomes, earlier marriages, better education, and more stable homes' were given as 'reasons for the decreasing illegitimacy' by W.H. Bury, director of child welfare for Ontario. Toronto *Telegram*, 24 November 1956.

59 '"Good" Mother May Be Single but Want Child,' Toronto *Telegram*, 21 November 1956.

60 Ontario, Department of Public Welfare, *Annual Report*, 1955–6, 42; '"Good" Mother May be Single But Want Child,' Toronto *Telegram*, 21 November 1956. Significantly, the department used the same logic of keeping families together to explain why unemployable fathers caring for dependent children would also be included for the first time under mothers' allowances in 1956. 'Previously, the only way that assistance could be provided for the children was to arrange for relatives or close friends to take the children into their care and then pay the regular foster mother's assistance on behalf of the children. If there were a number of children involved, it meant that possibly two or three foster homes had to be established to care for the children, thus defeating the very purpose for which Mothers' Allowance assistance was designed, namely, to keep the family together as a unit.' *Annual Report*, 1955–6, 43.

61 Ontario, Department of Public Welfare, *Annual Report*, 1955–6, 1956–7, 1957–8, 1958–9.

62 'New Welfare Plan Based on Need,' Toronto *Globe and Mail*, 1 October 1957; Ontario, Department of Public Welfare, *Annual Report* 1956–7, 1957–8; AO, RG 29-01, box 40, file 1623, Louis Cecile to Wm M. Nickle, 22 October 1957.

63 AO, RG 29-01, box 40, file 1621, M. Bannon, welfare administrator, Oshawa Public Welfare Board, to E.T. Plant, Mothers' Allowance Commission, 25 March 1953; E.T. Plant, director of mothers' allowances, to W.A. Goodfellow, 8 April 1953.

64 Clifford Williams, *Decades of Service: A History of the Ontario Ministry of Community and Social Services, 1930–80* (Toronto 1984), 79. 'The allowance must be a sum that will fit into the current pattern of wages and income,' Williams argued in a classic illustration of 'less eligibility.'

65 AO, RG 29-01, box 40, file 1623, James Band to all field workers, 'Re: Mothers' and Dependent Children's Allowance,' 25 September 1957; 'New Welfare Plan Based on Need,' *Globe and Mail*, 1 October 1957; Ontario, Department of Public Welfare, *Annual Report*, 1957–8; RG 29-01, box 40, file 1626, 'Budget Work Sheet' for L.G., 25 February 1960.

66 RG 29-01, box 40, file 1623, Louis Cecile to Wm Nickle, 22 October 1957.

67 Ibid.; James Band to field workers 'Re: Mothers' and Dependent Children's Allowances,' 25 September 1957.

68 James Band to field workers, 'Re: Mothers' and Dependent Children's Allowances,' 25 September 1957; Lorna Hurl, 'The Nature of Policy Dynamics,': Patterns of Change and Stability in a Social Assistance Program,' paper presented to the fourth National Conference on Social Welfare Policy, Toronto, 24–27 October 1989, 20. As Hurl points out, 1961 represented the high-water mark of adequacy within mothers' allowances, as the program in that year approached 74 per cent of the Toronto Social Planning Council's minimum standards of budgetary need. By the end of the 1960s, family benefits to mothers with dependent children in Ontario would approximate only 68 per cent of this standard (table 4). Case illustrations are from RG 29-01, box 40, file 1626, 'Budget Work Sheet' of E.S, mother of six, and Mrs D., mother of ten, nd but circa February 1962.

69 AO, RG 29-01, box 45, file 1807, Leslie Frost to Louis Cecile, 14 January 1960; Louis Cecile to Leslie Frost, 22 February 1960.

70 For a treatment of this issue in greater detail see James Struthers, 'Shadows from the Thirties: The Federal Government and Unemployment Assistance, 1941–1956,' in Jacqueline S. Ismael, ed., *The Canadian Welfare State: Evolution and Transition* (Edmonton 1987), 3–32.

71 AO, RG 29-01, box 23, file 953, 'Report of George Gathercole on the Second Meeting of the Preparatory Committee of the Federal-Provincial Conference, May 26, 27, and 30, 1955,' 6 June 1955, 11–12.

72 National Archives of Canada (NA), Canadian Council on Social Development Records, MG 28, I 10, accession 83, box 151, file 'Public Assistance and the Unemployed,' field report by William McGrath on visit with James Band, 10 February 1953.

73 NA, Department of Finance Records, RG 19, vol. 4663, file 187 EAC – 47, 'Report of the Economic Advisory Committee on the Reconstruction Committee's Recommendations Regarding Ministerial Responsibility for Reconstruction Planning,' 30 November 1942.

74 Ibid., vol. 3976, memo by Robert Bryce and Alex Skelton on 'Dominion Post-

War Policy,' for Economic Advisory Committee, 13 April 1943; vol. 4663, file 187, EAC – 46, 'Report of the Economic Advisory Committee on the Report of the Advisory Committee on Reconstruction,' 20 November 1943.

75 NA, W.L. Mackenzie King Papers, MG 26, J1, Graham Towers to King, 15 August 1940; Dominion-Provincial Conference on Reconstruction, *Proposals of the Government of Canada* (August 1945), 7, 21–6, 51. The Green Book Proposals noted that Ottawa wished to 'avoid the make-shift arrangements and controversy with provincial governments which otherwise would be almost certain to recur under the old [conditional grant] methods of providing relief'; NA, RG 19, vol. 537, file 135-0-167 (3), 'Dominion-Provincial Conference Co-ordinating Committee,' statement by the prime minister at the opening session, 28 January 1946.

76 AO, RG 29, series 74.1 – 1945, box 2, file 2.1, 'Preliminary Remarks Relating to Dominion-Provincial Proposals, August 1945'; H.J. Chater to George Drew and Leslie Frost, 'Dominion-Provincial Economic Committee, Report #5, 22 December 1945.'

77 NA, RG 29, vol. 918, 'Committee on Unemployment Questions: Draft of a Possible Memorandum to Cabinet on Unemployment Assistance Policy,' 15 October 1952, which noted that Ottawa's Green Book proposal on unemployment assistance was based on 'the anticipation of large scale unemployment in the immediate postwar years' as well as provincial 'acceptance ... of the taxation proposals put forward [in 1945] by the Federal Government'; Canada, House of Commons, *Debates*, 27 June 1946, 2913–14; NA, Privy Council Office Records, RG 2, series 18, vol. 187, file 50-60(d), 'Report of the Working Committee on Unemployment Insurance and Unemployment Aid,' 24 November 1950; MG 26L, Louis St Laurent Papers, vol. 165, file U-11-6, J.W. Pickersgill, 'Memorandum for the Prime Minister re Unemployment Assistance,' 21 October 1952; Canadian Council on Social Development Records, MG 28, I 10, accession 83, box 151, file 'Public Assistance and the Unemployed,' Louis St Laurent to Seely Eakins, executive secretary of the Ontario Association of Mayors and Municipalities, 23 October 1952.

78 NA, MG 28, I 10, accession 83, box 151, file 'Public Assistance and the Unemployed,' W.A. Goodfellow to R.E.G. Davis, 17 September 1952. In a complete reversal of Ontario's position at the 1945–6 Dominion-Provincial Reconstruction Conference, Goodfellow now argued that Ottawa should administer unemployment assistance itself, rather than rely on provincial and local welfare offices to do the job for it. 'With the machinery at their disposal ... the Employment Offices are located in each centre in Canada, they are well equipped to relieve the provinces and municipalities of duplication of effort ... They have full knowledge of all employable persons coming under their jurisdiction, including records of employment, occupation, whether they might be placed elsewhere, and other pertinent information ... Split authority ... would once more lead us to the worst

features faced by provinces and municipalities during the depression years'; see also accession 83, box 151, field report by William McGrath on interview with James Band, 10 February 1953.

79 MTRA, RG 5.1, file 46.1.73, 'General Welfare Assistance – District Work – Minutes of Meetings, Nov 49–May 53,' box 98, file 3, meetings 23 January 1952, 6, 28, 29 February 1952; NA, MG 28, I 10, accession 83, box 151, file 'Public Assistance and Unemployed,' C.A. Patrick to Lillian Thomson, 4 November 1954.

80 NA, RG 29, vol. 918, 'Committee on Unemployment Questions: Draft of a possible Memorandum to the Cabinet on Unemployment Assistance Policy,' 15 October 1952 This committee was chaired by Jack Pickersgill, St Laurent's senior political adviser.

81 NA, RG 29, vol. 921, copy of memo by J.F. Parkinson, Department of Finance, 'Unemployment Assistance: Proposal to pay a minimum federal share on a continuous basis,' 22 July 1954.

82 NA, MG 28, I 10, accession 83, box 151, file 'Public Assistance and the Unemployed,' *Public Assistance and the Unemployed*, February 1953. Deputy welfare ministers from Saskatchewan, British Columbia, Manitoba, and Nova Scotia and the chief commissioner of the Unemployment Insurance Commission served on the CWC committee, chaired by David Croll, which produced this report. Interestingly enough, no Ontario civil servant served on the commitee; however, the province was represented by its former deputy welfare minister, B.W. Heise, who was forced to resign his position in the wake of the repeal of the Welfare Units Act in 1951; George Davidson to R.E.G. Davis, 2 February 1953; field report by William McGrath on interview with James Band, 10 February 1953. McGrath was 'impressed by [Band's] sensitivity to public opinion.'

83 NA, MG 28, I 10, accession 83, box 151, file 'Public Assistance and the Unemployed,' John Morgan to Charles Hendry, 30 September 1952.

84 NA, RG 29, vol. 918, 'Minutes of the Interdepartmental Committee on Unemployment Questions,' 28 July 1954; George Davidson, 'Memorandum on Unemployment Assistance,' May 1954.

85 NA, RG 29, vol. 921, memorandum by J. Parkinson, 'Unemployment Assistance: Proposal to pay a minimum federal share on a continuous basis,' 22 July 1954; vol. 918, minutes of 'Interdepartmental Committee on Unemployment Questions,' 4 August 1954; Paul Martin, *A Very Public Life*, 2: *So Many Worlds* (Toronto 1985), 262.

86 NA, RG 29, vol. 921, 'Report of Meeting between Civic Representatives and Members of the Federal Cabinet Re: Unemployment Situation in Toronto,' 26 February 1955; Canada, House of Commons, *Debates*, 2 March 1955, 1656–7, 1690–1.

87 AO, RG 29-01, box 61, file 2411, cases selected from Neighbourhood Workers' Association, 'Homes without Work,' 28 April 1955.

88 AO, RG 29, series 74.1, file 3.1, W.A. Goodfellow to municipal clerks and welfare administrators, 8 March 1955; Canada, House of Commons, *Debates*, 1 March 1955, 1635; CTA, SC 40, box 168, file 7, Toronto Welfare Council Board Minutes, 9 March 1955, reporting discussions with the Ontario Welfare Council.

89 NA, MG 28, I 10, accession 83, box 151, Phyllis Burns, 'Record of Action re Public Assistance and the Unemployed, 1954–55,' 14 June 1955.

90 NA, RG 29, vol. 918, minutes of 'Interdepartmental Committee on the Federal-Provincial Conference, 1955,' 21 April 1955.

91 NA, RG 29, vol. 918, minutes of 'Federal-Provincial Meeting on Unemployment Assistance,' 20 June 1955; AO, RG 29-01, box 23, file 953, 'Report of George Gathercole on the Second Meeting of the Preparatory Committee of the Federal-Provincial Conference, May 26, 27, and 30 1955,' 6 June 1955; RG 29-01, file 953, 'Basic Details of Plan for Assistance for Unemployed,' 21 June 1955; NA, RG 29, vol. 918, Memorandum to the Cabinet, 'Re: Unemployment Assistance,' 18 October 1955.

92 AO, RG 3, Frost Papers, accession 9635, box 8, 'Statement of the Honourable Leslie M. Frost, Prime Minister of Ontario, at the Federal-Provincial Conference on Unemployment Relief, Ottawa, June 20, 1955'; NA, RG 29, vol. 918, minutes of 'Federal-Provincial Meeting on Unemployment Assistance,' 20 June 1955.

93 NA, RG 29, vol. 918, minutes of 'Federal-Provincial Meeting on Unemployment Assistance,' 20 June 1955; AO, RG 29, series 74.1, file 3.1, memo from W.A. Goodfellow to Leslie Frost, 'Re: Employable Unemployed Persons,' 12 October 1955; NA, RG 29, vol. 918, 'Memorandum to Cabinet re: Unemployment Assistance,' 18 October 1955.

94 AO, RG 3, Frost Papers, series E-16-A, accession 6521, box 37, file 76-G, W.A. Goodfellow to Leslie Frost, 3 November 1955; George Gathercole, 'Proposal of the Federal Government to Assist in the Cost of Relief for Unemployed Persons,' 2 September 1955; 'Statement of the Honourable Leslie Frost ... At the Federal-Provincial Conference on Unemployment Relief,' 20 June 1955; RG 29, series 74.1, file 3.1, memo from W.A. Goodfellow to Frost 'Re: Employable Unemployed Persons,' 12 October 1955; MS 728, COMSOC, Minister's Correspondence 1937–49, reel no. 2, microdex no. 1, memorandum on 'Unemployment Relief Assistance,' December 1955.

95 AO, RG 3, series E-16-A, accession 6521, box 37, file 76-G, George Gathercole to Frost, 'Revised Memorandum of Agreement Respecting Unemployment Relief,' 30 December 1955; NA, RG 29, vol. 918, memo from George Davidson to Paul Martin, 7 February 1956; AO, RG 29, series 74.1, box 3 – 1957 file 3.3, James Band to W.L. Clark, 23 December 1957, noting that 'several Provinces were keeping their fingers crossed with the hope that Ontario would serve them in obtaining a fair settlement'; MS 728, COMSOC, Minister's Correspondence 1937–49, memorandum on 'Unemployment Relief Assistance,' December 1955; as the *Toronto Star*, no supporter of Frost's administration, put it, 'it is generally

accepted that the strong representations made by Premier Frost have, to put it
bluntly, shamed the Federal Government into recognizing the obvious. It has been
difficult for the provincial delegations to appreciate why the Federal Government,
which has an annual budget of around $5,000,000,000 should be quarrelling with
the provinces over an expenditure which is not likely to be more than $7,500,000
and would not, in any event, exceed $10,000,000' (22 June 1955). See also
favourable accounts of Frost's position in the *Globe and Mail*, 21–22 June 1955,
and the *Telegram*, 22 June 1955. In fact, spending under the Unemployment
Assistance Act would top $215,000,000 by 1965. Kenneth Buckley and M.C.
Urquhart, *Historical Statistics of Canada*, 2nd ed. (Ottawa 1983), C404-16,
C391-416.

96 NA, RG, 29, vol. 2298, file 251-5-1, pt 1, copy of Louis Cecile to J.B. Adamac,
city clerk, Windsor, 1 May 1957; RG 29-01, box 45, file 1804, Leslie Frost to
Louis Cecile, 10 July 1957.

97 Roger Graham, *Old Man Ontario: Leslie M. Frost* (Toronto 1990), 353; AO, RG
29-01, box 45, file 1804, Frost to Louis Cecile, 10 July 1957, 17 July 1957.

98 AO, RG 3, box 201, file 292G, memo from Frost to W.M. McIntyre, 7 August
1957. Both James Band and his minister, Louis Cecile, were extremely reluctant
to negotiate any unemployment assistance agreement with Ottawa. As Cecile told
the premier that spring, 'I am also still adverse to entering into any overall
scheme with the Ottawa Government for the granting of direct relief to unemployed employable persons. I think such a step would weaken our position that
the Federal Government recognize the needs of the unemployed worker through
the National Unemployment Insurance offices.' RG 29-01, box 61, file 2412,
Cecile to Frost, 22 May 1957.

99 NA, RG 29, vol. 2298, file 251-501 pt. 1, memo from George Davidson to Waldo
Monteith, 'Unemployment Assistance,' 16 October 1957; Cecile and Band
initially argued that Ontario's willingness to participate in the Unemployment
Assistance Act would also be contingent upon Ottawa expanding unemployment
insurance entitlement from a maximum of thirty-six to fifty-two weeks, and the
launching of a federal public works program giving priority to municipalities
where relief rolls exceeded 3 per cent of the population. These demands were
quickly dropped. See NA, RG 29, vol. 2298, file 251-501 pt. 1, Louis Cecile to
A.J. Brooks, acting minister of national health and welfare, 12 August 1957;
Cecile to Waldo Monteith, 5 September 1957; Monteith to Cecile, 9 September
1957; on tax-sharing see Graham, *Old Man Ontario*, 337; AO, RG 3, series E-16-
A, box 158, file 228G, handwritten minutes of meeting on 'Unemployment,' 5
December 1957. Another major benefit of the agreement for Ontario was the
more than $1 million annually the province now received from Ottawa to cover
the cost of relieving unemployables in nursing and old age homes, which initially
made up two-sevenths of the province's relief load. See AO, RG 3, series E-16-A,

accession 6521, box 158, file 228G, James Band to Louis Cecile, 'Re: Federal-Provincial Agreement Respecting Unemployment Assistance,' 3 December 1957.

100 AO, RG 29-01, box 61, file 2418, memo from James Band to Louis Cecile 'Re: the Employable Unemployed,' 6 November 1957; Band estimated that the initial effect of the Unemployment Assistance Act would be to add 31,000 to Ontario's relief caseload at an estimated cost to the province of $9 million; RG 3, series E-16-A, box 158, file 228G, handwritten notes of meeting on 'Unemployment,' 5 December 1957. On problems of insufficient staff given the rapid rise in welfare caseloads see MTRA, RG 5.1, 46.17.3, 'GWA – District Work, Minutes of Meetings, Jan/58–Nov/65,' box 98, file 5, 25 June, 12 August, and 12 September 1958, as well as file 46.17, 'GWA – District Work – Jan/58–Mar/59,' box 97, file 1.

101 NA, RG 29, vol. 919, memorandum on 'Statistics of Unemployment and Social Need,' nd but circa January 1959 (my emphasis); Wismer, 'Public Assistance in Ontario, 1950–61,' 105–9. Ontario's expenditures on relief rose from $7.2 million to $18.7 million between 1956 and 1960; NA, RG 29, vol. 921, 'Discussions on Unemployment Assistance in Ontario, November 16th, 17th, and 18th,' 1959. As Dorothea Crittenden, executive assistant in Ontario's Department of Public Welfare, told federal officials, raising relief allowances in Ontario was a 'political decision based on financial considerations on the one hand and the weight of public opinion ... on the other.'

102 Pat Thane, *The Foundations of the Welfare State* (London 1982), 289.

CHAPTER 6   *'Work for Relief'*

1 K.J. Rea, *The Prosperous Years: The Economic History of Ontario, 1939–75* (Toronto 1985), 34.

2 National Archives of Canada (NA), RG 29, vol. 1527, file 201-16-2A, 'Canada Assistance Plan – Unemployment Assistance,' minutes of the first meeting of the 'Committee on Unemployment Assistance,' 26 March 1962; vol. 921, 'Estimate of Probable Unemployment Assistance Caseload,' 16 August 1954; vol. 1623, file 15, 'Background Paper for the Federal-Provincial Conference – Item 2(b), Categorical Assistance Programs,' 11 November 1963.

3 NA, RG 29, vol. 1623, file 15, 'Background Paper for the Federal-Provincial Conference – Item 2 (b) Categorical Assistance Programs,' 11 November 1963; Archives of Ontario (AO), RG 29-01, box 45, file 1809, James Band to R.A. Farrell, 'Re: General Welfare Assistance,' 31 July 1962. By that year general assistance made up 45 per cent of Ontario's welfare spending. Mothers' allowance and old age assistance, in contrast, cost only $13.5 million each per year.

4 Canadian Welfare Council, *Social Security for Canada* (Ottawa 1958), 3, 10–12. The council's first call for a national public assistance plan is contained in its pamphlet, *Public Assistance and the Unemployed* (Ottawa 1952).

5 AO, RG 3, Frost Papers, box 21, file 44-2G, memo from James Band to Glen Gordon, Premier's Office, 27 June 1958.

6 AO, RG 49, MS 755, reel 199, clipping from *Toronto Telegram*, 8 February 1961; NA, RG 29, vol. 2298, file 251-5-1 pt 2, 'Unemployment Assistance – Agreement with Ontario – Policy,' 1955–61, copy of Scarborough's work relief policy, March 1961. Fort William and St Thomas also developed detailed work relief policies, as did a number of northern Indian bands. See ibid., vol. 2299, file 251-5-1, vol. 3, James Band to R.B. Splane, 27 March 1962.

7 AO, RG 29-01, box 29, file 1193, 'Work for Relief,' clipping, *Globe and Mail*, 18 August and 1 September 1962; file 1192, 'General Welfare Assistance Act – Work for Relief 1961,' T. Gràham Reid to James Band, 22 June 1961; box 66, file 2568, 'Welfare Officers Association,' 'Notes on the Executive Meeting,' 12 February 1962.

8 AO, RG 29-01, box 29, file 1192, 'General Welfare Assistance Act – Work for Relief 1961,' James Band to Joe Willard, 8 March 1961.

9 NA, RG 29, vol. 1527, file 201-16-2A, 'Canada Assistance Plan – Unemployment Assistance,' memo by A.S. Abell, director of federal–provincial relations division, Department of Finance, on 'Unemployment Assistance,' 30 August 1962. As the federal director of unemployment assistance, Dick Splane, commented on this conference, 'Work for relief was in fact close to the surface of the discussions.' Splane to Joe Willard, 5 September 1962.

10 NA, RG 29, vol. 1526, file 201-16-2 pt 1, 'Unemployment Assistance, 1960–68,' R.F. Rintoul, national director of the National Union of Public Employees, to J. Waldo Monteith, 18 April 1961; AO, RG 29-01, box 61, file 2417, 'Unemployment Assistance Act 1958–1966,' Louis Cecile to John Robarts, 19 July 1963; NA, RG 29, vol. 2298, file 251-5-1, 'Unemployment Assistance – Agreement with Ontario – Policy,' 1955–61, R.B. Splane to Joe Willard, 19 April 1961. Splane also sent Willard a memorandum from the Canadian Labour Congress, presented to the federal cabinet, which set out a 'vigorous and ably-stated attack on the [work-for-relief] approach.' R.B. Splane to Joe Willard, memo on 'Work for Relief,' 11 December 1962.

11 AO, RG 49, MS 755, reel 199, clippings from *Belleville Intelligencer*, 15 February 1961; *Peterborough Examiner*, 18 June 1962; *Globe and Mail*, 22 February 1961; *Toronto Star*, 1 September 1962. 'Work for relief' enjoyed a tremendous come-back during the 1980s debates on welfare reform. In the United States, under the new name of 'workfare,' such programs became 'the new synthesis' in welfare reform at the federal and state level after 1981, as more than two-thirds of the states began implementing work or training requirements in exchange for relief under the new Community Work Experience Programs

fostered by the federal funding of the Reagan administration. On this phenom-
enon see Michael Katz, *The Undeserving Poor: From the War on Poverty to the
War on Welfare* (New York 1989), 225–6. The popularity of this approach has
now spread into Canada. Reform Party leader Preston Manning recently advocated 'a scheme whereby able-bodied welfare recipients would have to perform
some form of community service or agree to undertake training' in order to
maintain their welfare entitlement. *Globe and Mail,* 12 June 1992. In welfare
reforms aimed at addressing the province's $6 billion annual expenditure on
social assistance, Ontario's NDP administration has contemplated linking
community service requirements to welfare assistance as a means of 'encouraging
people who cannot find jobs to take volunteer work as a path to getting into the
work force.' As Marion Boyd, minister of community and social services, argued,
'There's lots of young, single moms who do have time that they could spend doing
some assistance in the community who don't dare do it because they're afraid that
they'll get caught. Well, there's something really wrong with the system.' *Globe
and Mail,* 27 January 1993. At the national level, newly elected prime minister
Jean Chrétien admitted he was 'impressed with a Danish program in which
welfare recipients have to work to get payments,' and he has argued that people
on unemployment insurance should be 'required to either upgrade their skills or
work at projects like cleaning brush in the country's forests.' According to
Chrétien, 'There's a lot of things that have to be done in society that are not done
because we don't have the resources and, on the other hand, a lot of people who
would like to work and there is no work. So why can we not match the need with
the availability of manpower?' *Toronto Star,* 21 September, 24 December 1993.

12 Dick Splane summed up the remarkable looseness of the Unemployment
Assistance Act in a 1962 memorandum. 'The broad terms of the [UA] legislation
make it clear that it was the intent of Parliament that the framework for federal
sharing of the general assistance costs should be flexible in recognition of the
wide variations in provincial programs which had developed over the years to
meet the special needs of the various provinces. No regulations were enacted
under this legislation when it was passed and none have been developed since
then. There is no general provision in the legislation for the enforcement of
standards of assistance nor is there any ceiling on the level of benefits in which
the Federal Government can share. The levels of benefits vary widely from
province to province and there are also considerable differences in the levels of
aid in different kinds of communities within the same province.' NA, RG 29, vol.
2311, file 251-15-1, vol. 6, memo by Splane, 'General Information on Unemployment Assistance,' 18 June 1962.

13 NA, RG 29, vol. 1526, file 201-16-2 pt 1, 'Unemployment Assistance, 1960–68,'
memo on 'Unemployment Assistance' from R.B. Splane to Joe Willard, 8 March
1961.

14 As the deputy minister of national health and welfare told his minister, Waldo

Monteith, in response to blistering criticism of the Unemployment Assistance Act in the auditor-general's 1959 report: 'He points out ... that the Act is confusing and ambiguous, and open to more than one interpretation, and that in consequence there is no way of determining whether the Department has adopted the correct interpretation or not. In my view, the Auditor General is quite correct in this.' NA, RG 29, vol. 2311, file 251-15-1, vol. 3, George Davidson to the minister, 26 February 1959.

15　Ibid., vol. 2299, file 251-5-1, vol. 3, James Band to R.B. Splane, 27 March 1962; vol. 2298, file 251-5-1 pt 2, Joe Willard to James Band, 10 March 1961, noting that the matter of work for relief 'has come to the attention of the Auditor General's staff in connection with the assistance practices of the Township of Scarborough where, it appears, recipients are being required to perform some work as a condition for the receipt of welfare aid.'

16　Ibid., vol. 2298, file 251-5-1, 'Unemployment Assistance – Agreement with Ontario – Policy,' 1955–61, Joe Willard to James Band, 10 March 1961.

17　AO, RG 29-01, box 29, file 1192, 'General Welfare Assistance Act – Work for Relief 1961,' Joe Willard to James Band, 17 March 1961.

18　NA, RG 29, vol. 1527, file 201-16-2A, 'Canada Assistance Plan – Unemployment Assistance,' memorandum to cabinet, nd but circa August 1962; vol. 1526, file 201-16-2 pt 2, R.B. Splane to Joe Willard, 17 January 1961; vol. 2298, file 251-5-1 pt 2, Joe Willard to James Band, 11 October 1961.

19　Ibid., vol. 1526, file 201-16-2 pt 2, R.B. Splane to Joe Willard, 17 January 1961; vol. 1527, file 201-16-2A, Joe Willard to J.S. White, deputy minister of welfare, Saskatchewan, 30 January 1963. See also vol. 2298, file 251-5-1 pt 2, Joe Willard to James Band, 11 October 1961, where he notes, 'It was the view of the Ministers that the federal government would not want to become involved in this way in the financing of functions which would normally be considered municipal responsibilities.'

20　Throughout 1961 and 1962, Health and Welfare deputy minister Joe Willard continued to equivocate on whether Ottawa should amend the Unemployment Assistance Act to permit 'work testing' in order to appease the provinces that wanted it. As he asked Splane, in response to Band's initial protests, 'If the Unemployment Assistance legislation were amended would it not be worthwhile to include a section on "Work for Relief" which would permit this type of assistance provided that the nature and scope of the types of projects to which it would apply were defined by the province?' RG 29, vol. 2298, file 251-5-1 pt 2, Willard to Splane, 22 June 1961. Reflecting his social work background, Splane's opposition to the idea was unremitting, however. In a lengthy memo to Willard, he made the excellent point that the provinces were mostly bluffing on this issue. The administrative difficulties standing in the way of comprehensive work-for-relief schemes, Splane argued, were 'sufficiently formidable that, while a number of provinces have seemed to favour such projects, we are not aware of any being in existence at the present time. *The federal government is, therefore, being asked to participate in a type of program which the provinces are themselves backing away from.* Because the projects seem, superficially, to have merits and because the problems of administering them are not obvious, the provinces may avow their willingness to participate in this type of program but assert that they are prevented from doing so by the federal government ... If the pressure continues from the provinces for federal participation in work-for-relief projects, however, *the federal government might properly ask the provinces to demonstrate their belief that they are necessary by first participating in and bearing the full cost of them, themselves* ... They would then be in a better position to ask the federal government to review the question of taking the necessary legislative steps to participate in them.' Ibid., vol. 1526, file 201-16-2 pt 2, R.B. Splane to Joe Willard, 'Some Considerations Concerning Work Programs and Work-for-Relief Programs,' 17 January 1961 (my emphasis). AO, RG 3, Frost Papers, box 158, file 228G, James Band to regional welfare administrators, welfare allowances officers, 'Re: Memorandum on Work in Return for Relief Assistance,' 31 May 1961; NA, RG 29, vol. 2298, file 251-5-1, memo for file by R.B. Splane, 'Re Meeting with Band and Crittenden on 27 October 1961,' 31 October 1961.

21 AO, RG 29-01, box 45, file 1810, 'General Welfare Assistance – Comparison of Case Load, May 1963 to May 1962,' in Louis Cecile to John Robarts, 19 July 1963; box 61, file 2417, 'Unemployment Assistance Act, 1958–1966,' copy of Department of National Health and Welfare memo, 'Annual Report of Expenditures and Administration in Connection with the Unemployment Assistance Act for the Fiscal Year Ended March 31, 1964'; NA, RG 29, vol. 2311, file 251-15-1, vol. 7, R.B. Splane to Joe Willard, 'The Unemployment Assistance Program,' 11 June 1963; vol. 1629, file 7, R.B. Splane to Joe Willard, 'Some Considerations Favouring the Amending of the Unemployment Assistance Act at the Next Session of Parliament,' 27 August 1962.

22 NA, RG 29, vol. 1526, file 201-16-2 pt 2, 'Factors Affecting the Increased Cost of Unemployment Assistance,' nd but circa 1962.

23 Ibid., 'Factors Affecting the Increased Cost of Unemployment Assistance'; vol. 2113, file 23-1-5, vol. 2, memorandum on 'Redrafting the Unemployment Assistance Act,' nd but circa 1963. By 1962 almost 14 per cent of unemployment assistance funding was going towards the support of the elderly and the disabled in homes for special care. In Ontario the figure was 21 per cent. Another 7 per cent went towards supplementing benefits under other categorical social assistance programs. AO, RG 29-01, box 45, file 1809, James Band to R.A. Farrell, Premier's Office, 31 July 1962.

24 Kenneth Buckley and M.C. Urquhart, *Historical Statistics of Canada*, 2nd ed. (Ottawa 1983), C404-16, C391-416.

25 NA, RG 29, vol. 1623, file 15, 'Background Paper for the Federal-Provincial Conference – Item 2(b), Categorical Assistance Programs,' 11 November 1963;

vol. 1526, file 201-16-2 pt 1, Joe Willard to Waldo Monteith, 'Ontario's New Assistance Program for Women over Sixty,' 24 April 1963. It is important to note that key policy-makers within Health and Welfare, such as George Davidson, Joe Willard, and Dick Splane, were quite conscious of these 'developmental' uses of unemployment assistance for liberalizing and modernizing public assistance programs across Canada, a goal not always shared by their colleagues in the Department of Finance or by the auditor-general. It was only through shared-cost categorical programs such as unemployment assistance, Davidson told finance department critics in 1958, 'that we were successful in getting the level of benefits above the present level of basic poor relief ... [T]he grants in aid approach has a very real function to perform as a stimulator of provincial action. While there may be a case for the merging of conditional grants into block grants or even into the tax adjustment grants when their purpose has once been achieved, the device of conditional grants should still be retained ... as a means of inducing provincial action in areas where the federal government thinks it is important that action should be taken.' Ibid., vol. 2113, file 23-2-4, 'Welfare – Federal-Provincial Continuing Committee on Fiscal and Economic Matters, 1958–1965,' George Davidson to R.M. Burns, 13 June 1958. Five years later, when finance department officials proposed scrapping all shared-cost programs in return for transferring tax points to the provinces, Health and Welfare once again vigorously defended the critical importance of federal program leadership through conditional grants. 'The ability and willingness of the provinces to establish assistance programs on an adequate basis, without federal support, has not been demonstrated. Since the establishment of the unemployment assistance program, there have been dramatic improvements in the provincial assistance programs. The provinces themselves and outside welfare observers, such as the Canadian Welfare Council, have attributed the improvements, in large measure, to the federal support available through a specific grant program.' Ibid., vol. 2311, file 251-15-1, vol. 7, 'Alternative Approaches in the Administration of Public Assistance Programs,' 24 July 1963. Given the virtual disappearance of shared-cost program initiatives by Ottawa in the social policy field in recent years, these arguments are worth reiterating.

26 Metropolitan Toronto Records and Archives (MTRA), RG 5.1, box 47, file 49A, 'Shelter – 1941–1965,' 'Minutes of meeting, Shelter Allowance Committee,' 9 February 1951, pointing out that 'monthly rental allowances on behalf of a family should not exceed $40.00.' Almost ten years later Toronto's welfare commissioner, Robena Morris, was still arguing that 'in so far as possible rental allowances be held to $40.00 a month for families of two, three, and four.' Ibid., 'Minutes of meeting of district welfare officers,' 11 August 1960; ibid., box 29, file 372B, 'Increases in Food Allowances,' 8 March 1960.

27 Social Planning Council of Metropolitan Toronto, *Social Allowances in Ontario: An Historical Analysis of General Welfare Assistance and Family Benefits (with*

special focus on adequacy of allowances) 1961–1976, July 1977, 21, 56. In making its calculations of minimum budgetary adequacy, the Toronto SPC study used estimates contained in its annual *Guides to Family Budgeting*, published regularly since 1949. These estimates remained the most detailed, indeed almost the only attempts to define and price a minimum budgetary standard of adequacy in Canada throughout the 1950s, 1960s, and 1970s and were regularly consulted (although never implemented) by federal and provincial welfare officials.

28 AO, RG 49, MS 755, Clippings, reel 199, 'Relief Too Low: Welfare Council,' *Toronto Telegram*, 31 January 1961; 'Relief Aid "Ridiculous,"' *Toronto Telegram* 12 January 1961; 'Relief System Can't Cope with Rising Poverty,' *Toronto Star*, 17 January 1961; 'War on Poverty Urged,' *Globe and Mail*, 13 February 1961; 'Demoralizing, Unjust, Attack Welfare Aid,' *Toronto Star*, 17 February 1961; 'They Live – On 50 Cents a Day,' *Toronto Telegram*, 30 January 1962.

29 Ibid., Pierre Berton, 'What You Don't Know about Relief,' *Toronto Star*, 3 February 1961; 'The Shame of Public Charity,' *Toronto Star*, 6 February 1961.

30 Ibid., Pierre Berton, 'The Shame of Public Charity – They Still Can't Pay the Rent,' *Toronto Star*, 27 February 1961.

31 Ibid., George Bryant, 'Hunger Never Far for Thousands on Metro Relief,' *Toronto Star*, 25 February 1961.

32 Ibid., 'Meals Poor But No Starvation,' *Toronto Telegram*, 10 March 1961; 'Degrading Lineups for Relief Blasted,' *Toronto Star*, 3 March 1961; 'Human Dignity,' *Niagara Falls Review*, 23 March 1961; 'Nate Rips Tales of Starved Tots,' *Toronto Telegram*, 22 March 1961; 'Cecile Backs U.S. Food Stamp Plan,' *Toronto Star*, 6 February 1961. Some of the press was less sympathetic. 'In many instances the difficulty is not lack of money but mismanagement of money; some families can manage on $50 a week, some cannot manage on $75. Every social worker knows of families which would be ill-housed, ill-fed, and ill-clad even if they were showered with gold. They are poor in character. What does one do about them?' asked the *Globe and Mail*, in 'Poverty in the Land,' 14 February 1961.

33 MTRA, RG 5.1, box 98, file 46.17.3, 'GWA Jan/58–Nov/65, "District Work – Minutes of Meetings,"' file 5, 3 January 1961, 25 August 1960; file 46.17.4, 'GWA–District Work–Financial Assistance, Dec/59–May/61,' box 99, file 2, memo from E. Songhurst, section supervisor, to Robena Morris, 9 January 1961.

34 Ibid., box 34, file 46.3, Robena Morris to Alderman Alex Hodgins enclosed in 'Board of Control Report no. 31, Adopted by City Council on Nov 7/60, Report no. 14 of the Committee on Public Welfare 20 October 1960.'

35 AO, RG 49, MS 755, reel no. 211, Clippings, 'Public Welfare' 1962, 'At Last a Break for our Heartbreak Homes,' *Toronto Star*, 10 February 1962; MTRA, RG 5.1, box 47, file 49A, 'Shelter 1941–1965,' memo from Robena Morris to Mary Temple, chairman, Committee on Public Welfare, 17 January 1963; file 83, Mayor Donald Summerville to Louis Cecile, 'Brief Respecting Adequacy of

Allowances Provided for Separate Individuals in the Regulations Made Under the General Welfare Assistance Act,' nd but circa 1961 pointing out that maximum shelter allowances for single people (including heat, light, and water) had been held at $25 a month; box 98, file 46.17.3, 'GWA – Jan/58–Nov/65, "District Work – Minutes of Meetings,' file 5, 1 June 1965; box 34, file 46.1, 'GWA 36-81,' 'Brief Respecting Contribution by Provincial Government Towards Administrative and Servicing Costs and Supplementary Assistance as Related to the General Welfare Assistance Act and Regulations,' n.d but circa 1961.

36 AO, RG 3, Frost Papers, box 158, file 228G, James Band to R.A. Farrell, Premier's Office, 7 March 1961; RG 29-01, box 45, file 1809, James Band to R.A. Farrell, 31 July 1962.

37 MTRA, RG 5.1, box 34, file 46.1, 'GWA 36-81,' report by Robena Morris for Fred Beavis, chairman, Committee on Public Welfare, 'Regulations Made under the General Welfare Assistance Act,' 12 January 1961.

38 AO, RG 29-01, box 63, file 2465, memos from Wanda Boor to A.T. Bosanquet, 23 August and 31 May 1960; E.W. Littleford to James Band, 'Re: City of Toronto Charge Backs,' 12 September 1960.

39 AO, RG 3, Frost Papers, box 158, file 228G, James Band to R.A. Farrell, 7 March 1961; R.A. Farrell to Leslie Frost, 9 March 1961; Leslie Frost to Louis Cecile, 9 March 1961.

40 The comment concerning 'the lack of data to determine the adequacy of the present old age pension of $55 a month' appears in Dr Robert M. Clark's advisory report for the federal government, *Economic Security for the Aged in the United States and Canada: A Report Prepared for the Government of Canada* (Ottawa 1960), as cited in memo on 'Minimum Family Budget(s): Project Outline,' Research Branch, Canadian Welfare Council, March 1960, City of Toronto Archives (CTA), SC 40, box 37, file 3; NA, RG 29, vol. 2311, file 251-15-1, vol. 7, memorandum for the Federal-Provincial Conference, 26 and 27 July 1963, 'Alternative Approaches in the Administration of Public Assistance Programs – Categorical Versus General Assistance: Means Test Versus Needs Test,' 24 July 1963.

41 AO, RG 29-01, box 51, file 2058, James Band to Louis Cecile, 6 July 1962 'Re: Budgetary Allowances'; MTRA, RG 5.1, file 83, Mayor Donald Summerville to Louis Cecile, 'Brief Respecting Adequacy of Allowances Provided for Separate Individuals in the Regulations Made under the General Welfare Assistance Act,' nd but circa 1962.

42 AO, RG 29-01, box 51, file 2058, James Band to Louis Cecile, 'Re: Budgetary Allowances,' 6 July 1962; RG 3, Robarts Papers, box 317, file 'Minister – Social and Family Services Nov 61–Dec 65,' Louis Cecile to Robarts, 11 July 1962. Under Old Age Assistance, individuals were allowed a basic liquid asset exemption of $1000 in calculating their eligibility. For married couples the liquid asset exemption was $2000. The assets of those getting benefits through blind

persons and disability allowances were calculated on the basis of the income they would yield if used to purchase a government annuity. Further evidence that Band's prime concern was restricting payment through these programs emerged in his subsequent discussions with Ottawa. As federal officials noted, 'Ontario's complaints about existing categorical programs were primarily related to the rigid regulations that have been developed for the treatment of property and income. There was concern that in some instances persons with large amounts of liquid assets may qualify for an allowance.' NA, RG 29, vol. 921, memo to file, 'Discussions with Officials of the Province of Ontario on Unemployment Assistance, 4th and 5th February, 1963,' 6 February 1963.

43 NA, RG 29, vol. 921, 'Discussions with Officials of the Province of Ontario on Unemployment Assistance,' 6 February 1963; Clifford Williams, *Decades of Service: A History of the Ontario Ministry of Community and Social Services, 1930–1980* (Toronto 1984), 80; Harvey Simmons, *Unbalanced: Mental Health Policy in Ontario 1930–1989* (Toronto 1991), 116–17.

44 AO, RG 29-01, box 66, file 2568, transcript of Welfare Officers Association meeting, 10 June 1963.

45 On the growing impact of the 'culture of poverty' thesis pioneered by anthropologist Oscar Lewis within the United States in the early 1960s see Katz, *The Undeserving Poor*, 9–35. Michael Harrington's *The Other America: Poverty in the United States* (New York 1962), became the most powerful source for disseminating the idea of a culture of poverty. As Harrington defined it, 'Poverty ... is a culture, an institution, a way of life ... The family structure of the poor ... is different from that of the rest of the society ... There is ... a language of the poor, a psychology of the poor, a world view of the poor' (20). As Katz points out, although the moralizing assumptions about the poor put forward by culture-of-poverty theorists were easily appropriated by conservatives as part of a backlash against welfare beginning in the 1970s, the idea really originated from within a liberal social science perspective. 'By defining dependent people as passive, in the 1960s liberal social science enhanced its own role. Without the assistance of liberal intellectuals, dependent people would remain mired in their own degradation' (22–3).

46 Ontario, Deputy of Public Welfare, *Long-Term Assistance Families: A Joint Study by the Departments of Public Welfare of the Province of Ontario and City of Toronto* (January 1964); *Long-Term Assistance Families: A Rehabilitation Project by the Department of Public Welfare of the Province of Ontario and the City of Hamilton* (November 1964); AO, RG 29, series 749, box 2, file 2-9, 'A Review of Public Welfare Services to Long-Term Assistance Families in the City of Windsor (March 1966).'

47 *Long-Term Assistance Families ... Toronto*, foreword.

48 Ibid., 9; *Long-Term Assistance Families ... Hamilton*, 4.

49 *Long-Term Assistance Families ... Toronto*, 22–5, 29–30, 32, 13; *Long-Term*

Assistance Families ... Hamilton, 3, 6, 10; 'A Review of Public Welfare Services ... in Windsor,' 28.

50 *Long-Term Assistance Families ... Toronto*, 37, 19, 21, 27; 'A Review of Public Welfare Services ... in the City of Windsor,' 27.

51 *Long-Term Assistance Families ... Toronto*, 6, 37–8. James Patterson has also pointed to the power of conservative assumptions about poverty within the United States which prevailed well into the 1960s. 'When Americans "rediscovered" poverty in the early 1960s social scientists were appalled to realize how little they knew about it ... Americans, once prosperity returned in the 1940s [were ready] to put the awful Depression years out of memory and to reaffirm the attitudes, only slightly altered, that had characterized progressives in the 1920s. Chief among these attitudes – one that always seemed to flourish in good times – was optimism that economic growth would ultimately conquer all. The market ... would soon eliminate privation. And welfare, blight on the good society, would "wither away."' Patterson, *America's Struggle against Poverty, 1900–1980* (Cambridge 1981), 79–80.

52 NA, RG 29, vol. 1527, file 201-16-2A, 'Canada Assistance Plan – Unemployment Assistance,' minutes of the first meeting of the 'Committee on Unemployment Assistance,' 26 March 1962; vol. 1629, file 7, 'Unemployment Assistance,' 'Meeting on Unemployment Assistance,' 8 November 1962; Waldo Monteith to George Nowlan, 23 August 1962.

53 Ibid., vol. 1526, file 201-16-2 pt 1, 'Unemployment Assistance, 1960–68,' R.B. Splane to Joe Willard, 'Committee on Unemployment Assistance Legislation,' 21 June 1962; vol. 2113, file 23-1-5, vol. 2, 'Redrafting the Unemployment Assistance Act,' nd but circa 1963, 17; vol. 1527, file 201-16-2A, 'Canada Assistance Plan – Unemployment Assistance,' minutes of the second and third meetings, 'Committee on Unemployment Assistance,' 6 April and 4 May 1962 (my emphasis); on the early planning for a new comprehensive general assistance act within National Health and Welfare see vol. 1629, file 7, R.B. Splane to Joe Willard, 'Considerations Respecting the Amendment of the Unemployment Assistance Act,' 6 October 1960, and Splane to Willard, 'Proposals for a Public Assistance Program in Canada,' 13 April 1961. As Splane argued in 1960, amending the Unemployment Assistance Act would 'make it difficult to approach Parliament a second time in a year or two with a proposal for the passing of a general assistance act.' It is important to point out, however, that even in their earliest planning for a new comprehensive public assistance act, Health and Welfare officials ruled out the possibility of defining and meeting the components of need on a national basis, as advocated by the Canadian Welfare Council. In his 1961 memoranda, for example, Splane argued that any comprehensive new public assistance act, like unemployment assistance, 'would continue to allow the province to set its own definition of need, income limits, and other conditions,' since this would 'meet the objections that have been expressed by certain

provinces, notably Ontario, over the extent to which the three categorical programs limit the provinces in deciding on income levels and similar matters.' Ibid., vol. 2311, file 251-15-1, vol. 5, Splane to William Hamilton, 10 May 1961.

54 NA, RG 29, vol. 1629, file 7, Joe Willard to the minister, 'Assistance Legislation,' 14 August 1962.

55 Ibid., vol. 2113, file 23-1-5, vol. 2, 'Redrafting the Unemployment Assistance Act,' nd but circa July 1963.

56 Ibid., vol. 2311, file 251-15-1, vol. 5, Waldo Monteith to William Hamilton, 10 May 1961 (my emphasis).

57 Ibid.

58 Kenneth Bryden, *Old Age Pensions and Policy-Making in Canada* (Montreal 1974), 128, 144. The further $10 hike in OAS by the Pearson administration in 1963 was something of a policy fiasco. The original idea was that it would be eventually funded through contributions levied under the proposed Canada Pension Plan, the centrepiece of Pearson's 1963 campaign. Once Quebec caught Ottawa by surprise in July 1963 by announcing that it was going ahead with its own contributory pension plan and would contract out of any federal scheme, this option was foreclosed. As Tom Kent later recounted in his memoirs: 'Our proposed [contributory pension legislation] included a prompt increase in OAS from $65 to $75 a month, to be financed from the contributory revenues of the CPP. In effect, the CPP included a small flat-rate benefit of $10 a month to be paid universally, irrespective of earnings. Clearly this could not be done, as an OAS benefit for all Canadians, if people in Quebec ... were not contributing to CPP. Contracting out meant ... that the extra $10 must be separated from the CPP and paid out of other federal revenue. This was financially unpleasant, but there was no point in delay. The promised $10 soon was what the public was most aware of ... In the event, the decisions were taken, just in time to be announced on 9 September ... [T]he $10 increase in OAS would be separated from the CPP and would be effective the next month.' Tom Kent, *A Public Purpose: An Experience of Liberal Opposition and Canadian Government* (Montreal 1988), 261–2.

59 NA, RG 29, vol. 1623, file 15, memorandum to cabinet 'Re: 1) Benefit Increases in Categorical Allowances; 2) A New Approach to Public Assistance,' 20 November 1963.

60 Ibid., vol. 1526, file 201-10-2 pt 2, Joe Willard to the Minister, 'Implications of Pension and Categorical Allowance Increases for the Administration of Public Assistance,' 15 July 1963.

61 Ibid.

62 Ibid., vol. 1526, file 201-16-2 pt 1, Joe Willard to the minister, 'Implications of Pension Increases for Other Provincial Assistance Programs and for Unemployment Assistance,' 29 April 1963.

63 NA, RG 29, vol. 1623, file 15, Background Paper for the Federal-Provincial Conference, 'Item 2 (b), Categorical Assistance Programs,' 11 November 1963;

vol. 2311, file 251-15-1, vol. 7, 'The Effect of the Levels of Benefit Under the Canada Pension Plan on Benefits Granted under Public Assistance Programs,' nd but circa August 1963. Health and Welfare officials argued in this memo that the inauguration of a contributory pension scheme would sever, once and for all, the linkage between federal old age security and allowance standards payable through provincial and local social assistance. 'While it cannot be said with certainty that the benefit levels under the insurance program will not affect the level of assistance payments, there is no necessary or direct relationship between the two ... While the maximum benefit levels under the categorical assistance programs have in the past been the same as those under the Old Age Security Act, this relationship will cease with the adoption of the Canada Pension Plan ... [A] clear distinction can be expected to emerge between benefits obtained through contributions under the Canada Pension Plan and benefits paid to meet minimum requirements under assistance programs. The Canada Pension Plan is designed to ... provide ... a benefit payment sufficient to support a living standard of modest comfort. General assistance measures of the kind developed by the provinces and their municipalities are designed on the other hand to provide, to persons able to pass a needs test, only a minimum level of adequacy. A wage related insurance program such as the Canada Pension Plan may be a factor in influencing public views on the concept of minimum adequacy. However, there is nothing to indicate how direct or immediate this influence may be.'

64 NA, RG 29, vol. 2113, file 23-1-3, Joe Willard to Ralph Andrews, 30 December 1963; vol. 2112, file 22-4-6 pt 2, Proceedings of Federal-Provincial Conference, 26–29 November 1963, 'Opening Statement by the Prime Minister of Canada,' 13–15.

65 Ibid., Proceedings of Federal-Provincial Conference, 26–29 November 1963, 'Opening Statement of Prime Minister of Ontario,' 15–16.

66 NA, RG 29, vol. 2311, file 251-151-1, vol. 5, Waldo Monteith to William Hamilton, 10 May 1961.

67 Ibid., vol. 2113, file 23-1-5, vol. 2, background memorandum to members of the Interdepartmental Committee on Public Assistance, 'Redrafting the Unemployment Assistance Act,' nd but circa autumn 1963. In its 1961 brief to the Senate Committee on Manpower and Employment, the Canadian Welfare Council called for the provision of general public assistance at adequate rates 'by allowing federal sharing of costs ... only if the procedures for determining rates of assistance assure the recipient at least a minimum standard of health and decency.' To establish what such a minimum standard might be, the council called upon Ottawa, through special studies and research, to 'establish uniform components for a public assistance budget ... that make provision for disparities in such living costs as rent.' Federal cost-sharing would only occur 'where these components are used as a basis for determining the actual amount of assistance to be granted.' On the provincial quest for greater 'flexibility' in setting assistance allowances

see vol. 1623, file 15, memorandum to cabinet 'Re: 1) Benefit Increases in Categorical Allowances; 2) a New Approach to Public Assistance,' 20 November 1963. The memo noted that 'several provinces' preferred the Unemployment Assistance Act's 'more flexible' approach to the 'provincial determination of rates and the establishment of conditions of eligibility.' Categorical programs had 'ensured a high degree of uniformity in benefits across Canada,' and the memo went on to point out the 'accompanying risk of less generous benefits' that might be paid through 'any new program ... administered at the municipal level.'

68 Ibid., vol. 1527, file 201-16-2A, minutes of the third meeting of the 'Committee on Unemployment Assistance,' 4 May 1962 (my emphasis).

69 Ibid., vol. 2113, file 23-105, vol. 2, 'Redrafting the Unemployment Assistance Act.' Within the United States, similar attempts to enforce national minimum standards of assistance for mother-led welfare families upon the states through the federal government's Aid to Dependent Children program were also defeated. As Patterson points out, 'the legislation had originally included a provision that required states, as a condition of getting federal aid, to provide a "reasonable subsistence compatible with decency and health" ... Conservatives, led by Virginia senator Harry Byrd, feared that federal intervention would destroy states' rights, especially over race relations ... The southerners joined fiscal conservatives to enlarge local discretion. As finally passed, the key clause merely asked states to fund the program, "as far as practicable under the conditions in such states."' By the 1960s, 'all but six states set their standards for AFDC below the federal definitions of poverty, and all but sixteen states failed to appropriate the money necessary to meet their own low standards.' Patterson, *America's Struggle Against Poverty*, 68, 163.

70 NA, RG 29, vol. 1623, file 15, Federal-Provincial Conference, 25–29 November 1963, 'Position Statement on Public Assistance (Item 2(b), Categorical Assistance Programs).' Leslie Bella argues that federal officials wanted the Canada Assistance Plan to contain 'a universal standard of adequacy in welfare programs across Canada,' but dropped this objective in response to Quebec's vehement opposition to the idea in 1965. However, it is clear federal Health and Welfare officials had abandoned the feasibility of such objectives as early as the spring of 1962 in discussions surrounding the reform of unemployment assistance; Leslie Bella, 'The Provincial Role in the Canadian Welfare State: The Influence of Provincial Social Policy Initiatives on the Design of the Canada Assistance Plan,' *Canadian Public Administration* 22, 3 (fall 1979), 447. As R.B. Splane, former director of unemployment assistance in National Health and Welfare and one of the key figures in the CAP negotiations, has subsequently pointed out, '"standards" was both a term and a concept that we sought to avoid. No serious consideration was given to a "universal standard of adequacy in welfare programs across Canada" for two reasons. First, because it would have been impossible to formulate in specific terms and, second, because it would have violated the principle that the

terms and conditions of assistance are for the provinces to decide.' Richard B. Splane, 'Social Development in Alberta: The Federal-Provincial Interplay,' in Jacqueline S. Ismael, *Canadian Social Welfare Policy: Federal and Provincial Dimensions* (Montreal 1985), 180. My interpretation of the origins of CAP also differs significantly from that given by Rank Dyck in his 'Canada Assistance Plan: The Ultimate in Cooperative Federalism,' *Canadian Public Administration* 19, 4 (winter 1976). Dyck ignores the critical importance of Ottawa's unhappiness with the Unemployment Assistance Act and provincial anger at federally inspired increases in categorical allowance programs as triggering factors in the quest for public assistance reform. Splane, in contrast, has argued correctly that the origins of CAP can be found as emerging 'primarily ... from the policy lines associated with the Unemployment Assistance Act. Both the strengths and the defects of that measure contributed to its being the fulcrum for the integration of public assistance' (178), although he also omits reference to the impact of categorical benefit increases upon provincial demands for a new and more 'flexible' social assistance framework.

71 Kent, *A Public Purpose*, 120, 266–9.

72 NA, RG 29, vol. 2114, file 23-3-5, memorandum from R.B. Splane to Joe Willard, 'Interdepartmental Committee on the Federal-Provincial Conference,' 23 September 1963; vol. 1623, file 15, memo by Robert Bryce for the Cabinet Committee on Federal-Provincial Relations, 'Proposed Position on Shared Cost Programmes and Their Relation to Fiscal Arrangements,' 19 March 1964.

73 Ibid., vol. 1623, file 15, Joe Willard to Judy LaMarsh, 'Public Assistance Shared Cost Programs,' 27 March 1964; vol. 2311, file 251-15-1 vol. 7, background paper for the federal-provincial conference, 26 and 27 July 1963, 'Alternative Approaches in the Administration of Public Assistance Programs,' 24 July 1963; vol. 2114, file 23-3-5, R.B. Splane to Joe Willard, 'Interdepartmental Committee on the Federal-Provincial Conference,' 23 September 1963, in which Splane noted 'there is a strong movement at the highest policy level below the Cabinet to terminate a number of these programs without sufficient consideration of the consequences'; vol. 1623, file 15, 'Federal-Provincial Public Assistance Programs,' 'Notes on the Discussion by Federal and Provincial Officials of the Relation between Conditional Grant Programmes and Fiscal Arrangements,' 13 February 1964. It is clear that, outside Quebec, the contracting-out proposal pitted federal *and* provincial officials in health and welfare departments against their counterparts in finance and treasury within both levels of government. As Finance officials recognized in 1960, 'it became obvious that representations made by the provinces [to end cost-shared programs] stem from the financial or Treasury Departments and that these representations are directed primarily to their counterparts in Ottawa ... Ontario officials also frankly admitted that Departments administering agreements were satisfied with arrangements and that dissatisfaction was essentially confined to the Treasury.' Ibid., vol. 2113, file 23-2-4, comptroller of the Treasury to Ken Taylor, deputy minister of finance, 'Re Conditional

Grants and Shared Cost Programmes,' 13 January 1960. Whereas fiscal control agencies found spending within cost-sharing programs hard to police, for exactly this reason operating departments liked them. The availability of '50 cent dollars' was a powerful incentive for program expansion, and the conditions attached by Ottawa provided provincial officials in line departments with useful arguments for extracting the resources needed to upgrade administrative standards, points explicitly acknowledged by federal and provincial officials in the discussions cited above. As Richard Simeon and Ian Robinson argue, 'far from weakening the provincial governments, shared cost programs strengthened them, allowing them to increase their revenues, expand their bureaucracies, and deliver programs that their citizens wanted ... [E]ven if there were disagreement on detail, there was fundamental agreement on the goals underlying these programs and in the legitimacy of federal leadership in promoting them.' See their *State, Society, and the Development of Canadian Federalism*, (Toronto 1990), 150.

74 NA, RG 29, vol. 1623, file 15, 'Notes on the Discussion by Federal and Provincial Officials of the Relation between Conditional Grant Programmes and Fiscal Arrangements,' 13 February 1964.

75 Ibid., memo by Robert Bryce, Department of Finance, 'Possible Alternative Approach to "Contracting-Out,"' 19 March 1964.

76 In him memoirs, Kent notes that he and other key advisers in the Pearson administration were 'very poorly prepared' for the November 1963 federal-provincial conference and that, at bottom, despite the rhetoric of 'co-operative federalism,' Pearson's government was not really committed to the 'opting out' proposals or significant fiscal decentralization. 'Our preparations had been stultified by the inhibitions, within the Ottawa system, to recognition of the provinces' need for a larger share of taxation.' On the one hand, seven out of ten provinces 'had governments of other parties ... It was not a political atmosphere conducive to the "surrender" of tax revenue to the provinces.' On the other hand, finance department and other key federal officials feared that 'if the federal government conceded financial resources at all quickly, it would lose its precious power to manage the economy.' Only intense anger from Jean Lesage at the April 1964 federal-provincial conference, including the threat of going it alone on contributory old age pensions, broke through this mentality to permit significant and unscheduled increases in federal income tax abatements to the provinces, along with a modest degree of contracting out for Quebec in extended family allowances and student loans. See the fascinating recounting of this episode in Kent, *A Public Purpose*, 269–79.

77 AO, RG 29-01, box 26, file 1084, Louis Cecile to R.A. Farrell, Prime Minister's Office, 13 November 1963; file 1089, Louis Cecile to W.M. McIntyre, secretary of the cabinet, 20 March 1964.

78 Proceedings of the Federal-Provincial Conference, 26–29. November 1963, 'Opening Statement by the Honourable John Robarts, Prime Minister of Ontario'; RG 29, vol. 2112, file 22-4-6 pt 1, 'Notes on Federal-Provincial Plenary Confer-

ence, November 26–29 1963,' 18; Ontario *Hansard*, 14 April 1964, 2074. Compare Robarts conciliatory statement in 1963 with this earlier lament from Ontario's Treasury Department in 1958: 'In general, conditional grants can be said to have the disadvantages of placing provinces under heavy political and economic pressure, affecting the authority of the provincial treasurers over their spending departments, establishing pressure groups and inhibiting reconsideration of long-established expenditures and of committing provinces to programs which, although nowadays rarely cancelled, are altered sufficiently often to create great uncertainty in the minds of budget planners as to just how large will be the grants each year which they will have to match.' AO, RG 6, series II–6, box 10, file 'Conditional Grants and Shared Cost Programs,' 5 September 1958.

79 'Notes on Federal-Provincial Plenary Conference, November 26–29, 1963'; Kent, *A Public Purpose*, 272–9; 'Notes on the Discussion by Federal and Provincial Officials of the Relation between Conditional Grant Programmes and Fiscal Arrangements,' 13 February 1964.

CHAPTER 7   *The War on Poverty*

1 Carl M. Brauer, 'Kennedy, Johnson, and the War on Poverty,' in Donald T. Critchlow and Ellis W. Hawley, eds., *Poverty and Public Policy in Modern America* (Chicago 1989), 232–5. Other good treatments of the American War on Poverty can also be found in Michael Katz, *The Undeserving Poor: From the War on Poverty to the War on Welfare* (New York 1989), 79–123, and Allan Matusow, *The Unraveling of America: A History of Liberalism in the 1960s* (New York 1984), chapters 4, 8, 9.

2 K.J. Rea, *The Prosperous Years: The Economic History of Ontario, 1939–75* (Toronto 1985), 34; Ontario *Hansard*, 18 March 1964, 1757; 'The U.S. War on Poverty,' *Globe and Mail* editorial, 20 March 1964; Norm Ibsen, 'Ontario War on Poverty Based on Specialization,' London *Free Press*, 18 August 1966.

3 Ontario *Hansard*, 18 March 1964, 1768–74; 14 April 1964, 2020–9. On the revitalization of the Ontario NDP in 1964 see Donald MacDonald's political memoirs, *The Happy Warrior: Political Memoirs* (Toronto 1988), 149–54.

4 Roger Graham aptly describes Cecile as 'the most inconspicuous' of Frost's cabinet ministers. See his *Old Man Ontario: Leslie M. Frost* (Toronto 1990), 308. The only reference to Cecile in Allan McDougall's biography of John Robarts is to his retirement. See his *John P. Robarts* (Toronto 1986), 178.

5 Ontario *Hansard*, 18 March 1965, 1760, 1775, 1785; 24 March 1965, 1940, 1945, 1978, 1981; 14 April 1965, 2035–6, 2040, 2043, 2046; *Globe and Mail* editorial, 16 February 1965.

6 Archives of Ontario (AO), RG 29, series 749, file 2.11, memo from B. Dymes to James Band, 'Statement on Supplementary Payments in Ontario,' 17 March 1967.

7 AO, RG 3, Robarts Papers, box 323, file 'Poverty: Social & Family Services, Jan–Dec 1965,' copy of Ontario Federation of Labour report, 'Poverty in Ontario,

1964,' adopted at 8th annual convention, October 1964. For the U.S. definition of a poverty line of $3000 (1961 dollars) annually for families see Brauer, 'Kennedy, Johnson, and the War on Poverty,' 227.

8 AO, RG 29-01, box 45, file 1811, Louis Cecile to John Robarts, 2 December 1964.

9 AO, RG 3, Robarts Papers, box 323, file 'Poverty: Social & Family Services, Jan–Dec 1965,' Louis Cecile to Robarts, 'What has been done to study the "War on Poverty" in the United States so as to attack the root causes of poverty,' nd but circa spring/summer 1965 (a memo written by James Band). Robarts's comment, 'A very interesting memo – Please file,' is handwritten on the margin.

10 For the ease with which 'culture of poverty' arguments could be transformed into blaming the poor for their plight see Katz, *The Undeserving Poor*, 124–84.

11 AO, RG 3, Robarts Papers, box 323, file 'Poverty – Social & Family Services, Jan–Dec 1965,' John Robarts to Patrick McGrath, 25 February 1965.

12 National Archives of Canada (NA), RG 29, accession 86-87/095, box 2, file 200-1-20A pt 1, Lester Pearson to all cabinet ministers, 27 January 1965.

13 Biographical background on Tom Kent and his role in the Liberal Party's post-1958 revival can be found in his memoirs, *A Public Purpose: An Experience of Liberal Opposition and Canadian Government* (Montreal 1988) as well as in a profile by journalist Scott Young, 'The War on Poverty: Latest Communique: All Quiet on the Canadian Front,' *Globe and Mail*, 29 October 1965.

14 Kent, *A Public Purpose*, 167–8.

15 Ibid., 354, 357 (my emphasis).

16 George Bain, 'The State of Welfare,' *Globe and Mail*, 16 April 1965; 'Poverty Fighters Posed,' *Toronto Star*, 22 May 1965; Scott Young, 'The War on Poverty.' As Young put it, 'this war is being fought only as an essential preliminary scouting operation by a tiny patrol ... Any dead-broke, uneducated Canadian leaning against a rotting slum doorpost should not raise his hopes too high. This war is not really for his generation.' In his memoirs, Kent is quite sensitive to the charge that 'Canada's "war on poverty" was ... a political gimmick: launched to meet a political need, winning much attention for a few months, and abandoned when the Liberals' main objective, to win a majority in the 1965 election, was not achieved. That perception became entrenched, naturally enough, with the abandonment.' Kent's own account of the launching of the War on Poverty gives considerable credence to this interpretation, however. Kent, *A Public Purpose*, 353–4.

17 Kent, *A Public Purpose*, 356–8; NA, RG 29, vol. 1606, file 7, 'The War on Poverty,' text of address by Tom Kent to provincial officials, second meeting, 18–19 October 1965.

18 Kent, *A Public Purpose*, 356–64; RG 29, vol. 1606, Kent, 'The War on Poverty'; vol. 2110, file 21-2-2, vol. 1, 'The Profile of Poverty,' December 1965. The absence of any reference to native people or immigrants by the Special Planning Secretariat was picked up early on by officials from National Health and Welfare.

See vol. 1626, file 5, memo from R.B. Splane to Joe Willard, 'Meeting with Mr. Tom Kent on the work of the Special Planning Secretariat for the War on Poverty,' 19 April 1965. Apart from the work of the Company of Young Canadians, however, the SPS generally ignored poverty within aboriginal communities, nor were officials from Indian Affairs or Citizenship and Immigration included within its departmental representation. As the bureaucratic constituencies represented within the SPS suggest, Kent's interests in fighting poverty lay almost exclusively within the twin spheres of labour market training and regional economic development. The real end-products of his War on Poverty would be the Department of Manpower and Immigration, which he established and headed as deputy minister, and the Department of Regional Economic Expansion, a department he would also work closely with as the first head of the Cape Breton Development Corporation following his departure from government in 1971.

19 Kent, 'The War on Poverty,' 18–19 October 1965; Kent, *A Public Purpose,* 382–4.

20 NA, RG 29, vol. 2111, file 21-1-3, vol. 4, 'Income Maintenance Measures in Canada,' background memo prepared for the Conference on Poverty and Opportunity, November 1965.

21 Ibid., vol. 2110, file 21-1-2, vol. 1, R.B. Bryce to Joe Willard, 15 November 1965; Joe Willard to R.B. Bryce, 23 November 1965. Willard agreed that 'some of the statements in the document might prove embarrassing to the government if they were used in a critical way by the members of the opposition.' John Osborne eventually published his critique of federal social programs as a private article the following year. See ibid., vol. 2104, file 20-P-22, copy of John Osborne, 'Canada Combats Poverty Through Social Policy,' *Journal of the American Public Welfare Association,* April 1966; AO, RG 3, Robarts Papers, box 323, file 'Poverty – Conference on Poverty & Opportunity: Jan-Dec 1965,' memo from Don Stevenson to Robarts, 'Notes on the fed-prov meeting of Sept 8 1965 in Ottawa to plan the Agenda of a conference on poverty and opportunity,' 10 September 1965.

22 Kent, *A Public Purpose,* 383; AO, RG 3, Robarts Papers, box 323, file 'Poverty: Conference on Poverty & Opportunity, 1965,' copy of opening statement by Ian Macdonald at the Conference on Poverty and Opportunity, December 1965; file 'Poverty: Conference on Poverty & Opportunity, Jan–Dec 1965,' memo from H. Ian Macdonald to J.K. Reynolds, 30 September 1965; memo from Don W. Stevenson, director, Economics Branch, Department of Economics and Development, 'Notes for the Meeting Organizing the Poverty and Opportunity Conference, 3 September 1965.'

23 AO, RG 3, Robarts Papers, box 323, file 'Poverty – Conference on Poverty & Opportunity: Jan–Dec 1965,' memo from Ian Macdonald to J.K. Reynolds, Premier's Office, 'A Suggested Ontario Approach to the Problem of Poverty,' 30 September 1965; memo by Don Stevenson, 'Notes for the Meeting Organizing

the Poverty and Opportunity Conference,' 3 September 1965; memo by Don
Stevenson, 'A Few Facts on Income Distribution in Ontario,' 7 September 1965;
RG 29-01, box 45, file 1790, 'Notes for the Federal-Provincial Conference on
Poverty and Opportunity, December 1965.'

24 Ibid., memo by Department of Labour, 'Labour Standards and Poverty in
Ontario,' 22 November 1965. As the labour department pointed out, maximum
ceilings for assistance established by the Department of Public Welfare assumed
that '[basic] needs ... for a single person living in Toronto [can be met] by an
income of $77.00 per month and for a family of four (2 adults and 2 children ages
10 to 15 years) by $190.00 per month. On the other hand, findings of the Toronto
Social Planning Council of Metropolitan Toronto suggest that a health and
decency budget for a family of four ... is approximately $85.00 per week.'

25 Ibid., box 323, file 'Poverty: Conference on Poverty & Opportunity, 1965,'
'Notes for the Federal-Provincial Conference on Poverty and Opportunity,'
prepared by Department of Public Welfare, December 1965.

26 Ibid., box 323, file 'Poverty: Conference on Poverty & Opportunity, 1965,'
opening statement by Ian Macdonald, chairman of Ontario delegation, to the
conference.

27 Ibid., box 323, file 'Poverty – Conference on Poverty & Opportunity: Jan–Dec
1965,' Ian Macdonald, 'A Suggested Ontario Approach to the Problem of
Poverty,' 30 September 1965.

28 On Kent's views of promoting 'opportunity' rather than 'welfare' models towards
poverty see his A Public Purpose, 354–7, as well as his draft of Pearson's covering letter to the premiers re the poverty conference. NA, RG 29, vol. 2110, file
21-1-2, vol. 1, Lester Pearson to all provincial premiers, 16 August 1965; Scott
Young, 'The War on Poverty.' AO, RG 3, Robarts Papers, box 323, file 'Poverty – Conference on Poverty & Opportunity: Jan–Dec 1965,' memo by Don
Stevenson, 'Notes on the fed-prov meeting of Sept 8 1965 in Ottawa to plan the
Agenda of a conference on poverty and opportunity,' 10 September 1965. As
Macdonald told Robarts: 'I heard some rumours in Ottawa of the formation of a
new Department of Manpower to take over manpower aspects of labour, immigration, and perhaps ARDA. Such a department would presumably also speak on
matters of educational discussion with the Provinces ... In designing our own
approach to regional development ... we must be in a position to take the initiative
in areas that the federal government has a related interest.' In this same memo,
Macdonald also told Robarts that 'my emphasis [at the conference] was placed on
opportunity as a positive and dynamic concept rather than on poverty as a static,
welfare concept.' Ibid., memo by Ian Macdonald to John Robarts, 'Conference on
Poverty and Opportunity,' 16 December 1965.

29 NA, RG 29, vol. 2110, file 21-1-2, vol. 1, 'Federal-Provincial Conference on
Poverty and Opportunity, Ottawa, December 7–10 1965: Summary of Panel
Reports,' Special Planning Secretariat, 9 February 1966.

30 Kent, *A Public Purpose*, 384; AO, RG 29-01, box 26, file 1085, C.J. Williams to James Band, 'Report on the Federal-Provincial Conference on Poverty and Opportunity, Ottawa, December 7 to 10 1965,' 13 December 1965 (original emphasis).

31 NA, RG 29, vol. 2116, file 24.1.2, John Osborne to Joe Willard, 'Special Planning Secretariat – Review of Operations,' 19 May 1966 (a scathing summary of the views of NHW officials on the irrelevance of the SPS and its work). See also file 24.1.2, memo by R.J. Phillips, director, Special Planning Secretariat, 'The Special Planning Secretariat,' 10 March 1966, which embodies the vagueness of the SPS mandate. According to Phillips, the purpose of the secretariat was to promote 'a continuous flow of information and ideas tending to bring individual provincial plans into some kind of relationship. This process can best be described as community development on an inter-provincial scale.' NHW officials rightly criticized the 'attitude of paternalism' implicit in this definition of the SPS mandate.

32 As cited in Clifford Williams, *Decades of Service: A History of the Ontario Ministry of Community and Social Services, 1930–1980* (Toronto 1984), 118 (my emphasis). Full equality of entitlement and treatment was not, in fact, extended. Deserted and unwed Indian wives were denied eligibility for mothers' allowances between 1958 and 1962, unlike their white counterparts, because welfare department field staff argued that the 'prospect of substantial income tempted unmarried Indian women to produce babies.' Ibid., 119.

33 AO, RG 29-01, box 45, file 1810, James Band to John Robarts, 31 July 1963; James Band to John Robarts, 30 August 1963; Louis Cecile to John Robarts, 8 November 1963. Band pointed out that Ontario's aboriginal population had jumped 15 per cent over the past four years; 35 per cent were living off-reserve and thus outside the responsibility of the federal government. He estimated that perhaps two-thirds of Ontario's northern native reserve population were 'absent therefrom and camping on the fringes of small municipalities.'

34 Ibid., James Band to Robarts, 30 August 1963; Louis Cecile to Robarts, 8 November 1963.

35 Ibid., Louis Cecile to John Robarts, 8 November 1963; James Band to Robarts, 30 August 1963. 'It may be advisable to consider an agreement with the Ottawa Government to transfer the total Indian question (with the exception of property rights) to the province, providing the Indians consent,' Band advised. 'At the same time, federal authorities might favour the transference of the necessary funds, which they now dispense through their own officers, to provincial jurisdiction. Almost all the matters which relate to the well being of these more or less primitive people are susceptible of treatment under legislation common to the province as a whole.'

36 Ibid., James Band to John Robarts, 30 August 1963.

37 AO, RG 3, Robarts Papers, box 317, file 'Social and Family Service, Dept of,

Minister, 1961–67,' press release, 6 January 1966; RG 29-01, file 1107, verbatim
proceedings of 'Meeting of Federal-Provincial Working Group,' February 1964;
RG 29-01, box 45, file 1813, James Band to R.A. Farrell, 2 August 1966; Louis
Cecile to R.A. Farrell, 27 July 1966.

38 AO, RG 3, Robarts Papers, box 317, file 'Social and Family Service, Dept of,
    Minister, 1961–67,' press release, 1 January 1967; Williams, *Decades of Service*,
    120–1; RG 29-01, box 45, file 1813, Louis Cecile to John Robarts, 19 October
    1966. As Cecile initially interpreted the agreement, it provided federal cost-
    sharing for 'general services such as education, training, job placement, housing,
    health measures, recreation, and some phases of law enforcement ... together with
    any capital construction cost or the cost of purchasing buildings for community
    development purposes.' He also argued that 'if the native Indian population in a
    development area reached a 90% per capita figure, the Federal Government will
    be responsible for 90% of the expenditure in that development area.' Ottawa had
    no interest in such a wide-ranging and open-ended commitment to provincially
    administered northern development projects.

39 Williams, *Decades of Service*, 120–1.

40 Ibid.

41 AO, RG 29-01, box 26, file 1092, C.J. Williams, 'Confidential Report on the
    Federal-Provincial Conference of Welfare Ministers, January 18 & 19, 1968,'
    22 January 1968.

CHAPTER 8   *The Canada Assistance Plan*

1 National Archives of Canada (NA), RG 29, accession 86-87/095, box 2, file 200-
   1-20 A pt 1, Judy LaMarsh to Lester Pearson, 5 February 1965. There have been
   several good but somewhat conflicting accounts published on the origins of the
   Canada Assistance Plan. The four most important are Rand Dyck, 'The Canada
   Assistance Plan: The Ultimate in Cooperative Federalism,' *Canadian Public
   Administration* 19, 4 (winter 1976), 587–602; Leslie Bella, 'The Provincial
   Role in the Canadian Welfare State: The Influence of Provincial Social Policy
   Initiatives on the Design of the Canada Assistance Plan,' *Canadian Public
   Administration* 22, 3, (fall 1979), 439–52; Richard B. Splane, 'Social Welfare
   Development in Alberta: The Federal-Provincial Interplay,' in J.S. Ismael, ed.,
   Canadian Social Welfare Policy (Edmonton 1985), 173–87; and Rodney
   Haddow, 'The Poverty Policy Community in Canada's Liberal Welfare State,' in
   William Coleman and Grace Skogstad, eds., *Policy Communities and Public
   Policy in Canada: A Structural Approach* (Mississauga 1990), 212–37. Haddow
   argues that 'during the 1960s the policy network in the poverty sector was ...
   state-directed,' pointing out that 'officials who worked in the sector usually
   shared a common professional background in social work and, when they did not,
   quickly became assimilated to the reformist norms that predominated in welfare

departments ... CAP emerged from this cooperative group of welfare officials. They reached a general consensus on reform in the [Public Welfare Division of the Canadian Welfare Council] in the late 1950s, and elaborated this in direct federal-provincial negotiations from 1960 to 1964' (218–219). None of Haddow's characterizations fit the role, personality, or training of Ontario's deputy minister of welfare, James Band.

2 Archives of Ontario (AO), RG 29-01, box 27, file 1107, verbatim proceedings of the 'Meeting of the Federal-Provincial Working Group on Welfare Programs,' Ottawa, 14–15 February 1964, 18, 27 (my emphasis). In pressing the need for action on public assistance reform on his minister, Judy LaMarsh, following the February meeting, Joe Willard also argued that 'some action in respect to public assistance is ... imperative in view of the repeated observations of the Auditor General on unemployment assistance in his recently tabled Report for 1963' as well as the 'attention ... being given by President Lyndon Johnson and the Government of the United States to measures to relieve and combat poverty.' NA, RG 29, vol. 2113, file 23-1-3, Joe Willard to Judy LaMarsh, 24 February 1964. At the February working group meeting, Nova Scotia deputy welfare minister Fred MacKinnon also commented on the importance of the growing public backlash against welfare because of its rising costs and inability to get at the roots of poverty: 'The public image ... of what we have been able to accomplish in this area is ... not good across Canada ... This is the area in which the magazines attack us. Maclean's magazine publishes articles about the growing relief mess; the Saturday Evening Post, Reader's Digest and so on, never miss an opportunity to take a poke at this ... We have made far less progress than we sometimes deceive ourselves into thinking we have made ... Our operation is a minimal one to determine eligibility and that only' (55–6).

3 NA, RG 29, vol. 2113, file 23-1-3, 71, 76, 201, 216. Unless mothers' allowances were included in shared-cost funding there could be no agreement on a new public assistance framework, James Band bluntly told federal officials. Federal officials conceded that Ottawa's complicated mothers' allowance deduction factor designed to exclude women and children on welfare from shared-cost unemployment assistance funding made little sense and was an administrative nightmare. 'I do not know of any agreement which appears to have a more complicated formula ... I have to reread it and reread it and think it through each time to understand what it really means,' Joe Willard observed (30–1). Band was the only provincial representative at the meeting to favour the reinstitution of 'work for relief' as a category eligible for shared-cost funding. 'During the depression days I had a program myself which I thought worked out very well ... I do not see anything wrong with that kind of operation,' Ontario's deputy minister argued. Other provincial officials did not agree. 'Work for relief is based on a myth,' Alberta's K.O. Mackenzie replied. 'There are not enough sidewalks to be

shovelled and not enough lawns to be cut.' The whole idea reminded New Brunswick's deputy minister 'of a system we had in New Brunswick where they used to auction off the poor in the fall ... So far as I am concerned this work for relief is exactly the same philosophy.' 'This turns into something like the workhouse days,' agreed Nova Scotia's deputy minister Fred MacKinnon (129–36).

4 Ibid., vol. 1623, file 15, 'Federal-Provincial Public Assistance Programs,' 24 March 1964; vol. 2113, file 23-1-3, Joe Willard to Judy LaMarsh, 24 February 1964, noting that 'in view of the criticisms that have been repeated recently by two or three of the Provincial Premiers about the failure of the [Canada Pension] Plan to provide for some of the groups most in need, it will be helpful to be able to refer to important action being taken in the field of public assistance'; ibid., accession 86-87/095, box 2, file 200-1-20 A pt 1, Joe Willard to Judy LaMarsh, 'Memorandum to Cabinet on the Canada Assistance Plan,' 8 November 1965; on the linkage between Old Age Security and categorical assistance see AO, RG 29-01, box 27, file 1107, verbatim proceedings of the 'Meeting of the Federal-Provincial Working Group on Welfare Programs,' statement of Fred MacKinnon, Nova Scotia deputy minister of welfare, that 'the average payment now in Nova Scotia under the old age assistance, the blind, and disabled persons allowance is somewhere between $800 and $900 ... per individual and the average payment under social assistance ... including what is called mothers' allowance ... is something slightly in excess of $200 a year per person. So there is a discrepancy between the two which we could not possibly catch up with. It will take years before this discrepancy can be ironed out. This is not the only argument, but it is one of the arguments for a generalized assistance program. It is totally unbalanced' (202). For a similar Ontario argument see AO, RG 29-01, box 26, file 1089, introductory statement by Louis Cecile at the 'Federal-Provincial Meeting of Welfare Ministers on Public Assistance,' 28–29 May 1964. Rand Dyck goes so far as to argue that 'in its initial stages CAP was not seen as a major innovation, but merely as a "tidying up" exercise in the wake of CPP,' but this is surely an overstatement given the longstanding concern within Ottawa for some alternative to unemployment assistance. Dyck, 'The Canada Assistance Plan,' 590.

5 NA, RG 29, accession 86-87/095, box 2, file 200-1-20 A pt 1, Judy LaMarsh to Lester Pearson, 5 February 1965 (my emphasis). The importance of the War on Poverty to CAP's approval by cabinet is noted by all commentators on the legislation. See Dyck, 'The Canada Assistance Plan,' 590; Bella, 'The Provincial Role in the Canadian Welfare State,' 445–6; Splane, 'Social Welfare Development in Alberta,' 180; Tom Kent, *A Public Purpose: An Experience of Liberal Opposition and Canadian Government* (Montreal 1988), 360. As Kent later recalled, 'No program involved less federal-provincial controversy. The battles had to be fought within Ottawa ... with those who disliked so large an extension of the federal role.' Kent's reference here is undoubtedly to the Department of

Finance, which mustered only faint support for an expensive new shared-cost program at a time when it was devising new tax-sharing agreements through which provinces would be allowed to 'opt out' of all such agreements.

6 NA, RG 29, accession 86-87/095, box 2, file 200-1-20 A pt 1, memorandum to cabinet, 'The Canada Assistance Plan,' 9 February 1965, 2, 50, 52–3.

7 Ibid., Robert Bryce to Joe Willard, 17 February 1965 (my emphasis); Inter-departmental Committee on Social Security, memorandum for the cabinet, 'Canada Assistance Plan,' 2 April 1965 (my emphasis). Willard replied that 'in view of the fact that the provinces will be able to terminate their categorical assistance programs and obtain sharing under the Canada Assistance Plan which will be based on need, it is essential that some support for the principle of adequacy in meeting need be included in the proposal ... We hope to do this through requiring that the provinces submit program and administration plans that will meet qualitative rather than quantitative standards.' Willard to Robert Bryce, 19 February 1965.

8 Ibid., 'Note on Cabinet Document No. 361/65 re Welfare Services under the Canada Assistance Plan,' 12 July 1965.

9 Metropolitan Toronto Records and Archives (MTRA), RG 5.1, file 46.17.3, 'Instructions for Computation and Issuance of Allowances under the General Welfare Assistance Act and Regulations, 1967' (my emphasis).

10 Ottawa's commitment to national standards in social welfare by the mid-1960s had been so weakened by the spectre of Quebec's demands for autonomy that two months after CAP received parliamentary approval, federal finance minister Mitchell Sharp presented the provinces with a new, comprehensive tax-sharing proposal that envisaged the complete elimination by 1970 of all federal conditions from shared-cost programs including CAP, hospital insurance, and national health grants, once their ongoing program costs could be determined, in return for an additional transfer of seventeen points of income tax. Sharp said he was 'hopeful that the provinces will want to accept the additional fiscal freedom this plan provides and assume the fiscal responsibility that is theirs ... to secure full freedom of action in the management of these programs.' NA, RG 29, vol. 1538, file 1003-C1-3, 'An Approach to Federal-Provincial Relations in the Fields of Fiscal and Economic Policy,' statement presented by Mitchell Sharp to the Tax Structure Committee, Ottawa, 14 September 1966. This proposal represented the apex of fiscal decentralization in the 1960s. As Richard Simeon and Ian Robinson observe, 'when more generalized conditions proved inadequate to meet Quebec's demands without conceding *de facto* special status, opting out was extended to all provinces for all major programs, without their ever having asked for it ... Thus, the imperatives of responding to Quebec and avoiding special status, led to greater decentralization than the federal government and most of the provinces wanted.' Simeon and Robinson, *State, Society, and the Development of Canadian*

Federalism (Toronto 1990), 201. These proposals were rejected by Ontario and the other provinces, principally because they did not wish to run the risk that their actual program costs in these areas would outpace whatever formula was calculated (on the basis of past expenditure patterns) for the transfer of equivalent income tax points. The momentum for centralization temporarily shifted back to Ottawa, particularly in response to the growing influence of Pierre Trudeau in cabinet and as prime minister. However, the negotiation of Established Programs Financing in 1977 effectively brought about the degree of fiscal and administrative decentralization first put forward *by Ottawa* in 1966. Henceforth, 'the mechanism for maintaining national standards was to be the will of the provincial governments and the expectations of their citizens, rather than federal controls,' according to Simeon and Robinson (288). Significantly, however, CAP was left out of the 1977 EPF agreement.

11 NA, RG 29, vol. 1538, box 27, file 1107, verbatim proceedings of the 'Meeting of the Federal-Provincial Working Group on Welfare Programs,' 14–15 February 1964; Ontario *Hansard*, 21 June 1965, 4439. René Lévesque, speaking for Quebec on the matter of adminstrative cost-sharing, told Ottawa that 'I would take a chance and buy your full child welfare coverage and get the hell out of this administration jungle any time.' Cecile agreed. 'I would second Mr. Lévesque's motion and countersign it very quickly.' NA, RG 29, vol. 2115, file 23-4-5, verbatim proceedings of 'Federal-Provincial Conference of Ministers of Welfare,' 7–8 January 1966.

12 NA, RG 29, accession 86-87/095, box 2, file 200-1-20 A pt 1, Joe Willard to Judy LaMarsh, 'Memorandum to Cabinet on the Canada Assistance Plan,' 8 November 1965; vol. 2115, file 23-4-4, verbatim proceedings of the 'Federal-Provincial Deputy Ministers of Welfare Conference, 19–20 October 1965.'

13 University of Toronto Archives (UTA), Charles Hendry Papers, box 11, copy of memo from M. Borczak, acting deputy minister, to H.I. Macdonald, chief economist, 'Re: Proposed Canada Assistance Plan,' 2 July 1965.

14 NA, RG 29, vol. 2115, verbatim proceedings of 'Federal-Provincial Deputy Ministers of Welfare Conference,' 19–20 October 1965; verbatim proceedings of 'Federal-Provincial Conference of Ministers of Welfare,' 7–8 January 1966; accession 86-87/095, box 2, file 200-1-20 A pt 1, Judy LaMarsh, memorandum to cabinet re 'The Canada Assistance Plan,' 28 October 1965.

15 Ibid., verbatim proceedings of the 'Federal-Provincial Conference of Ministers of Welfare,' 7–8 January 1966; vol. 2115, file 23-4-5, vol. 2, memorandum from R.B. Splane to Joe Willard, 'Summary Comments on Federal-Provincial Conference of Ministers of Welfare, January 7 and 8, 1966,' 17 January 1966.

16 K.J. Rea, *The Prosperous Years: The Economic History of Ontario, 1939–75* (Toronto 1985), 34, 84.

17 AO, RG 3, Robarts Papers, box 323, file 'Poverty: Social and Family Services,

Jan–Dec 1970,' draft speech by J. Keith Reynolds, CEO, PMO, 'Social Security and the Distribution of Powers: Some Ontario Views,' prepared for the federal-provincial conference on income security and social services, nd but circa 1970.

18 AO, RG 29-01, box 45, file 1813, Louis Cecile to Robarts, 7 June, 31 August 1966.

19 AO, RG 3, Robarts Papers, box 323, file 'Programs – Department Jan–Dec 1967,' memo on 'The General Welfare Assistance Act and Regulations as Revised in July 1967'; memo, 'Welfare Maintenance of Living Allowances – Introduction,' 25 September 1967; RG 29-01, box 4, file 143, W.S. Groom to M. Borczak, 21 July 1970.

20 Ontario *Hansard*, 21 June 1966, 5008, 5012–13, 5028, 5082, 5084, 5106–7.

21 Ibid., 20 March 1967, 1538–9, 1544; 21 May 1968, 3181.

22 AO, RG 29-01, box 26, file 1084, Louis Cecile to R.A. Farrell, PMO, 13 November 1963 (letter drafted by James Band); box 51, file 2058, James Band to Albert Rose, 20 April 1966; Senate of Canada, Special Senate Committee on Poverty in Canada, *Proceedings of Hearings*, 25 May 1970, brief of the Ontario Department of Social and Family Services, 43:65–7. This last quotation is actually taken from the Report of the Ontario Committee on Taxation, 1967, vol. 2, 424, and is reproduced in the Department of Family and Social Services' brief as one argument against provincial administration of general welfare assistance.

23 Special Senate Committee on Poverty, *Proceedings of Hearings*, 21 May 1970, 43:55–7, 43:67–8; Senate of Canada, Report of the Special Senate Committee, *Poverty in Canada* (Ottawa 1970), 79.

24 Ontario *Hansard*, 27 October 1970, 1763; 21 May 1968, 3168–9; 26 October 1970, 2633.

25 AO, RG 29-01, box 4, file 143, W.S. Groom to M. Borczak, 21 July 1970; Special Senate Committee on Poverty, *Proceedings of Hearings*, 25 May 1970, appendix, table 4.

26 Richard Harris, *Democracy in Kingston: A Social Movement in Urban Politics, 1965–1970*, (Montreal 1988), 138. Harris gives a particularly insightful account of the growing welfare backlash in Kingston's community politics between 1965 and 1971.

27 Ontario *Hansard*, 15 April 1969, 3079, 3039–42; 1 April 1969, 2944, 2950; 22 April 1969, 3448. Harris, *Democracy in Kingston*, 78–9. As Harris correctly observes, during the welfare backlash of the late 1960s, 'the main target was the young.' Kingston's administration argued bluntly that so many of the young were on relief because they were simply too lazy to work. The 'problem [was] one of motivation,' exacerbated by welfare allowances that were 'unduly generous.' As Stella Buck, the local welfare administrator put it to a conference near the decade's end, 'what we need here is another depression.' Quoted in Harris, *Democracy in Kingston*, 140; MTRA, RG 5.1, file 82, 'Ontario Task Force on Community and Social Services Report on Selected Issues and Relationships:

Response from the Committee on Community and Social Services of the Association of Municipalities of Ontario,' May 1975.

28 MTRA, RG 5.1, box 98, file 46.17.3, 'GWA – District Work – Minutes of Meetings, 27 February 1968; 2 May 1968; 17 October 1968; 9 October 1969; 24 November 1969.

29 Harris, *Democracy in Kingston*, 138–9; Senate of Canada, *Poverty in Canada*, 85; Social Planning Council of Metropolitan Toronto, *Social Allowances in Ontario: An Historical Analysis of General Welfare Assistance and Family Benefits (with special focus on adequacy of allowances), 1961–1976* (Toronto 1977), 33.

30 Clifford Williams, *Decades of Service: A History of the Ontario Ministry of Community and Social Services, 1930–1980* (Toronto 1984), 81; Social Planning Council of Metropolitan Toronto, *Social Allowances in Ontario*, 31–5. The divorce rate in Ontario jumped by 295 per cent in the same time period.

31 Diana Pearce, 'Welfare Is Not For Women: Why the War on Poverty Cannot Conquer the Feminization of Poverty,' in Linda Gordon, ed., *Women, the State and Welfare* (Madison 1990), 267–71.

32 Ontario *Hansard*, 17 June 1965, 4383; 21 June 1966, 5058; Williams, *Decades of Service*, 102.

33 Ontario *Hansard*, 20 March 1967, 1528; 18 March 1964, 1758.

34 Ibid., 18 March 1964, 1760; 21 June 1966, 5062, 5057.

35 Ibid., 27 October 1970, S-1754, S-1758. On 1 May 1970 women out of the workforce for three years and on welfare became eligible for Manpower training grants for the first time without loss of welfare eligibility.

36 Ibid., 21 June 1966, 5008; 22 June 1966, 5084.

37 Ibid., 22 June 1966, 5108; 27 October 1970, S-1761.

38 AO, RG 29-01, file 2574, 'Manifesto of Women Trapped in Poverty,' nd but circa 1970.

39 Lorna Hurl, 'The Nature of Policy Dynamics: Patterns of Change and Stability in a Social Assistance Programme,' paper presented to the 4th National Conference on Social Welfare Policy, Toronto, 24–27 October 1989, 20–1, 28; Social Planning Council of Metropolitan Toronto, *Social Allowances in Ontario*, 56. Hurl's study and that of the Metro Social Planning Council disagree on the extent to which Family Benefits Act allowances either approximated to or fell away from the council's *Guide to Family Budgeting* during the 1961–71 period. According to Hurl's calculations, FBA benefits dropped from 74 per cent to 68 per cent of adequacy over the decade. The council calculated the drop as from 60 per cent to 59 per cent of adequacy. Similarly, according to Hurl, 'in 1961 a family on Mothers' Allowances received approximately 35.5% of the average family income in Ontario ... by 1971 they received only 28.9%.' The Social Planning Council's own calculations from *Social Allowances in Ontario* (66), however, show that, including federal family allowances, the income of a typical family of

four on FBA remained constant at 34 per cent of the average Ontario family income over the decade 1961–71. As Hurl points out, this paradoxical pattern of 'change and no change' is consistent with American research on welfare reform in this era. As a U.S. study puts it, 'reforms intended to help the poor ... have principally changed the rules of the game under which some people come to be known as deprived and others as "normal" without altering the basic pattern or outcomes of this game.' D. Street, G. Martin, and L. Gordon, *The Welfare Industry: Functionaries and Recipients in Public Aid* (Beverly Hills 1979), 29, as cited in Hurl (29).

40 Ontario *Hansard*, 1 April 1969, 2954; 15 April 1969, 3076-77.

41 NA, RG 29, vol. 2115, file 23-4-4, verbatim proceedings of 'Federal-Provincial Deputy Ministers of Welfare, Conference, 19–20 October 1965.'

42 Ontario *Hansard*, 21 March 1967, 1600.

43 Ibid., 2 April 1969, 2992–5, 2999–3010; 15 April 1969, 3074. Margaret Renwick also noted that throughout Ontario, only in Scarborough, Brantford, Peterborough, and Kingston were the poor organized and aware of their rights. Ibid., 15 April 1969, 3079; 26 October 1970, S-1679. As the Senate report on *Poverty in Canada* put it, 'Generally speaking, appeal boards seem to be treated as extensions of the provincial welfare departments, and not in any way as independent entities. They are naturally geared to act in the interests of the welfare system, and not in the interests of the welfare recipient' (88).

44 AO, RG 29-01, box 66, file 2573, 'Welfare Rights Groups – Action 70, 1969–70,' Clifford Williams to John Yaremko, re 'Community Action Groups in Ottawa,' 16 February 1970; Williams, *Decades of Service*, 124. Peterborough's United Citizens, a local organization of the unemployed and those on welfare led by Ray Peters, dated from the severe local unemployment crisis of the late 1950s. Peters had been an activist within the United Electrical Workers at General Electric since the 1940s. Action 70, the product of Ottawa's Neighborhood Improvement Committee, 'developed as a result of housing problems encountered by a number of residents of the Preston area ... [who] received eviction notices and subsequently organized into a committee.' It was led by a local priest 'working on the principles of social animation.' AO, RG 29-01, box 66, file 2573, 'Comments on Correspondence re: the Neighborhood Improvement Committee of Ottawa,' J.G. McLellan, deputy minister's office, 10 July 1969. In Kingston, ATAK emerged out of the combination of New Left activists from Queen's University and the burgeoning anger of the welfare and working poor against the high cost and poor quality of rental housing. Its initial organizers were funded through the Company of Young Canadians. On the CYC see Ian Hamilton, *The Children's Crusade: The Story of the Company of Young Canadians* (Toronto 1970), and Margaret Daly, *The Revolution Game: The Short, Unhappy Life of the Company of Young Canadians* (Toronto 1970). For a superb recent study of the

coming together of the New Left, the CYC, urban redevelopment, and welfare rights in Kingston see Harris, *Democracy in Kingston.*

45 NA, RG 29, vol. 1524, file 201-16-1 pt 5, memo on 'Minimum Living Standards,' nd but circa September 1968. Experienced National Health and Welfare officials were somewhat alarmed at Trudeau's Throne Speech statement on defining minimum standards. As Dick Splane pointed out, the idea of conducting such a study and giving it 'maximum public exposure' was dubious. 'The "satisfactory standard" may be fixed in the public mind long before the Task Force has reached its final conclusions ... More serious is the danger that such a public study would pre-judge the whole question of a guaranteed minimum income before all its ramifications have been considered. The question of impact on incentives to work, to save, to invest needs thorough examination before any figure becomes fixed in the public mind as the "satisfactory standard of living" to which all are entitled.' Splane also asked whether the government was 'prepared to accept the cost increases (and attendant tax increases) consequent upon the establishment of such minimum standards? Furthermore provincial programs will also be brought under pressure when minimum standards are set. Is the government prepared to face provincial reaction in terms of cost increases in shared-cost programs?' Finally, Splane asked, 'Is the goal one standard or a matrix of standards varying from region to region, from rural to urban to metropolitan, from age group to age group, and from one family size to another?' If so, political leaders should make this point clear 'by consistent use of the word "standards" in the plural. Otherwise, the goal is unrealizable,' NA, RG 29, vol. 2116, file 24-1-1, vol. 1, R.B. Splane to N. Prefontaine, 'Comments of Officials of the Department of National Health and Welfare on the Draft Memorandum "Minimum Standard for Satisfactory Living Study,"' 24 December 1968. As for the Canada Assistance Plan's promise to 'prevent and remove the causes of poverty,' health and welfare minister Allan MacEachen also conceded to provincial welfare ministers by 1968 that this 'maybe [was] a bit too ambitious.' AO, RG 29-01, box 26, file 1094, verbatim proceedings of 'Federal-Provincial Conference of Welfare Ministers, Ottawa, January 18–19 1968'; Williams, *Decades of Service,* 124.

46 NA, RG 29, vol. 1524, file 201-16-1, vol. 5, N.F. Cragg to Joe Willard, 'Implications for the Canada Assistance Plan of the 5th Annual Review of the Economic Council of Canada,' 20 September 1968. Officials within the federal government were not enamoured of the Economic Council report, soon noting that 'where systematic evaluation (and proposals for new approaches) is vested in an organization independent of the government, the 'Economic Council of Canada syndrom' [sic] is likely to develop. Responsible Ministers are inevitably forced onto the defensive by published reports which fail to take account of many related considerations. Worthwhile contributions to policy formulation become clubs with which the opposition beats the government ... Social policy cannot be

developed in isolation from economic policy, foreign policy, budgetary problems, constitutional issues, etc.' Ibid., vol. 1614, file 4, 'The Departmental Position with Regard to the Report of the Special Senate Committee,' nd but circa 1970.

47 Special Senate Committee, *Poverty in Canada*, xiii-xviii; Christopher Leman, *The Collapse of Welfare Reform: Political Institutions, Policy and the Poor in Canada and the United States* (Cambridge 1980), 59. In fact, the Senate Committee was wrong. Absolute poverty had diminished throughout the 1960s, but this fact was disguised by the committee's decision never to compare the Economic Council's income estimates for families and individuals living in poverty in 1961 with the situation in 1969 in terms of the same constant dollar standards and definitions. Instead, the Senate Committee used a different, although defensible, relative definition of what constituted a poverty line in 1969 and found that one out of four Canadians lived below it. A detailed 1970 study of poverty in Hamilton, Ontario, in contrast, did update the council's original 1961 data for 1970 and found the proportion of all families and individuals living in poverty within that city had shrunk from 19 per cent to 13 per cent over the course of the decade, approximately the same as for the province as a whole. See brief to the Special Senate Committee on Poverty by the Social Planning and Research Council of Hamilton, 12 March 1970, 28:76; vol. 2104, file 20-P-22, memo from John Osborne to Joe Willard, 'Brief to the Senate Committee on Poverty,' 11 April 1969; Special Senate Committee on Poverty in Canada, *Proceedings of Hearings*, 25 May 1970, 43:51; speech of John Munro cited in Ontario *Hansard*, 26 October 1970, S-1694. National Health and Welfare officials were not enamoured with much of the Senate Committee's report, in particular its central recommendation that Ottawa's existing income security programs be scrapped in favour of one single guaranteed annual income. As the department argued, 'The present system is not perfect, but it is a good system which is continually being improved ... The existing structure should not be lightly tossed aside in favour of a technique which is largely theoretical and as yet untried in practice except in certain limited areas, unless there is a considerable amount of research and investigation into all aspects of the guaranteed annual income.' Like Ontario officials, NHW pointed to the central dilemma in formulating any guaranteed annual income poverty line. 'The higher the standards, the greater will be the cost ... If the benefit is less than the income gap, it will be less costly ... but may not be adequate.' Other problems with the Senate guaranteed income proposal, according to NHW officials, were that their definition of a poverty line set at $3500 for a typical family and the 70 per cent 'clawback' proposed on earned income to reinforce work incentives were 'arbitrary' and not based on any research; that the proposal made no provision for 'regional adjustments in the poverty line'; and that its recommendation for a scheme exclusively financed and administered by the federal government was 'not ... possible' and 'naïve' because of certain Quebec opposition to such a proposal. NA, RG 29, vol. 1614, file 4, 'Guaranteed Annual Income,' 2 June 1969;

'The Departmental Position with Regard to the Report of the Special Senate Committee,' nd but circa 1970.

48 Social Planning and Research Council of Hamilton, *The Hamilton Study of Poverty*, volume 2 of a Brief to the Special Senate Committee on Poverty, March 1971, 5-25, 5-46-49.

49 Ontario *Hansard*, 26 October 1970, S-1677-1681.

50 AO, RG 29-01, box 66, file 2573, 'Welfare Rights Groups – Action 70 1969–70,' verbatim transcript of the 'Welfare Seminar Workshop' at the Action 70 conference, 17 January 1970; clipping from *Ottawa Journal*, 'Poverty Conference to Bid for Income Supplements,' 21 February 1970; 'Report of the Workshops, March 7 1970, Action 70.'

51 Social Planning Council of Metropolitan Toronto, *Social Allowances in Ontario*, figures 5–7, 46–9, table 9, 56; Social Planning and Research Council of Hamilton, *The Hamilton Study of Poverty*, 7-22, 6-2; Special Senate Committee, *Poverty in Canada*, xv–xvii, chart 4, 26; Special Senate Committee on Poverty in Canada, *Proceedings of Hearings*, 25 May 1970, 43:81. In 1961, general welfare assistance allowances for single people and families of four were only 29 per cent and 48 per cent of adequacy (including family allowances), respectively, to meet budgetary needs as calculated through the council's *Guide to Family Budgeting*. By 1970 allowances for single people had risen to 38 per cent of adequacy, and for families of four to 59 per cent of adequacy, according to the cost of meeting the same budgetary standards. *Social Allowances in Ontario*, table 9, 56.

52 Senate of Canada, *Poverty in Canada*, 179–83.

53 AO, RG 29-01, box 27, file 1107, verbatim proceedings of the 'Meeting of the Federal-Provincial Working Group on Welfare Programs, Ottawa, February 14 and 15 1964,' 120.

54 NA, RG 29, vol. 2115, file 23-4-3, Federal-Provincial Conference of Ministers of Welfare, 8–9 April 1965, memo re 'Considerations in the Development of an Improved Public Assistance Plan'; vol. 1622, file 2, memo 'Canada Assistance Plan: Explanatory Notes, Contributions for Assistance Costs,' 12 May 1966. Exactly the same contradictions surrounding income supplements persist today within Ontario's welfare policy. In 1989 the province began allowing those receiving welfare to retain a larger proportion of any earnings without deductions from their monthly allowances. As of 1 August 1992, however, low-wage earners were cut off from applying for 'top-up' welfare benefits through this same program. The program had a 'costly flip side,' program director John Stapleton explained. 'Besides allowing welfare recipients to keep outside earnings it also allowed the working poor to top up their salaries with welfare benefits ... A woman with four children ... earning $800 a month at a waitressing job ... could also apply to the program for a welfare supplement.' As a result, the number of working poor in Ontario receiving welfare benefits jumped from 28,600 before the program to 62,300 after it was introduced. 'You have to ask yourself, are you

saving money by encouraging people to get off welfare? Or are you attracting people to welfare who are earning money?' Stapleton observed. 'That's the conundrum.' Through the new changes, however, anomalies persist. Although a low-income mother working as a waitress can no longer apply for welfare supplements, 'another woman with the same number of children could keep a large portion of her welfare benefits – including child care – if she got that same waitressing job.' *Toronto Star*, 31 July 1992.

55 AO, RG 29-01, box 4, file 141, 'Canada Assistance Plan 1968,' N.F. Cragg to M. Borczak, 7 May 1968.

56 Ibid., box 26, file 1094, verbatim proceedings of the 'Federal-Provincial Conference of Welfare Ministers,' 18–19 January 1968; Ontario *Hansard*, 21 May 1968, 3167.

57 Special Senate Committee on Poverty, *Proceedings of Hearings*, 25 May 1970, 43:14–16, 81–4. Yaremko's resistance to the idea of further enhancing welfare allowances was also evident at the January 1968 conference of welfare ministers. As he told his colleagues, 'giving money to people is no longer as acceptable and popular in the minds of the general public as it was even a decade ago.' If a family was having difficulty making ends meet at the present level of FBA benefits, 'which are considerable, – that to give them an extra hundred, two hundred, five hundred, thousand dollars may not be the answer.' Instead, his department 'intend[ed] to lay so much stress on this social service and rehabilitation program that we will eliminate from the minds of the public the fact that there may be somebody on the maintenance rolls that shouldn't be there.' AO, RG 29-01, box 26, file 1094, 'Federal-Provincial Conference – Welfare Ministers, Ottawa, January 18–19 1968 – Proceedings,' 76–7, 83.

58 AO, RG 3, Robarts Papers, box 323, file 'Poverty – Social and Family Service, Jan–Dec 1970,' John Yaremko to Robarts, 14 April 1970.

59 Special Senate Committee on Poverty, *Proceedings of Hearings*, 25 May 1970, 43:97–9.

60 Ibid.

61 Ibid., 43:98–104, 43:18; AO, RG 3, Robarts Papers, box 323, file 'Poverty: Social and Family Services, Jan–Dec 1970,' Mary Collins, executive officer, PMO, to H.R. Hanson, deputy secretary to the cabinet, 'Re: Question from Mr. Gisborn to the Prime Minister,' 10 April 1970; RG 29-01, box 29, file 1201, 'Guaranteed Annual Income – Background Material, 1966–69,' John Yaremko to James Auld, 8 November 1968.

62 AO, RG 29-01, box 29, file 1201, James Band, 'Statement on Guaranteed Annual Income,' October 1967.

63 AO, RG 3, Robarts Papers, box 323, file 'Poverty: Social and Family Services, Jan–Dec 1970,' J. Keith Reynolds, 'Social Security and the Distribution of Powers: Some Ontario Views' (a response to the federal White Paper on 'Income Security and Social Services'), nd but circa 1970.

64 AO, RG 3, Robarts Papers, box 323, file 'Increase in Welfare Benefits, Social and Family Services, Jan–Dec 1970,' J. Patrick Boyer to John Yaremko, 9 April 1970.

65 Ibid., file 'Poverty, Social and Family Services, Jan–Dec 1969,' John Robarts to M.H. Crone, 29 May 1969; Ontario *Hansard*, 15 April 1969, 3156; Leman, *The Collapse of Welfare Reform*, 117, 149. Interview with Dorothea Crittenden, 23 July 1990. As Leman observes, throughout the Social Security Review discussions between 1973 and 1976 Ontario's 'Progressive Conservative leaders were unhappy with the very idea of expanding the social assistance rolls to new groups and did not want the welfare rolls to lose their "categorical" nature.' Provincial officials instead wished to see the working poor aided by refundable tax credits paid through the regular tax system. The province also wanted the cost of such credits financed through ending universality within the existing family allowances and Old Age Security programs, an option ruled out as politically unacceptable by Ottawa (128–31). Finally, Ontario costed Ottawa's income supplementation scheme in 1976 at $3 billion a year, three times the level of spending forecast by Ottawa. 'We are convinced that our figures are the more realistic ones,' provincial treasurer Darcy McKeough argued. MTRA, RG 5.1, file 83, 'Remarks by the Honourable Darcy McKeough to the Community Planning Association of Canada Annual Conference,' 8 November 1976. On the failure of the 1973–6 Social Security Review see also Rodney S. Haddow, *Poverty Reform in Canada, 1958–1978* (Montreal 1993).

66 *Social Allowances in Ontario*, 1977, appendix A, 77–82; NA, RG 29, vol. 1524, Memo on 'Minimum Living Standards.'

67 Ibid., table 9, 56. For a father-led family of four the improvement in welfare allowances was less marked, reaching only 53 per cent of basic adequacy by 1970. Rea, *The Prosperous Years*, 131.

68 *Social Allowances in Ontario*, appendix A, 78–83, figures 4–7, 46–9. As this exhaustive analysis of welfare allowances in the province between 1961 and 1977 concludes, 'almost all increases in the adequacy of allowances were ... achieved prior to 1970' (76); Senate of Canada, *Poverty in Canada*, 'Part 1 – The World We Leave Behind.' See also chart 4, 26.

69 Special Senate Committee on Poverty, *Proceedings of Hearings*, 25 May 1970, 43:25, 43–4, 46, 48. As John Yaremko put it in his testimony, 'Even in 1970 we still have not come to a delineated definition of what it is to be poor in Canada or to be poor in Ontario ... Once we have a definition that everybody understands, then we can arrive at how many people there are in that category. We know what they need, and we will know how much is going to be needed at the national-provincial level to bring all these people up. But we have to start out with a definition that is scientifically sound.'

70 *Social Allowances in Ontario*, 75. The assumption that because welfare allowances do not meet basic needs and are so far below existing poverty lines, they

must be 'irrational,' permeates most social policy writing on welfare programs. See, for example, the most recent Report of Ontario's Social Assistance Review Committee, *Transitions* (Toronto 1988), which argues that 'our current social assistance programs have evolved ... without a coherent set of principles and objectives to guide their development.' Welfare in Ontario lacked any 'overall rationale or secure policy framework,' the committee concluded (27, 126). This assumes, as governments never have, that welfare programs that do not reach a standard of basic adequacy must be 'illogical' or 'irrational.' In fact, the preeminent rationale of keeping welfare entitlement in some kind of rough alignment with income available through the private labour market is all too apparent.

71 Senate of Canada, *Poverty in Canada*, table 28, 81. See also the 'Hamilton Study of Poverty,' 4–14, which noted in 1970 that among the 'very poor,' shelter costs accounted for more than 80 per cent of family budgets.

72 Special Senate Committee on Poverty, *Proceedings of Hearings*, 25 May 1970, 43:66–7.

CONCLUSION

1 Michael Katz, *In the Shadow of the Poorhouse: A Social History of Welfare in America* (New York 1986), 290.

2 Ontario, Report of the Social Assistance Review Committee, *Transitions* (Toronto 1988), 27.

3 On the concept of political learning and the centrality of state officials to shaping policy see Hugh Heclo, *Modern Social Politics in Britain and Sweden: From Relief to Income Maintenance* (New Haven 1974), particularly 301–7.

4 However, James Pitsula's analysis of the CCF's modest record of accomplishment with respect to welfare reform in Saskatchewan after 1944 serves as a caution against assuming that dramatic changes in welfare might have occurred had the party formed a government in Ontario in 1943. See Pitsula, 'The CCF Government in Saskatchewan and Social Aid, 1944–1964,' in J. William Brennan, ed., *'Building the Co-operative Commonweath': Essays on the Democratic Socialist Tradition in Canada* (Regina 1984), 205–26.

5 For a recent revisionist analysis of the impact of the Cold War and prosperity on the collapse of the Ontario CCF, see Dan Azoulay, '"A Desperate Holding Action": The Survival of the Ontario CCF/NDP, 1948–1964,' *Ontario History* 85, 1 (March 1993), 17–42.

6 T.H. Marshall, 'Citizenship and Social Class,' in his *Class, Citizenhip, and Social Development* (Chicago 1977), as well as his 'The Right to Welfare,' in his *The Right to Welfare and Other Essays* (London 1981), 83–94. See also J. Donald Moon, 'The Moral Basis of the Democratic Welfare State,' in Amy Gutmann, ed., *Democracy and the Welfare State* (Princeton 1988), 27–52.

7 As Theda Skocpol notes in her study of mothers' pensions in the United States, 'clients ... were too busy with struggles of daily life, and too morally cowed, to demand higher funding for these programs'; *Protecting Soldiers and Mothers: The Political Origins of Social Policy in the United States* (Cambridge 1992), 478.

8 See Frances Fox Piven and Richard Cloward, *Poor People's Movements: Why They Succeed and How They Fail* (New York 1977).

9 On the critical importance of developing the state's admininistrative capacity for reform see Stephen Skowronek, *Building a New American State: The Expansion of National Administrative Capacities, 1877–1920* (New York 1980), and Ann Shola Orloff, *The Politics of Pensions: A Comparative Analysis of Britain, Canada, and the United States, 1880–1940* (Madison 1993).

10 Skocpol, *Protecting Soldiers and Mothers*, 479.

11 Heclo, *Modern Social Politics in Britain and Sweden*, 284–322.

12 The term 'polity-centred framework' is from Skocpol, *Protecting Soldiers and Mothers*, 531. On the importance of federalism to Canadian social policy development see Christopher Leman, 'Patterns of Policy Development: Social Security in the United States and Canada,' *Public Policy* 25, 2 (spring 1977), 260–91.

13 For the arguments surrounding this point see Keith Banting, *The Welfare State and Canadian Federalism* (Montreal 1982), and Leslie Pal, *State, Class, and Bureaucracy: Canadian Unemployment Insurance and Public Policy* (Montreal 1988).

14 For the longevity of distinctions between the deserving and undeserving poor in the shaping of welfare policy see Michael Katz, *The Undeserving Poor: From the War on Welfare to the War on Poverty* (New York 1989), and Clarke Chambers, '"Uphill All the Way": Reflections on the Course and Study of Welfare History,' *Social Service Review* (December1992), 492–504. As Chambers points out, 'American society has been resistant to change in welfare, owing in some substantial part to the persisting belief that the needy are somehow different from the "rest of us"' (500).

15 As James T. Patterson observes in his history of welfare policy in the United States, 'attitudes toward the welfare poor had not changed very much since the 1940s and 1950s. In this sense ... the growth of the welfare rolls cannot be traced to the rise of a more liberal public opinion about the poor or welfare.' See his *America's Struggle against Poverty, 1900–1980* (Cambridge 1981), 178.

16 Rodney Haddow, 'The Poverty Policy Community in Canada's Liberal Welfare State,' in William Coleman and Grace Skogstad, eds., *Policy Communities and Public Policy in Canada: A Structural Approach* (Mississauga 1990), 212–37. See also Rand Dyck, 'The Canada Assistance Plan: The Ultimate in Co-operative Federalism,' *Canadian Public Administration* 19, 4 (1976), 587–602.

17 James Band, Merian Borczak, and Dorothea Crittenden, the department's three deputy ministers between 1951 and 1974, were all trained in bookkeeping or accounting. Burne Heise was the only social worker to hold the position of deputy minister within the department.

18 This is the core argument in Dyck, 'The Canada Assistance Plan,' and, to a lesser extent, Haddow, 'The Poverty Policy Community in Canada's Liberal Welfare State.' While not disputing the important contributions of National Health and Welfare's social policy elite, I believe both authors overstate their influence in interpreting the origins of the Canada Assistance Plan.

19 Skocpol, *Protecting Soldiers and Mothers*, 478.

20 Linda Gordon, 'What Does Welfare Regulate?' *Social Research* 55, 4 (winter 1988), 609–30, and her 'Social Insurance and Public Assistance: The Influence of Gender in Welfare Thought in the United States, 1890–1935,' *American Historical Review* 97, 1 (February 1992); Skocpol, *Protecting Soldiers and Mothers*. Arguments for a 'patriarchal' welfare state controlling women through the enforcement of a 'family ethic' are from Mimi Abramovitz, *Regulating the Lives of Women: Social Welfare from Colonial Times to Present* (Boston 1989), and Jane Ursel, *Private Lives, Public Policy: 100 Years of State Intervention in the Family* (Toronto 1992). For a major new analysis of gender and welfare in Ontario see Margaret Hillyard Little, '"No. Car, No Radio, No Liquor Permit": The Moral Regulation of Single Mothers in Ontario, 1920–1993' (PhD dissertation, York University 1994).

21 As Skocpol points out, the importance of gender solidarity as a rallying point for expanding social entitlement in our own era is also critical; *Protecting Soldiers and Mothers*, 531–9.

22 Ibid., 476.

23 Gordon as cited in Alan Wolfe, 'The Mothers of Invention,' *New Republic*, 4 and 11 January 1993, 34.

24 Skocpol, *Protecting Soldiers and Mothers*, 478–9.

25 A point acknowledged by Skocpol as well. See *Protecting Soldiers and Mothers*, 467–70.

26 Frances Fox Piven and Richard Cloward, 'Welfare Doesn't Shore Up Traditional Family Roles: A Reply to Linda Gordon,' *Social Research* 55, 4 (winter 1988), 639. Piven and Cloward point out that in the 1920s, only 55,000 families were receiving mothers' pensions in all the United States. 'Clearly, mothers' pensions didn't matter much, one way or the other' (639).

27 On the moral regulation of men within welfare programs see Ann Shola Orloff, 'Gender in Early U.S. Social Policy,' *Journal of Policy History* 3, 3 (1991), 249–81. On the 'less eligibility' components of mothers' pensions in the United States see Piven and Cloward, 'Welfare Doesn't Shore Up Traditional Family Roles,' 639.

28 Piven and Cloward, 'Welfare Doesn't Shore Up Traditional Family Roles,' 636.

29 Gordon, 'Social Insurance and Public Assistance,' 32, 35.

30 Ibid., 44.

31 Hugh Heclo, 'Towards a New Welfare State?' in P. Flora and A. Heidenheimer, eds., *The Development of Welfare States in Europe and America* (London 1981), 393.

32 Heclo, 'Towards a New Welfare State?' As Heclo points out, 'In the era of austerity, consolidating the welfare state had required strong political backing ... In an era of affluence, passive acquiescence could suffice ... As the political price of social policy declined, the need to build and maintain a strong, positive political coalition behind the expanding welfare state diminished ... [C]ommitment to struggling with the inevitable tensions among such values went soft' (397–8). Similar points are made by Moon, 'The Moral Basis of the Democratic Welfare State,' and by Skocpol, *Protecting Soldiers and Mothers*, 531–9.

Index

negative income tax, 255
Neighbourhood Workers' Association,
    21, 78, 104, 170, 173
Nelles, H.V., 7
Nelson, Barbara, 32, 296–7 n18, 298 n38
New Democratic Party (NDP): and
    daycare, 243; and guaranteed annual
    income, 255; and poverty, 264–6; and
    War on Poverty, 212–13, 218; and
    welfare appeal boards, 246–7. See also
    CCF, CCF–NDP
New Left, 247, 346 n44
New Liberalism (British), 310 n54
New Zealand, 7, 64
Noel, S.J.R., 7
nursing homes, 348 n99
nutrition: conference on, 1957, 148; and
    food allowances after World War II,
    142–3, 145, 180; and mothers' respon-
    sibility for, 82, 102, 105–6, 110, 114,
    116, 143, 327 n121; and relief diets,
    88, 127; and social work, 268, 273–4;
    and women reformers, 101–5, 271; and
    World War II, 108. See also Campbell
    Report, Cost of Living, McHenry
    Report, E.W. McHenry, minimum
    standards of need, Tisdall-Willard-Bell
    Report

O'Connor, John, 310 n57
Office of Economic Opportunity, 211, 220
old age, 47–63, 64–5, 68, 76, 108, 302
    n3, 302 n9, 303 n15; and housing,
    302–3 n10, 304 n21, 306 n 33, 306
    n36, 307 n44; political voice of, 311
    n63; and poverty, 144, 153, 179, 214,
    216, 223, 225, 232, 268, 332 n29;
    and women, 114–15, 197–8, 237, 301
    n77, 304 n22, 332 n29. See also
    charitable homes for the aged,
    geriatrics, gerontophobia, Houses of
    Refuge, nursing homes, Old Age

Assistance, old age pensions, Old Age
    Security
Old Age Assistance, 190, 196–7, 204,
    208, 227, 233, 237, 239, 349 n3, 356
    n42
old age pensions, 4, 8; administrative
    weakness of, 309 n53, 312 n71; and
    Australian scheme, 308 n49; benefits
    and eligibility, 64–75, 120, 314 n79,
    308 n50; and British scheme, 308 n79,
    310 n54, 314 n79; and cost-sharing,
    62, 65, 71, 75, 314–15 n81; and
    criticism by elderly, 308 n50; and
    farms, 313 n73; and gender, 63, 310
    n58; local administration of, 60–76;
    and parental maintenance, 45, 66, 68,
    71–2, 76, 307 n41, 311 n61, 312 n65,
    313 n75, 314 n78; and patronage, 315
    n81; and Reconstruction Conference,
    1946, 118, 120, 126; and relief, 144;
    and welfare units, 128, 136; and work
    ethic, 311 n59
Old Age Pension Act, 71
Old Age Pension Commission, 66, 70–2,
    75, 314 n79
old age pensioners' organizations, 205
Old Age Security, 268; adequacy of,
    356 n40; and Canada Assistance Plan,
    259; and eligibility, 232; increases in,
    204–6, and inflation, 142, 180; and
    universality, 381 n65; and welfare,
    203–5, 233, 360 n63, 371 n4
Oliver, Farquhar, 112
Ontario Conference on Social Welfare,
    133
Ontario Department of Labour, 367 n24
Ontario Department of Public Welfare,
    130, 133; and Conference on Poverty
    and Opportunity, 222–3; creation of,
    70; and home visiting, 194; and
    long-term assistance families, 199–
    202; male authority within, 271; and

THE ONTARIO HISTORICAL STUDIES SERIES

Peter Oliver, *G. Howard Ferguson: Ontario Tory* (1977)

J.M.S. Careless, ed., *The Pre-Confederation Premiers: Ontario Government Leaders, 1841–1867* (1980)

Charles W. Humphries, *'Honest Enough to Be Bold': The Life and Times of Sir James Pliny Whitney* (1985)

Charles M. Johnston, *E.C. Drury: Agrarian Idealist* (1986)

A.K. McDougall, *John P. Robarts: His Life and Government* (1986)

Roger Graham, *Old Man Ontario: Leslie M. Frost* (1990)

John T. Saywell, *'Just call me Mitch': The Life of Mitchell F. Hepburn* (1991)

A. Margaret Evans, *Sir Oliver Mowat* (1992)

Joseph Schull, *Ontario since 1867* (McClelland and Stewart 1978)

Joseph Schull, *L'Ontario depuis 1867* (McClelland and Stewart 1987)

Olga B. Bishop, Barbara I. Irwin, Clara G. Miller, eds., *Bibliography of Ontario History, 1867–1976: Cultural, Economic, Political, Social.* 2 volumes (1980)

Christopher Armstrong, *The Politics of Federalism: Ontario's Relations with the Federal Government, 1867–1942* (1981)

David Gagan, *Hopeful Travellers: Families, Land and Social Change in Mid-Victorian Peel County, Canada West* (1981)

Robert M. Stamp, *The Schools of Ontario, 1876–1976* (1982)

R. Louis Gentilcore and C. Grant Head, *Ontario's History in Maps* (1984)

K.J. Rea, *The Prosperous Years: The Economic History of Ontario, 1939–1975* (1985)

Ian M. Drummond, *Progress without Planning: The Economic History of Ontario from Confederation to the Second World War* (1987)

John Webster Grant, *A Profusion of Spires: Religion in Nineteenth-Century Ontario* (1988)

Susan E. Houston and Alison Prentice, *Schooling and Scholars in Nineteenth-Century Ontario* (1988)

Ann Saddlemyer, ed., *Early Stages: Theatre in Ontario, 1800–1914* (1990)

W.J. Keith, *Literary Images of Ontario* (1992)

Cornelius Jaenen, ed. *Les Franco-Ontariens* (Les Presses de l'Université d'Ottawa 1993)

Douglas McCalla, *Planting the Province: The Economic History of Upper Canada, 1784–1870* (1993)

R.D. Gidney and W.P.J. Millar, *Professional Gentlemen: The Professions in Nineteenth-Century Ontario* (1994)

J.E. Hodgetts, *From Arm's Length to Hands-On: The Formative Years of Ontario's Public Service, 1867–1940* (1994)

A.B. McKillop, *Matters of Mind: The University in Ontario, 1791–1951* (1994)

Edward S. Rogers and Donald B. Smith, eds., *Aboriginal Ontario: Historical Perspectives on The First Nations* (Dundurn 1994)

James Struthers, *The Limits of Affluence: Welfare in Ontario, 1920–1970* (1994)